SUMMER DAYS PROMISE

PAUL EDWARDS

fairfield books

First published by Fairfield Books in 2022

fairfield books

Fairfield Books
Bedser Stand
Kia Oval
London
SE11 5SS

Typeset in Garamond
Typesetting by Rob Whitehouse
Photography by Getty Images unless stated

Every effort has been made to trace copyright and any oversight
will be rectified in future editions at the earliest opportunity

The views and opinions expressed in this book are those of the author
and do not necessarily reflect the views of the publishers

ISBN 978-1-915237-10-1

A CIP catalogue record for is available from the British Library

Printed by CPI Group (UK) Ltd

for David Sleight

Sometimes, on certain evenings in London, I imagine I hear the distant rumble of Brighton-bound trains hurtling through Clayton Tunnel. I know it is an illusion, but the sound is immured in me, as once were the hooting of trains over Howrah Bridge, the sirens of Bengal river steamers, the cawing of crows. The noise sets the night into ferment, restoring the past as if it were animated, like the murals in Clayton church. Others may live in the village now, but the beeches still turn for me, clouds lighten along the skyline, summer days promise.

Alan Ross – Coastwise Lights

CONTENTS

Foreword – George Dobell   10

Introduction   12

1 Covid: Cricket in the Plague Months   18

The Glorious Treasure House in Perilous Times   19

A Different Type of War   22

When Play Resumes   27

Chorley v Littleborough – July 10, 2020   30

Lancashire v Derbyshire – September 2020 – Aigburth, Days 1 and 4   32

The Bob Willis Trophy – Lord's – Lingering Snapshots   38

Worcestershire v Nottinghamshire – April 2021,
Worcester, Days 1 and 4   40

Gloucestershire v Somerset – May 2021, Bristol, Day 1   45

**2 THE BIG MATCH. Shantry's Match – Worcestershire v Surrey,
September 2014, New Road**   48

3 Southport   62

Lancashire v Durham – July 2016, Days 3 and 4   63

Lancashire v Middlesex – June 2017, Day 4   68

Lancashire v Worcestershire – August 2019, Day 4   71

**4 THE BIG MATCH. Carrying On – Kent v Sussex, May 2017,
Tunbridge Wells**   74

5 Odd Men In   88

Lionel Palairet – Standing Out   89

Ian Folley – The Folley of Youth   92

Charlie Parker – The Lure of the Leftie   97

VVS Laxman – Blackpool Illumination   102

Frank Chester – How Was It?   106

Martin Donnelly – New Zealand's Oxford Don   111

George Cox – GOSBTS   116

John Edrich – Reporting for Duty   120

Alan West – Notching   124

David Essenhigh – Coach – The Smoked Salmon is Under the Canaletto   126

6 Matches from the Day   **131**

Lancashire 2007 – Ramped Up   132

Somerset 2016 – Great Days Indeed   136

Glamorgan 1948 – Wales, Wales   140

Hampshire 1961 – What Larks, Shack   144

Essex 1979 – It Must be Cricket   149

Worcestershire 1965 – Tom, Doug and Dolly   154

Surrey 1954 – Infantry   159

Sussex 1963 – No Going Back   164

Surrey 1925 – Got it at Last, Jack   168

7 THE BIG MATCH. When We Count at All – Sussex v Durham,

June 2018, Arundel   **174**

8 Great Days and Finals Days   **184**

2015

Glamorgan v Lancashire – Colwyn Bay, July   185

T20 Finals Day – Edgbaston, August   187

Somerset v Hampshire – Taunton, September   189

2016

Gloucs v Essex – Cheltenham, July   192

2017

Sussex v Gloucs – Eastbourne, May   194

Northants v Notts – Northampton, September   198

2018

Somerset v Hampshire – Taunton, May   200

Yorkshire v Surrey – Scarborough, June   202

T20 Finals Day – Edgbaston, September   204

Sussex v Warwickshire – Hove, September   207

2019

Middlesex v Lancashire – Lord's, April   209

Hampshire v Nottinghamshire, Newclose, May   212

Lancashire v Leicestershire – Aigburth, June   216

T20 Finals Day – Edgbaston, September   218

9 Bookish   **222**

Alan Ross – Preserving a Style   223

Alan Ross – Alan and his Friends   229

Alan Ross – Finding his Voices   234

David Foot and Alan Gibson – Such Stuff as Dreams are Made on   243

Stephen Chalke – Summer's Crown   250

Chris Arnot – The Past is More Important   252

Andrew Renshaw – Too Young to Fall Asleep For Ever   254

Christian Ryan and Patrick Eagar – Feeling is the Thing that
Happens in 1000th of a Second   257

**10 THE BIG MATCH. The Joy of Living – Lancashire v Durham –
June-July 2019, Sedbergh**   **260**

**11 THE BIG MATCH. Live at Leeds – England v Australia –
August 2019, Headingley**   **274**

12 Has   **298**

Lancashire v Hampshire – Old Trafford, May 2016   298

Lancashire v Warwickshire – Old Trafford, June 2016   301

Lancashire v Yorkshire – Old Trafford, August 2016   303

A Château Lafite Cricketer in a Wine-Box World   306

Lancashire Yearbook 2017   310

Lancashire v Middlesex, April 2019   311

13 Season's End   **314**

Lancashire v Middlesex – Old Trafford, 2014   315

Yorkshire v Sussex – Headingley, 2015   317

Somerset v Nottinghamshire, 2016   320

Worcestershire v Durham, 2017   323

Somerset v Essex, 2019   325

14 Envoi   **329**

Oxford UCCE v Worcestershire, March 2022   331

Acknowledgements   **335**

Foreword

Like a jobbing decorator being hired to paint Michelangelo's bathroom ceiling, it is with some trepidation I write this foreword.

On good days, I 'do' words. But many days they do me. Editors often say 'the piece will write itself.' But it never bloody does. Usually the words have to be hacked out of my soul with a blunt spoon. I find it hard.

Paul seems to find it easy. He's a writer, you see. And a beautiful one at that. He can express the moods and emotions of a day as well as anyone I've sat alongside in a press box. It's always a pleasure to see him but it's also a little intimidating. I saw the crescent; he saw the whole of Leonard Moon.

I flatter myself I played a minor part in Paul's progress, though. When David Hopps was appointed editor at *ESPNcricinfo*, he asked me to find him 'some young and trendy writers'.

Paul wasn't young or trendy, really. Sure, he sports that jumper round his shoulders with a certain ramshackle *je ne sais quoi* but he isn't one of those journos with vast numbers of contacts, a deep understanding (or even interest in) every franchise tournament across the globe or the ability to use Stasguru to uncover statistical gems. It's only a couple of years since we convinced him he required a mobile phone.

But what he does have is a deep and abiding love of the game. And because of that, he has been immersed in its characters and characteristics for as long as he can remember. He once told me that, on Christmas Day, he likes to visit Lancashire League cricket grounds and savour the encounters long past and imagine those yet to come. That's unusual, isn't it? But it illustrates his love for the sport. The expression 'cricket mad' could have been coined for him.

That love for the game – and those involved in it – pours off every page of this book. But because he has interests far beyond the boundary – in politics and people, in music and history – he is as likely to quote Mott the Hoople as Herman Melville; as likely to cite the repeal of the Corn Laws as regulations regarding Kolpak registrations. His work is all the richer and more satisfying for it.

We always knew we could send him to a damp day in Derby or a Lord's final and he would treat it with the same respect and reverence. We knew you would be able to feel how much he wanted the players to succeed; we knew you would be able to feel his pain when they struggled. We knew he'd care and we knew he would produce a piece that would capture the spirit of the day better than anyone. His pieces soon developed a cult following. He almost never has a bad day.

We live in an era when it seems some think that everything in cricket – and beyond, actually – can be expressed by statistics. The quality of a new-ball spell? Oh, that's a 7.9. The aggression of that innings? Well their bat speed was 9.4 and the elevation on their stokes a 6.8. Some of that stuff is brilliant. Some of it is people touching because they can't feel.

Paul knows that not everything that counts can be counted. He knows you can't define love or loyalty or a million things in between. So he tells us how a day's play feels. He tells us about the people and places. He tells us why it matters but knows it doesn't matter too much.

This is a beautiful book: a gem; a joy. The game is lucky to have Paul Edwards and I feel lucky to have a copy of this book.

George Dobell

Introduction

"There's enough in the game to justify sending you," said David Hopps, *ESPNcricinfo*'s UK editor. "I hope you get something good to write about." It was the second Friday in May 2012. For months I had been pestering David and asking if there was a chance of covering the County Championship. Finally, with one of his regular writers opting to report on a football match, he packed me off to New Road for the final day of the game between Worcestershire and Surrey.

The irony is that I was not that keen to go. The journey to Worcester from my home in Birkdale is long and messy and includes a change at Smethwick Galton Bridge, arguably the ugliest railway station in the land. I was also very busy tutoring students for their final exams. But within five minutes of arriving at New Road the following morning I was shamed by the memory of my weak-hearted reluctance. In his marvellous book *Engel's England*, Matthew Engel describes Worcestershire's home as "an ugly ground in a beautiful setting" and one appreciates his point. The place is a hotchpotch of architectural fashions, and all the more so since a Premier Inn was built in the northern corner. Yet the stroll across Worcester Bridge, the sight of the horse chestnut tree to the right of the Ladies' Pavilion and, of course, that view over to the cathedral, trump any well-meaning brutalities. I thought of past Aprils and of young Australian tourists, seemingly wearing every cricket sweater they possessed, walking out in freezing disbelief to begin their first-class programme. Then I ambled round to the press box.

Worcester's haphazard modernity extended to technology. There was Wi-Fi but it went down soon after the start of play and remained absent without hope of recall. In those days I didn't own a mobile router and was therefore reduced to taking notes for my report and phoning through comments to whoever was on duty. Alex Winter dutifully turned my fragments into English sentences and put them on the blog. Even that stopped after lunch. I eventually filed my copy at around one o'clock on Sunday morning. David might observe tartly that I had started as I meant to go on.

But at least my editor's hopes for some good cricket were fulfilled. Anyone caring to spend their Sunday morning finding out what *ESPNcricinfo*'s correspondent thought of Saturday's play could have read about Tom Maynard and Rory Hamilton-Brown extending their fifth-wicket partnership to 215, thereby giving Surrey a chance of victory after following on. Eventually needing 260 to win, Worcestershire scraped their way to 150-8 with Matt Pardoe and Richard Jones surviving the last 45 balls of the match to seal the draw. Four of the wickets fell to a 19-year-old Championship debutant, George Edwards, whose pace with the new ball was too much for Michael Klinger and Vikram Solanki. Quite properly, we all wrote about Edwards' abundant promise but he would play only two more first-class matches for Surrey before being released in 2014 and joining Lancashire. Some 15 months later Edwards and his new colleague, Gavin Griffiths, were in the side that won the T20 Blast. The following August they were both released and in the 2019/20 season Edwards was playing for Stoneyford CC in Victoria.

Maynard's century was the fourth and last of a career blessed with promise and hope. Having joined Surrey from Glamorgan in 2011, he made a thousand first-class runs in his maiden season at The Oval and would add another 635 in eight matches in 2012. Five weeks after that game at New Road his body was found on the tracks near Wimbledon Park tube. He was 23. "Not since the death in 2002 of Ben Hollioake – also of Surrey, also youthful, good-looking and precocious – had English cricket been so numbed by tragedy," wrote Richard Whitehead in *Wisden*.

I am finishing this introduction in December 2021. There is a cutting wind and slashing rain outside. But inside my writing room Jones is bowling to Thomas Lloyd Maynard and is being driven straight to the boundary. It is a shot that brooks no dispute. Then Aneesh Kapil is lifted over long-on and the always generous New Road crowd applauds a century. It is nearly a decade ago. It is yesterday.

* * *

Since that game at Worcester I must have covered hundreds of matches for *ESPNcricinfo* and this book hopes to reflect some of the joy and fulfilment derived from watching county cricket over the last decade. Some of the pleasure came from the variety of venues at which first-class matches are still played and from the reaction of the spectators watching the games. But most of the delight was taken from seeing skilled cricketers struggle for dominance over four days in matches which, while frequently fierce and brutal, were also played in a relatively civil atmosphere. On such days my contentment was boundless: to watch James Hildreth play a cover-drive at Taunton or Glen Chapple bowl on a cloudy afternoon at Liverpool is as good as I expect my life to get. (Neither Chapple nor Hildreth has played Test cricket for England and there should be a public enquiry about the matter.) Even the wet days offered something. My friend Chris Waters, the cricket correspondent of *The Yorkshire Post*, occasionally suggests I would garner some satisfaction from four days' rain. He may be right, although Lancashire's match against Surrey at Blackpool in 2008 tested that theory severely.

Summer Days Promise offers one writer's impressions of professional domestic cricket in England. Fortunately, there are many other perspectives: coaches, analysts, statisticians, spectators and players all have their own standpoints on a game while the players' own views on their work will be diverse indeed. Of course, such perspectives need not be utterly separate: one of the very best cricket books of recent years, *The Test*, was a novel written by one of England's white-ball analysts, Nathan Leamon. And I acknowledge that a county cricketer's life is often far more demanding than these reports sometimes suggest; amid all the beauty and skill, the professional game can be bloody tough.

In the autumn of 2021 it became clear how very hard the game had been for a few cricketers. The testimony of Azeem Rafiq to the Digital, Culture, Media and Sport Select Committee regarding his treatment at Yorkshire appalled people who love cricket. The apologies from some of Rafiq's colleagues and disclosures at other counties in 2021 made it plain that our game has a problem with racism. It is not the purpose of this book to suggest possible policies to cut such a poison out of cricket. Nevertheless, it was instructive to review the one or two reports in *Summer Days Promise* that mention Rafiq and then think how life might have been treating him while folk in press boxes and pavilions were enjoying their sport.

There is also a broader context to this book, one that has determined its structure. When it was first suggested to me that some of these reports on county matches might be collected within hard covers, I suspect the existence of Covid was known to a few hundred scientists. In early December 2021, the virus continues to affect the lives of almost everyone on the planet. When the great history of the pandemic is written, its impact on cricket might be a phrase in a footnote at the end of one of the shorter chapters. And yet never has sitting in a press box seemed a greater privilege than in the four months spanning two seasons when no spectators were allowed in grounds and venues as rich in history as Trent Bridge and Headingley became sombre, almost alien, places.

One recalled matches at Scarborough, Taunton and Nottingham and longed for the return of the cheery hubbub and the generous applause for the spectators' favourites. At the same time, it is important to keep attendance figures in perspective. In *White Heat – A History of Britain in the Swinging Sixties*, Dominic Sandbrook identifies *county* cricket as "England's national sport" in the first half of the 20th century, but not since the early 1950s have matches been regularly watched by large crowds, and the domestic first-class game will never again attract anything remotely approaching the mass support seen at professional football. In 2019/20 the average attendance at Rotherham United, a Division One club, was 8,906; the total attendance at Leicestershire's seven home four-day games in 2019 was 8,994. But the number of people turning up at a ground is not always a true measure of the general interest in it.

When cricket restarted in August 2020 many counties live streamed their matches to supporters. A few communications officers were astonished by the viewing figures but the more savvy ones expected such a response; Somerset, for example, have been streaming their games for four years and the live streams at both Taunton and Old Trafford are exceptionally professional operations. Other counties are quickly catching up. But watching any sport on a screen will never match being present at a ground. For one thing, you see only what a director decides you will see; for another, you miss the atmosphere, the company, the weather – the whole experience. When I covered Worcestershire's game against Nottinghamshire in April 2021 I wrote that "county cricket is about the game and about

15

everything around the game". That partly explains why watching cricket in the Covid seasons was a privilege wreathed in sadness. Writers like Alan Gibson and Alan Ross have shown that a day at the cricket is always about more than sport.

All these reports were written on the day of the game. I have corrected a few statistical errors and tidied up a few phrases but no assessments have been changed. A few sentences have been deleted because their references were very topical, never because their judgements now appear a little strange. When the vast majority of these pieces were written the words "batsman" and "batsmen" were in general and uncontested use. I viewed it as strange and unnecessary to change them to batter (s) although I happily acknowledge that the latter words have been employed frequently by others over the years. David Essenhigh (See *Odd Men In*) often referred to someone he liked as "a good batter". As ever, dogmatism and certainty are my enemies.

Most of the reports on county matches were filed within an hour or so of close of play. Above all, I hope they communicate something of the joy felt by a writer who could scarcely credit his good fortune. The book is a small thank you to the cricketers whose skills still garland our summers. It is also, in December 2021, a wager on the hope that a more normal life will soon be possible and that professional cricket will play its part in that.

Paul Edwards

COVID – CRICKET IN THE PLAGUE MONTHS

On March 9, 2020 I travelled to Old Trafford for a press conference with Glen Chapple. Chatting with the journalists, Lancashire's coach talked about "this Covid business" and the possibility of wearing a face mask but at no time did anyone suggest that the forthcoming season might be seriously disrupted. Within ten days it was plain that no cricket could be played anywhere in England for some months, maybe a year. None of the counties complained. Before long, some furloughed cricketers were wondering what they could do to help folk who were struggling. Some delivered food, others drove the elderly to hospital.

What follows is a series of pieces written over the 14 months from March 2020 to May 2021. A few focus directly on the pandemic and a couple are reflective pieces on cricket during and just after the 20th century's two World Wars. There are reports from four first-class matches. In the first, Lancashire met Derbyshire at an almost deserted Aigburth; an outground that is normally vibrant with comment and life suddenly acquired the atmosphere of a country house in which a private game was being played. In the third, some seven months later, Haseeb Hameed made two hundreds at Worcester and was applauded only by those who were professionally obliged to be on the ground. There are other pieces, too. When club cricket returned in July 2020 The Times *sent me to Chorley to cover the match; it was the first morning in decades that a report on the recreational game had appeared in the paper. And in May 2021 spectators were allowed in to watch county cricket for the first time in 20 months. Less than a session's play was possible at Bristol that morning but it was one of my favourite days in the whole season.*

When covering the 2019 Headingley Test for Yorkshire's website I had written that "it is the people we remember." As the pandemic tightened its hold those words were suddenly freighted with fresh significance. I looked again at the people among whom I was proud to live: at the scientists in their laboratories working absurd hours to develop the vaccines that have saved countless lives; at the doctors and nurses, some of them my friends, who found themselves dealing with fresh hell every day; at the pupils I taught on Skype who retained their buoyant spirits and optimism even at a time when their hopes of university were in the hazard; at the folk who rang the lonely, shopped for the shielding and did what they could.

And it was important to remember that cricket still mattered to very many people, particularly during the months when there was no chance of the game resuming. Sir Jeremy Farrar, director of the Wellcome Trust and therefore one of the experts frequently interviewed about the pandemic, expressed the hope he might play a game of village cricket before the summer of 2020 was over. I hope he managed to do so. Encouraged by such enthusiasm, I wrote about the game and the pandemic has become a sub-text for this book. Even in the darkest months, summer days still held their promise and so, when possible, I turned my attention back to the game I loved. "Between my finger and my thumb / The squat pen rests. / I'll dig with it." wrote Seamus Heaney.

Cricket's glorious treasure house can sustain us in perilous times

The April issue of *The Cricketer* arrived last week. Folded within was the annual wallchart presenting the fixtures for a season which will begin three months late at best. By September that multi-coloured graphic is normally frail as medieval parchment; I doubt it will be treated so roughly this summer. And this morning the postman delivered the *Second XI Annual*, another companion on a six-month odyssey which normally sees me tarry in Taunton, Cheltenham, Hove. But until July at the earliest, I doubt my travels will take me outside Southport. The only first-class cricket ground visited will be Trafalgar Road, where Paul Parker and his helpers were due to be putting up the outdoor nets next weekend. That happy ritual had already been postponed by Thursday evening, when the whole club was closed until a date only a loon would predict.

And quite right, too. The innings we should applaud at the moment are being played over 24 or 48 hours by people whose personal protective equipment is not made by Kookaburra or Gray-Nicolls.

The shot I liked most this past week was produced by the young lad who followed his mother's instruction to grab a supermarket's last two packets of pasta but then placed them in the trolley of the elderly shopper who had arrived just too late. The notion we might play sport at such a time is glaringly obscene and bloody dangerous.

But even in these perilous days, cricket still matters. As my colleague, Sambit Bal, explained so eloquently, sport is one of humanity's most glorious enterprises. It is an outlet for skill, courage and endeavour; it is revelatory of character; it has endowed the lives of many men and women with vital purpose. It has been a profitable business for many and a glorious escape for many more. It has even inspired a few half-decent writers. And for perhaps the majority of those who visit this website cricket remains the incomparable game. It charmed us before we knew it and the attachment has only deepened with the years.

For the moment, though, we must find other outlets for our unspoilt love and should only make use of even those channels when we have dealt with our new priorities. Over less than a fortnight our lives have changed utterly. In seven days the smart paradox that we should stick together even while we keep our distance became something of a cliché. We have gradually become more of a community even as we have grown anxious about our own livelihoods. When I have cancelled hotel bookings owners have wished me well and exhorted me to "Stay Safe", the words' gentle sibilance never disguising the anxious imperative. It is time to press the sleep button on a cricket season that has not begun and to resolve that when it awakens – as it will – the counties and clubs we treasure will all be there to celebrate the moment. The cricket fields of England remain the countries of my heart.

All the same, we must deal with difficult months before that day arrives and some have compared the present struggle against this accursed virus to the Second World War. That is both dangerous and useful. Only the other day Andrew Carney, the excellent chairman of Southport and Birkdale CC, expressed the hope that he and I might meet for a "two-metre coffee" quite soon. It is a grand idea and I was tempted to reply that perhaps we could have a takeaway snook fishcake as well. Yet you combat fascism by arguing against it, ridiculing it, defying it and, if necessary, engaging in physical combat with it. We will deal with coronavirus by doing our very best to ensure we are not infected by it and by waiting for a vaccine to be developed. The two battles – if we must employ a military lexis – are quite different yet the qualities they require may still be compared to the last global conflict. That point was made with particular acuity by the always excellent Bagehot in *The Economist*: "Britain's greatest resource is the character of ordinary people rather than the genius of élites; and… character is reflected in the way you go about your daily business – keeping calm and carrying on; resisting the temptation to hoard or shirk – as well as in war heroics." One might only add that such qualities are, thank heavens, not a British preserve. One thinks of Lombardy, of Madrid, of New York State. Compared to the situation in Bergamo and Brescia the absence of cricket in England this spring does not amount to Rick Blaine's hill of beans.

But in our quiet moments we can still think about our game, read about it and yes, write about it. We cannot follow the example of Squadron Leader Les Ames and Sergeant Keith Miller, who were among the many professional cricketers to seize opportunities to play cricket during the Second World War. But we can recall memorable games and relish afresh the players we have watched. Such an exercise is immeasurably enriched by a familiarity with the work of Alan Ross, who spent most of the Second World War in the Royal Navy, a time he describes in *Blindfold Games,* the first volume of his autobiography. In the sequel, *Coastwise Lights*, he remembers how his beloved Sussex soothed him, even when he was thousands of miles away from the county. "During my sea-time I used to dream of Sussex; not so much a specific Sussex as a generalised, romantic image conjured out of memory and hope. Sussex cricket played a large part in it, to the extent that I had only to see the word Sussex written down, in whatever context, for a shiver to run down my spine."

For Ross it was the county of Hugh Bartlett and George Cox; for others it may be the cover drives of Ian Bell and the many skills of Jeetan Patel; for others again, it may be the bowling of Ryan Sidebottom on a cloudy Leeds morning or the batting of James Hildreth on a summer Saturday at Taunton. And yes, it has just this moment struck me that it may also be Shantry's Match. Please take your pick from cricket's glorious treasure house. And be assured that when they have all discharged their daily obligations, others will be comforted by similar thoughts. The rich memories will sustain us and the firm hope will warm our days. Stay safe.

ESPN*Cricinfo – March 2020*

A Different Type of War

> MAINWARING: We're walking out here as free men, to play a friendly British game. That's what we're fighting for, you know.
> WILSON: Yes, of course, sir. Amongst other things.
> *Dad's Army – "The Test"*

Neville Cardus's fourth book, *Cricket*, was published in 1930. Its first pages find him in Dover at the very end of the season. He has, apparently, spent that final afternoon watching Frank Woolley make a century, so perhaps we can understand the rhapsodic mood.

"It was all over and gone now, as I stood on the little field alone in the glow of the declining day. 'The passing of summer,' I thought. 'There can be no summer in this land without cricket.' "

Well, we shall see. This might be the year when the old boy's blithe assertion is disproved. Ninety and more seasons since Cardus stood on the Crabble, his reverie assisted by King Lear, we are facing the near certainty that no cricket will be played in England for three months, and there remains a possibility the whole shebang might be lost. Faced with such gloomy prospects, writers have cast around for similar seasons and many have cited the ten years covered by the two World Wars as offering useful comparisons. But plenty of cricket was played in each of the wartime summers, even if the County Championships of 1914 and 1939 were prematurely ended and first-class matches did not resume until the first year of peace. The game was certainly disrupted and some cricketers wondered if it was proper to play sport at a time when friends were losing their lives. Yet cricket eventually came to be seen as a means of raising funds for the war efforts and even as offering reassurance there would always be an England people could recognise.

So perhaps we should make allowances for Cardus and his serene optimism, even if the specific match he had been watching is difficult to pin down. Turned down for military service in the First World War because of his myopia, he had nevertheless witnessed the effects of that conflict on the game he loved. Of the 377 men who played County Championship cricket in 1914, 40 had given what Abraham Lincoln called at Gettysburg "the last full measure of devotion". All the same, cricket had continued in England, albeit that the Championship was suspended. The last summer of the war saw St Peter's School, York take on The Army Pay Corps, Sefton play The South Wales Borderers and FS Jackson's XI meet PF Warner's XI. That last-named game was one of a handful played at Lord's and all matches were one-day affairs, but it didn't matter. For many the game had come to symbolise a mixture of fortitude and confidence; to play cricket was to bet on the future.

It took the clear eye of Siegfried Sassoon and his poem "Dreamers" to put such ideas in a grimmer context.

> *I see them in foul dug-outs, gnawed by rats,*
> *And in the ruined trenches, lashed with rain,*
> *Dreaming of things they did with balls and bats,*
> *And mocked by hopeless longing to regain*
> *Bank-holidays, and picture shows, and spats,*
> *And going to the office in the train.*

Cricket's reaction to the outbreak of hostilities in 1914 had been both confused and regional. The County Championship continued for nearly a month after the declaration of war and it needed WG Grace's famous article in *The Sportsman* to halt it. But enormous misconceptions still abounded. The first was that the war was a great adventure, a jaunt which any sporting cove would be daft to miss. "I am waiting to go off any night now," wrote the Etonian, Oscar Hornung, to his uncle, Arthur Conan Doyle in 1914. "I am longing to go – it is a chance for us chaps isn't it?" In the following spring Oscar's father EW Hornung, the creator of Raffles, took his cue from Sir Henry Newbolt.

No Lord's this year, no silken lawns on which
A dignified and dainty throng meanders.
The Schools take guard upon a fiery pitch
Somewhere in Flanders.

On July 6th 1915 Oscar Hornung was struck by a shell near Ypres and died without recovering consciousness.

The other misconception, one which young Hornung might well have shared, was that the war would be over relatively quickly. The 1915 County Championship was not officially abandoned until January, by which time The Oval had been commandeered by the military. Nevertheless, Surrey made it clear that "in the event of the war coming to an early conclusion it is hoped that some matches will be played in July and August." It was a fond notion.

The situation was rather different for many clubs and there is a fair argument that some northern leagues prospered. There was an organised programme of games in both the Lancashire and Central Lancashire Leagues, and Jeremy Lonsdale's fine book, *A Game Sustained,* shows how the Bradford League thrived, with clubs regularly hiring a host of county cricketers who were not otherwise occupied. Large crowds paid to watch players of the quality of Sydney Barnes, Ernest Tyldesley, Frank Woolley and Jack Hobbs albeit *The Yorkshire Post* thought such recreation to be "out of harmony with the spirit of the times, directly opposed to the serious interests of the nation and a melancholy response to the dominating and inexorable call." One might assume the *Post*'s view would have commanded general support during summers in which Pals regiments from northern towns were being mown down on the Western Front but officers and soldiers alike drew comfort from the fact that sport was still being played. In April 1917 a member of the Windhill team, who was recovering in Leeds General Infirmary from his war injuries, wrote as follows in the *Shipley Times and Express*:

"I would just like some of those people who croack (sic) about cricket in warfare to see these chaps when the sporting papers arrive. I should like these people to understand that there are men out there, face to face with death every day, who, when they have half an hour to spare, are discussing the merits etc. of their favourite clubs. If the Bradford League does nothing else in 1917... it will take away for a short time from the horrible nightmare of war."

That nightmare had come as a brutish revelation to soldiers like Oscar Hornung and his successors in 1915. Emboldened by *Tom Brown's Schooldays,* Newbolt's verses and the novels of GA Henty, they had been gulled by the notion that world war would be something of a quick kill. Twenty years later cricketers were not burdened by such illusions. The reality of mechanised conflict and the obvious power of the German armed forces made it plain to county sides travelling around England in August 1939 that they were probably playing their final games together. Many writers sought to capture the strange atmosphere that enfolded those matches but none succeeded so well as JM Kilburn in his description of the Yorkshire team as it completed its southern tour in Hove, where Hedley Verity (1905-1943) played his last game for the White Rose.

"They travelled to Brighton, cricket continuing because no authority had stopped it. The match was well attended, partly no doubt because it was for the benefit of James Parks, partly because pre-arranged routines remained in existence. Batsmen went to the crease, bowlers bowled, spectators assembled and applauded and nobody felt that cricket mattered in the least.

"Play was not casual, watching was not indifferent, but behind the bowling and batting lay concerns for another way of life... Fine weather broke on the second evening and Sussex played their second innings on a softened pitch. It was completed in less than 12 overs for a total of 33 and Verity's last bowling analysis in first-class cricket was o6 m1 r9 w7."

Few newspapers argued that cricket should not be played during the Second World War. On the contrary, matches were seen as part of the attempt to keep everyone's spirits up, especially during the early years of the conflict, when it seemed Nazism might prevail. Servicemen seized every chance they got to play cricket, even starting matches against local teams soon after returning from action. That was the case when Bill Edrich's squadron spent a morning attacking German ships near the Dutch coast and the afternoon playing a match at Massingham Hall in Norfolk. The RAF side included two substitutes for the men who had been shot down a few hours previously. Edrich's account of that game is perhaps the most evocative piece of cricket writing to emerge from the war years.

"At times it seemed like a strange dream…" he writes, "Both cricket teams played well, and it was a hard and exciting game. Every now and then would come the old, accustomed cry – 'OWZATT' – and then one's mind would flicker off to the briefing, and to joking with a pal whose broken body was now washing in the long, cold tides, and one saw again his machine cartwheeling down, flaming from nose to tail; and then a ball would roll fast along the green English turf and in the distance the village clock would strike and the mellow echoes would ring through the lazy air of that perfect summer afternoon."

Yet even as we search for similarities it is plain that our current situation is different. These words are being written exactly a week before the scheduled start of the 2020 County Championship season. An unusually balmy spring beckons. Yet the most defiant act most of us can accomplish is to ring our colleagues and enquire after their welfare or take some essential supplies to vulnerable friends. These are important acts, yet they seem insignificant when set beside the work being done in the intensive care wards or the homes for the elderly. Cricket offers merely a pleasant reminder of what life might be like once again if we stay at home and give the modellers, doctors and scientists time to do their work.

One consequence of such obedience is that for the first time since cricket became an organised pursuit the game will not be played anywhere in England this spring. Our veterans may make comparisons with the Second World War but the obvious truth about the Nazis was that you could get to grips with them. None of us have been here before. The best that cricket can offer us is its history; the best that we can supply is our memories and our determination than when this virus departs – as it will – the 18 first-class counties and the thousands of clubs will all have survived to mark the moment. Until then we must dream of balls and bats.

The Cricketer – May 2020

When Play Resumes

BASIL: Who won the bloody war, anyway?
Fawlty Towers – "The Germans"

There were times after 1945 when some British people queried the reasons for their many sacrifices in the Second World War. As they endured years more rationing and became reconciled to the United Kingdom's diminished position in the hierarchy of global powers, they wondered, sometimes intemperately, often in pubs, whether the nature of victory justified the price paid. As free people sometimes do, they took their freedom for granted. (Some may argue that until a few months ago a comparable complacency informed the outlook of healthy folk.)

In 1945, though, the predominant emotions were relief and joy, feelings which cricketers expressed as boisterously as anyone. Only 11 first-class matches could be played that season but five of those were three-day, unofficial Victory Tests in which an England side took on a strong Australian Services team, and a sixth, the contest against The Dominions in late August, was described by *Wisden* as "one of the finest games ever seen". No one thought that view hyperbolic, not when they recalled Walter Hammond's two hundreds, Martin Donnelly's century for the visitors or Doug Wright's ten wickets in the match. Yet it was not those achievements they would most vividly remember in later years; rather, it would be the 185 made in 168 minutes by Keith Miller, a former fighter pilot who had once walked away from a crash landing with the words: "Nearly stumps drawn that time, gents."

English spectators knew something of Miller's ability from his performances in wartime games. But in 1945 he not only made two centuries and took ten wickets in the Tests but also established himself as the most charismatic cricketer in the world. His three first-class centuries that season were all made at his beloved Lord's but in truth he had only to stand at slip in Eastbourne to attract attention from men who wanted to be like him and women who simply wanted him. On the third morning of that game for The Dominions he made 124 runs in 90 minutes, adding half a dozen more sixes to the one he had powered onto the top tier of the pavilion the previous evening. Although Miller's team won that game by 45 runs the vast majority of the crowd would remember the spectacle long after they had forgotten the details.

It was a year in which cricket managed to reflect public joy and distract people from the various debts that even victors in war have to pay. The mood on VE day, which was celebrated only 11 days before the first Test, was memorably captured by Alan Ross in his book *The Forties*.

"The actual end of the war, between a stutter of imaginary and real celebrations, came almost as an anti-climax. Everyone had been emotionally prepared for it for too long. But a kind of ruthless determination to celebrate, to achieve some sort of catharsis that would satisfy the cumulated frustrations of half a decade, in the end won through. Bonfires were lit from Trafalgar Square to the Old Kent Road; people danced and sang and kissed one another in a way they would never do again."

The Victory Test series was drawn two-all and the matches did what was promised on the posters advertising them. They celebrated a great triumph. Few people thought them inappropriately named, certainly not the English players when they thought of Hedley Verity, nor the Australians when they remembered Ross Gregory. Unlike the First World War, the reasons for this conflict had been clear and it had been less easy to understand conscientious objection when one thought of what totalitarian governments of any stripe did to citizens who obeyed their consciences.

Just as cricket had bolstered the morale of both players and spectators during the war, now it offered affirmation of the return of peacetime. First-class games may have been scarce but the following year's *Wisden* contains details of all manner of one-day matches, many of them played for the simple joy of doing so. Such an emotion would have been well understood by writers like Jim Swanton who had spent three years in a Japanese prisoner-of-war camp. In his article "Cricket under the Japs" for the 1946 *Wisden* Major EW Swanton recalled how the game had "inspired many a daydream, contrived often in the most gruesome setting, whereby one combated the present by living either in the future or the past."

Miller and his fellow Australians lived gratefully in the world for which they had fought. Although based in Eastbourne, they travelled the country, playing two games in High Wycombe in May and three in Scotland in July before signing off with a match in Middlesbrough in mid-September. In all there were 48 contests of various lengths and descriptions, each of them appreciated by people eager to welcome sport as some small restoration of normality.

Except that things were not normal and not even the presence of Australian cricketers in England could make them so. Albeit the tour was arranged at very short notice, it had been decided to play one of the Tests at Sheffield and another at Old Trafford in addition to the three at Lord's. (The Oval was still being turned back from a prisoner-of-war camp into a cricket ground.) But the pavilion and two of the stands at Lancashire's home ground had been badly damaged by bombs. During the war Old Trafford's carpets were sent to North Wales for safe keeping and the heavy roller conscripted for active service in the Western Desert, where it helped flatten airstrips. Of course, none of these factors blunted Lancastrians' enthusiasm for their first top-level cricket in over six years. A grand total of 72,463 spectators attended the three-day game and saw Lancashire's Eddie Phillipson take nine wickets in England's victory. One wonders how many of those watching the game knew that Old Trafford had been dolled up by German prisoners, who were paid three farthings an hour for painting the ground's outside walls.

Almost all counties and clubs had been affected by the war and some even viewed the return of a full peacetime wage bill with apprehension. Derbyshire and Northamptonshire launched appeals for £10,000 with the latter noting bleakly that only 120 out of 900 members were still on their books. Taunton had been pressed into service during the war by Ministry of Food and National Fire Service. The pavilion at Chelmsford had been damaged and 138 incendiaries had fallen on the outfield at Canterbury, although some said they had improved the Kentish grass. Most poignantly of all, the season's only first-class county fixture was a Roses match during which £3,000 was raised for the family of Hedley Verity. By the end of the summer the fund stood at £7,000 and *Wisden* would later devote seven pages to a Roll of Honour listing deaths, prisoners and decorations. "By 1945 the photographs of my Haileybury and Oxford XIs scarcely bore looking at," wrote Ross.

Some reminders of war were yet more terrible. On August 6 over 10,000 people were locked out of Lord's on the first day of the fourth

Victory Test and thus missed seeing Miller complete his century just before close of play. At roughly the same time it was announced that an atomic bomb had been dropped at Hiroshima. Three days later Nagasaki was flattened. Japan surrendered on August 15 and the end of world war was properly toasted during the first day of the Australians' game against the North of England at Blackpool. Over the Pennines in Leeds, the eight-year-old Tony Harrison watched the revels in the streets of Beeston and the poet later preserved his memories in "The Morning After".

> Though people weep, their tears dry from the heat.
> Faces flush with flame, beer, sheer relief
> and such a sense of celebration in our street
> for me it still means joy though banked with grief.

And yet it was peace and over the next few seasons cricketers of all standards would enjoy the freedoms that came in its train. The following spring Nettlefolds, manufacturers of spikes for sporting shoes, would take out advertisements reminding potential customers that they hadn't forgotten how to make them. In 1946 the County Championship would resume and, as ever, some people invested far too much importance in cricket while others paid the game too little attention. In future years war memorials would appear in county pavilions and on perfect summer mornings lads would attend their first matches. They would look up at the new boards and ask their fathers about the men whose names shone out in gold leaf.

The Cricketer – July 2020

Club season back with cheers, beers and surface wipes

Windsor Park: Chorley beat Littleborough by eight wickets

"Play," said Alistair Davies, his command clearly audible on the boundary at Windsor Park. Rarely can an umpire have been obeyed so gratefully.

Chorley and Littleborough's cricketers played. They gave themselves to their sport with the enthusiasm of men who once feared their summer would never start. Joe Barker's first ball of the match beat Littleborough's Zac Perren outside the off stump; his second was clipped forward of square towards the sycamores and Norway maples on the far side of Chorley's lovely cricket field. There was gentle applause from a large group of spectators who had been determined not to miss the start of this strangest of seasons. By the end of the afternoon there would be well over a hundred folk on the banks and decking areas that surround this Northern Premier League ground.

The oddity of a pre-season game taking place in July was soon forgotten. The ECB's protocols for club cricket in a time of Covid were quickly absorbed into the natural rhythm of the play. They were noticeable only when the cricketers repaired to the boundary every six overs to sanitise their hands. By the first such break Perren and his skipper, Travis Townsend, had helped themselves to some easy runs as Chorley's opening bowlers struggled to find a good length. By the second young seamer Jimmy Lee had taken three wickets and the home bowlers had exerted a grip on the game.

Every wicket was celebrated safely. Huddles were out. Many spectators took the opportunity to amble round the boundary and among them were Wayne Barclay, Chorley's vice-chairman, and committee member, Oliver Smith, who had been on the ground since 8.30 making sure the changing rooms were stocked with anti-bacterial wipes and that the one-way systems were set up. Recreational cricket has been hit hard by Covid but most clubs have people like Barclay and Smith, who keep things going. "We had to cut our expenditure wherever we could and sometimes in ways we'd never envisaged," said Smith. "But about two thirds of annual subscriptions were paid within a month by people who could not be sure they'd see any cricket at all this year. They just wanted to support the club."

Covid protocols meant that no food was available at Windsor Park on Saturday but the bar opened and many home supporters were nursing pints as they watched the home bowlers throttle the life out of Littleborough's youthful lower-order batting. Decently placed on 72 for three halfway through their 40-over innings, the visitors collapsed to 97 all out, medium-pacer Andy Flear helping himself to four very cheap wickets. Rather more significant, though, was the fact that both teams included a clutch of young players. Reviving and maintaining the interest of junior cricketers will be vital over the next couple of months and tomorrow, Alex Howarth, is taking an Under 15 team to Southport. "The nice thing is that some dads are now netting with their sons because they've been allowed to do that," said Barclay "We have just adapted to whatever restrictions were in place."

The next generation of club cricketers dominated the play after tea. Matthew Hernon's one-bail leg-side stumping to remove Zane Nirodi off Joe Kershaw's medium pace was as good a piece of wicketkeeping as you might see in the professional game. And having claimed five victims in Littleborough's innings, Harry Barclay took his team home in comfort with 54 not out.

Did the result matter? Of course, it did. Otherwise there would have been no point Dave Hindle and Stuart Roberts, the socially-distanced scorers, doing their jobs so well. However, the outcome took its place within a broader context, one that was also appreciated in Fleetwood, Toft and Instow, just three of the other grounds where matches took place on Saturday. But maybe Chorley has been preparing for this sort of crisis for longer than we know. In 1988 the town's motto was changed from "Beware" to "Be Aware": watchwords for a Covid summer that even Dominic Cummings could not better.

The Times – July 12, 2020

Lancashire v Derbyshire – September 2020

North leaders Derbyshire seize momentum despite Josh Bohannon's 94

———————————— DAY ONE ————————————

Lancashire 206 for 8 (Bohannon 94, Melton 3-46) against Derbyshire

It is September, yet this cricket season, such as it's been, has run little more than half its course. On Liverpool's great ground, Lancashire and Derbyshire are playing a match the result of which might help to determine the destiny of an utterly new trophy. Inside Aigburth barely a hundred people have gathered for a game which, in normal times, would be a major event, even in this football-crazed city. But instead of the babble of hospitality there is the dull hum of a generator; instead of the chatter of expectation, shouted encouragements ring out in the crisp air: "That's the way, Sammy boy! Backing you, pal." As a backcloth to these sounds, the first ambers of autumn settle on the trees that line Beechwood and Riversdale Roads. "As on this whirligig of Time / We circle with the seasons," wrote Tennyson.

This is a bigger game for Derbyshire, who still have hopes of contesting the Bob Willis Trophy final at Lord's, than it is for Lancashire, whose chance has gone. Yet for nobody do these four days carry more significance than George Lavelle and Jack Morley, who are making their first-class debuts for the home side. So our cricket was freighted with both personal and collective aspirations and when this first day was done, Derbyshire held the advantage, a judgement reinforced by the loss of George Balderson and Danny Lamb's wickets in the final quarter-hour of play. For all that Josh Bohannon's 301-minute 94 had frustrated the visitors, a total of 206 for eight should not daunt them, especially as Lancashire are fielding one of their greenest bowling attacks in recent memory. And as the evening session ended, the cries of the players still rang out as loudly as they had in the gentle warmth of afternoon. "Yes Fynny! Come on Critcher!"

Such encouragements enriched the day but they had barely been voiced at all at 11 o'clock when Sam Conners swung the first ball of the match into Keaton Jennings' pads. Steve O'Shaughnessy did not have to think too long about his decision. His colleague, Graham Lloyd, pondered a little longer when Luis Reece brought one back off the seam to Alex Davies in the fourth over but his finger went up, too, and both openers had gone for nought. Derbyshire sought more breakthroughs with the new ball but were resisted by Bohannon and Rob Jones, both of whom are in their early twenties yet might think themselves old hands in a Lancashire team five of whom had not played first-class cricket prior to Lammas. And thus the rhythm of the morning was set: Bohannon and Jones, watchful yet unwatched, except by perhaps 80 other souls; Bohannon and Jones, rebuilding an innings, driving sweet fours to a silent boundary. It was like that for most of a session in which early drizzle gave way to broken cloud and brightness.

The visitors took their third wicket when Jones edged Dustin Melton to Leus de Plooy at slip and would have had more if Mattie McKiernan had held on to difficult chances at slip off Melton. But Bohannon and Vilas survived those alarms and after 2 for 2 Lancashire would have taken 71 for 3 at lunch. They would not, however, have accepted the departure of Vilas in the over after the resumption when the Lancashire skipper was surprised by the lift Reece coaxed from the pitch and feathered a catch to Harvey Hosein. That wicket brought Lavelle to the wicket and he batted without much fuss or worry to make 13 runs in nearly an hour before being pinned on the back foot by Melton. Certainly he did not look out of place but then neither have most of the six young cricketers who have made their first-class debuts in Lancashire's colours this season. One of the first was George Balderson, who has settled into county cricket with almost unnerving ease and now played with easy composure and good footwork for 36 until his slash at a ball from Conners gave Madsen a catch just before the close.

Five runs were scored in nearly half an hour after tea but no one thought the cricket dull. This arm-wrestle was interrupted when Bohannon not only square-drove Reece to the boundary but in the process managed to lose the ball under the media tent. It took Anuj Dal a couple of minutes to locate the thing and he then threw it back to the umpire Lloyd, who decided it still looked like a cricket ball and tossed it back to Reece. Lloyd is rarely dazzled by life's complexities. Neither, you might argue, is Bohannon and that is why both men are so good at their jobs. The Lancashire cricketer once wondered if this game was for him but he now looks every inch a professional batsman, fond of drives but not in thrall to them and, as we saw again at Aigburth, always ready to grit it out if that is required. Although dropped by McKiernan on 29, and again by Wayne Madsen, an easier one on 40, Bohannon was six shy of his second first-class century when he clipped Melton to midwicket where Fynn Hudson-Prentice took a diving catch. Buoyed by this vital wicket,

Derbyshire's bowlers dominated the final hour of the day. Jack Morley came out to play his maiden innings in first-class cricket and ended the session with no runs to his name but his wicket intact. One imagines he is looking forward to the morning; he is not by himself.

Young bowlers seal Lancashire win after Derbyshire batsmen make them sweat

—————————————— DAY FOUR ——————————————

Lancashire 219 (Bohannon 94, Melton 3-46, Reece 3-54) and 356 for 6 declared (Davies 86, Jennings 81, Balderson 61*, Lamb 50*; Critchley 4-126) beat Derbyshire 195 (Hosein 84; Lamb 4-60, Balderson 3-63) and 202 (Reece 69; Morley 4-62, Lamb 3-12, Hartley 3-79) by 178 runs

This was one of those days when watching first-class county cricket on an outground is just about the best thing on earth. Some of us have always maintained this to be true, of course, but when the sun first dappled and then enriched the Aigburth beeches and Derbyshire's batsmen battled against perhaps the youngest attack Lancashire have ever fielded, our case was surely made.

The afternoon offered us September's gentle, generous warmth and it brought particular joy to the slow left-armers, Tom Hartley and Jack Morley, who eventually shared seven wickets in Lancashire's 178-run victory. Yet it was also heartening that Derbyshire's last three batsmen made the home bowlers sweat for their spoils: there was less than half an hour left in the game when Mattie McKiernan's 130-minute innings of 52 was ended by Steve O'Shaughnessy's raised finger in answer to Danny Lamb's appeal. It was McKiernan's maiden half-century but you can be certain he would have swapped it for the draw.

On Tuesday evening the headlines had been dominated by the possibility of the ECB changing the regulations for the Bob Willis Trophy should teams finish equal on points. What was allotted rather less attention was the argument that Derbyshire's chances of winning this game and thereby achieving such parity were remote in the extreme. That prospect receded even further with Dane Vilas's decision to bat on this morning and to extend Lancashire's lead to 381 before declaring. Danny Lamb used the long handle to good effect, reaching his maiden first-class fifty off 49 balls and by the time Derbyshire's openers came out to begin the game's last innings the main discussion revolved around whether the visitors could avoid defeat and go through a first-class season unbeaten for the first time since 1874. It transpired they couldn't.

Derbyshire's pursuit – if pursuit it ever was – got off a woeful start. Lamb slanted one across Billy Godleman and the visiting captain departed much as he had done in the first innings: caught in the slips when pushing a little across the line. Four overs later Lamb brought one back to Wayne Madsen and Graham Lloyd decided it was not doing too much to miss leg stump. Luis Reece and Leus du Plooy shepherded the innings to 56 for two at lunch and batted with relative restraint for an hour on the resumption. Vilas brought on his spinners and du Plooy cover-drove Hartley for successive boundaries when he overpitched. The contest was never less than keen and one sensed that both young bowlers were gaining in knowledge with every over they delivered. It was an afternoon when a man might think himself young again and once more 'prince of the apple towns', the figures in white making the hours memorable even as the season slipped away.

Then Derbyshire lost the match in little more than half an hour, their extraordinary decline beginning in an incident-crammed 41st over bowled by Morley. Off the first ball Reece, who was well set on 55, went down on one knee and clumped the ball over midwicket for six. The third and fifth balls were reverse-swept to the boundary but the opener then attempted an orthodox sweep to the final delivery and top edged a catch to Keaton Jennings at slip. For a while batsmen came and went like drivers collecting car park tickets. Du Plooy played all around a low full toss from Hartley and was leg before; Fynn Hudson-Prentice was beaten by a well-flighted delivery from the same bowler and nicked a catch to Jennings; Matt Critchley played down the soft fruit aisle only to find the spinning ball was in chocolate and biscuits. Morley thus collected his second wicket and later picked up his third when Harvey Hosein went back fatally. By then, Dal had also been leg before to Hartley, although there was a suspicion he'd hit it. Derbyshire had lost six wickets for 17 runs in barely nine overs.

All this drama lacked was the appreciation of a crowd. The live streams have been invaluable this season but they are one-way media. One notices the absence of loyal spectators, their smiles, their applause and, yes, their grumbles. There would have been joy from home supporters when Hartley and Morley were running through Derbyshire this afternoon but also appreciation for the determination shown by McKiernan and Sam Conners in a 36-over stand which bridged the tea interval. McKiernan hit eight boundaries but eventually shut up shop; his partner, by contrast, had never been open for business.

With 40 minutes left in the game – Lancashire would have bowled something like 100 overs had the innings run its full length – Conners went back to Morley and thereby became his fourth victim of the innings. By then the trees on Beechwood Road, which had been dark and shadowed in the early morning, carried the sunlight of early evening. Lancashire's players shouted in hope at almost every thick edge and traces of impatience were showing before McKiernan became Lamb's third wicket of the innings, thus giving him match figures of 7–72; they are the best of his career and it suddenly seemed a long time since he had completed that rapid fifty in the opening overs of the day. Having made certain they could not lose the game, Lancashire had duly succeeded in winning it and no one was asking about a late declaration when they interviewed the young spinners, their faces shining with the sweat of triumph.

The cricketers are gone now and Aigburth has been made ready for other matches. There is that soft melancholy that accompanies the final month of any cricket season. Yet the sight of Morley and Hartley and McKiernan playing with such passion and skill offered us portents of next spring and we are blessed in this of all summers that we have had so much to remember and enjoy afresh.

The Bob Willis Trophy

Lingering snapshots of summer will carry cricket's family through an uncertain winter

Many people who love cricket hope to see something in the season's final match that they can take with them into winter. If nothing substantial or obvious is available, they will pick a single stroke, a fine catch or even the sight of the players leaving the field on a long-shadowed evening. Such romanticism may be mocked by more cynical folk but they are just as vulnerable. To examine a scorecard is to read a short story; to scan career averages in a county yearbook is to see a record of both fulfilled promise and dashed dreams. "My God, he was some batsman! Do you recall that century against Surrey? Whatever went wrong…?"

Fortunately, those of us privileged to watch last week's Bob Willis Trophy Final at Lord's will not need to ransack our minds for sustaining images. Here is Eddie Byrom straight driving Sam Cook on the first day; there is Tom Lammonby easing James Porter through midwicket on the fourth; and what about the close catching of Craig Overton, the eight wickets of Lewis Gregory, the steel-hearted resilience of Ryan ten Doeschate? Above all, though, above even the unpriced bravery of youth, there was an opening batsman who had already shown us all his shots many times but then, on Friday, played them again, only this time with renewed grace and fresh poise. "Do you ever remember seeing him bat so fluently before?" one journalist asked his colleagues, all of them with a few hundred Tests on their clocks. And on the instant, as though to answer the query, Alastair Cook threaded another cover drive to the Grand Stand boundary. It was as though one's accountant had burst into popular song.

Even the statisticians had their little jest, pointing out that only Worcestershire's 11 batsmen had taken more runs off Somerset's tight-fisted bowlers in an innings than Cook managed in his 172 at Lord's. All that was missing from the day was the supporters from Chelmsford and Colchester, who had to be content with their live stream. The rows of empty seats in the pavilion reminded us that one of the innings of the season was being played in a year like no other. The newly built stands honouring Denis Compton and Bill Edrich loomed like the players' reputations over the Nursery Ground and one wondered when they would be filled.

The historians and collectors of oddities will probably have sport with these months. They will ask at which of Lancashire's grounds their home game against Leicestershire was staged. (Answer: Worcester.) They will query why Derbyshire and Hampshire didn't play first-class games at their headquarters in 2020. The pandemic will be a prism through which the season will always be viewed. Biosecurity, self-isolation and bubbles have entered the cricket's language, too. *Wisden*'s style council has already decreed that the virus is to be known as Covid-19. Thank God that's been sorted out.

Optimism is a dangerous intoxicant at such times. We await a vaccine and confident prediction about the course of this crisis is the hallmark of the halfwit. Cricket is only one among many sports, and sport itself is only one aspect of social life which has yet to return to anything approximating to its usual condition. And yet, when club games resumed in July and when the Bob Willis Trophy began in August, all cricketers of whatever stamp reclaimed something precious to them, even if it was not yet the game they knew. In March, when we were certain of even less than we are now, I wrote this:

"It is time to press the sleep button on a cricket season that has not begun and to resolve that when it awakens – as it will – the counties and clubs we treasure will all be there to celebrate the moment. The cricket fields of England remain the countries of my heart."

The words were a fusion of hope and belief. Yet after we had locked ourselves down, reordered our libraries, redecorated our spare bedroom, turned our gardens into passable imitations of Hidcote Manor and labelled our cassettes – ask your parents – the counties and clubs were indeed all there, ready to resume the incomparable game. Social media featured photographs and home-cooked videos of matches at beautiful cricket grounds, a large number of them, so it appeared, in Devon. Across in Oxfordshire the captain of Middleton Stoney played the last game of his career in his club's President's Day on Sunday and was given a guard of honour by both teams.

A parochial matter? Not really, no. Life is composed of such social pleasantries. They are among the things we missed.

And youth was given its chance in both recreational and professional cricket. Much has been written about the wonderful fact that 30 cricketers made their first-class debuts in the Bob Willis Trophy. Many clearly have fine careers ahead. But thanks to the diligence of the ACS's Mike Goulder we also know that 29 other county players, who had made fewer than five first-class appearances prior to this summer, also got another chance in 2020. Necessity has rarely garnered so rich a harvest. Tom Lammonby would probably agree.

But so would most people who have managed to play or watch any cricket in England this year. Today I saw the Sussex players preparing for their T20 game against Lancashire and memories of that autumn in Hove will sustain me through the winter. For others it may be a President's Day in Oxfordshire, a cricket ground in the West Country or a club match in Lancashire. And for some, it may even be the sight of England's former captain playing a cover drive on a Friday evening at Lord's as one of the last suns of the season set behind the pavilion and the old ground shone in its light.

ESPNCricinfo – October 2020

Worcestershire v Nottinghamshire – April 2021

Jake Libby lives up to the scenery with century against former team-mates

——————————— DAY ONE ———————————

Worcestershire 305 for 7 (Libby 117, Mitchell 59) against Nottinghamshire

There are times when one thinks no cricket ground could carry the weight of emotion that is borne each April by New Road. Flooded in many Februarys, it emerges on mornings like this, sparkling in springtime, a testament to hours of labour on bleak days. In drier years broadsheet editors hoped the season would begin here, for then they could dispatch their photographers to Worcester, comfortable in the knowledge that their back pages would feature sweatered cricketers against the backcloth of the cathedral. And a scene already laden with connotation and symbol was further enhanced today when some marvellous sport was fittingly enriched by Jake Libby and Luke Fletcher, two of the county game's very many good guys.

Libby dominated the first half of our cricket and made his second century in four innings, thereby bringing his aggregate for this immature campaign to 318 runs. Until Ed Barnard and Alzarri Joseph put on an unbroken 89 for Worcestershire's eighth wicket in the final 100 minutes or so of the evening, the former Nottinghamshire opener's batting had done most to determine the early shape of this contest. Libby's cuts and drives had been firm and well-chosen and his leaving the ball was particularly judicious. Nothing expressed his superiority more clearly than the manner with which he reached his hundred after nearly four hours' batting. That came when Dane Paterson, Nottinghamshire's South African seamer, attempted an ill-advised bouncer. Instead of being hard and potent, though, the delivery was limp and useless: a clear case of projectile dysfunction. Libby heaved the ball over square leg for six and clenched his fist, a shade ostentatiously, perhaps.

At Chelmsford nearly a fortnight ago Libby made 180 and was at the crease for longer than it takes the traffic-jams to clear in that city. The first-class season has now occupied nine days and he has batted for nearly three of them. But while Libby will have taken pleasure from the fact that this hundred was scored against his former colleagues at Trent Bridge, one rather doubts he gloated over the matter. And in any case his innings of 117 was countered by Fletcher, another of the English game's noble servants, who bowled tightly, took two good wickets, including Libby's, and pulled off a run out that will surely feature when Steven Mullaney's players hold their Christmas party.

Fletcher's value to his team's attack had been plain well before he enjoyed obvious success. While the other Nottinghamshire bowlers were conceding more than 3.5 runs an over Fletcher was leaking barely a single. It was, therefore, simple justice that he took the first wicket when Daryl Mitchell drove at a wideish ball ten minutes after lunch but merely feathered a catch to Tom Moores, who was standing up to the stumps, thereby chaining Mitchell to the crease. Nottinghamshire's need for a breakthrough was becoming desperate; Libby and Mitchell had put on 140 for their side's first wicket. Home supporters watching on the live stream will have enjoyed the opening overs when the pair's cover-drives and cuts ran to the off side boundaries and Mullaney had been forced to post only a single slip after 16 overs.

Fletcher's removal of Mitchell for a well-made 59 began Nottinghamshire's best period of the day. Almost immediately Tom Fell was leg before when he overbalanced while trying to clip a ball from Zak Chappell to leg. Then Gareth Roderick groped rather stiffly at a wideish delivery from Paterson. But that most conventional of dismissals, an edge to the keeper, was followed by a quite extraordinary one as the formidably proportioned Fletcher ran out Brett D'Oliveira for three when the batsman hesitated over an achievable single and was beaten by a direct hit from backward point. Fletcher's reaction when he saw Russell Warren's finger raised was to hold his arms aloft in triumph and gallop madly towards the cathedral. Perhaps he thought God would like to exchange a few high-fives with an equal; certainly there was something miraculous about the event.

Worcestershire lost their fifth wicket as the Earl Grey was brewing when their slow left-armer, Liam Patterson-White, produced a beauty that turned and hit the top of Riki Wessels' off stump. Ten minutes into the evening Libby nibbled at a ball he didn't have to play and Moores completed the catch. But any thought that Nottinghamshire might have to bat tonight on a wicket that is already taking spin was dispelled by Barnard and Joseph, whose partnership offered something of a gentle epilogue to this rich day. Both batsmen resisted any temptation towards wanton aggression, instead settling for careful accumulation in the sunlight. Once again one's eye was taken by the towered tracery of the cathedral, the improbable beauty of the setting, the familiar things at Worcester of which one never tires. The Ladies' Pavilion remains closed, of course, but we still had cake for tea.

Haseeb Hameed and Ben Slater enrich dour draw with stats for the ages

———————————————— DAY FOUR ————————————————

Worcestershire 436 (Libby 117, Leach 86, Joseph 61, Mitchell 59, Barnard 58 Patterson-White 4-114) drew with Nottinghamshire 276 (Hameed 111, Moores 62; Morris 3-30) and 236 for 0 (Slater 114*, Hameed 114*)

Ed Barnard bowls to Ben Slater. The match in which they are playing will soon be drawn as firmly as Excalibur was fixed in the stone. Yet the contest will soon be of particular interest to statisticians, for all three innings will boast century opening partnerships and Haseeb Hameed will make two hundreds in a game for the second time in his young career. He and Slater, another centurion, will put on an unbroken 236, thus breaking Nottinghamshire's first-wicket record against Worcestershire, the now-expunged mark of 220 having been set by George Gunn and 'Dodger' Whysall in 1924. No wicket will fall for over a day at New Road and in his two innings Hameed will bat 13 hours 41 minutes and face a total of 635 balls, a new record for County Championship matches.

In other worlds brilliant men and women are developing advanced vaccines and wise leaders are reaching tentative agreements about climate change.

But this afternoon, in crystal sunlight at New Road, Ed Barnard bowls to Ben Slater and number crunchers move into helpful overdrive about a deeply drawn cricket match. What can it matter?

For the answer to that question one must consider, as others have done, the wider impact of the past year. Recreation – in part, the act of re-creating valuable experience – has been shown to have a value beyond even our previous conception of that myriad. It has bound us together in the darkest times. Unable to enjoy it in conventional fashion, we have experienced it remotely, thus sustaining the rich sense of community upon which so much else, not least mental health, depends. And community is what we're preserving in these spectator-free weeks. The doors will be closed for a few weeks yet but the county clubs are available to their supporters in every other way. My colleague David Hopps, no one-eyed optimist he, put it perfectly in a superbly balanced essay written for *Wisden Cricket*

Monthly: "Community and heritage… is why county cricket matters… Discover it, nurture it, save it. It has never been more vital."

And county cricket still commands the loyalty of unsuspected thousands of supporters. The live streams and the websites have revealed that. Some Worcestershire loyalists and very many more Nottinghamshire ones would have paid double the usual entry price to watch Hameed and Slater become the first Trent Bridge openers since Tim Robinson and Matthew Dowman in 1995 to share century opening stands in each innings of a game. There is already speculation as to how big the crowds will be for four-day games when spectators are allowed in on May 20. Those that haven't booked probably needn't bother. After May 16 they can admit 895 spectators here; after June 21 there are hopes of full houses, maybe even for Championship games. Who'd have thought it?

Today, though, neither the efforts of Joe Leach's bowlers nor the occasional eccentricities of a fourth-day pitch were enough to bring Worcestershire a victory. One suspects the teams could have played another dozen hours and not produced a winner on a surface that always promised more help than it delivered. Six of the 12 sessions in this game were wicketless. Stump and bail flashed and flew… infrequently. Batsmen rarely departed, pensively or otherwise. So we were left to ponder Slater's mercilessness when dealing with short balls and his powers of concentration in making a century on the ground where he revived his career with a 172 for Leicestershire less than a year ago. Loan spells are rarely so pivotal in a player's career.

As for Hameed, the mannerisms remain. Between each delivery there is still the farmer's gentle amble to square leg with the bat balanced, scythe-like, on his shoulder. He is still occasionally inclined to play two shots to every ball, one real and one yet more perfect as the bowler returns to his mark. The trigger movements and technique have undergone small but significant modifications: the slightest of forward presses, for example. More notably, there is more intent to score by angled cuts to third man or glances to fine leg: they are his staple diet when his punches through midwicket or cover drives are not on offer. Most importantly of all, there is trustworthy judgement and a lovely greed for batting.

"Just as we were about to follow-on Ben Duckett told me it was an opportunity to go out and get another century," said Hameed. "Peter

Moores said the same not long after but it's a great leveller when you go out there and the scoreboard says '0'. Thankfully, though, I was able to start again and go through the processes again. It wasn't overly difficult to focus because I was disappointed I'd got out in the first innings and I was in the moment as soon as they asked us to go out there."

And so two of these four days have been about a 24-year-old cricketer rebuilding his career with the sort of studious, attentive batsmanship that some sceptics doubted they'd see again. That enriching sight has taken its place amid timeless pleasures. So much has changed on this ground but the essential aspect remains the same. A couple of diseased trees have had to be felled; nature does not exist to satisfy poets or painters. But the chestnut in front of the marquee remains and stood in young-leafed grace as Hameed and Slater extended their partnership into its fifth, sixth and seventh hours.

And it mattered because county cricket is about the game and everything around the game. This week it has been about listening with agnostic piety to evensong in the cathedral on Wednesday evening, when the choristers gave us George Herbert's "The Call" in the Vaughan Williams setting that was first performed at Worcester during the Three Choirs festival in 1911. It has been about peregrine falcons in the cathedral tower. It has been about Hameed embracing the rich talent he still possesses. It has been about the black pear tree and the damasked tulips in Cripplegate Park. It has been about chilly mornings on Bromwich Parade and gentle dusks with the Malverns fading from view. And it has been about Ed Barnard bowling to Ben Slater in crystal sunlight.

Gloucestershire v Somerset – May 20, 2021

Applause will be remembered fondly as Bristol welcomes spectators back

———————————————— DAY ONE ————————————————

Somerset 45 for 1 against Gloucestershire

45

Of all the sweet sounds we shall hear this season few will be recalled more fondly in autumn than the rich applause that greeted the fall of Somerset's first wicket at Bristol today. This will be hard on Tom Lammonby, whose incautious skitter down the pitch led to his run out for three off the eighth ball of the game; but it will be pleasant indeed for Ian Cockbain, whose clean pick up and accurate throw at a single stump from midwicket was a rather brilliant piece of work. It is still the applause we will remember, though, for it came from the 700 or so souls who had braved poor weather and a worse forecast in order that they could return home this evening and say, for the first time in 602 days, that they had watched some cricket on this ground.

A few people arrived early, of course. At 9.18am a man in a red anorak took up residence in the Mound Stand and at roughly the same moment a chap in a light tweed jacket on the opposite side was branding the weather "ridiculous". A lovely couple parked their white Honda before spending the next two minutes smiling contentedly at the world. Another fellow arrived sporting a Somerset flag with the wyvern defiantly salient. But there are probably folk who would have turned up at the County Ground today if Armageddon had been 20/1 on and their homes had been washed away in God's kerfuffle. There were even times when one felt roles had been reversed: that the spectators were performing for the players by demonstrating their loyalty, even as rain drove in from the west.

Cockbain's run out of Lammonby cheered home supporters before some of them had settled in but the following 45 minutes' cricket was less obviously eventful as Tom Abell and Eddie Byrom resisted a Gloucestershire attack led by David Payne and Ryan Higgins. The Somerset pair's tenacity and patience were admirable; this was the sort of morning on which sides can lose half their wickets while a spectator drinks his flat white.

Byrom's leg glance off Dan Worrall brought us our first boundary of the match but that delight was followed by a ten-minute break for bad light. During this time the umpires remained in the middle, their trousers fluttering in the breeze, much like the garments deliberately quivered by Eric Morecambe, Ernie Wise and Francis Matthews in their pastiche of 1930s detective fiction. As though momentarily in tune with that mood the clouds soon rolled by and Somerset's batsmen marked the occasion with a trio of fours. Abell's straight drive off Matt Taylor was the pick of them but our joys were brief. A little before half past twelve the rain fell from squabbling clouds and before long a groundsman was grappling with a tarpaulin much as a first-year undergraduate struggles with a duvet cover.

It turned out that we had seen our last cricket of the day. There was an early lunch and an early tea. There were also several inspections but the brief dry spells and snatches of blue sky played everyone false. During the worst of the rain the spectators crouched in the stands shielded by their umbrellas or they found shelter and talked quietly of the past year or so.

Some of the people present had spent many of those long months in their houses, guarding their loved ones, waiting for better days. And now the absolute imperative to stay at home had been replaced by the gentler injunction that they must go to the cricket. Neither the rain nor a breeze lacking charity could deter them. They are among the salt of the earth.

SHANTRY'S MATCH

Worcestershire v Surrey – 2014

If you walk east down New Road towards the County Ground early on a perfect summer morning, the full glory of Worcester's famous cathedral is often shadowed by the rising sun. One ambles down Kleve Walk in the hope of enlightenment, much as one might arrive at any ground on the first morning of a County Championship match. There is every reason to think the next few days will be rewarding but the precise architecture of the contest has still to become clear.

What follows are my ESPNcricinfo reports about a match whose shape was as improbable as most in the history of cricket. Needing a win against Surrey to be sure of promotion in September 2014, Worcestershire were in progressively more trouble on each of the game's four days, yet their players eventually secured victory on the fourth afternoon and toasted their success deep into the night. They sat on the outfield as the light faded and indulged in the good-natured playfulness that is so often characteristic of successful cricket teams. That this could have been possible was largely due to Jack Shantry, who made increasingly remarkable contributions on each day of the game: on the first afternoon Shantry's eighth-wicket stand of 44 with Joe Leach, one of the game's less lauded heroes, helped Worcestershire put up 272 in their first innings; on the second Surrey were 373-4 when Shantry took five wickets in 30 balls to restrict the visitors' first-innings lead to 134; on the third day Worcestershire were 171-7 in their second innings, only for Shantry to make 101 not out off 89 balls and give his side a lead of 216; and on the final afternoon, after Surrey had been 131-2 just after lunch, Shantry took four vital wickets as the visitors collapsed to 189 all out. He thus became only the third Worcestershire cricketer after Ted Arnold and Imran Khan to score a century and take 10 wickets in a first-class match. He was the first in the history of the game to do so when batting at No.9.

But as ever with cricket, statistics offer only a partial reflection of matters. Those who watched the third and fourth days of that game exulted in the sheer improbability of it all. Even more significantly, supporters could see that Shantry's fiery intensity and deep joy were entirely consonant with their own emotions. He cared as much as they did. If he hadn't been playing, he might well have been sitting amongst them. So when he reached his hundred or took a wicket they roared their approval and Shantry responded as if newly aware of the reciprocal bond between himself and those in the stands. And some of those giving it large at the Diglis or New Road Ends were unlikely candidates for such frolics. Some seemed to be of an age when sensible chaps visit grandchildren or garden centres. Yet here they were, bless their cotton-rich M&S socks, bouncing around like kids in the mosh pit. Such kinship between players and supporters is by no means unique in county cricket yet rarely is it expressed with such fervour. What is more, it lives on, even when the players have put their kit away. Memories of cricket matches can fade or be embroidered but they never die as long as there are folk willing to share their tales of days in the sun. Jack Shantry gave more enjoyment to cricket lovers than some players who have won a bagful of Test caps. You don't forget such things. They transcend retirement.

The deep affection for Shantry was also felt in press boxes and other dressing rooms. On the morning he announced his retirement I was covering Yorkshire's match against Surrey at Scarborough. "Oh no! Jack Shantry's had to retire. That's awful," said Jon Surtees, the visitors' head of communications. And one of the most rewarding interviews I conducted after the 2014 game at New Road was with Vikram Solanki, Shantry's first skipper at Worcestershire, who courteously pushed aside any regret he might have felt that his new team had been defeated and replaced it with warm appreciation for Jack's efforts. And then there are my colleagues, so many of whom are Shantry fans. Not all of them, however, endow him with such miraculous powers as Vithushan Ehantharajah, who watched Shantry begin another innings in explosive fashion and tweeted: "Jack Shantry's hit another six. And now everyone's pregnant". Vish also offered a typically insightful comment in the aftermath of the Surrey game. Stealing a good line from Ricky Gervais in The Office, *he wrote: "People in Worcester will see Jack across the street and say*

'Oh look, there goes Jack Shantry, I must remember to thank him.'"
The truth, of course, is that Worcestershire supporters have never
stopped thanking Jack Shantry for his efforts. Neither have I.

DAY ONE

Worcestershire's promotion getting nervy

Surrey 59-0 trail Worcestershire 272 (Leach 70, Ali 54,
Kohler-Cadmore 51; Dunn 3-68) by 213 runs

This is the season of bounteous abundance yet Worcestershire's
players may feel they have been altogether too generous of late.
It is normal for the Ladies' Pavilion at New Road to be laden with
delicious cakes and only expected that the boughs of the chestnut
tree shadowing the corporate marquee should bend with leaf and
conker at this time of year. It is quite another matter when Daryl
Mitchell's players take such charity across the boundary, as they have
done when losing to Gloucestershire and Derbyshire in their last two
Championship games. Those results, combined with Hampshire's
resurgence, have narrowed the gap between the top two from 45
points to a mere seven. Even more significantly, both Surrey and
Essex treasure hopes that they will be playing Division One cricket
next summer. So while the county's fields are packed with crops and
the branches in orchards bend with fruit, Worcestershire's cricketers
have yet to harvest their year's labours. Promotion, which once
seemed so probable, cannot yet be toasted.

The initial skirmishes of the vital game against Surrey did nothing
to calm home supporters. Mitchell probably knew that he was
taking a slight risk in choosing to bat first in a game beginning at
10.30; yet his players could be comforted that it was their captain, the
season's leading scorer in Championship cricket yesterday morning,
who would be facing Surrey's seamers on a wicket offering early
help. Four balls into the game, though, Mitchell was trooping off
after edging a ball from Jade Dernbach which hardly required a
stroke to the safe hands of Rory Burns at second slip. He was one
of four Worcestershire batters not to bother the scorers on a day
which raised plenty of questions about their techniques against
the moving ball. By lunchtime, which always seems to be a major

50

occasion in these parts, the home side were 132-5 in a mere 27 overs. Although Dernbach and Matt Dunn had bowled some good deliveries, Worcestershire's top order had hardly looked of First Division calibre. Richard Oliver fell into a trap about as subtle as a kick up the bum when he pulled Dernbach straight to the studiously positioned Gareth Batty as deep square leg; Tom Fell was lbw on the crease to Dunn playing a barely recognisable shot; and Alexei Kervezee drove limply at the same bowler only to nick the ball to wicketkeeper Gary Wilson.

Yet the curious thing was that the day also offered the fine crowd three half-centurions in Moeen Ali, Tom Kohler-Cadmore and Joe Leach, who hit a total of 27 fours in reaching their fifties. However, while both Ali and Kohler-Cadmore were dismissed a few balls after reaching these modest landmarks, Leach went on to make a more major contribution. Indeed, the No.8 was ninth out, caught by Vikram Solanki in the gully, bat and pad off Batty, for a carefully constructed 70. Leach it was who was responsible for more than doubling the Worcestershire score from 133-6, when Ben Cox edged Stuart Meaker to Zafar Ansari just after lunch, to 272-8, when the cheerfully obdurate Jack Shantry could only fend a vicious bouncer from Meaker to Jason Roy at silly point. By then, though, Shantry had added 44 runs in 24 overs with Leach and he had also been received a meaty whack on the helmet from the bowler who dismissed him.

Shantry's good work followed a seventh-wicket stand of 95 in just over 22 overs between Leach and Kohler-Cadmore and this offered Worcestershire's loyal supporters their pleasantest viewing of the day. As the pair competed with each other to play the most sweetly-timed drive, the public address announcer contributed to the mood: "Tea is served in the Ladies' Pavilion," he informed the crowd, thus prompting the rapid growth of the most civilised queue since the 2012 Vermeer show at the Fitzwilliam. From the steps of the tea-room the panama'd ravenous applauded Kohler-Cadmore and Leach's fifties, which were brought up within six balls of each other. However, Kohler-Cadmore, who was playing schools cricket for Malvern only last summer, turned left-arm spinner Ansari into Burns' hands at short leg only three overs later and it was left to Leach to help secure a second batting bonus point.

Worcestershire lost their last three wickets for no runs in five balls and their modest effort seems 50 or more runs short of par on this wicket. Indeed, a total of 272 was put into context by the eventless first-wicket partnership of 59 in 17 overs between Surrey's openers, Burns and Ansari; eventless, that is, unless one includes some stock-in-trade nudges and deflections that ensured the scoreboard was kept ticking over without risk. The pair will be there on the second day, too, when Surrey's slim hopes of promotion may be advanced. Either way, there are likely to be a few more fraught days before Worcestershire discover what rewards their season's work will garner.

--- DAY TWO ---

Shantry counters Roy hundred

Worcestershire, 272 and 12-0 trail Surrey, 406 (Roy 103, Burns 91, Wilson 77, Davies 69; Shantry 6-87) by 122 runs

This is both a cricket match and a poignant reunion. Four Surrey players once sported the pears sable on their shirts and three of them, Vikram Solanki, Steve Davies and Aneesh Kapil are graduates of Worcestershire's academy. The trio therefore came under the tutelage of Damian D'Oliveira, a distinction they share with seven of their current opponents. The game is thus a most fitting tribute to the ability and influence of D'Oliveira, who died, aged a mere 53, in late June. Probably the last time some of the Surrey cricketers visited New Road was for their former coach's thanksgiving service, which was held on the outfield and included a rousing rendition of the team song.

D'Oliveira would probably have found much to applaud on the second day of this game but also plenty to criticise. For a few players, the importance of the contest in resolving promotion issues seemed to be a trifle inhibiting. A couple of cricketers who rose to the moment, however, were Jason Roy, whose third Division Two century of the season helped Surrey establish what may yet be a match-winning lead of 134, and Jack Shantry, who took 6-87, thereby collecting his 50th Championship wicket of the season in the process. Shantry's wickets, the last five of them taken in 30 balls for 15 runs, prevented Gary Wilson's side establishing what had seemed likely to be a match-defining advantage when they were 373-4. The removal of Wilson himself, caught and bowled for 77 off a sharp drive, began an almighty collapse which saw the last six batters depart in 10 overs for 33 runs.

Rather than going out tomorrow thinking that they might have to bat five sessions to save the game, Worcestershire batters will see 12-0 on the board and they will know they have a chance of building a respectable lead in advance of the final day. Surrey may still hold the whip here but Shantry's spell has changed this contest markedly. It also, incidentally, ensured that Worcestershire gathered a full haul of bowling bonus points for the 27th successive match. Four Surrey batsmen reached fifty but no one played more fluently than Roy whose 105-ball innings included 14 boundary fours, most of them cleanly struck, and a magisterial six off Moeen Ali that disappeared over long-off at the New Road End of the ground and might have taken out a few Tour of Britain cyclists had it been struck only a little harder and a few hours earlier. (As it was, the lycra'd horde had passed in a pleasing blur.) Arriving at the crease after Steven Davies had been caught at slip by Tom Kohler-Cadmore for 69, the 24-year-old Roy batted with the easy assurance and command that has caught the notice of the England selectors. Regarded as a short-form specialist, Roy now needs 58 runs to reach a thousand in the Championship; he is an exciting work in progress.

It would, though, be an error to think that there was anything inevitable about the establishment of Surrey's modest supremacy on Wednesday. They had lost the stabilising influence of Zafar Ansari in the fourth over of the morning when the opener's uncharacteristically sloppy drive only edged Mitchell McClenaghan to Ben Cox behind the stumps. Vikram Solanki then stroked four boundaries in an hour-long innings of 28 but his innings was more a divertissement than the substantial sonata his team required, and his slash at Joe Leach's first ball of the day nicked a catch to Kohler-Cadmore at slip.

Having added 127 runs in the morning session – this remains a wicket on which careful stroke-makers can flourish – Surrey lost Rory Burns for 91 three overs after the resumption when the opener attempted a drive at a wideish ball but merely gave Cox another present. Nevertheless, Burns could be comforted with the knowledge that he had reached a thousand first-class runs in a season for the first time in his career. Forty minutes later Davies had gone, too, and Wilson was joined by Roy in the 151-run fifth-wicket stand that offered the many travelling Surrey supporters their very best watching of the day. Both batsmen played with fluent control on a pitch that had completely lost its early morning devil. Roy hit two commanding boundaries off Ali, who had Wilson badly dropped by Kohler-Cadmore at midwicket when the Surrey skipper had made only 21.

Ten overs after tea, when the second new ball was taken, that spill appeared more expensive than it was to prove. But Shantry's removal of Aneesh Kapil and Gareth Batty with successive deliveries sparked a measure of panic among the Surrey lower order with Stuart Meaker following his colleagues to the pavilion and Matt Dunn being taken at slip by Mitchell off Ali. Yet the limitations of Worcestershire's batters have already been exposed once by their first-innings total of 272 when taking first use of a good pitch. Equally worrying may be the likelihood that Moeen Ali will be on England duty for most of next summer. It is these considerations that have prompted the New Road hierarchy to sign Gloucestershire batsman Alex Gidman on a two-year contract. In the short term, Daryl Mitchell's side must also cope with the absence of fast bowler Mitchell McClenaghan, who is returning home to New Zealand at the end of this game following the death of his father on Tuesday.

DAY THREE

The joy of 'Shantry's Match'
*Surrey, 406 and 30-1, need 187 runs to beat Worcestershire, 272
and 350 (Shantry 101*, Ali 51, Leach 50, Dernbach 4-72)*

They will call it "Shantry's Match" and those reading about it will think themselves accursed they were not there.

For on a mellow September afternoon, when Worcestershire's hopes of winning promotion were in severe and unexpected peril, the county's No.9 batsman, Jack Shantry, fresh from taking his 50th wicket of the season on the previous evening, strode out to the middle at New Road and struck his maiden first-class century with some of the cleanest and simplest hitting you are likely to see. In company with Joe Leach, Shantry extended Worcestershire's second innings total from 171-7, which represented a paltry lead of 37, to 279-8 when Leach was lbw to Zafar Ansari for 50. Then Shantry added a further 71 with Mitchell McClenaghan, who added to the mood of fiesta at New Road by playing a scoop shot and a reverse sweep off Jade Dernbach. In case it has escaped your notice, Dernbach is neither a slow bowler nor a terribly placid soul on the field. He was not pleased by the New Zealander's temerity.

But no one else's strokeplay, however outrageous, could detract from Shantry's innings in all its mad, "up guards and at 'em" glory. He began by taking 14 off a Stuart Meaker over with an orthodox drive over mid-on, a top edge for six over third man and a curious heave, seemingly of his own devising, which may have some place in a book on baseball. Before long, Leach, who had made 70 in the first innings, took his cue from his partner and their stand became something of a hitting contest. When Shantry slashed a drive through point, Leach responded by whacking Gareth Batty cleanly off his length and over long on for six. The fifty partnership came up in 45 balls and Surrey's bowlers began to wilt. The crowd, as crowds will when enraptured by the utterly unexpected, cheered every blow as it cracked around New Road. Before Leach and Shantry came together it had seemed likely that Worcestershire's season would end in anti-climax with a third-day defeat and promotion nothing like secure.

Nor has Shantry's innings changed everything: Surrey are 30-1 and need another 187 runs to win the game but they have already lost Rory Burns, lbw to McClenaghan for 5. All the same, the pitch has been lively in the first hour of these golden early autumn mornings and there is work for Gary Wilson's men to do. And there will at least be cricket on the last day of the season here....

That it should be so is credit to Shantry's daring, underpinned by the support of Leach and McClenaghan. When Dernbach was recalled to the attack, Shantry glanced him to leg before thrashing him over mid-wicket. A single off Batty took him to his fifty off 37 balls. The hundred partnership came up after the pair had been batting for 15 overs and Leach reached his fifty off 67 balls. Inexplicably, Ansari's left-arm spin was only introduced into the attack in the 71st over but he garnered an immediate reward with the wicket of Leach. Nothing, though, could stop Shantry now. It was as if he knew that this was his day and he was damned if he was not going to enjoy it. He cut Batty for four to overtake his previous first-class best of 55 not out and then he hit Ansari over long on for six. Encouraged by McClenaghan's shot selection, which seemed to come from an emporium of the bizarre, Shantry drove, cut and slashed on. He reached his century, which came off 86 balls with 18 fours and two sixes, by leg glancing Dunn to the boundary.

New Road rose and cheered and clapped. Don Kenyon, Tom Graveney and Graeme Hick have made centuries on this ground and not received ovations more warm or heartfelt. Shantry, a beam on his face as wide as the Severn, raised his bat to the pavilion, to the new hotel and to the Basil D'Oliveira stand. Old Dolly would have loved this knock, you know. He then raised his bat one more time for good measure and he even lifted it towards the cathedral, as if expecting divine applause; who knows, perhaps he got it. When Dernbach ended the innings a few minutes later, we went through the whole bally rigmarole again but nobody minded a bit. Not even Surrey. Well, not much.

And all this followed a half-day's cricket in which Worcestershire had looked nothing like a First Division batting side. From the moment Daryl Mitchell inside-edged Dernbach on to his wicket in the fourth over of the morning to Ben Cox's obliging hoick to deep square leg the home team's players had looked unnerved by what was at stake. There was also anxiety among spectators watching their last day's cricket at this cricketing Elysium. They experienced relegation here only two years ago and even if they secure a top division place over the next fortnight, the loyal supporters at this gentle, lovely, homely club with its cakes, bookstalls and postcard views have no wish to spend their winter fretting over what might lie ahead.

Well, if all their players show Jack Shantry's courage, and if they also recruit an effective overseas player this winter, they need not worry too much. Promotion has yet to be clinched, and with Vikram Solanki batting serenely, Surrey may still be favourites to win this game; but the happy boisterous crowd who streamed out of New Road on Thursday evening knew they had seen something which will warm them should fog wreathe the Severn and Teme in a few months' time.

Worcestershire promoted amid extraordinary drama

Worcestershire 272, (Leach 70, Ali 54, Kohler-Cadmore 51; Dunn
3-68), and 350 (Shantry 101*, Ali 51, Leach 50; Dernbach 4-72) beat
Surrey 406 (Roy 103, Burns 91, Wilson 77, Davies 69; Shantry 6-87)
and 189 (Ansari 64, Solanki 58; Shantry 4-44, Ali 3-63) by 27 runs

They wept.

Whether from tension, disbelief or joy, some Worcestershire members gathered under the Graeme Hick Pavilion on Friday afternoon had tears on their cheeks as they watched their heroes drench each other with champagne after they had defeated Surrey by 27 runs.

They cheered.

The victory ensures that Daryl Mitchell's side will be promoted after two seasons in Division Two. That in itself was sufficient to prompt hurrahs from the few hundred loyalists on the outfield.

They applauded.

Maybe some of the loudest clapping honoured Jack Shantry, who had just added match figures of 10-131 to his second-innings century. But, of course, the whole squad was being saluted after a season in which they had won eight of their 15 matches, the last of these victories being one of the most dramatic and wonderful in the county's history.

So they wept, cheered and applauded. And I swear that if the Ladies' Pavilion had been open, someone would have rattled the cake-stands.

On occasions cricket takes the inevitable, the probable and even the merely quite likely and stuffs them with little ceremony in sport's deepest dustbin. This was such a match and its last day was no less extraordinary than the preceding three. When play began Surrey were 30-1, needing another 187 to win the game and keep their own hopes of promotion alive. Already it seemed that the chance wicketkeeper Ben Cox had dropped off Vikram Solanki the previous evening would be crucial. The former Worcestershire skipper was 21 not out overnight and batting ominously well.

The New Road pitch was still pretty flat, although there had been help for swing bowlers, particularly in the first hour of each day's play. So it was seen as a blow to the home side's hopes when Solanki and his partner, Zafar Ansari, negotiated the first 90 minutes of the session with skill and aplomb. By midday the mood inside the ground was quiet, resigned, almost peaceful. The crowd was smaller than that which had cheered Shantry's hundred to the echo and it seemed to accept what was thought inevitable. After every party comes a reckoning.

Even the dismissal of Solanki, bowled when he inside-edged Charlie Morris onto his stumps did not change matters much. Surrey lunched on 122-2 and a few people bade farewell to friends they would not see for six months or so. Ansari was batting beautifully and playing an admirable opener's innings. The win had always been a long shot, after all. Mitchell was among those who thought matters were settled. "I think the lads kept believing but deep down I thought that we were dead and buried," he said later. So it's safe to say that what followed in the next two hours came as something of a shock to the affable Worcestershire skipper. For yet again the second part of a day's play in this match bore little relation to what had taken place in the first.

In truth, though, we should have expected something to occur when Shantry was given the ball and asked to bowl from the Diglis End. The 26-year-old struck in the third over after the resumption when Steven Davies pushed forward and edged a catch to Mitchell at slip. Already those behind the arm could see that the ball was now swinging; they dared to hope. Two overs later, Gary Wilson lost his off stump when he played inside a delivery from Shantry that curved away from him. 131-4. "Can it still be done?" asked some. "No, but at least we've made it respectable," came the rejoinder from their hard-headed neighbours. This, though, was no occasion for hard heads or good sense.

From the New Road End England's Moeen Ali had also taken up the attack and he and Shantry were to operate unchanged for the rest of the game. The over after Wilson had departed, Jason Roy, as though overawed by the situation, drove at the off-spinner and gave a return catch. Barely 10 minutes later, Aneesh Kapil had no price at all when he played back to a ball which both turned and kept low. 144-6.

Now the game was in the hazard. Perhaps for the first time on Friday, home supporters began to believe that they would not have to go to Chelmsford needing a draw to guarantee promotion. More significantly, the psychological balance of the match had changed, too. Suddenly Surrey's players could see victory becoming less likely and their season effectively ending at New Road. Gareth Batty, though, began coolly, taking advantage of two loose balls from Ali and then congratulating Ansari when he reached his fifty off 171 balls. The Surrey opener, it should be noted, batted with perfect poise for almost his entire innings on Friday. If only others had done the same…

Having hit four boundaries, Batty was drawn forward by Ali and bowled for 17. Thirteen runs were added in the next half hour but by now it was difficult to see where Surrey's win was going to come from. The innings was almost becalmed as neither Ansari nor Stuart Meaker could get the bowlers away. Then, after facing 31 balls Meaker played back to Shantry when he should have gone forward. His off stump slumped back. Two overs later Matt Dunn was pinned by the left-arm seamer whose awkward round the wicket bowling has posed problems all season. 179-9. Nearly there, now.

Joined by last man Jade Dernbach, Ansari changed his approach and the last pair added 10 runs with a boundary and some scurried singles. The cricket became panicky, frenetic. Ansari drove a return catch back to Ali, who dropped the thing. Was that the key moment?

It was not. At three o'clock Ansari drove Ali to Alexei Kervezee at mid-off and called Dernbach for a run. The fielder's throw hit the stumps. Umpire Nigel Cowley merely nodded and with one nod of an umpire's head something like a year's work bore the sweetest fruit.

And yes, they will call it "Shantry's Match". Already his Worcestershire's teammates have dubbed the all-rounder "Beefy". They have folk festivals in these parts, and in Pershore or Bewdley, they may already be writing songs in Shantry's honour. For the moment, though, the disarmingly pleasant architect of one of his county's most famous victories will be content to celebrate long and hard with his teammates. In that pursuit he will be joined by many others across this county over the coming weekend. And when the jubilation abates players and supporters alike may reflect on these four days under a September sun and consider whether they have ever seen a game quite like it. One suspects they have not.

WORCESTERSHIRE V SURREY
Worcester, September 09 - 12, 2014
LV= County Championship Division Two
Worcestershire 272 & 350 – Surrey 406 & 189 (T:217)
Worcestershire won by 27 runs

WORCESTERSHIRE 1ST INNINGS

BATTING		R	B	M	4s	6s	SR
Daryl Mitchell (c)	c Burns b Dernbach	0	4	2	0	0	0
Richard Oliver	c Batty b Dernbach	23	24	51	4	0	95.83
Moeen Ali	b Dunn	54	73	89	10	0	73.97
Tom Fell	lbw b Dunn	0	9	18	0	0	0
Alexei Kervezee	c †Wilson b Dunn	18	31	45	2	1	58.06
Tom Kohler-Cadmore	c Burns b Ansari	51	95	118	9	0	53.68
Ben Cox †	c Ansari b Meaker	0	9	13	0	0	0
Joe Leach	c Solanki b Batty	70	135	167	11	0	51.85
Jack Shantry	c Roy b Meaker	21	76	81	3	0	27.63
Mitchell McClenaghan	not out	0	1	5	0	0	0
Charlie Morris	b Batty	0	2	2	0	0	0
Extras	(b 12, lb 12, w 11)	35					
TOTAL	76.3 Ov (RR: 3.55)	272					

BOWLING	O	M	R	W	E	WD	NB
Jade Dernbach	18	6	54	2	3	0	0
Matt Dunn	15	2	68	3	4.53	0	0
Stuart Meaker	17	0	85	2	5	3	0
Gareth Batty	20.3	8	31	2	1.51	0	0
Zafar Ansari	6	3	10	1	1.66	0	0

FALL OF WICKETS:
1-0 (Daryl Mitchell, 0.4 ov), 2-59 (Richard Oliver, 10.6 ov), 3-70 (Tom Fell, 15.2 ov), 4-99 (Moeen Ali, 19.6 ov), 5-131 (Alexei Kervezee, 25.5 ov), 6-133 (Ben Cox, 29.2 ov), 7-228 (Tom Kohler-Cadmore, 51.3 ov), 8-272 (Jack Shantry, 75.5 ov), 9-272 (Joe Leach, 76.1 ov), 10-272 (Charlie Morris, 76.3 ov)

SURREY 1ST INNINGS

BATTING		R	B	M	4s	6s	SR
Rory Burns	c †Cox b McClenaghan	91	141	198	15	0	64.53
Zafar Ansari	c †Cox b McClenaghan	18	70	77	2	0	25.71
Vikram Solanki	c Kohler-Cadmore b Leach	28	44	56	4	0	63.63
Steven Davies	c Kohler-Cadmore b Shantry	69	90	101	12	0	76.66
Gary Wilson (c)†	c & b Shantry	77	139	165	11	0	55.39
Jason Roy	c Kervezee b Shantry	103	105	172	14	1	98.09
Aneesh Kapil	c Fell b Shantry	10	8	10	2	0	125
Gareth Batty	c †Cox b Shantry	0	1	2	0	0	0
Stuart Meaker	lbw b Shantry	0	15	17	0	0	0
Matt Dunn	c Mitchell b Ali	0	4	4	0	0	0
Jade Dernbach	not out	4	9	10	1	0	44.44
Extras	(b 1, lb 2, nb 2, w 1)	6					
TOTAL	104.1 Ov (RR: 3.89)	406					

BOWLING	O	M	R	W	E	WD	NB
Mitchell McClenaghan	17	2	87	2	5.11	1	1
Charlie Morris	21	4	79	0	3.76	0	0
Jack Shantry	28.1	5	87	6	3.08	0	0
Moeen Ali	26	5	99	1	3.8	0	0
Joe Leach	12	1	51	1	4.25	0	0

FALL OF WICKETS:
1-70 (Zafar Ansari, 20.5 ov), 2-122 (Vikram Solanki, 34.1 ov), 3-190 (Rory Burns, 51.3 ov), 4-222 (Steven Davies, 62.4 ov), 5-373 (Gary Wilson, 94.2 ov), 6-387 (Aneesh Kapil, 96.1 ov), 7-387 (Gareth Batty, 96.2 ov), 8-393 (Stuart Meaker, 100.4 ov), 9-394 (Matt Dunn, 101.3 ov), 10-406 (Jason Roy, 104.1 ov)

WORCESTERSHIRE 2ND INNINGS

BATTING		R	B	M	4s	6s	SR
Daryl Mitchell (c)	b Dernbach	3	27	37	0	0	11.11
Richard Oliver	c †Wilson b Dernbach	24	45	67	5	0	53.33
Moeen Ali	lbw b Batty	51	66	92	5	2	77.27
Tom Fell	b Batty	9	22	29	1	0	40.9
Alexei Kervezee	lbw b Dunn	38	68	103	4	0	55.88
Tom Kohler-Cadmore	run out (Davies)	20	23	23	3	0	86.95
Ben Cox †	c Dernbach b Dunn	11	62	68	1	0	17.74
Joe Leach	lbw b Ansari	50	73	90	7	1	68.49
Jack Shantry	not out	101	89	119	18	2	113.48
Mitchell McClenaghan	lbw b Dernbach	23	37	46	3	0	62.16
Charlie Morris	b Dernbach	0	3	2	0	0	0
Extras	(b 14, lb 2, nb 2, w 2)	20					
TOTAL	85.4 Ov (RR: 4.08)	350					

BOWLING	O	M	R	W	E	WD	NB
Matt Dunn	21	5	77	2	3.66	0	0
Jade Dernbach	18.4	4	72	4	3.85	1	1
Stuart Meaker	10	0	59	0	5.9	1	0
Gareth Batty	31	7	103	2	3.32	0	0
Zafar Ansari	5	1	23	1	4.6	0	0

FALL OF WICKETS:
1-17 (Daryl Mitchell, 9.2 ov), 2-46 (Richard Oliver, 15.2 ov), 3-63 (Tom Fell, 21.4 ov), 4-110 (Moeen Ali, 29.4 ov), 5-139 (Tom Kohler-Cadmore, 35.6 ov), 6-164 (Alexei Kervezee, 48.5 ov), 7-171 (Ben Cox, 54.3 ov), 8-279 (Joe Leach, 72.6 ov), 9-350 (Mitchell McClenaghan, 85.1 ov), 10-350 (Charlie Morris, 85.4 ov)

SURREY 2ND INNINGS

BATTING		R	B	M	4s	6s	SR
Rory Burns	lbw b McClenaghan	5	16	18	1	0	31.25
Zafar Ansari	run out (Kervezee)	64	217	284	8	0	29.49
Vikram Solanki	b Morris	58	102	143	8	0	56.86
Steven Davies	c Mitchell b Shantry	14	18	23	2	0	77.77
Gary Wilson (c)†	b Shantry	0	5	6	0	0	0
Jason Roy	c & b Ali	5	4	5	1	0	125
Aneesh Kapil	b Ali	2	17	14	0	0	11.76
Gareth Batty	b Ali	16	17	16	4	0	94.11
Stuart Meaker	b Shantry	4	31	31	0	0	12.9
Matt Dunn	lbw b Shantry	0	11	8	0	0	0
Jade Dernbach	not out	8	12	13	1	0	66.66
Extras	(b 5, lb 8)	13					
TOTAL	75 Ov (RR: 2.52)	189					

BOWLING	O	M	R	W	E	WD	NB
Mitchell McClenaghan	11	3	26	1	2.36	0	0
Charlie Morris	12	5	28	1	2.33	0	0
Jack Shantry	24	9	44	4	1.83	0	0
Moeen Ali	24	5	63	3	2.62	0	0
Joe Leach	4	0	15	0	3.75	0	0

FALL OF WICKETS:
1-6 (Rory Burns, 4.4 ov), 2-106 (Vikram Solanki, 40.5 ov), 3-131 (Steven Davies, 47.4 ov), 4-131 (Gary Wilson, 49.3 ov), 5-136 (Jason Roy, 50.1 ov), 6-144 (Aneesh Kapil, 54.2 ov), 7-164 (Gareth Batty, 58.6 ov), 8-177 (Stuart Meaker, 69.2 ov), 9-179 (Matt Dunn, 71.4 ov), 10-189 (Zafar Ansari, 74.6 ov)

3

SOUTHPORT

In 1965 I watched my first County Championship cricket at Trafalgar Road, the home of Southport and Birkdale CC. In 1981 I joined S&B and played for the club for 20 years, during which time I learned more about the game than I have anywhere else. Many other writers have proved that it is not necessary to have played first-class cricket in order to write well about it; my own experience is that it helps to have played at as a high standard as possible. The vast majority of league cricket is far removed from the boozy knockabout some imagine it to be. But my debt to S&B goes far deeper. For the past 17 years I have lived around 600 yards from the ground and I visit it as often as possible. In winter I walk several circuits of the boundary almost every day and try to understand the place afresh. "To know fully even one field or one land is a lifetime's experience," wrote Patrick Kavanagh. "In the world of poetic experience it is depth that counts, not width. A gap in a hedge, a smooth rock surfacing a narrow lane, a view of a woody meadow, the stream at the junction of four small fields – these are as much as a man can fully experience."

When I return from away trips, Trafalgar Road is often my first port of recall. During the season I watch games and chat to members and players, many of whom have become friends. In 1992 my first piece of paid cricket writing was a report on an S&B game against Oxton and it is a fair wager that the last thing I write about the game will also be a report for the Southport Visiter, *our local paper. That would be very fitting. It is difficult to explain and impossible to assess what I owe to S&B. But it seems plain to me that without the club this book would never have appeared.*

What follows are four reports from three Championship games played at Trafalgar Road. I hope they tell their own stories. There are two pieces from the Durham game in 2016 when the triumphant visitors decided to stay at the ground after their victory and played an impromptu game on the outfield with two S&B juniors, Peter and Tom Crew. The match against Durham and its magical aftermath still seem to me perfect illustrations of the many benefits outground cricket has to offer. I hope Ben Stokes remembers that evening; Peter and Tom certainly do.

Lancashire v Durham 2016

Of summer, and beauty and community... and cricket

———————————————— DAY THREE – JULY 18 ————————————————

Durham, 291, need 247 runs to beat Lancashire, 204 and 333
(Procter 122, Hameed 53, Stokes 3-50, Borthwick 3-98)

To appreciate the full perfection of this day's cricket, it may be useful, just for a moment please, to recall this ground in December: the grass is tussocky and barely green at all; the outfield is marked out for junior football games; there are dishcloth skies and lowering dusks; and crows are perched in the bare balsam poplars like black commas punctuating the winter.

Now a Monday in July and summer is suddenly emerging from grey bedragglement. The sycamores at the Grosvenor Road End stand as if saluting its tardy arrival. In the middle Haseeb Hameed and Luke Procter are building the 114-run partnership that will take Lancashire into the lead. Harrod Drive at his back, Ben Stokes is running in, determined to win the game for Durham and prove his fitness for the Manchester Test. But for all that Stokes and Borthwick may be in the selectors' minds, this is not an international occasion. It is Lancashire and Durham badges that proliferate, along with those of fine local clubs: Ormskirk, Fleetwood Hesketh, Sefton Park. Then Hameed, having taken 14 runs off a frolicsome four balls from Graham Onions and passed fifty for the sixth time in 15 innings this season, arches back but can only fend a fearsomely nasty short ball from Stokes to the substitute fielder, Jeremy Benton – almost a utility cricketer? – at third slip. Hameed, his sadness momentarily infinite, troops off without waiting for Rob Bailey's finger. He receives a warm round of applause and the crowd settles again. Blue pastels and panamas are almost a uniform in the marquees. Alviro Petersen opens his account with a swept four off Borthwick, who is getting ever more joy from the Grosvenor Road End. There is a rattle of crockery as lunchtime approaches.

Dreams may, indeed, take their time to arrive and be gone in a casual glance but that is no reason not to enjoy the reverie, be it a day at the cricket or the scent of a once familiar perfume. Decembers come soon enough.

But this day held its flawlessness through the afternoon session and on into the evening. A sip of manzanilla before lunch Petersen was leg before to Borthwick when attempting to force the ball to leg and that dismissal heralded a Durham fightback on the resumption. Bowling from the Harrod Drive End, 19-year-old Adam Hickey, he of Benwell Hill CC, took his first Championship wickets when Steven Croft underclubbed a drive to Borthwick at mid-on and Karl Brown prodded him to Keaton Jennings at short-leg. Poor Brown is struggling badly at the moment and it is sad to see. Those reverses left Lancashire with a lead of just 121 and only five wickets in hand but Tom Moores proved his mettle first by driving his ninth ball, bowled by Borthwick, for six and then by accompanying Procter to his second century of the season. Frankly Lancashire's No.3 needed all the nursemaiding that was on offer. Already he had nearly run himself out twice, once when simply dawdling and once, on 73, when his misunderstanding with Croft was unpunished thanks to Hickey's fumble.

Procter, though, is a true fighter and he has developed a method that suits him. True, he crouches in his stance not so much like a fierce tiger about to pounce as an aged butler about to keel over. But like others with bizarre comportment at the wicket – Michael Yardy, Shivnarine Chanderpaul – his technique works for him and when he plays his cover-drives and pulls, the final execution is as classical as Palairet could have wished. A scrambled single was called by the alert Moores and Procter sprinted to the bowler's end before giving a little leap of joy and holding his bat aloft to all and to sundry. He had batted for four minutes less than five hours and he may have played an innings which sets up a victory. The crowd stood to Procter when he reached three figures and they stood again nine overs after tea when he returned to the pavilion having made 122 off 282 balls. They applauded as well when the details of his innings were announced over the public address system, for this was a day when people seem determined to relish every good thing. One saw their point.

Two overs after Procter was out Moores failed to make his ground when called for a single by Kyle Jarvis. It says something about the

19-year-old's sangfroid during his second first-class innings that a run out seemed his most likely mode of dismissal. He had made 35 and had looked the part of a Division One cricketer. On the final day of this game, he will keep to Simon Kerrigan and Matt Parkinson on a turning pitch. Every day offers young Moores a new test, a new adventure and he looks as if he is enjoying every dashed minute of it. When he was out Lancashire's lead was 196, competitive perhaps but nothing like the 250 for which Ashley Giles was looking. That was all but achieved thanks to a 27-run stand for the ninth wicket between Kerrigan and Nathan Buck and then thanks to Buck levying 16 runs off four balls from Borthwick, one of the sixes sailing over the Indoor School. Unlike the enjoyment derived by the crowd from this day, that ball is gone for ever. Stokes ended the innings when Parkinson was caught at short leg but, as a bowler anyway, the all-rounder does not look quite at his fighting weight. Whether his batting is ready for the challenge of Mohammed Amir and Yasir Shah… well that, as Alan MacGilvray used to say, "is for tomorrow."

This evening spectators can smile ruefully at their sunburn and reflect on their day's cricket. Tennis players are on their courts now but the light is still crystal-bright at a blessed Trafalgar Road. On the patio there is excited chatter and more clinking glasses as people discuss the several glories of the day. Someone is belting out "Flower of Scotland" although God knows why. On second thoughts, there should be songs.

Collingwood's Durham drink to victory as county game values its roots

———————— DAY FOUR – JULY 19 ————————

Durham 291 (21pts) (Borthwick 64, Collingwood 50, Anderson 3-58) and 247 for 8 (Jennings 82, Burnham 52, Smith 5-25) beat Lancashire (4pts) 204 (Croft 54, Petersen 51, Rushworth 4-30) and 333 (Procter 122, Hameed 53, Stokes 3-50, Borthwick 3-98) by two wickets.

This game ended with small eruptions of blue and yellow joy in front of the pavilion and on the railway side of Trafalgar Road.

They were accompanied a larger and more boisterous outburst of triumph from Durham's players in the dugout as Chris Rushworth cover-drove a Kyle Jarvis half-volley to the boundary, thus placing a seal on his side's two-wicket victory.

But, no, the occasion in its proper sense did not end there. For Paul Collingwood and his players later threw their bags on the coach that had arrived to take them home and told the driver they were staying in Southport. They played cricket with some of Southport and Birkdale's most junior players on the outfield and one just wished that Colin Graves, the chairman of the ECB, had been there to see it. "Look", one could have said, "this is what can happen when you take four-day cricket back to its roots. Now, would you like a pint, Colin?"

Having been invited to Southport, the Durham players did not overstay their welcome. They won the match, had a few drinks, then a few more, and regaled the Southport and Birkdale members with "Blaydon Races", many, many verses of it, and then "American Pie" and "I'm Gonna Be." On a golden evening when players made common cause with those who watched them, photographs were taken amid the rich choruses. It made a wonderfully tuneful conclusion to the sweetest of weeks. The Durham players have asked if they can come back to Southport next year.

Suddenly summer is in full sail and she has a following wind.

Of course the eagerness of Durham's players to return may be something to do with the fact of their victory. Yet Lancashire's cricketers were also deeply appreciative of everything that this outground experience had offered them and they will certainly return to honour their county's three-year staging agreement at Trafalgar Road. All that spectators can hope is that the match is as stuffed with delights as this 2016 game managed to be. The final day began with the visitors needing 247 to win and when Paul Collingwood's side were 170 for two, it looked as though this match might deviate from the pattern of damp-palmed tension which had characterised games between these sides. Even when Jack Burnham was leg before to a full-length ball from Simon Kerrigan, few reckoned the game was about to be blown off course. After all, Burnham had made 52 and he had looked increasingly comfortable as he lifted both Steven Croft and Kerrigan for sixes.

Lancashire did not look like taking wickets. "Bang, bang," said the players on the ground as they encouraged each other. But it did not happen. Then Keaton Jennings, after cutting and pulling his way to 82 off 140 balls in this season when his warm-ups are preludes to success, skied a pull off Tom Smith. The wicketkeeper, Tom Moores, tottered under it, shielded his eyes and clung on. In Smith's next over Michael Richardson perished down the leg side. 175 for five. Ho hum. Enter Durham's captain to warm and respectful applause. For all his 40 years, his 68 Tests and his trademark jig-and-squat as he goes out to bat Paul Collingwood still marches to the wicket with the air of a no-nonsense PE teacher on the way to sort out strife in the playground. You know the sort, the type who announces himself with: "I don't care who started it *lad* but I know who's going to finish it."

For nigh on two decades Collingwood has been playing this sort of role in Durham cricket: ending collapses, calming mayhem. But not on this occasion. For he was pinned on the back foot by Smith having made only four, and when the same bowler had Paul Coughlin quite brilliantly caught by Moores diving to his right, Durham were 195-7, still 52 short of victory. This glorious match was back in the hazard.

Moores's third catch was his best but in its way hardly better than that mighty skier which he could hardly see but still pouched to remove Jennings. For his part, Smith was in the middle of an eight-over spell in which he took four wickets for 12 runs and would finish with 5-25. But it was another 19-year-old in this game filled with promising young cricketers who then shared in the stand which all but decided the match. Until he took a couple of wickets on the third afternoon, Adam Hickey had enjoyed – or not enjoyed – a quiet first-class debut, Now, he walked out to join Ben Stokes, who had already deposited Simon Kerrigan over the railway line and into Dover Road.

As Hickey later explained, the two batsmen calmed things down before tea and went on the attack when play began again. But in truth, with Durham on 197 for seven, the spectators needed the tea break as much as the players. On the resumption Stokes hit two more sixes over deep midwicket off Kerrigan, and Hickey lifted Kyle Jarvis onto the roof of the pavilion with a much mightier blow. Steven Croft rotated his bowlers but the game was gone. Or was it? Suddenly Hickey called Stokes for a quick single and the

England all-rounder was run out for 36 at the bowler's end. Four runs needed. Rushworth dealt with business and another county match at Trafalgar Road was over.

And all this drama followed a morning session which was as tense as most folk expected. Lancashire savoured the first success as early as the sixth ball of the day when Mark Stoneman played across the line to one from Jarvis which pitched middle and leg only to hold its line and take him on the pad. Durham responded by taking 26 off Nathan Buck's four overs, forcing Croft to call Smith into the attack. Another good fourth-day crowd was held by the cricket and the ground grew in a stillness broken only by the action in the middle. Necessity, though, benefitted Lancashire as Smith squared up Scott Borthwick, whose previous three innings against Lancashire had been 134, 103 not out and 64. The left-hander was caught in the gully by Alviro Petersen for 28, so that more or less qualified as under-achievement.

But failures of any sort have been thin on the ground this extraordinary week. And the thing is that while Southport and Birkdale may be very special, it is not unique. There are many clubs who would welcome first-class counties and all they are looking for is the chance to put on a show. Outground cricket is enjoyed by spectators and appreciated by players. Amid the entirely understandable desire to maximise the revenue from other formats, someone should think a little more about taking the game back to the people who are its lifeblood.

Lancashire v Middlesex 2017

Hameed puts seal on Lancashire's outground triumph

DAY FOUR – JUNE 12

Lancashire 309 (McLaren 75, Bailey 58, Murtagh 6-63, Harris 4-119) and 111 for 2 (Hameed 38*, Croft 34*) beat Middlesex 180 (Simpson 53*, Clark 3-36, Mahmood 3-63) and 236 (Malan 52, Parry 5-45, McLaren 3-48) by eight wickets

Lancashire and Middlesex's cricketers reported back for pre-season training last November. A few weeks later officials at Southport and Birkdale CC heard they would be hosting this game, which ended in mid-afternoon on the final day when Steven Croft's straight six off Ravi Patel completed an eight-wicket victory for the home side. It was Middlesex's first defeat since they lost to Worcestershire in September 2015. So for four June days these three groups of people, all of them professional in their particular ways, have been joined in closely-related endeavours: one of them in preparing to stage a cricket match, the other two in competing against each other to win it. And thus we have a link between Bev Baybutt's careful editing of the programme and Stephen Parry's maiden five-wicket haul in Championship cricket, his first such return in the first-class game for a decade.

It was Parry's two wickets late on the fourth morning which ensured that Lancashire would need only 108 to win. Until those final breakthroughs there seemed a chance that Tim Murtagh and Toby Roland-Jones' shrewd hitting would set Lancashire a target in excess of 150. But Murtagh's cautious venture down the pitch ended in his being stumped by Alex Davies for 27 and Roland-Jones swung across a straight one and was leg before for 31.

Davies walked rather proudly off the field knowing that only Warren Hegg among Lancashire wicketkeepers had completed more dismissals in a match than the ten he had managed at Southport. On the stroke of lunch he cut a rather more disappointed figure after he had been caught by John Simpson off Roland-Jones for 13 but one doubts he lunched on water-biscuits and self-pity. Liam Livingstone was the only other Lancashire batsman to lose his wicket and he had the consolation of knowing that he had been selected for England's T20 squad. Haseeb Hameed helped himself to 104 minutes' batting practice and made a pleasingly serene 38 not out, the sort of innings that suggests big runs are not far away. Within an hour of the game ending Paul Parker and his battalion of workers were stacking the chairs they had so carefully set out less than a week ago. Lindsey Bridge's tremendous alliums were still blooming but there were only a few spectators left on the ground to admire such floral delights.

No one could doubt the justice of the result of this game. If Middlesex had replaced their suspicious glances at the pitch with a little more tenacity, they might have scored more than the 180 they managed in the first innings; if they had bowled with better lines and lengths Lancashire may not have replied with 309. Resuming on 156 for six on the final morning, the visitors lost their overnight batsmen, Dawid Malan and James Harris, to effort balls from Ryan McLaren which bounced more than the batsmen expected. Both were caught at the wicket, Malan when attempting to play no shot at all. Those reverses left the responsibility for building a defendable total in the hands of Roland-Jones and Murtagh; they did what they could in typically aggressive fashion and Glen Chapple admitted that his players were getting "a little twitchy". Parry settled their nerves and left Chapple praising the way his whole team had responded to their ten-wicket towsing at Headingley.

This result will be a fillip to Lancashire's players as they prepare to meet Hampshire at Emirates Old Trafford; Middlesex's next match is at home to Yorkshire, which should bring back some happy memories for them. Before long Southport and Birkdale will return to being a club ground once again although its members will retain warm memories of the 2017 game, albeit such recollections will not be as precious as those they cherish in their hearts of Durham's visit last year. In December pied wagtails will be scuttering along the outfield in the gathering dusk; trains laden with Christmas presents will be rattling into Birkdale station; and the lights in Dover Road will stretch away in the winter darkness. And on one morning in that month S&B's indefatigable chairman, Tony Elwood, will be told which county will be visiting his ground in 2018.

Outground cricket is threatened when it should be encouraged. For many it remains a precious feature of the English season, something which no other sport can match. The game is taken back to a few of the clubs who produce the players. It remains, as Philip Larkin wrote of the Bellingham show in 1958, "something people do, / Not noticing how time's rolling smithy-smoke / Shadows much greater gestures; something they share / That breaks ancestrally each year into / Regenerate union. Let it always be there."

Lancashire v Worcestershire 2018

Dane Vilas and Josh Bohannon
script the impossible

———————————— DAY FOUR – AUGUST 31 ————————————
Lancashire, 161 (Tongue 5-63, Parnell 3-42) and 317 for 6 (Vilas 107*,
Bohannnon 78*) beat Worcestershire 222 (D'Oliveira 65; Bailey 4-41) and
252 (Parnell 50; Bailey 3-53, Maharaj 3-64, Onions 3-76) by four wickets

Early this morning, before any spectators had arrived, a Lancashire cricketer strolled out to the middle at Trafalgar Road. He took up his batting stance at the Harrod Drive End, then at the Grosvenor Road. He played a few shots to imaginary balls and, so one assumed, contemplated that which he might be called upon to do later in the day. His name was Dane Vilas.

Now let us scroll forward some eight hours. Vilas is facing Josh Tongue and there are some two thousand pairs of eyes upon him. He clips the ball crisply to the square leg boundary to reach his third century of the season. The applause drowns out the rumble of a passing train but even that cacophony is exceeded a few minutes later when Josh Bohannon hits Tongue for consecutive boundaries to seal the four-wicket victory over Worcestershire that administers the kiss of life to Lancashire's chances of avoiding relegation. Perhaps just as significantly, the victory gives unbounded joy to most folk in the crowd at Trafalgar Road. They cheer and will not stop. The suited ones cheer in the corporate marquee and men in daft shorts cheer on the popular side. The players in the dug-out cheer and shake hands with anyone they can find. Fifty-year-old songs from a great age in Lancashire cricket are resurrected and belted out anew. Few have seen this coming. Vilas finishes on 107 not out while Bohannon, the deuteragonist in the great drama and a Boltonian battler to his marrow, ends unbeaten on 78. The pair have added an unbroken 139 for the seventh wicket and if you had told Lancashire supporters early this morning that their team would be bowled out for that many, they would have grunted an acceptance.

It was impossible, of course. No one had ever chased down 314 to win at Trafalgar Road and the pitch was nipping around. But records are there to be eclipsed and the view that this wicket was a mere club surface on which centuries were impossible was exposed as utter bunkum. It turned out that all you needed was a tight technique and faith in your own ability. So Vilas anchored the innings and gave one difficult chance to slip on 84 while Bohannon stayed true to his pugnacious nature and took the game to Worcestershire. And Worcestershire's bowlers did not like it up 'em. In his book *On Form* Mike Brearley remembered Tony Greig's first Test century, at Bombay in 1973. "He played calmly, from his own centre," writes Brearley. Both Vilas and Bohannon played from their own centres today. Dear God, they made it look almost easy.

But surely it was impossible. That much had been clear when Lancashire had withered to 63 for four inside the first 75 minutes of play. People talked of an early afternoon finish. First to go was Haseeb Hameed who hit three sweet fours, two of them cover-drives, but then came forward a little woodenly to Ed Barnard and edged behind for 14. Two deliveries later Rob Jones attempted a similar stroke with the same result and collected an eight-ball pair. Any lunatic optimism felt by spectators on this blissful morning was thoroughly doused twenty minutes later when Alex Davies tried to pull a ball but only skied a catch. "Mine" called Ben Cox loudly enough to petrify Formby's red squirrels. Four down and some in the corporate hospitality marquee decided to make their early sharpener a large one. And who could blame them on this last day of meteorological summer? "Gone, gone again, / May, June, July, / And August gone" wrote Edward Thomas in "Blenheim Oranges". Soon we will be deep in the month when cricketers harvest their year's work. September also brings other farewells. It was announced on Friday morning that this game would be the last in the 27-year career of Matt Proctor, Lancashire's PA announcer. Ever the loyalist, Proctor attempted to destabilise Lancashire's opponents by announcing that Hameed had been "caught Cox bowled *Barnyard.*" Matt will be missed but the catch wasn't. Steven Croft, another faithful servant, began to play himself in.

It was surely still impossible, so why wouldn't Vilas be told? Worcestershire's bowlers remained threatening and their fielders lively. Cox kept wicket with the brim of his sunhat tilted back and looked for all this precious world like an echo from the Golden Age:

I Zingari, perhaps, or the Worcestershire Occasionals. Croft made 36 before he could do nothing with a fine ball from Tongue and edged behind. Jordan Clark made 31 but then lofted the slow left-armer Ben Twohig to Brett D'Oliveira at deep mid-off. Bohannon, bristling with "Are you looking me?" strode out to join Vilas. Quite soon he had driven boundaries and the crowd warmed to him. Vilas, untroubled by anyone, continued to bat just as he had visualised early in the morning. Club members who have worked for months to make this game a success realised that dear old Trafalgar Road was singing more tunes of glory.

It is nearly dark on the last day of August. The lights are bright on the tennis courts on the day when Lancashire mounted their highest run chase for 13 years. But those songs are heard still as out in the middle Dane Vilas plays shadow shots to the bowling of a ghost.

4

CARRYING ON

Tunbridge Wells – Kent v Sussex – 2017

On May 22 2017 I covered the final day of the Roses match at Old Trafford and watched Yorkshire's Peter Handscomb brighten an otherwise unremarkable afternoon by making a sublime century. Among those sitting with me in the press box was Chris Ostick, who was then the Manchester Evening News's *assistant print production editor. Chris's very dull job title did nothing whatever to reflect his commitment to Lancashire cricket or his willingness to cover games, even on his days off. That evening we filed our copy on the draw and went home.*

The following morning I awoke early to the news that a bomb had been detonated at the Ariana Grande concert in the Manchester Arena, killing 22 people and injuring over a thousand. When my initial horror became manageable I wondered how Chris, a proud and emotional Mancunian, was coping with it all. As it happened my old friend had seen the news on his television in the small hours of the morning and had immediately rung his desk to ask if he should come in to work. "No, thanks," he was told. "We reckon we can cope for now. And we'll need you to be fresh in the morning." It was a wise reply. For over a week the staff of the MEN worked beyond exhaustion to tell the people of a great city about the horror that had been visited upon them. Whole editions were devoted to the aftermath of the bombing. They contained no advertisements. Football matches were covered with unprecedented brevity. It was the biggest story that journalists on the paper were ever likely to cover and one about which they would have to write while their own emotions were raw beyond words. But they got the paper out.

Two days after the atrocity at the Arena I travelled to Tunbridge Wells to cover Kent's game against Sussex. The nation was in mourning but there was a clear determination that as far as possible, normal life should continue. Nevertheless, events in Manchester were never far from my thoughts as I made my way to Kent and I rang ESPNCricinfo's *UK editor, Andrew Miller, to let him know that my report on the first day would contain references to the bombing and its impact. He told me to go ahead. But I didn't have a clue what I might write and wondered how I could presume to say anything at all.*

I filed four days' copy on an absorbing match played on one of the loveliest grounds in England. Whatever enjoyment I took from the cricket was mixed with a deep awareness that 260 miles away some people's lives had been changed utterly. On the third afternoon I rang Chris and we had a brief chat. He told me he was coping, as I knew he would. I ended the call and looked around me. It was a warm Sunday evening and the pubs were full, as were most of the restaurants. People were going about their lives and even the most trivial act seemed suddenly precious.

Denly century caps cathartic day for Kent, and country

———————————————— DAY ONE ————————————————

Kent 316-8 (Denly 119, Wiese 3-54) v Sussex

Joe Denly may play finer innings for Kent but he will make no century more treasured than that which he completed just before five o'clock on an afternoon borrowed from Elysium. Denly's hundred was constructed in the style of former Kent openers: Wally Hardinge, Arthur Fagg, Brian Luckhurst. It anchored his side's effort when choppy seas threatened and it was largely responsible for his team ending the day moored in the relatively safe harbour of 316-8. Yet Denly's 119 was freighted with more than statistical significance and this day's cricket embraced more than deep enjoyment. Tunbridge Wells, you see, is quite gloriously the same but England is different. We did not need the early announcement of evacuation procedures over the public address to remind us of our new reality. Those travelling to this match by train from the north on Thursday were privileged to take part in a perfectly observed minute's silence when the only noise was the gentle hum of the Pendolino. Then there were the extra police at Euston and a quiet capital city with its Union flags at half-mast. We are suddenly more alert and newly protective of our liberties.

Those liberties include sport, of course, and so it was with a special pleasure that folk arrived to watch the cricket on a day when rugs were needed only to prevent the sun's glare reflecting off windscreens. The game began with a succession of four faultless maidens, which sounds rather like a medieval ceremony of purification. A sun-hatted slip cordon remained in vigilant attendance throughout a first hour in which Kent scored 25 runs off 15 overs and lost Sean Dickson for nought, the opener being caught behind when failing to cover Jofra Archer's movement and bounce. Archer, of whom fulsome panegyrics have already been written, bowled well throughout the day yet enjoyed no more success.

The next wicket fell instead to David Wiese, who sent down a nondescript bouncer to Daniel Bell-Drummond and was no doubt gratified to see the Kent opener waste his 65 minutes' watchfulness and slap the thing to Danny Briggs at backward point. The French Open begins at Roland Garros this weekend so maybe that was on Bell-Drummond's mind. Twenty minutes later Sam Northeast followed Vernon Philander's fine away-swinger – a shot more from Hamelin than Harrow – and gave Michael Burgess the second of his three catches.

Denly, meanwhile, was batting with studied precision, driving the Sussex seamers through the off side when they overpitched but otherwise protecting his stumps and playing shots only when they appeared necessary or without risk. At least he obtained full value for his aggression; the ball ran away across the square like a marble on glass. Kent lunched on 69-3 and many spectators promenaded contentedly on the outfield. This was "keeping calm", and few places in our land are more conducive to serenity than the Nevill Ground; and this is "carrying on", though we did so in the painful knowledge that there are people for whom the mere idea of getting through any day has become almost inconceivable…

Kent dominated the afternoon session, scoring 126 runs in a style which brought pleasure to many of the near-as-dammit 3,000 spectators. The pitch eased a shade and the ball softened. Joe Weatherly hit six pleasant boundaries and promised more before he was caught behind off a good delivery from Wiese. Darren Stevens, who is having the time of his life this season, batted with much greater aggression, taking three successive fours off Wiese and whacking eight in all during a run-a-ball 44 which was ended when he went down on one knee but only miscued Briggs to Chris Nash at short midwicket. Denly, meanwhile, had reached his fifty with a straight drive off Archer and the ball was beating his bat infrequently. The temperature settled in the seventies and the crowd basked in their sport. It was the sort of day when the gods turn up and watch the cricket while enjoying a pint of Goacher's mild in the CAMRA tent.

The honours in the evening session were shared, Kent scoring 121 runs but losing three batsmen to leg before decisions. Briggs was cut without mercy by Will Gidman whenever he pitched short but gained his revenge when he trapped the all-rounder for 42, the ball striking the pad just prior to the bat. Denly reached his century off 188 balls after 290 minutes of fierce concentration but he then played tiredly across the line to Philander. James Harris became Wiese's third victim and the day ended with Adam Rouse unbeaten on 32 and batting for Saturday morning in partnership with James Tredwell.

The spectators drifted away, though many will be here again on Saturday; the county match is prized in these parts. And the crowd who watch their cricket at Tunbridge Wells over the weekend will share a bond with the thousands attending concerts or the slightly fewer turning up to Tredwell's hog-roast at Pembury tomorrow evening. The same association links them to those going to the Cup Final at Wembley or the athletics events in the scarred city of Manchester. So perhaps such a day at the end of such a week even gives one licence to paraphrase very slightly the greatest cricket poem of all, "J M Parks at Tunbridge Wells" by Alan Ross: "Kent 316 for eight. Moss roses on the hill / A dry taste in the mouth, but the moment / Sufficient, being what we are, ourselves still."

Clerical Stevens leaves Sussex without a prayer

Kent 369 (Denly 119; Wiese 3-54, Philander 3-78) and 116-0 (Bell-Drummond 68*) lead Sussex 164 (Stevens 5-40, Harris 3-37) by 321 runs

Darren Stevens rumbles to the wicket like a taxi-driver bilked of a good fare and in warm pursuit of the miscreant. The ball, when it emerges from one of his many skilful grips, is travelling at little more than 70 miles per hour; yet it swings and seams with the craft of the ages. Five Sussex batsmen were baffled and beaten by Stevens' ruseful cunning on the second day of this match, bringing his total of Championship wickets for the season to 29 at an average of 12.08, statistics that suggest he is the best medium-pacer in the land. Stevens is the Vicar of Dibbly-Dobbly.

If such an accolade seems even faintly derogatory, that is not one's intention. (Perhaps a bishopric would better reflect our subject's stature and eminence.) Stevens takes the new ball for Kent and his bowling against the Sussex batsmen, most of whom could make nothing of him, was one the best things seen this glad season. He has now taken five wickets on 16 occasions in first-class cricket, all of them since celebrating his 35th birthday. Stevens is 41 and his powers show no sign of declining. As much as the centurion, Joe Denly, he is responsible for Kent being in utter control of this game, a position they strengthened by establishing a 205-run first-innings lead and extending it to 321 without the loss of a wicket by stumps. Only a cheek-cracking, steeple-drenching tempest on one of the last two days will make the decision not to enforce the follow-on look foolish.

But for all the serenities of Kent's batting on the second evening, this was Stevens' day, albeit one on which he was helped a trifle by the conditions at the Nevill Ground. There was rain at breakfast time and the air remained heavy and very faintly tropical. Droplets of water fell from the trees which threshed in the fresh breeze and this added to the mildly subcontinental atmosphere; it even recalled a more distant age when, so some of the stories go, this Regency spa was a favoured haunt of colonial governors with their fearsome curries and crested ties. The day remained a trifle steamy deep into the morning and this is often advantageous to bowlers of Stevens' pace.

But the session had been crammed with good things for Kent ever since the first ball of the day when Adam Rouse's square cut off Vernon Philander offered the crowd a rifle-shot reveille to their day's cricket. Rouse followed that blow with two more fours in very short order and was probably a trifle unfortunate to be given out leg before to the final ball of that same over. He trooped off with 44 good runs against his name and some say he was rubbing his thigh pad. James Tredwell and Matt Coles ensured that Kent collected a fourth batting point before Chris Jordan ended the innings.

Sussex's reply began in sickly fashion and was never off the danger list after James Harris's second ball of the innings nipped back and plucked out Chris Nash's off stump. The batsman looked a little bemused at his dismissal but that was nothing to the general confusion when Stevens moved into full throttle. That began in the seventh over when Luke Wells pushed defensively at a ball of good length but only edged a catch to Coles at second slip. Twenty-five minutes later, Finch, whom Stevens had tortured for most of his 30-ball innings, received two outswingers followed by an in-ducker. Peter Hartley's lbw decision was almost merciful.

As if to add variety to the home crowd's entertainment Coles took the fourth wicket when Luke Wright's slash nicked a catch high to second slip's left. Such chances frequently fly to the boundary unmolested but Tredwell dived and held the bullet two-handed. Such catches win games and shape seasons. It reminded one of the days when Ian Botham stood at second slip for England with the air of a man who could slay the Stymphalian birds before breakfast.

Even lunch at Tunbridge Wells might have seemed like hard commons for Sussex's cricketers but things got worse for them on the resumption. Stevens, whose figures had at one point read 8-5-9-2, splattered Michael Burgess's stumps when the batsman attempted a loose drive, probably out of desperation. Chris Jordan lasted eight balls before he simply played across the line, which is almost always an error against a bowler whose line is so tight. "Jordan has disturbed the scorers because I've got to put his nought up as last man," said one of the scoreboard men with impish glee.

For his last trick Stevens persuaded the resolute left-hander Stiaan van Zyl to play inside one which drifted away. There was another tumble of ash and Sussex were 109 for seven. Stevens ended his 17-over spell, which admittedly had been bridged by luncheon, with figures of 5-40. There was great applause, of course, and the ovation was repeated at the end of the innings when the smiling bowler produced the ball from his pocket and waved it to the crowd. He had scarcely bowled a delivery which did not require a response and here he was again, knowing exactly what he should do with a cricket ball.

The end of Stevens' spell was followed by something of a siesta as Philander and David Wiese added 55 good runs in 17 overs. Any hopes of further resistance, though, were quickly ended as Sussex lost their last three wickets in 11 balls. Tredwell had Philander snapped up at slip by Coles before Harris removed Wiese and Archer with successive deliveries. Most of the crowd then watched the final session in blissful contentment. The many hundreds of trees, most of which have overlooked every Kent v Sussex match on this ground, buffeted each other in the gentle breeze, as if chuckling at Kentish dominance. It will take batting beyond the merely resolute for Sussex to save this game and with Stevens in such delicious form, one cannot fancy their chances.

Kent bask in Nevill dominance with festival's future uncertain

———————————— DAY THREE ————————————

Sussex 164 and 182-6 (van Zyl 78) trail Kent 369 and 298-2 dec (Bell-Drummond 90, Dickson 74, Denly 72) by 322 runs*

"There will be days and days and days like this," says Susan Traherne at the end of *Plenty*, the film David Hare adapted from his own stage play. Susan is wrong, of course; that final scene is a flashback and we know that her later life will be filled with unhappiness. All the same, as spectators watched Kent's bowlers press hard for victory over Sussex on the third evening at Tunbridge Wells it would have been easy for them to echo Susan's blamelessly optimistic sentiments as she looked over the French countryside. The ovations that greeted Matt Coles' two early wickets and Joe Denly's two late ones were also outpourings of pleasure from people grateful to be watching their sport at one of English cricket's other Edens. And surely there will be more Sundays like this?

Such assumptions are dangerous. As my colleague, Mark Baldwin, reported in *The Times* on Friday, this game was nearly moved to Canterbury because of concerns about both the outfield and the pitch, the latter having flooded because of inadequate covering by employees of Tunbridge Wells council, the body that "owns" this ground. Hours of work by Kent's groundstaff and members of the Tunbridge Wells club saved the Festival but it was a damn close-run thing and the county's officials are clear they will not go through such a shemozzle again.

All of which may not have troubled some of those who had seen Kent's batsmen do much as they wished with Luke Wright's bowlers in the morning session. Sean Dickson had made 74 when he was leg before on the front foot to Danny Briggs. The batsman looked down at his leg and back at the stumps when Peter Hartley gave his decision; perhaps he was regretting all those Friday afternoons when he dozed off during geometry lessons. Daniel Bell-Drummond seemed set for a hundred when he inside-edged an attempted square-drive onto his stumps and departed with 90 runs against his name. At that point Kent were 188 for two but the real entertainment was to come as Joe Denly and Sam Northeast scored 70 runs in 35 minutes before lunch. The crowd enjoyed this, too, although their pleasure was alloyed somewhat by the need to protect their strawberries and Sancerre from cricket balls travelling at ferocious velocities. Denly cleared the rope three times in successive overs as he and Northeast sought to pile up the sort of lead that would allow them to set very aggressive fields while giving Sussex nothing but a draw on their dance card. Thirty years ago the picnics may have been more modest: Scotch eggs and Blue Nun, perhaps, but no one doubted that the Tunbridge Wells festival would continue, rather as it had since 1901…

Northeast and Denly brought up their century partnership in 72 balls and the declaration was applied 20 minutes after the resumption. Sussex were challenged to score 504 to win and one or two Kent supporters may have pledged that they would breakdance in the Pantiles if Darren Stevens and his congregation of bowlers allowed this one to slip. Immediately the self-respect of the Sevenoaks faithful, not to mention the ambience of Tunbridge Wells' most stylish quarter, seemed secure. Harry Finch was leg before to a full delivery from Matt Coles in the third over of the innings; ten minutes later Luke Wells played too early at a delivery from the same bowler and gave an shin-high return catch to the Maidstone mountain. Poor Wells, his misery seemed measureless. He dropped his bat, bowed his head in his hands and took longer to leave the ground than a substituted Premier League footballer when his team is winning 1-0 and there are moments to play. Two balls later Chris Nash could offer his sympathy. His foot movement restricted by Adam Rouse's decision to stand up to the stumps, the Sussex opener had his off stump knocked back and its bail broken by a good ball from Stevens which nipped away a shade. Sussex were then 8-3 and we were wondering whether we might be home before evensong.

It did not turn out that way. Partly this was because Luke Wright hit Stevens' more attacking deliveries for eight boundaries in 38 before he nicked a leg side catch to Rouse off Harris. More persuasively, however, it was explained by Stiaan van Zyl and Michael Burgess's obduracy, the pair batting for 30 overs and deep into the evening session as they sought to make Kent fight for their points. Van Zyl's shot selection was particularly impressive and he had made 78 off 134 balls when he was judged caught behind off Denly's part-time off-spin. To say that he was not pleased by Hartley's decision does little justice to his apparent ire.

Next over, Chris Jordan collected a pair when he gave a gentle return catch to Denly and, once again, a three-day finish threatened. But David Wiese and Michael Burgess batted stoutly through the final 11 overs and Burgess in particular will have gained more than 44 runs from his 157-minute innings. Kent's victory, though, should be confirmed at some stage tomorrow and one could wish that the future of cricket at the Nevill was as certain. One hopes, indeed, that the banks of dark asperatus cloud which encircled this sacred place in the late afternoon did not symbolise something.

There is clearly a need for all parties to talk and to do so soon. More responsibility should be given to Steve Niker and his staff; they would break their backs to ensure that the festival continues. It would be easy to demonise the local authority but they have pressing financial priorities and may wish to delegate responsibility to people who actually know something about cricket outfields and pitches. On the other hand, Tunbridge Wells council may be under the misapprehension that they own this blessed plot. They do not; rather, they are the guardians of one of the finest cricket grounds in England and they are properly charged with the task of ensuring that the Nevill's full glory is available to the next generation. Kent, meanwhile, are doubly blessed: God or whatever means the good has granted them the use of the St Lawrence and Nevill grounds; they must honour such gifts and do whatever they can to stay at both venues. Tunbridge Wells is a demi-paradise and we have seen so much good cricket this weekend. Surely there will be days and days and days like this?

Harris ends resistance as Kent march on

<hr>

DAY FOUR

Kent (23pts) 369 (Denly 119, Wiese 3-54, Philander 3-78) and 298-2 dec (Bell-Drummond 90, Dickson 74, Denly 72) beat Sussex (3pts) 164 (Stevens 5-40, Harris 3-37) and 356 (van Zyl 74, Philander 73, Burgess 68; Harris 4-103, Coles 3-85) by 147 runs*

The 55th match to played between these teams on this ground took its place in one of county cricket's most treasured lineages at precisely 2.40 pm with the raised index finger of Steve Gale and the slow departure of Danny Briggs, who may have felt that the ball had struck his pad a little high or a little outside leg or both. What no one doubted was the justice of the overall outcome. Kent's superiority, which had been evident since Saturday lunchtime when Darren Stevens ripped the vitals out of Sussex's first innings was confirmed in the only way that really matters to professional cricketers: Sam Northeast's team gained the points which enabled them to keep pace with Nottinghamshire and Worcestershire at the top of the Division Two table.

Yet there were times on this final day when we toyed with the thought that this might be one of those games when the whole current of a contest is mysteriously reversed. As though seized with a sudden reluctance to leave Tunbridge Wells – and who would not be? – Sussex's batsmen made Kent work hard for their wickets on this fourth morning at the Nevill Ground. Resuming on 182-6, the visitors lost David Wiese and Michael Burgess in the first session but Wiese made 34 before was bowled by a ball that kept a little low from James Harris, and Burgess revealed an admirable temperament in batting 252 minutes for 68, his second fifty of the season. That innings was ended when Burgess was leg before to Matt Coles but by then Vernon Philander had played himself in and was finding the gaps in Northeast's attacking fields.

Sussex had added 81 runs to their overnight total when that eighth wicket fell and the reverse did nothing to blunt the batsmen's attacking instincts. Twice in an over Matt Coles tested Jofra Archer with bouncers; on both occasions he was deposited into the white bucket seats 30 yards to the left of the Bluemantle Stand. Archer and Philander added 49 runs in 25 minutes before lunch and we wondered if all this was something more than a game's frolicsome last knockings. Yet the irony was that all this occurred in atmospheric conditions which favoured seam bowlers. The atmosphere was heavy and steamier than at any stage in the match. Perhaps it recalled the early hours of the morning when a super-storm crashed around the town like a keyless drunk trying to get into his hotel room.

There was even a little rain during the luncheon interval and the resumption was delayed by 20 minutes. But Archer profited little from his extended rest. Instead, he played across the line to the second ball of the afternoon session and was leg before to Harris for 27. Briggs batted capably with Philander who reached his fifty off 67 balls and celebrated the moment by taking fours off three consecutive balls from Harris. But it was the Middlesex loanee who had the last word and it will be Kent's cricketers who move on to their next game, at home to Durham in ten days' time, in better heart.

Kent have shown themselves to be a team with a mission over the past four days; Sussex have sometimes looked a collection of talented individuals in need of a common purpose. It rather recalled their distant days of endearing fallibility when they could beat the champions only to come a cropper against a county without a win all season. Their weaknesses were most in evidence with the bat in their first innings and with the ball in Kent's second: on Saturday evening when Bell-Drummond and Dickson did more or less as they wished. Tunbridge Wells, meanwhile, has revealed itself, once again, to be one of the great venues in the English game. Memories of this match will be with some of us throughout the next four months, even when we watch cricket on more famous fields. The Nevill Ground's traditions are revered but none of them are as important as the next first-class game to be played at this place.

"That summer ground, so rhododendron-proud, / Where Woolley (they said), in one tremendous basting, / Lifted his longest six – over the crowd / Into a coal truck rumbling down to Hastings." So wrote John Hall in his poem "A Bouquet for Tunbridge Wells". The bouquets were different this May. They were delivered by Joe Denly, Darren Stevens and Daniel Bell-Drummond. Echoes of dreamland, indeed.

KENT V SUSSEX

Tunbridge Wells, May 26 - 29, 2017
Specsavers County Championship Division Two
Kent 369 & 298/2d – Sussex 164 & 356 (T:504)
Kent won by 147 runs

KENT 1ST INNINGS

BATTING		R	B	M	4s	6s	SR
Daniel Bell-Drummond	c Briggs b Wiese	14	65	81	2	0	21.53
Sean Dickson	c †Burgess b Archer	0	3	7	0	0	0
Joe Denly	lbw b Philander	119	208	320	16	0	57.21
Sam Northeast (c)	c †Burgess b Philander	9	15	20	2	0	60
Joe Weatherley	c †Burgess b Wiese	33	61	67	6	0	54.09
Darren Stevens	c Nash b Briggs	44	44	46	8	0	100
Will Gidman	lbw b Briggs	42	99	90	6	0	42.42
Adam Rouse †	lbw b Philander	44	58	83	10	0	75.86
James Harris	lbw b Wiese	7	27	45	1	0	25.92
James Tredwell	c Nash b Jordan	18	38	43	2	0	47.36
Matt Coles	not out	15	14	30	3	0	107.14
Extras	(lb 12, nb 12)	24					
TOTAL	**87.3 Ov (RR: 3.47)**	**304**					

BOWLING	O	M	R	W	E	WD	NB
Vernon Philander	21	7	78	3	3.71	0	4
Jofra Archer	26	9	72	1	2.76	0	0
Chris Jordan	18.1	1	65	1	3.57	0	2
David Wiese	15	3	54	3	3.6	0	0
Danny Briggs	18	1	65	2	3.61	0	0
Chris Nash	3	0	14	0	4.66	0	0
Stiaan van Zyl	3	0	9	0	3	0	0

FALL OF WICKETS:
1-0 (Sean Dickson, 1.3 ov), 2-45 (Daniel Bell-Drummond, 19.6 ov), 3-58 (Sam Northeast, 24.3 ov), 4-115 (Joe Weatherley, 41.2 ov), 5-175 (Darren Stevens, 51.6 ov), 6-260 (Will Gidman, 78.4 ov), 7-281 (Joe Denly, 84.4 ov), 8-315 (James Harris, 94.4 ov), 9-330 (Adam Rouse, 96.6 ov), 10-369 (James Tredwell, 104.1 ov)

SUSSEX 1ST INNINGS

BATTING		R	B	M	4s	6s	SR
Chris Nash	b Harris	4	2	2	1	0	200
Harry Finch	lbw b Stevens	5	30	54	1	0	16.66
Luke Wells	c Coles b Stevens	25	27	30	6	0	92.59
Stiaan van Zyl	b Stevens	31	72	95	3	0	43.05
Luke Wright (c)	c Tredwell b Coles	12	14	20	2	0	85.71
Michael Burgess †	b Stevens	22	23	28	4	0	95.65
Chris Jordan	lbw b Stevens	0	8	10	0	0	0
David Wiese	c Dickson b Harris	36	72	94	5	0	50
Vernon Philander	c Coles b Tredwell	20	45	72	2	0	44.44
Jofra Archer	b Harris	0	6	8	0	0	0
Danny Briggs	not out	0	0	3	0	0	-
Extras	(lb 9)	9					
TOTAL	**49.5 Ov (RR: 3.29)**	**164**					

BOWLING	O	M	R	W	E	WD	NB
James Harris	8.5	2	37	3	4.18	0	0
Darren Stevens	17	7	40	5	2.35	0	0
Matt Coles	17	5	51	1	3	0	0
Will Gidman	5	1	23	0	4.6	0	0
James Tredwell	2	1	4	1	2	0	0

FALL OF WICKETS:
1-4 (Chris Nash, 0.2 ov), 2-37 (Luke Wells, 7.5 ov), 3-46 (Harry Finch, 13.3 ov), 4-69 (Luke Wright, 18.2 ov), 5-100 (Michael Burgess, 25.1 ov), 6-100 (Chris Jordan, 27.3 ov), 7-109 (Stiaan van Zyl, 31.3 ov), 8-164 (Vernon Philander, 48.1 ov), 9-164 (David Wiese, 49.4 ov), 10-164 (Jofra Archer, 49.5 ov)

KENT 2ND INNINGS

BATTING		R	B	M	4s	6s	SR
Daniel Bell-Drummond	b van Zyl	90	150	204	10	0	60
Sean Dickson	lbw b Briggs	74	169	192	4	0	43.78
Joe Denly	not out	71	49	67	5	4	144.89
Sam Northeast (c)	not out	46	40	55	3	2	115
Joe Weatherley							
Will Gidman							
Darren Stevens							
Adam Rouse †							
James Harris							
James Tredwell							
Matt Coles							
Extras	(b 4, lb 1, nb 12)	17					
TOTAL	**67 Ov (RR: 4.44)**	**298/2d**					

BOWLING	O	M	R	W	E	WD	NB
Vernon Philander	8	1	36	0	4.5	0	2
Jofra Archer	8	1	19	0	2.37	0	0
Chris Jordan	14	1	65	0	4.64	0	3
David Wiese	12	1	63	0	5.25	0	1
Danny Briggs	16	0	68	1	4.25	0	0
Stiaan van Zyl	9	1	42	1	4.66	0	0

FALL OF WICKETS:
1-172 (Sean Dickson, 51.2 ov), 2-188 (Daniel Bell-Drummond, 54.1 ov)

SUSSEX 2ND INNINGS

BATTING		R	B	M	4s	6s	SR
Harry Finch	lbw b Coles	5	9	10	1	0	55.55
Chris Nash	b Stevens	3	13	22	0	0	23.07
Luke Wells	c & b Coles	0	8	11	0	0	0
Stiaan van Zyl	c †Rouse b Denly	78	134	172	13	1	58.2
Luke Wright (c)	c †Rouse b Harris	38	32	55	8	0	118.75
Michael Burgess †	lbw b Coles	68	212	252	9	0	32.07
Chris Jordan	c & b Denly	0	3	8	0	0	0
David Wiese	b Harris	34	72	76	6	0	47.22
Vernon Philander	not out	73	93	124	12	1	78.49
Jofra Archer	lbw b Harris	27	30	30	2	2	90
Danny Briggs	lbw b Harris	18	28	41	3	0	64.28
Extras	(lb 12)	12					
TOTAL	**105.4 Ov (RR: 3.36)**	**356**					

BOWLING	O	M	R	W	E	WD	NB
Matt Coles	23	2	85	3	3.69	0	0
Darren Stevens	22	5	72	1	3.27	0	0
James Harris	26.4	2	103	4	3.86	0	0
James Tredwell	17	4	35	0	2.05	0	0
Joe Denly	17	5	49	2	2.88	0	0

FALL OF WICKETS:
1-6 (Harry Finch, 2.2 ov), 2-8 (Luke Wells, 4.5 ov), 3-8 (Chris Nash, 5.1 ov), 4-73 (Luke Wright, 18.2 ov), 5-158 (Stiaan van Zyl, 48.5 ov), 6-160 (Chris Jordan, 50.2 ov), 7-211 (David Wiese, 73.4 ov), 8-263 (Michael Burgess, 88.2 ov), 9-312 (Jofra Archer, 95.2 ov), 10-356 (Danny Briggs, 105.4 ov)

5

ODD MEN IN

During the first Covid-19 lockdown in the spring and summer of 2020 there seemed no end to the making of lists. Needing to fill their pages with something to entertain their readers, sports editors asked their chief correspondents to rate players, goals, innings, sets, rounds, teams, tries and matches of every variety. You name it and somebody ranked it. Rather than join in this exercise – okay, nobody invited me – I asked ESPNcricinfo *if they would be interested in my writing about some of the cricketers and county sides that had always intrigued me. To the relief of my bank manager they agreed and so for about four months I wrote two essays a week. I suggested the title Odd Men In for one series and the excellent Alan Gardner chose Match from the Day for the other. Some of the essays from each series comprise two of the chapters in this book. Odd Men In, of course, was originally A A Thomson's title for a very fine book subtitled 'A Gallery of Cricket Eccentrics'. It was then in Gideon Haigh's words "shamelessly borrowed" for his own series on* ESPNcricinfo *about cricketers that had caught his attention but about whom he had "never previously found a pretext to write". Conforming to the very valid theory that writers are thieves, I also nabbed Thomson's idea.*

I coped with lockdown fairly well. Perhaps a single man who is used to working alone and lives in a huge book-stuffed flat was never going to find it too onerous. Though my cricket club was closed I still had access to the ground through a private gate. On the one hand that allowed me to take my exercise in peace and I rarely saw more than one or two other people on the ground; on the other, the sight of the unscarred square and the deserted nets was painful until I thought of what other people were going through, either at home or in the intensive care units. Writing the pieces that appear in these two chapters allowed me to research and revisit players and matches from treasured summers. They helped get me through.

Lionel Palairet – Standing Out

The pose, if pose there ever was, suggests a studied casualness. The batsman still has his pads on and one leg is a little in front of the other, indicating the balanced ease so characteristic of his cricket. The blazer recalls its owner's four summers in The Parks, and the Harlequin cap is his favourite headgear. Instead of an orthodox belt he has a sash tied round his slim waist and its colours may be those of MCC, another of his clubs. The only article of clothing missing from his usual garb is the white linen kerchief he is wearing around his neck in the only film of him, which was shot during Lancashire's game against Somerset at Old Trafford in 1901, when he is seen walking from the field and talking to his chum, Archie MacLaren. Such friends nicknamed him 'Coo' or, occasionally, 'Stork'; the professionals called him Mr. Palairet and perhaps one or two other things behind his back.

The luxuriant moustache might owe something to Trumper (not Victor, you understand, but Geo. F, the gentleman barbers of Curzon St, Mayfair). The hands are thrust deep in the flannels' pockets, the gesture of a man who has rarely needed to ask anyone's permission to do so. Our tall cricketer seems to be watching something – it might even be the game – yet he is doing so with a superior, perhaps slightly arrogant, eye. In any event this *Vanity Fair* cartoon helps to explain why the work of its artist, Sir Leslie Ward ("Spy"), is still collected. For it perfectly captures the essence of Lionel Charles Hamilton Palairet's character. And so, naturally, it has *style*.

Virtually everyone who saw Palairet play cricket commented on the beauty of his batting. Harry Altham deserves some sort of posthumous hosanna for managing to do so in *A History of Cricket* without mentioning the word 'style', yet over half a century after he first saw Palairet bat at Taunton, the old boy stood by the rapture he first felt as a child at the turn of the century.

Of Lionel Palairet I confess that I cannot write with any pretence to judicial impartiality…of all the great batsmen I have been privileged to watch and admire, none has given me quite the sense of confident and ecstatic elation as Palairet in those days. Whenever I came to the ground he made 50, often 100; once I followed him to the Oval, and was rewarded with an innings of 112 against Lockwood and Richardson at their best, for which even the sternest critics were beggared for epithets. A perfect stance, an absolutely orthodox method, power in driving that few have equalled and withal, a classic grace and poise, unruffled even in adversity. Even now I can recapture something of a thrill when I recall that gorgeous off-drive, with a flight like a good cleek-shot, swimming over the low white railing of the Taunton ground. From the day on which I first saw it, his Harlequin cap took on the colour of all earthly ambition.

It seems cheap to ruin a good tale but Bill Lockwood wasn't actually playing in that 1898 game, which Surrey won by nine wickets, but Altham's mention of a cleek, an early version of the one-iron, reminds one that Palairet was a multi-talented sportsman who ran the three miles for Oxford University, played football for Corinthians and was celebrated in his later life for his contributions to golf in Devon. The short profile attached to the *Vanity Fair* cartoon reflects its Edwardian age by mentioning that he was also "a good shot and a capital billiard player".

Palairet's host of other interests place him ever more firmly in cricket's Golden Age, when amateurs often had to balance any commitment to the game against their other enthusiasms and even – dash it all – their need to make a living. In his case this latter requirement involved him first in directing the Newton Electrical Works in Taunton and then by working as a land agent for the Earl of Devon, a job he later combined with being Secretary of the Taunton Vale Foxhounds. His sporting prowess and that annoying requirement for paid employment also allow him to be bracketed with CB Fry, who was at both Repton and Oxford at the same time as Palairet and who would write about his contemporary in *The Book of Cricket* and the far more notable *Great Batsmen – Their Methods at a Glance*. The latter book is famous for capturing the dynamic power and grace of Victor Trumper but George Beldam's photographs achieve a similar feat with Palairet's lesser talent.

And so, perhaps inevitably, we return to reality and, eventually, its pictorial representation. Palairet's statistics were respectable but they hardly fork lightning. In 267 first-class matches over 19 seasons he scored 15,777 runs at an average of 33.63 – though it should be remembered that many innings were played on pitches which would attract ECB penalties today. He scored 27 centuries, five of them against Yorkshire and another four against Surrey, the most powerful counties in the land at that time. His 292 against Hampshire in 1896 remained Somerset's highest individual score until Harold Gimblett beat it in 1948, and his 346-run first-wicket stand with Herbert Hewett against Yorkshire at Taunton in 1892 remains his county's second-highest partnership in first-class cricket. He played only two Test matches, both in 1902, but they are ranked among the great ones. In the first, at Old Trafford, Victor Trumper made 104 and Australia won by three runs; in the second at The Oval, Gilbert Jessop's 75-minute century set up England's one-wicket victory. Palairet's aggregate from four innings was 49 runs.

All but one of Palairet's hundreds were scored in the 13 seasons from 1891, Somerset's first in the County Championship, until 1904; the other came against Kent in 1907. That was the year he agreed to captain a weak side only to resign when his team finished the campaign with only Northamptonshire and Derbyshire below them. Like many skippers who lead teams for one season, he fell into the trap of staying on a year too long. "This season is the most disappointing I have had to face in my life. Throughout the season this team has had no fighting spirit, there is a distinct lack of ability and the team is ageing with no talent coming through to compete at a first-class level," he moaned in the *Taunton Gazette* that autumn. Historians have interpreted events differently. "Colleagues found Palairet somewhat aloof, a reserved fellow, incapable of inspiring affection, save among his closest friends," wrote Peter Roebuck.

Yet to Altham, and almost everyone else who saw their hero bat, none of this mattered. Jessop told of the game against Somerset when a young Gloucestershire amateur tried to stop one of Palairet's powerful off-drives and got a ball in the face for his pains when it ricocheted off his hand. The same thing happened to the substitute who replaced the naïve freshman. There is little suggestion of that power in the posed shots taken by Chaffin for *The Book of Cricket*. But there is an abundance of graceful ease in Beldam's two photographs of Palairet's off-drive in *Great Batsmen*. That impression supplies a slight but important corrective to Patrick Morrah's cautionary note that "the peculiar distinction of his style can only be taken on trust".

The matter is further clarified by David Foot, who spoke to anyone he could find who had seen Palairet in his pomp. Typically, Foot offers a daring modern comparison, too: "Perhaps his manner wasn't flamboyant enough [to get more than two England caps] – he got his runs with the minimum of extrovert flourish and had no quaint mannerisms to amuse or intrigue the spectators. His stance was perfect, and motionless. Everything about him epitomised grace; there was never a superfluous movement. One obvious point of comparison with Viv Richards, in fact, was his obvious *stillness* at the crease. The back lift, the quiet and assertive advance of the front foot, the overall co-ordination were near perfection…"

Foot eventually joins the ranks of writers who think Palairet the most stylish English batter ever to have played the game. Golden Age contemporaries like Fry, Plum Warner and Ranji were also effusive in their praise. And yes, their beau ideal scored most of his runs on the posh side; he might also have been a snob and one of RC Robertson-Glasgow's one-way critics. His presidency of Somerset in 1929 was marked by his claim that batting in that era of Walter Hammond and Frank Woolley was marked by a "siege mentality".

But none of that counted for much to the boys at Taunton, who realised some 60 years before Sammy Cahn that you've either got or you haven't got style. And Lionel Palairet had it. It stood out a mile. Everybody said so.

ESPNCricinfo April 2020

Ian Folley – The Folley of Youth

On June 28, 1988, Lancashire's manager, Alan Ormrod, was watching a second-team game at Elland CC when he received a phone call from his England counterpart, Micky Stewart. There was a Test match against the West Indies taking place at Old Trafford in two days' time and Nick Cook had failed a fitness test. Ormrod was therefore asked whether he thought his left-arm spinner, Ian Folley, was ready to make his international debut. The Lancashire coach replied that while Folley was bowling very well and worth his place in a touring party, he was, perhaps, not quite at the level he had reached the previous summer. The selectors eventually plumped for John Childs, the 36-year-old Essex spinner.

Folley never did receive a call to England colours. Although he finished that season with 57 first-class wickets, he started the next virtually unable to bowl spin at all. His deliveries might bounce four times or sail high over the wicketkeeper's head. The yips had claimed another victim and Folley's first-class career was all but over. Within two years of leaving the professional game in 1991 he was to die under anaesthetic at Cumberland Infirmary, where he was having surgery for a perforated eyeball. He had been hit when batting for Whitehaven but had been able to walk off the ground. The operation should have been relatively routine. And the final sadness is that if you mention Folley's name today, many good-natured folk are likely to recall only the way his career ended and the dreadful tragedy of his death, aged 30.

But that's no way to remember you at all, is it, Ian?

For one thing, it leaves out all the fun, such as the times you went in as nightwatchman and tried to score the fastest fifty of the season. Let's put them right, shall we? Let me start again.

"Fol!...Bloody hell, can't he hear me? FOL!...Next over, this end."

There were many summers in the 1980s when those words brought happiness to Ian Folley; and at least a couple of seasons when they may have sparked particular joy in his heart. The pleasure was shared, too. It was felt by his Lancashire colleagues, who knew their tousle-haired, not-so-slow left-armer was one of the best spinners in the land; and the delight was known in abundance by supporters, who thought, like thousands before them, that they were watching Lancashire play title-winning cricket.

The 1987 season is just such a time and on July 22, Lancashire are playing Warwickshire at Southport. Folley is bowling from the Harrod Drive End and the ball is turning on the first afternoon. (Mike Atherton describes the pitch as a "sandpit".) But it isn't just that; players of the quality of Dennis Amiss and Asif Din are reaching forward to where they think the ball will land, only to find it pitching a trifle shorter, thus allowing the bounce and turn to do their work.

"Fol started as a seamer and you could see that in his action because he ran quite energetically to the crease," said Atherton, who was making his first-class debut for Lancashire in that game.

"He had a fast arm action and I think that's where he got his dip from. The one thing I remember from my debut was the number of people he beat by getting the ball to drop and having batsmen searching for it. He was landing it on a sixpence, he was spinning it sharply and he had that lovely drop on the ball. He was dangerous."

"He had this knack, a little bit like Simon Kerrigan, that when he got into a good place, you thought you were going to get a wicket every ball," added the former Lancashire wicketkeeper, John Stanworth. "His consistency was that strong. I remember stumping Graeme Hick off Fol and the ball spun that much Hick nearly got back. He had this uncluttered knack of being able to produce really good spinning deliveries."

Lancashire win the game at Southport by 10 wickets inside two days. Folley takes 12-57 and finishes the season with 74 first-class wickets at a tad over 25 runs apiece, an achievement which had not eluded the notice of the selectors. "At the end of that year I'm pretty certain he was on a list for the England tour to Pakistan," said Atherton. "I think Fol was on an initial long-list of about 30 players and in those days not many Lancashire cricketers were playing for England. I remember it being a big thing in the dressing room when he got the letter."

Folley's recognition was all the more remarkable given that almost every county possessed at least one high-quality finger-spinner in that era; and his achievement was vaguely astonishing given that he had only turned to slow bowling the previous winter on the shrewd suggestion of Jack Bond, Lancashire's manager. There is evidence he had mixed his usual left-arm quicker stuff with a few twisters during his time in Lancashire's junior sides but the Burnley-born youngster had signed his first contract in 1982 primarily as a swing bowler. For a season or two it worked well enough for him but Bond recognised that Folley's career would be limited if he stuck to his first discipline and therefore suggested he try spin. The change would be the making of him... and yes, probably the breaking as well.

The players at Old Trafford accepted Folley's decision and waited to see what sort of progress he would make in his new trade. In truth, they were already accustomed to a large dollop of eccentricity from him. "Fol was away with the fairies at times," said Warren Hegg,

Lancashire's former wicketkeeper and captain. And one can see what Hegg means. This, after all, was the lad who had been Graeme Fowler's runner when he made two centuries against Warwickshire in 1982 game at Southport and had raised his own bat to milk the applause of the large crowd when Fowler reached three figures. "I've never scored a century before," he told his mates in the dressing room. Folley's innings as nightwatchman also mocked expectations: they were noted for a flurry of boundaries carved through the slips or for calls to take quick singles early in an over, invitations which his partner, often Gehan Mendis, brusquely declined. But this sense of fun never strayed over into the sort of self-indulgent indiscipline that blights a team. Indeed, Folley was so renowned for retiring to bed early in his first few years with Lancashire that his most popular nicknames were "Vicar" or "Reverend". The extrovert Fol arrived at more or less the same time as he turned to spin.

But gradually, maybe even during that last golden season, the fun began to stop. Rather than hoping Folley would take wickets, his teammates and spectators started to expect him to do so. This is, of course, a perfectly normal response to a colleague's success but Ken Grime, Lancashire marketing executive in the late 1980s, offers invaluable testimony that Folley felt pressured by it.

"When Ian started to struggle with a loss of confidence, my mind went back to a lunch time conversation we'd had during the winter of 1987. I'd always found him to be approachable, outgoing, with an impish sense of fun and happy to chat cricket. But somehow that day we got talking about playing under 'pressure' and he recalled the first time it had really crystallized in his mind. It was during that charge for the title in 1987.

"'You want to know about pressure?' he said. 'You turn up at a ground and realise if it's a spinning track everyone's looking at me and Simmo [Jack Simmons] to win us the game,' he said. 'That's real pressure.' He mentioned the game in question but I can't recall it now. Although that situation is probably true for many spinners, and indeed many cricketers, it showed a serious side to Ian I'd not seen before. And I got the impression it was something that was on his mind."

In 1989 the ball was going everywhere and anywhere when Folley bowled spin. He could put his fingers down the seam and land it on a putting marker but he knew he was never going to make a career in professional county cricket doing that. Once he tried to tweak it again the yips would have him by the throat. And such was cricket's sadistic generosity in those days that a head-high no-ball or wide delivered by a spinner merely gave the bowler another opportunity to experience the agony.

"It was the most heartbreaking thing to see from a guy who was only that far from playing for England," said Warren Hegg. "When the pressure was on he'd lose it, but even in the nets he'd lost it a bit. Pressure affects people in different ways and I think it was a real big burden for Fol because people were talking him up as the next England spinner."

Folley did not play another County Championship match for Lancashire after 1988. There were four first-class games for Derbyshire in 1991 but he was released at the end of that season and had to build a new career in the licensing trade while playing cricket in the leagues. In the years since his death there have been serious academic studies of the yips, including a chapter in the philosopher David Papineau's excellent book *Knowing the Score: How Sport Teaches Us About Philosophy* and an outstanding paper written by Mark Bawden and Ian Maynard in the *Journal of Sports Sciences* (January 2002). The latter identifies "15 general dimensions" that are "descriptive of the overall 'yips' experience". But to a layman, or even to an amateur sportsman who has suffered from the yips, the whole business is raw agony and not many recover from it. When the body cheats on the mind, reconciliation is rarely achieved. "It's like a worm in your brain that's hard to get rid of," said Atherton.

You would be 57 this year, Fol. No doubt, you would be attending Lancashire's former players' reunions, admiring the talent of Matt Parkinson and hoping he does well. But the simple pleasures of the ex-pro were denied you. What you could enjoy, though, was those few seasons when you were very near the top of your profession. What's more, the folk who saw you bowl shared your pure delight that life could be so much fun. And when they recall such days, to borrow a phrase from Michael Frayn, the past becomes the present inside their heads. A choir of close catchers lies in wait and you are once again bamboozling Warwickshire's batsmen on a July afternoon in Southport.

ESPNCricinfo April 2020

Frank Chester signals a leg bye, 1948.

VVS Laxman in action for Lancashire, 2009.

Haseeb Hameed avoids a short one against Essex, 2016. Photo: Simon Pendrigh.

Charlie Parker, cigarette in hand, 1920.

David Essenhigh in his Wiltshire days.

Ben Stokes after his Headingley miracle, 2019.

Lancashire scorer Alan West, 2011. Photo: Simon Pendrigh.

Jack Shantry hits out, 2015.

Ian Folley in action. Photo: Simon Pendrigh

Charlie Parker – The Lure of the Leftie

In the clearing stands a boxer
And a fighter by his trade
And he carries the reminders
Of ev'ry glove that laid him down
Or cut him till he cried out..."
"The Boxer" – Simon and Garfunkel

The number of first-class matches played in England has declined so markedly in the last half-century that some records stand like monuments from antiquity. Likewise, a few giants of the past have become shadowy figures, their achievements mentioned by current historians but seldom properly investigated. What might be said, for example, about the third-most successful bowler in the game's history, a slow-medium left-arm spinner who took 3,278 first-class wickets in 635 matches but bowled in just one innings of Test cricket? Well, for a start do not be fooled by his three faintly distinguished first names: Charles Warrington Lennard; or by his fine reputation as a golfer; or by the fact that he was born in Prestbury, Gloucestershire, and died in Cranleigh, Surrey, both of them apparently affluent locations. Charlie Parker was the son of a general labourer, an admirer of the Russian Revolution and a gut radical who, in 1929, nearly stuck one on Pelham Warner, the former England captain and an epitome of his country's cricketing establishment.

Immediately there is a danger that our subject's fondness for communism, if not pugilism, will overshadow an appreciation of his skills. (This is not a frequent hazard for students of English county cricket.) Let us therefore allow Grahame Parker, Gloucestershire's historian and someone who played with his namesake for three seasons in the 1930s, to give us a picture of Charlie in his pomp:

"Lithe and over six feet tall, he would glide through a day's bowling with unbuttoned shirt sleeves flapping about his wrists, always with a cap pulled down at a rakish angle over his right eye and a smooth effortless rhythm that did not change as the overs passed... His was a classic action – left arm hidden behind the body as he approached the wicket, brought over fully extended at the moment of delivery in a lazy circular arc that defied analysis from the other end."

But our observant historian can have seen Parker only after he started bowling spin in 1919. He had joined Gloucestershire in 1903 as a left-arm seamer and for over a decade he left the twirling to George Dennett, a bowler who picked up a mere 2,147 first-class wickets in his 19 English summers. Before that first post-war season, however, the 36-year-old Parker informed officials at Gloucestershire – negotiation was rarely his style – that he would be turning to spin. So began a decade or so in which Parker became one of the finest cricketers in the world, an achievement which RC Robertson-Glasgow (Crusoe) assessed in his inimitable style: "On a sticky wicket…[Parker] was the greatest bowler I have seen; for, then, there was no man whom he could not make to look like a child batting with a pencil… Slim and angular, he was a sad-eyed executioner."

The statistics of Parker's career after 1919 might initially strain the belief of the 21st century cricket lover. In every season from 1920 until his retirement in 1935 he took over a hundred wickets; in each of the three seasons plumb in the middle of the 1920s he picked up over two hundred. In 1925 he took five wickets in an innings and 10 in a match more often than Simon Harmer, a very fine current bowler, has managed in his entire career. But such facts burst out from Parker's career like clothes from an over-filled cupboard. He took five wickets in an innings 277 times and 10 in a match on 91 occasions. "He wasted nothing," wrote Crusoe, "to every ball some stroke had to be offered; and there was Walter Hammond roaming, predatory, at very short slip."

Parker was shrewd enough to choose the Yorkshire game for his benefit in 1922 and then skilful enough to take 9-36 in his opponents' first innings. During the course of that 10.2-over spell he hit the stumps with five successive deliveries, one of which was a no-ball. That sequence included his first hat-trick; two years later he managed three in the same season, including two in the home game against Middlesex, a match Gloucestershire won after being bowled out for 31 in the first innings. (Hammond chipped in with 174 not out in the second dig.) Parker bowled a total of 7,719 maidens; Jimmy Anderson, a great modern bowler, has so far delivered 8317.5 overs in his entire career. Having taken 467 wickets in nine seasons before 1914 Parker picked up another 2,811 after the war until a modest return of 108 wickets at 26.04 in 1935 convinced him it was time to retire. He was 52.

The consensus of Parker's fellow professionals was that on a damp pitch he was the best bowler in the country and on a dry one he was merely among the top three or four. He was unfortunate that the first decade of his spin-bowling career overlapped with Wilfred Rhodes' last and also unfortunate that his latter seasons coincided with Hedley Verity in his pomp. The very shrewd Bob Wyatt thought him a less dangerous bowler when attacked. "You had to know how to play him," said Wyatt. "Move down the wicket...and hit the ball over his head. It could affect him. His next delivery might be short, then."

Parker's great liking for damp English wickets and the availability of other slow bowlers offers an explanation as to why he was not selected for any MCC tours but it is scarcely a satisfactory one. Crusoe was certainly having none of it: "The silly saying went that Parker could not bowl on a plumb pitch; as if so great an artist were a sort of one-pitch man, like some elder who must occupy but one certain chair in the room, and if that be taken, cannot sit down at all." What defied conventional comprehension, then as now, was that Parker was selected for only one home Test and that he was not picked when conditions suited him perfectly.

He certainly believed playing for Gloucestershire didn't help his cause. Even when naming him as one of Wisden's Cricketers of the Year, Sydney Pardon confessed: "I have seen so little of Parker that I can say little about his bowling from personal observation." Yet in 1922, the season for which he was honoured, Parker had taken 206 wickets. One can imagine Charlie bridling in resentment at the editor's admission before ascribing such ignorance to the fact that he played at least half his games in Bristol, Gloucester and Cheltenham.

Other occasions offered him perfect opportunities to publicise his deep grievance. At his county's Annual Dinner in February 1926 he was presented with a trophy to mark his achievement in taking 17-56 in the match against Essex the previous season. Earlier the same evening Pelham Warner, the principal guest and an England selector, had spoken of his country's chances against Australia in the forthcoming Ashes series. As recorded by David

Foot in *Cricket's Unholy Trinity* Parker concluded his acceptance speech by saying that "the selection committee would do well not to overlook some of the players in the less fashionable counties".

No one could argue the barb was out of character. Parker had a good mind and he frequently spoke it, particularly on his favourite topics: music, politics and cricket. Sometimes the last two subjects could be combined. Foot's typically fine essay, which itself is based on a series of conversations with his subject's teammates and opponents, records several occasions when Parker had execrated the unearned privilege in which inter-war English cricket was soaked. Annual dinners like that held at Bristol's Grand Hotel were a perfect example of an occasion when the dividing line between cricket's officers and men was very clear. More often than not, the amateurs were placed with the guests of honour and the county's officials. The professionals sat together and drank their beer.

Five months after that dinner England's players gathered at Leeds for the third Ashes Test. The first two matches had been drawn and all the signs were that the unprotected sections of the Headingley pitch would be wet, "marshy" *The Times* called them. They were classic Charlie Parker conditions and there was little surprise he was among the 12 players picked for the game. There was, though, astonishment when he was omitted from the team and disbelief when the England captain, Arthur Carr, then opted to bowl first. Australia made 492 and the game was eventually drawn. The England selectors for that series were Arthur Gilligan, Percy Perrin and Pelham Warner.

"Leaving out Parker at Headingley in 1926 was the most extraordinary mistake in all Test history," concluded Bob Wyatt, who was himself to omit Parker from his own England side at The Oval in 1930. "If it was thought proper to invite him to the ground, it was an act of lunacy not to play him when you had decided to put the opposition in because it was a wet wicket," wrote Alan Gibson.

Charlie Parker rarely forgot a batsman's weakness and he never forgot a slight. In April 1929 Warner attended Gloucestershire's annual dinner once again. Once the formal proceedings had ended Parker went to the lift with his teammate and close friend, Reg Sinfield. The pair were hoping to take some fresh air on one of the balconies.

Suddenly an obsequious lift attendant announced that room should be made for "Mr Pelham Warner", who was approaching the lift and wished to go up to his room. Let us allow David Foot to take up the story:

Parker flung his arms out and grasped Warner by the lapels. "I'll never once in my life make way for that bugger. He's never had a good word to say for me. This so-and-so has blocked my Test match career. I played once in 1921 – and he made sure I'd never play for England again. He even got me up to Leeds in 1926 and then left me out. Make way for him…? Mr Bloody Warner will go to bed when I've finished with him.

Foot admits that he has heard various versions of the story but none that contradicted its basic elements. (He even toned down some of the language.) Parker's hands were trembling. For several seconds it seemed possible he was going to give one of cricket's most eminent statesmen a punch up the bracket.

"Come on, Charlie. Tisn't worth it." said Sinfield. Parker released his grip.

Cricket's historians might do well to pay more attention to Charlie Parker but it would be fatuous to turn him into either a paragon or a martyr. He was sharp-tempered, irascible and quick to criticise other fielders while being fairly inept himself. And for all that he might have argued about politics his career displays the conventional characteristics of the inter-war professional. He admired some of Gloucestershire's amateur captains – Bev Lyon is a good example – and his benefit brought him £1,075 (worth about £50,000 today). After retirement he served the game as a first-class umpire and then as a coach at Cranleigh School. Yet he remains one of the most intriguing characters from an age when the English professional cricketer was notable for his silent deference. And on a warm afternoon at Nevil Road it is wonderfully easy to imagine that rhythmical approach to the crease and Charlie wreaking quiet havoc in the only republic he ever knew.

ESPNCricinfo April 2020

VVS Laxman – Blackpool Illumination

There were days when VVS Laxman gave the impression his art was no more than simple ease; it was probably the only deceptive thing about him. Everything else, the quality of his batting, the honesty of his statements, the warmth of his friendship, possessed such deep integrity that only a sad cynic might doubt its presence. For Indian supporters the best examples of Laxman's cricketing skills were perhaps his first two Test centuries: the 167 against Australia at the SCG in January 2000 and then his 281 against the same opponents at Kolkata 14 months later. As any fule kno the latter innings was played in perhaps the greatest Test of all; indeed, DVDs of India's victory at Eden Gardens after following on 274 runs behind offer balm to lovers of the game in these strange cricketless months. England fans were less fortunate. None of Laxman's 17 Test centuries were made against their side and even the barmiest member of the army regretted the fact. Loyal Lancashire followers, on the other hand, were rather luckier: they saw Laxman make six hundreds in the County Championship. And do you recall that 55 not out at Blackpool...?

September 7, 2007: The second day of Lancashire's home match against Durham at Stanley Park. The pitch being used for the game is difficult, its devilry caused by small semi-detached chunks of soil on the surface which move every time the ball hits them. The results are lateral movement and inconsistent bounce, features which both Glen Chapple and Ottis Gibson are cheerfully exploiting. By teatime on Friday it seems plain the game is unlikely to stretch into a third day, a fact which grieves Blackpool's hoteliers and publicans. Shortly after the resumption Lancashire are 44-3 and their victory target of 169 seems more distant than the top of the famous Tower. At which point Laxman strides out to join Stuart Law. It is the Indian's third first-class match for Lancashire...

Across the decades overseas players in English county cricket have come in many shapes and all sizes. Some have arrived looking to earn all they could; others to learn all they could. The latter group have been especially keen to understand conditions they have rarely encountered before. Put even more simply, some look to take while others – the majority, I believe – look to give as much as possible to their counties while making a decent living. It did not take Lancashire's players long to find out to which camp "Laxy" belonged.

"When an overseas player arrives, they command your respect for what they have done in the game but you wait to see how they go about their business," said Luke Sutton, who made 66 not out in the first innings of the game at Blackpool. "VVS was everything you would imagine. He was brilliant in training, assiduous in practice and very happy to share what he knew. He wasn't the most athletic guy but he made up for that with his enthusiasm and cricketing intelligence."

"He would be right up there both as a player and a person," added Mark Chilton, who was Laxman's captain in the first of his two seasons at Emirates Old Trafford. "I hold him in very high regard. He was an outstanding player, one of the best with whom I played. But more than anything he was an outstanding person."

What is slightly remarkable – at least, until you have spent any time in Laxman's company – is that Sutton and Chilton's judgements were made on the strength of little more than a full season's cricket with VVS, who played just 16 championship games in his two spells for Lancashire in 2007 and 2009. During the second of these he was capped, which is almost always a great occasion for any English cricketer born in their county but has not always been so significant a moment for overseas players. (Indeed, one or two would probably have preferred to get the money spent on the cap.) Laxman, by absolute contrast, understood very clearly the honour he was being paid in front of the famous pavilion. "He had some very strong values," said Chilton. "He understood the importance of playing for Lancashire and respected our environment. He wanted to be a good ambassador for the club."

However, neither an abundance of talent nor a sense of your county's ethos will help a player if he does not possess the courage to face fast bowling on a pig of a pitch. "Ticker", the pros call it....

Gibson is steaming in from the Parched Peas End at Blackpool. The ball is still flying around but Laxman is getting inside the line and wristing it through mid-wicket or driving on the up through the covers; at the other end Stuart Law is displaying equal courage, maybe even more, given that he is carrying a painful finger injury. "It burst like a sausage on the barbie," he later observed drily. Durham's other new-ball bowler is Liam Plunkett and it is easy to see that on other days Lancashire could have been rolled for a few more than bugger all. But Laxman and Law are facing down the visiting bowlers and the balance of the game is shifting decisively. Batting appears almost straightforward until another ball rears off a length…

"In those situations you needed great skill but you also had to be brave because you couldn't trust the bounce and the ball was going through the surface," said Sutton, who had put on 43 with Laxman in the first innings. "You hear that Indian players might struggle in such conditions but VVS showed amazing application and supreme ability. You particularly noticed his balance at the crease. The ability to transfer your weight, both forward and back, is a skill of top batsmen which often goes unnoticed, especially in difficult conditions. There is a temptation to sit back but his balance was so good he could play off either foot. And when you lose any trust in the bounce, you have to second-guess everything. You have to have a strong mind to maintain your technique and play that well at times like that.

"But Laxman is up there with anyone I played with. When you batted with him, he made you bat better because he helped you and encouraged you and shared information. It was very much like he was in the trenches with you. This guy had an abundance of talent yet he had the humility to be simply your teammate."

That humility extended into the press box. Rather than taking refuge in end-of-day clichés – and who blames a player for doing so? – Laxman listened intently to questions and answered each of them thoughtfully. Once he even gave us an insight into his own development as a cricketer who had chosen sport instead of the medical career once marked out for him. We had been asking him about the Test prospects of a young Lancashire player.

"The first thing you must do is knock on the door," he said. "If there is no answer you knock more loudly." Suddenly Laxman's voice became a little louder and more insistent, an unusual occurrence for this mildest of men. "But then if there is still no answer, you smash the door down and demand to be let in."

Lancashire win the game at Blackpool by seven wickets, Law finishing unbeaten on 82. His unbroken partnership with Laxman is worth 125 runs; the next highest stand in the match is worth 69 and that included a palpably unhinged 41 from Sajid Mahmood. It is a golden late summer evening as the press write up their reports and the freelancers come to terms with the loss of two days' work. Suddenly, my colleague Graham Hardcastle turns to me in the press tent, which is now a wreckage of coffee-cups and cold chips. "Do you think I'm okay to call Laxman and Law 'brilliant'?" he asks. I reply that he is fine to do exactly that.

It is strange to realise that game at Blackpool took place nearly 13 summers ago and stranger still that it is eight years since Laxman announced his retirement. Then one talks to his former colleagues and realises their memories are as fresh and generous and unforced as one's own. Laxman is 45 now and one of Indian cricket's mature statesmen. If the game has any sense it will make use of his wisdom and intelligence He has recently written his autobiography *281 and Beyond*, a title which has a faintly Star Trek feel to it. But then Laxman has a life to live and one expects he has fresh ambitions to realise. Next March it will be two decades since that innings at Kolkata.

There was far more to Laxman's batting than he revealed that evening at Blackpool. One could write a separate piece about his skill against spin bowling and how he made something that was plainly very difficult look terribly easy. ("It was quite demoralising bowling to him in the Lancashire nets," said Gary Keedy. "You would pitch one on middle and leg that was turning square and he would just step back and whack you through mid-wicket with a flick of those famous wrists. You'd be thinking: 'Yeah, okay then. I'll have to produce something a bit different, here.'")

It is not my place or purpose to give Laxman his position in a hierarchy of Indian batters that, in living memory, includes Sunil Gavaskar, Dilip Vengsarkar, Mohammad Azharuddin, Sachin Tendulkar, Virat Kohli. All the same I will risk one gentle judgement in these troubled times: if Rahul Dravid is still the man many Indian supporters would choose to bat for their lives, VVS Laxman may well be the player they would select to remind them that those lives were so abundantly worth living.

ESPNCricinfo May 2020

Frank Chester – How Was It?

In the pre-avian era, sales of *Tom Smith's Cricket Umpiring and Scoring* far outnumbered those of autobiographies that actually described what it was like to stand in Test matches. To an extent this was a tribute to the success of the famous instructional book that was first published in 1957 without Smith's name in its title, yet quickly grew in both length and popularity. But the absence of umpires' personal tales also reflected the status of officials in first-class cricket. Of course they were essential but the game was not about them; rather like children in well-ordered Edwardian nurseries they were better seen than heard. This was perfectly understandable but it also risked neglecting an important strand of the game's social history. That danger was first clear when Frank Chester's *How's That!* appeared in 1956 and we had the reflections in retirement of the man who, in the words of Bob Arrowsmith, "set new standards and raised the whole conception of what an umpire should be".

Immediately after the Second World War the majority of those professionally involved in English cricket shared Arrowsmith's view. Tourists, too, had benefitted from Chester's acute discernment. In the 1938 Trent Bridge Test, he judged that Sir Donald Bradman was caught at the wicket by Les Ames off Gloucestershire's Reg Sinfield. As it happened, it was one of only two wickets off-spinner Sinfield took in his single England appearance. But Chester's decision also had an impact on Bradman, who described it as the cleverest ever made against him. And there was no sly criticism lurking within that complement. Rather, it was a salute from the best batsman in the world to the official he regarded as the finest umpire he ever encountered. Nearly 12 years later, Bradman recalled the incident with characteristic precision.

The ball turned from the off, very faintly touched the inside edge of the bat, then hit my pad, went over the stumps and was caught by Ames. Whilst all this was happening amidst a jumble of feet, pads and bat, I slightly overbalanced and Ames whipped the bails off for a possible stumping. There was an instant appeal to the square-leg umpire, who gave me not out, whereupon Ames appealed to Chester at the bowler's end, and very calmly, as though it was obvious to all, Chester simply said, 'Out, caught,' and turned his back on the scene.

Frank Chester was only 43 years old when he sent Bradman on his way quite late on the second evening of that game. Had things turned out differently it is not absurd to think he might have been playing, albeit enjoying a swansong, in that Ashes series. A quarter of a century earlier Chester's three Championship centuries and 44 wickets for Worcestershire had brought him praise from WG Grace and a tribute in *Wisden*. "Having begun so well, Chester should continue to improve, and it seems only reasonable to expect that when he has filled out and gained more strength he will be an England cricketer," said the Almanack. Chester was 18 years old and everyone at New Road called him "Nipper"; 12 months earlier he had been awarded his Worcestershire cap. He had wanted to be a cricketer since his childhood in Bushey. "My future seemed stocked with happiness," he reflected.

In 1914 Chester made his career-best 178 not out against Essex at New Road but a few months later he joined the 22nd Division of the Royal Field Artillery and was soon packed off to join the general madness in France. Having survived the second battle of Loos, he was sent to Salonika, where he was wounded in the right arm by a piece of shrapnel. Gangrene set in and the arm was amputated. Had penicillin been available, Chester's career as a professional cricketer might have been saved. "When the bitter truth had penetrated my number brain in the hospital ward in Salonika, I wondered whether life was worth living," he wrote. "My case was psychological as well as physical, for nothing could restore my ability to follow the only trade I knew and loved. The initial shock was as much as I could bear...My young heart was bursting with the desire to resume where I had left off but on the bitter battlegrounds overseas I met disaster...To adjust myself physically to new employment was not the only necessity; somehow I had to submerge the mental anguish of not being able to play the game which had been my life."

Chester first umpired a match at the Oval on August 5, 1918. It had taken some persuasion to get him to Kennington and he was wearing a white coat over his hospital blues. The game was nothing more than a one-day single-innings match between an England XI and the Dominions, but Jack Hobbs, Frank Woolley and Charlie Macartney were all playing. The young umpire found his duties fairly congenial and he was moved to be back among cricketers again. It was the only world he knew. "Take it up seriously, Chester," said 'Plum' Warner. "One day you'll make a fine umpire."

It would be nearly four years before Warner was proved right. In 1919 Chester just about survived on his small pension. His marriage and the birth of a son then made the need for proper employment all the more pressing. In *How's That!* he revealed without explanation that but for the death of his father he would have become a poultry farmer. Instead, he was accepted onto the umpires' list for 1922.

Chester was 27 when he made his first-class debut as an umpire in the match between Essex and Somerset at Leyton. Almost all his colleagues on the list were over 50 and had begun wearing white coats when their services in cream flannels were no longer required. "He regarded it not as a retirement job, but as his life's work and applied to it a shrewd brain and a forceful character," wrote Arrowsmith. But Chester's character was to be tested. His account of life as a rookie umpire surrounded by time-served former professionals reveals yet again the extent to which inter-war cricket was saturated by status and deference.

Although complimented on his umpiring by JWHT Douglas and John Daniell, the captains in that game at Leyton, he gave out two other skippers on the first day of a game later that season. (Chester is not specific about the match in question but research suggests it may well have been the Roses match at Old Trafford.) The reaction of his partner made it clear that for some umpires unwritten rules had more power than printed laws:

As we walked off the field my colleague said to me,

"Boy, you won't last long as an umpire."

"Why not?" I demanded in great concern.

"Because," came the amazing reply, "if you give skippers out, you sign your own death-warrant."

Now this was a slant on the game which was entirely new to me and I urged my fellow umpire to tell me what happened when he had to deal with a sound appeal against a captain. He disappeared into the pavilion without answering, so I came to my own conclusion.

There were other tough lessons. For example any sense of solidarity that existed between umpires in that era plainly did not extend to a young novice who was rapidly proving himself fitter, more alert and sharper than almost all his colleagues:

Whereas at the start of my playing career I received nothing but the wisest counsel and kindest consideration from the old professionals, I was favoured with little, if any, advice from the old umpires. They criticized my concentration and complained that I was taking the game too seriously. What rot! Even as a player I realized it was essential for an umpire to concentrate as much as any batsman, that his job was specialized and required the maximum efficiency of all faculties. I made it plain that I would set myself only the highest standards.

County cricketers, on the other hand, warmed to Chester. This was partly, perhaps, because he was a former colleague, but more likely because he plainly knew what he was doing. Just over two years after his first-class debut he was standing in the first of what were to be 48 Tests. All these games were played in England, of course, but they included some of the greatest encounters in Anglo-Australian sporting history: Percy Chapman's team winning the Ashes in '26; Bradman's 254 at Lord's in 30; Hedley Verity's 15 wickets at Lord's in 34; Stan McCabe's 232 at Trent Bridge and Len Hutton's 364 at The Oval, both in '38; Australia chasing down 404 at Leeds in '48; Trevor Bailey batting 262 minutes for 38 and then bowling down the leg-side to secure the draw at Leeds in '53.

Cricket matches as vintages...and Chester tasted them all. Only that last encounter had little bouquet but by then the pain from a stomach ulcer was impairing his judgement and making him far less tolerant of what he saw as histrionic appealing. "Nor were the Australians satisfied with the umpiring of Frank Chester, for so long the greatest of his kind but now in such poor health that he should not have been allowed to stand," wrote EW Swanton of the umpire's single appearance in his last Ashes series.

Yet Chester was only 58 in 1953; in other words he was at the age when some of his contemporaries in the 1920s were just getting used to their white coats. For most of the previous three decades he had established new measures of excellence by which umpiring was to be judged. He did so partly because he saw the job as a profession rather than a means of making a few bob when the main business of one's life was done. One wonders whether anyone before Chester had watched a game of cricket with greater intensity.

"Sometimes you might say he was over-zealous and rhetorical," wrote Neville Cardus, who was not averse to a drop of zeal and rhetoric himself. "He would give an lbw decision with his finger pointing vehemently down the pitch, as though detecting the batsman in some really criminal practice, and denouncing and exposing him on the spot."

It was, Chester might have argued, the best way he knew of doing his work. But he also knew it didn't make up for Salonika. "There were often times when umpiring was anything but true enjoyment," he wrote. "This was for a variety of reasons, among them the irritating conduct of the players, the poor remuneration between the wars for such long, intense hours, and the fact that it was always to me a poor substitute for the joys of playing."

When the Second World War broke out Chester grew vegetables to make a little cash and umpired for the London Counties team. His fee for each of those games was £1. Only when his 1948 testimonial raised £3171 9s 5d did he know any measure of financial security. Before long, though, the game was to lose a little of its attraction for him. He saw no reason for the gesticulations of the 1948 Australians and sometimes gave his opinion on what he saw as ignorant appeals. By the mid-1950s it was time to go.

Some might wonder what Chester would make of modern umpiring. It is a little like asking whether Neville Chamberlain would have gone on Twitter. Even in the late 20th century the job of officials was changing. "I couldn't see why I should stand there and have players looking at me as if I were a leper," said Tom Brooks when he retired in the middle of the 1978-9 Ashes series. A few months later Cec Pepper also saw what was coming and stepped down. "Umpiring at the top now is full of comedians and gimmicks," said Pepper, a notoriously flatulent official who was wont to ask non-striking batters if they wouldn't mind kicking his farts to the boundary.

Yet all umpires today owe something to the bloke from Bushey who used to put on a white coat over his civvies and umpire with his trilby at the slightly rakish angle favoured by National Hunt trainers. Occasionally his false arm might remind him of Salonika and the life he had been denied. But then he would crouch down again and watch Verity bowling to Bradman.

Martin Donnelly – New Zealand's Oxford Don

If you were to seek solace in these strange days by going for a walk in the Parks at Oxford you might notice that a few of the benches around the cricket ground have been placed there in memory of former Blues. One has been dedicated to Martin Donnelly but even were you reasonably well-versed in the game you might still not be able to name his achievements with much precision. And you would not be alone. Among the hundreds of lists compiled in these cricketless months, one table sought to rank the finest left-handed batters in history. It is a ticklish task given that the candidates include Lara, Sobers, Pollock and Clive Lloyd. Pardonably perhaps, no one mentioned Donnelly. Who would have thought that in those joyous post-war summers of abundance and shortage he was reckoned the finest leftie in the world?

Please take your walk again. It is a May morning in 1946. Oxford are batting against Lancashire, who will become one of Donnelly's favourite opponents. Suddenly the university lose their second wicket and he strides from the pavilion wearing the lucky multi-coloured cap he picked up in a Cairo bazaar during the war. Before long the ground will be ringed with spectators. A few tutorials have been hastily postponed but this, it turns out, has been to the perfect satisfaction of both parties, for undergraduates soon notice that some of their tutors are also watching the cricket. One of the latter may be JC Masterman, the Provost of Worcester; he helped arrange Donnelly's two-year stay at Oxford, where he is reading Modern History at Masterman's college. The Parks may not be thronged like this again until the mid-1970s when Imran Khan is in residence and the proximity of two all-women colleges helps to increase the number of spectators watching the cricket or something. Now, though, Dick Pollard drops a shade short and Donnelly square-cuts him for four. The undergraduates settle into their seats and some wonder if they can fit in a lunchtime pint at The Lamb and Flag.

"Bare figures can give no idea of the electric atmosphere in the Parks when that short, sturdy figure went out to bat," wrote Geoffrey Bolton. "A lucky spectator might have half an hour to spare between lectures... In that half hour he might well see Donnelly hit nine boundaries, each from a different stroke… If Oxford were fielding the spectator's eyes would turn to cover point."

The students were watching Donnelly at close to the peak of his powers. Within four years he had all but retired from the first-class game and moved to Australia to become Cortaulds' sales and marketing manager in that country. He joined the Coventry-based firm on going down from Oxford and they allowed him to play for Warwickshire in 1948 and to join the New Zealand tour the following summer. But by 1950 Donnelly was 32 and had decided to make a career in business. He played his last County Championship match at the Cortaulds Ground in early July. For something like five years he had flamed across the English game and now he was gone. "It was as if all his own cricket had been a student pastime, a youthful wheeze not worth mentioning any more," wrote Frank Keating.

The promise, however, had been clear since the early 1930s when Donnelly was a pupil at New Plymouth Boys High School in the North Island. At that stage it was unclear whether cricket or tennis would be his major summer sport but a letter he received from Australia in 1933 may have settled matters. "Dear Martin," it read, "Having heard that you were a very keen little cricket enthusiast, I thought I would write and encourage you into even greater deeds. New Zealanders love the game as much as we do, and I am looking forward to seeing your name among their champions in the future." The 15-year-old Donnelly kept that letter from Don Bradman under his pillow. Less than four years later he was selected for New Zealand's tour of England, the decision to include him in the party being made on the strength of his innings of 22 and 38 and some brilliant fielding in a Plunket Shield game for Wellington against Auckland. It had been his first-class debut.

Donnelly was 19 years old when he arrived in the country where he would play all seven of his Test matches and make all but two of his 23 first-class centuries. His height had long earned him the nickname "Squib" but his maiden hundred against Surrey revealed a different type of stature and *Wisden* announced that he was "decidedly a 'star' in the making". He managed 120 runs in the three matches against England and although New Zealand lost the series 1-0, Donnelly's innings were already crafted as occasion required. He was beyond promising. All the same, he began his Test career with a duck at Lord's, an indignity he shared with one of England's debutants, Leonard Hutton. In view of the innings he played on the ground after the war, Donnelly probably viewed that nought with a wry smile. And on the way back to New Zealand he was able to thank Bradman for his earlier letter when the tourists played at Adelaide. It would be one of only two first-class games he would play in Australia

Although he returned home having scored 1,414 first-class runs in his first English summer, it was by no means clear how Donnelly's cricket career would develop. He read for a BA degree at Canterbury University and transferred his allegiance to the province for the 1938-9 season. But he played only six Plunket Shield games for his new team before being commissioned in 1941 and posted first to Cairo where Major Donnelly commanded a squadron of tanks and was a star of the Gezira Club. Having later served in Italy, he returned to England in 1945 to represent New Zealand Services during a four-month tour that would take them from village greens to the Test grounds. None of the players minded and all the spectators were grateful. Though the war against Japan continued until August, cricket seemed as good as way as any of celebrating peace in Europe, even if The Oval still looked more like the POW camp it had recently been. Austerity and even the Iron Curtain were problems for other years. Donnelly was 27 and had played just 41 first-class matches.

In late August he represented the Dominions against England at Lord's. It was a three-day match which featured two centuries by Wally Hammond, 10 wickets for Doug Wright and an extraordinary innings of 185 in 168 minutes by Keith Miller. *Wisden* described it as "one of the finest games ever seen". Donnelly made 133 in 10 minutes over three hours and although overshadowed by Miller's extraordinary hitting on the final morning, that century had been as clear a proclamation of talent as anyone could desire. Denzil Batchelor was clearly sold: "You sat and rejoiced, hugging the memories to your heart and gradually letting the dazzle fade out of your eyes."

Over the next four years there would be at least three more such occasions, all of them at Lord's. At Oxford strong county XIs found a mature batter of international class waiting for them when they arrived to take on the undergraduates. Journalists returning late from the war hurried to the Parks to see what the fuss was about, only to find it was not a fuss at all, but the real thing. Given his fame, it would have been easy for Oxford's best cricketer to trade on his status and become something of a star but after Donnelly's death in 1999, Professor Douglas Johnson, a contemporary at Worcester, penned an addition to the obituary in the *Independent*:

"In college, Martin was universally liked. He was a quiet, modest man who was interested in the same things as the rest of us. At a college society meeting he talked about folk-music and folk-songs. He was not too grand for college games, and, if he was available, he would play in the college teams for cricket and rugby, at a time when they were far from strong. In one such match he hit five sixes in one over, against a visiting team that had not expected to encounter a Test batsman."

Donnelly made six centuries for his university in 1946, including 142 in front of 8,000 spectators in the Varsity Match at Lord's. The following season there were four more hundreds and a three-hour 162 not out for the Gentleman against the Players. Hubert Preston's account of that innings in *Wisden* suggests why Donnelly was one of the almanack's cricketers of the year: "Apart from a chance to slip off [Doug] Wright when 39, he played practically faultless cricket and hit twenty-six 4's, his punishment of any ball not a perfect length being severe and certain; he excelled with off-drives; hooked or cut anything short."

Yet however glittering his talent, cricket was always an amateur pursuit for Donnelly. Perhaps that was one reason why he struggled in 1948, his one full season for Warwickshire. He certainly found Bradman's Australians no more vincible than anyone else had: his eight innings for four different teams produced an aggregate of only 116 runs with a best score of 36 at Scarborough. That letter of encouragement had become a fond memento of another time.

But one reason why Donnelly had played cricket during his first year with Cortaulds was in the hope he might be selected for the New Zealand tour in 1949. Despite a degree of opposition in a homeland where he had not played for nearly a decade, he achieved his aim and that trip would become his glorious farewell to the game's great occasions. While his fellow tourists may have been met by a team mate who spoke with an English accent when they arrived in April 1949, they also found a cricketer determined to prove that New Zealand should no longer be fobbed off with three-day Tests while Australians were granted five-day fixtures.

Martin Donnelly made 2,287 first-class runs in his last full summer of cricket. The tally included four centuries and the first double-hundred made by a New Zealander in Test matches. That was scored at Lord's, of course, and it took him five minutes short of six hours. The final stages of Donnelly's last great innings, which was completed on a Monday morning of dry London heat, were described by Alan Mitchell, the correspondent who travelled with the team on their tour.

"His pulling was bloodthirsty, coldly calculated, executed with both strength of wrist and perfect timing and balance, and a graceful swinging body. His off-driving was full of weight and his newly perfected late cutting a thing of joy and a suppleness of wrist that D'Artagnan could have admired. Bailey pounded up to the stumps, dragging a foot and spurting dust, only to be battered and in one over alone, hit for 12; Hollies lowered his trajectory and added speed to his spin, only to be cut or driven straight.; Gladwin glistened but with mere perspiration and the new ball lost its shine; Young was pulled and cut. The Don was alive in Donnelly."

Perhaps so but Mitchell also knew his comparison was momentary; Bradman's statistics belonged in a category of their own. As Alan Gibson reflected in 1964: "He [Donnelly] had certain similarities with Bradman: the build, the hawk-eye, the forcing stroke square of the wicket on the leg side, the determination to establish a psychological supremacy over the bowler as soon as possible. But Donnelly did not share Bradman's passion *never* to get out." Then again, it is difficult to imagine the Don singing folk songs.

New Zealand drew all four of the Tests in 1949 and Donnelly made 462 runs from No.5 in their batting order. By now the best cricket writers of the day were searching carefully for appropriate references and ransacking their store of metaphors. As ever, RC Robertson-Glasgow found the words for the moment: "It is a position where the player must be equally able and ready to arrest a decline or to blaze an attack, to be Fabius or Jehu at need and in turn. In this exacting role Donnelly went from triumph to triumph. He was, as it were, both the gum and the glitter; and he carried his burden like a banner."

After his retirement Donnelly spoke about his own cricket only to those who made a point of asking about it. He made a new career in Australia and set about the serious business of raising three sons and a daughter. Occasionally, though, the past would be revived. There were reunion dinners and in 1990 he was elevated to the New Zealand Sports Hall of Fame   "They said he had everything as a Test batsman," read the citation, "Style and grace, confidence and determination, success and modesty."

Yet still you would be forgiven if you did not quite understand Donnelly's place in the history of cricket in two countries. Perhaps you needed to live through those post-war years to understand their mixture of relief and guilt, exultation and grief, responsibility and abandon. Peace levies its own tariffs. Maybe the best we can do is find Donnelly's bench in his beloved Parks and imagine his feelings as he strode out to bat in the few summers the gods allowed him.

George Cox – GOSBTS

The simplicity of George Cox's career is not misleading in the slightest. Rather, it suggests a deep attachment to Sussex and Sussex cricketers which lasted more or less from Cox's birth in Wernham in 1911 until his death in Burgess Hill in 1985. He was a good enough batsman for his many supporters at Hove to talk up his England prospects, but as things turned out he played all but seven of his 455 first-class games for Sussex and scored all his 50 centuries for his much beloved county. Those other matches were festival encounters and five of them took place at either Eastbourne or Hastings. So much, so unremarkable, you might say. After all, Cox made his debut in 1931 and played his final County Championship game in 1960. It was an era in which cricketers were expected to stay local and show loyalty. But Cox took things further: after a stint helping Hubert Doggart with Winchester's first XI, he returned to Sussex as coach and later as president of the county's Junior Cricket Festival and its Cricket Society. He skippered the second team when

116

well in his fifties and even led the side against Middlesex when three months short of his sixtieth birthday. He sat on committees; he spoke at dinners whenever he was asked. And even now, the story is nothing like complete.

For there are the little matters of the poem, the Memorial Service and the Garden.

The poem "A Cricketer in Retirement" begins as follows:

> *The marine and the regency, sea frets*
> *And somewhere the Downs backing a station*
> *Like a Victorian conservatory. I come upon*
> *A scorecard yellow as old flannels and suddenly*
> *I see him, smilingly prowling the covers*
> *In soft shoes, shirt rolled to the forearm,*
> *Light as a yacht swaying at its moorings,*
> *Receptive to breezes.*

Alan Ross published only 10 poems about cricket. Six of them focused quite directly on Test players such as Walter Hammond, Len Hutton, David Gower and Richie Benaud. Another considered an 1852 engraving of Alfred Mynn, "the Lion of Kent", who died 16 years before England lost to Australia at Melbourne. But the Sussex cricketers of the 1930s were Ross's "First and Last Gods" and his bond to them never weakened. After the war Cox became a friend whose glorious hospitality he would enjoy at his farm on the edge of Ditchling Common, where they would talk of the Sussex cricketers they both knew. They would recall the county's famous kinships and shake their heads at the team's skittish form:

> *One apart, yet part all the same,*
> *Of that familiar pattern of families,*
> *Parkses and Langridges, Tates and Oakes and Gilligans,*
> *Griffiths and Busses, Sussex is rich in,*
> *The soft air phrased by their fickleness.*

"A Cricketer in Retirement: For George Cox" was one of the readings chosen for Cox's Memorial Service, which took place at Hove Parish Church on May 7, 1985. It was read by Johnny Barclay, then the

Sussex captain, and it followed an address given by Dennis Silk, the Warden of Radley College. Silk began with a series of images those attending the service would know well:

"George was a man of Sussex, with cricket in his blood and a gift with people of all ages that I have never seen equalled. Wherever he went there was sure to be laughter, a feeling of mellow well-being and a mischievous sense of fun. Crowds sat up in their deckchairs at Hove and the Saffrons when George walked to the wicket. When his turn came to speak after dinner there would be a ripple of excitement, whether it was at The Hilton or in Ditchling Village Hall."

But Silk knew very well that Cox had struggled in his early seasons at Sussex, not managing a fifty until nearly two years after his debut and only making his first century, 162 against Hampshire at Southampton, in 1935. Another two summers were to pass before Cox could be sure of his place in the Sussex team but his 1891 first-class runs in 1937 included four hundreds. He then scored at least a thousand runs in every peacetime season until his effective retirement from first-team cricket in 1955.

"Not many cricketers gave more pleasure to more people than did George," said Silk "and most of his finest innings were played against the toughest opposition: Yorkshire before the War, Surrey after it...He could be downcast by failure. Which cricketer isn't? But he had all these emotions under control, though he used to say with whimsical wistfulness that there wasn't a county ground in England in the lavatory of which he had not cried his eyes out having made nought."

Gradually the tears would give way to shy smiles and raised bats at Hove, Eastbourne and Hastings. Cox's batting flourished and his fielding at cover point revealed the athleticism that had once enabled him to play professional football for Arsenal, Fulham and Luton Town. He would make four hundreds against Lancashire and take another six centuries off the powerful Yorkshire attack. The pick of the latter was probably his 198 in 200 minutes in the final county match before World War Two ended championship cricket for over six years. However, Cox had to share the top score in Sussex's second innings; he and Harry Parks both made 9 as the home side were bowled out for 33 on a wet pitch. Hedley Verity took 7-9 in the last first-class match of his life.

The runs continued to flow for Cox in the first peacetime summers. Yet again there was talk of an England cap as delicacy and nous were added to power and yielded 2,369 runs in 1950 when he turned 39. But journalists noticed that while the best teams brought the best from him, struggling sides were often presented with his wicket. "Indulgently negligent against parachuting spinners," wrote Ross of the batsman whose 754 first-class innings included 98 noughts. "I cannot think of anyone who was as good a player as he who seemed to lose form for such long periods," added David Sheppard in *Parson's Pitch* in 1964. Some 21 years later it would be the Right Reverend Sheppard, Bishop of Liverpool, who would conduct that memorial service at Hove.

"In many ways he was my closest friend in cricket, and I learned a great deal from him, not only about the technique of the game, but about the whole approach to it," he had written. "If cricket wasn't fun you felt George would have no part in it. He has always been intensely interested in people and their problems. He used to go regularly to coach in South Africa and it was he who first started me thinking seriously about problems there."

It is a mistake to judge the deceased by the presence of good people at their funerals or memorial services. Obligation frequently trumps everything and some thorough skullduggers have been given virtue-scented send-offs. With George Cox, however, it was the real thing. There was a bishop, a headmaster, a duchess, a bevy of writers and a fine collection of establishment figures at Hove that day, but also the villagers for whom Cox had always made time and who now took a final opportunity to make time for him.

The cricketers remembered the batsman and the rather useful bowler of slow-medium floaters who frequently apologised to the batter he had dismissed. His father, Old George, had taken 1,843 first-class wickets, most of them in cricket's first golden age. Young George managed 192 victims and might have taken more had he approached the business more seriously. Yet he was ever the professional who played like an amateur. "He could have bowled respectable medium pace as well," said John Woodcock. "George Cox was a lovely cricketer – in many ways he personified summer days at Hove."

And so a garden seemed – and seems – a fitting memorial to a player that most of those attending a match at Hove today will never have met, let alone seen walk out to bat, his cap set at a permanently rakish angle. Originally it was a spacious affair from which members of the Cricket Society could watch a game and hold their Annual Party. But when land was needed for the indoor nets in 2002 the garden was reduced to a narrow rectangle – some call it a corridor – wedged between the outdoor and indoor practice facilities deep in the north-west corner of the ground.

It is easy to miss. The more fanciful might suggest it is like platform nine-and-three-quarters in the Harry Potter books; one doesn't see it unless one has been inducted into the gentle magic that informs Sussex cricket. Yet there is no more tranquil place on the circuit than Young George's garden. The foliage is sometimes so abundant that on quiet days you could sit on the bench at the far end and not be aware you were near a cricket field at all. Cox, of course, might be rather amazed that anyone has sought to commemorate his life in this way. For him it was always Sussex, and whether he was playing, coaching or speaking that devotion remained gently absolute, woven into his personality like Wealden wool in a fine suit.

John Edrich – Reporting for Duty

John Edrich began his Test career at Old Trafford, facing Wes Hall and Charlie Griffiths. He ended it on the same ground 13 years later, batting against Michael Holding and Wayne Daniel. Some of his innings in the intervening period were more hazardous.

Edrich accepted every blow from fast bowlers as the price he must pay for the trade he had chosen. "Some of my best friends have put me in hospital," are the first words of his 1970 autobiography *Runs in the Family*. "Fred Trueman did it the first time we met. He broke my hand. Frank Tyson…broke it again and a surgeon had to scrounge a piece of bone from my leg to mend it. A spring-heeled South African called Pollock crumpled me like a puppet without a string, with a broken head. Big boisterous Charlie Griffiths rushed me into a casualty ward with an arm like a balloon."

Yet every ruddy time Edrich returned, undaunted and unflinching. Eleven days after Peter Pollock hit him on the temple and "broke his head" in the 1965 Lord's Test he was back at St John's Wood, opening Surrey's batting against Middlesex. The lexis of military conflict does not seem insensitive or tasteless when applied to some of his innings. Batting was frequently analogous to trench warfare where Edrich was concerned and by the end of a career which comprised 20 English seasons and four full MCC tours he had accumulated 39,790 first-class runs. That puts him 19th on the all-time list, while Frank Woolley and Philip Mead are the only left-handers to have bettered his total of 103 centuries. He was the highest run-scorer in three English seasons in the 1960s; no one else in the decade managed it more than once.

As ever with left-handers it is tempting to accept the conventional distinction between artist and artisan, and then place Edrich firmly in the latter category. Yet his unbeaten 310 against New Zealand at Leeds in 1965 included 52 fours and five sixes, and although it took him only 30 fewer balls to make his 175 against Australia at Lord's 10 years later, the final stages of that innings included some cover-drives Woolley might have envied. It's just that Edrich was something like five hours into a seven-hour marathon before he felt confident enough to play them.

One could see his point. The Australian attack in that match included Dennis Lillee and Jeff Thomson, against whom Edrich had some scores to satisfy. The previous winter, Lillee had fractured his hand in the first Test at Brisbane and broken two of his ribs in the fourth match at Sydney. But that series, which England lost 5-1, encapsulated Edrich's valour and value. He "dug in grimly", reported Christopher Martin-Jenkins, making 48 in 210 minutes at the Gabba and then returned to the team for the third Test. Even with his ribs fractured he came back to the crease at the SCG – he was captaining England in place of Mike Denness – and was unbeaten on 33 when both the game and the Ashes were lost. A month later he was in the side again for the final game at Melbourne and made 70 in the visitors' only victory. They'd knocked him down but he'd got up again. "I am tattooed with scars but unfortunately pain is something you cannot remember," Edrich had written nearly five years earlier. What he didn't know when he returned from Australia was that the most severe test of his courage was yet to come.

For those who remember the garish highlights of that 1974-5 series – it was the early days of colour TV and those Tests were a blood sport – images of Edrich's innings come easily to mind. They include the England cap, never a helmet, and the MCC touring sweater, but they also feature the high right shoulder and straight right arm in his stance, the latter almost brandished like a knightly shield towards the bowler. Runs came without flourish and were often worked slightly forward or backward of square in the classic opener's fashion. Edrich's forearms were hawsers and his wrists cracked down like the bolts on a miser's strongbox. He used one of the heaviest bats in the game and played a thousand square cuts with it. When he first netted at The Oval, most of the professionals looked at his technique and doubted he'd ever get near the professional game. Then Bernie Constable, who always looked more closely than anyone else, pointed out that he'd not yet missed the ball. "It was all unspectacular, thoughtful, determined and sound," wrote John Arlott of Edrich. "He had many technical limitations, knew them, and played within them, never assuming too much; knowing invariably what to hit, what to play and what to leave."

In his first Championship match Edrich batted at No.5 for a Surrey team that included eight current or future Test cricketers and would end that 1958 season celebrating its seventh successive title. In the second innings the home side needed 171 to beat Worcestershire but were 7-3 when the 21-year-old debutant went out to face Jack Flavell, one of the most underestimated fast bowlers on the circuit. Edrich could not prevent his team being bowled out for 57 but he was unbeaten on 24 when the last wicket fell. A small marker had been put down. The following May, Edrich offered a rather larger indication of his talent when he made a hundred in each innings of the match against Nottinghamshire. He finished that summer with 1,799 first-class runs, his second *lowest* aggregate in his first 11 seasons. In 1963 he was capped by England.

For something like five years Edrich was never quite an automatic pick in the Test side. Unsurprisingly, he was more likely to play in the tough series overseas and didn't miss a five-day match on the West Indies tour of 1967-8 or the Ashes trips of 1965-6 or 1970-1. That latter adventure was arguably his finest hour (and perhaps explains the special attention Lillee and Thomson paid him four years later.) In Ray Illingworth he had a captain who prized his approach to his craft and he responded by making 648 runs in the six matches. That series included two of his 12 Test centuries and only twice was he dismissed for less than 30. The following summer he found the Indian spinners more of a challenge but still made over two thousand first-class runs as Surrey won the County Championship.

His final Test innings was viewed by many as his most famous, even if it was played on an infamous Saturday evening at Old Trafford. Accompanied by Brian Close, a man who sought out challenges rather than funking them, he faced the West Indian trio of Daniel, Holding and Andy Roberts for 80 minutes on an atrocious Manchester pitch. By the close England were 21 without loss with Edrich unbeaten on 10 and Close having a single to show for his many wounds.

"[Edrich] was thirty-nine years old, and that evening he came back in after taking the biggest physical hammering anyone ever saw inflicted on a batsman," wrote Arlott. "He ducked sometimes but rarely took evasive action. That performance was, without exaggeration, heroic; though that kind of comment generally persuaded him into a broad and friendly grin, or some wrily (sic) dismissive remark."

Edrich had ended his Test career rather as he had begun it: squeezing every run out of a gruelling game while also being overshadowed by more charismatic colleagues. That Saturday evening people in Tommy Ducks, a famous Manchester pub, were chattering about Close's bravery; the following days' papers were filled with pictures of the Yorkshireman's bruises and tales of the medicinal Scotch he had drunk to ease the pain. So it had been in 1968 when Edrich had made 164 in the Oval Test against Australia but everyone was talking about Basil D'Oliveira's 158 and the forthcoming South African tour; and so it had also been in that 1975 Ashes Test at Lord's where the opener's century was a sidebar in papers celebrating David Steele's half-century on debut; and, yes, so it had been in 1977 when Geoffrey Boycott's 100th first-class hundred caused far more fuss than Edrich reaching the same mark.

Perhaps he was content with that. Fame and celebrity were never Edrich's style. He remained to a strong degree the 17-year-old

Norfolk cricketer who had asked for a trial at Surrey so that he could not be compared to his cousin, Bill, who was at Middlesex. He had even written to The Oval in the winter of 1954-5 when Bill was on an Ashes tour and was therefore unable to put a word in for cousin John. Geoff Edrich, another cousin and a warrior batter for Lancashire, would have understood such behaviour very well. He might also have acknowledged that the youngest of the five Edrich cousins to play first-class cricket was also the best of them.

There is a poignant postscript to Edrich's career, albeit his afterlife featured some of the usual honours, including the presidency of Surrey. In 2000 he was diagnosed with a rare form of leukaemia and given seven years to live. "You can't fight it," he said, for maybe the first time in his life. "You have to have faith in your consultant and the treatment. They said I would feel tired from time to time and would have to live with it. I think we've got to be grateful for what we've had. I did something which I loved and had the ability to play cricket at the highest level."

In 2012 Edrich announced that injections of mistletoe extract had cured his cancer. He now lives in Aberdeenshire. One wonders how many people in his small town know their neighbour is one of the bravest cricketers England has ever produced.

Alan West – Notching

It was almost always "Westy" and the nickname denoted acceptance rather than any lack of respect. Moreover, the warm, easy friendship that Old Trafford's cricketers extended to the first-team scorer, Alan West, was shared in other counties and in press boxes across the country. It seemed to me that he was liked throughout the game. Indeed, if you couldn't get on with Westy, there was probably something up with you. Which all helps to explain why, when it was announced on Sunday that Alan had died, aged 76, social media was filled with tributes: "Lovely bloke…true gentleman…legend" were some of the most popular comments and their repetition only reinforced our awareness of loss.

A county cricket team's changing room is their private space, a sanctum where outbursts of anything from cold anger to wild joy can be released with no fear that an unguarded comment will reach prying ears. Quite rightly, the media are almost never allowed in. Scorers, of course, are different. They may need to give coaches and players important statistics and they are permitted greater access; they stay at the team's hotel and they might have other administrative duties. Yet few scorers listen to team-talks, as Alan did before one morning's play at Taunton in 2011. There he was, though, sitting on a batting pad as Peter Moores chatted to the players before one of the more important days in the club's recent history. One of the boys.

A day or so later Alan was on that outfield again, hoisting the County Championship trophy aloft as proudly and gleefully as any of the players. He was always, you see, a trusted member of the squad, and if his relations with his scoring colleagues were always utterly cordial, they never concealed his passionate desire to see Lancashire win cricket matches. This partisanship, while it never veered into one-eyed bigotry, sometimes found splendidly candid expression. After the first day of the 2008 game against Sussex at Hove Lancashire were 67 for four in reply to the home side's 253. Then Stuart Law put on 160 with nightwatchman Gary Keedy and Lancashire finished the final session on 382 for eight. Graham Hardcastle and I were waiting at the foot of the pavilion steps to speak to Law when Alan approached. "Bloody marvellous!" he said, without breaking step, and marched up to give the players any information they needed. Lancashire won the match by eight wickets; that was probably bloody marvellous, too.

When I was writing a few pieces for the book celebrating Lancashire's championship, I decided to focus on the non-players closely associated with the squad. I recorded a long interview with Alan and learned about his career in education, latterly with the JMB examination board. It was easy to see how factual accuracy had always been a vital part of his life. I also discovered that he had watched cricket in the late 1940s and knew some of Lancashire's players personally. He later wrote the semicentennial book on the Lancashire Cricket Federation and another marking the centenary of the Ribblesdale League. His pet project was to write a book about the spinners Malcolm Hilton and Bob Berry. Yet for all that closeness, all those days with the cricketers, he never imagined that he would end his working life professionally involved with the game. I thus discovered that we shared rather more than a great school in Rusholme.

There are plenty of things I don't know about Alan's life. This is a tribute, not an obituary. Although his private life was something of a *hortus inclusus*, he was more than willing to talk about the musical achievements of his three sons and he tried to be modest about them. He failed by an innings. I never asked him if he met Cardus. Damn. I've not said too much about scoring but the truth is that I don't feel any great need to do so. Alan was one of the best scorers on the circuit and he took pride in the provision of accurate information to players first and foremost, but journalists, too, whenever he could. There are many pieces that would be the poorer had we not had the chance to check a statistic or two with Westy. He also, I think, looked after Lancashire's flag during away games and that was more than a mere task, for there could have been no more vigilant guardian of the Red Rose.

We last saw Alan in the press box during the game against Yorkshire. He was in good spirits but it was clear that the hateful disease was upon him. However, he and we had the consolation that he spent his final years doing a job he loved among people he liked very much and watching a game to whose welfare he was quietly devoted. Bloody marvellous, wasn't it, old friend? Bloody marvellous.

Lancashire County Cricket Club website – October 2014

The Smoked Salmon is under the Canaletto
David Essenhigh – Coach

"Do you shoot at all, Paul?"
  "Denis, I've never shot a live animal in my life."
  "Well, there's not much bloody point shooting a dead one."
  Touché

In the early 1980s I taught History for four mostly blissful years at Rendcomb College, a small school in the south Cotswolds.

Gloucestershire's postcard villages – Bourton-on-the-Water and all that crush – lay some 20 miles away but from my rooms on the top floor of the old mansion which housed the school's main building, I could look across the Churn valley, west to the village of Woodmancote, or north to Elkstone, where the poet P J Kavanagh lived. It was a good half-hour's walk to The Bathurst Arms, and Cirencester was another five miles distant. There was an Irish invasion every March and the other Cheltenham Festivals were even greater delights. I was a town boy who had fetched up in the middle of the countryside. Perhaps it was not surprising that those four years changed my life.

But it is people who really make the difference. For a school that had around 260 pupils Rendcomb turned out some good cricket teams. That it should have been so was partly due to facilities: "Up Top", the playing fields, accommodated about five matches on good pitches with some ease. But I soon discovered that the seriousness with which the game was taken also reflected the commitment of the school's groundsman, who was also the keenest and most natural coach I have ever known. After I was made master-in-charge of cricket at the end of my first year it was rare for a couple of days to pass without us having a conversation about the school's teams or who had taken our attention in the first-class game. Whether the boys he coached recall their afternoons with David Essenhigh is something I expect never to know; but I remember him.

He was a small, deep-chested man who carried the permanent tan of someone who spent most of their working day in the open air. But in contrast to the reticence frequently characteristic of groundsmen, David was positively gregarious, even if you had to prove you knew something about cricket to earn his full respect. Once he realised my love of the game matched his own he was difficult to keep away – but then I rarely wanted to. My only regret was that I didn't question him more deeply about his early career, which had included at least 85 Minor County championship games for Wiltshire. What I did discover was that he was born in Folkestone in 1936 and that he had nurtured some hopes of playing for Kent. But neither as an opener nor as an off-spinner was he ever quite of first-class standard and he told me Colin Cowdrey had advised him to try coaching. That changed his life, too.

To see him running a coaching session was to see a man in perfect concert with his world. It didn't matter to him if his pupils were talented boys or novice members of staff looking to gain their first badge. He encouraged them all and managed to tailor his advice to their specific requirements. I wonder if it ever occurred to my colleagues in the staff-room that one of the most gifted teachers at their school was the bloke who cut the grass. As soon as anybody showed a keenness to play cricket David was their friend. The "bloody Bursar" who blighted his life with crackpot economies during morning break became the recipient of his kindly encouragement during a Staff match on the same evening. "Well bowled, Edward!" he would enthuse should the ball bounce only once on its way to the wicketkeeper.

But in truth both David and I had to work hard to feel at home among Gloucestershire's gentry. One evening the entire staff were invited for drinks with one of the governors and his wife. We attempted to make small talk about A Levels, pastoral care and horse trials but were failing dismally. "I think we could all do with some food," said the lady of the manor. "Can you bring some, darling? The smoked salmon is under the Canaletto."

On another occasion we were playing five-a-side football in the gym when someone rushed in.

"Come quick! We need help! The horse!"

Bemused and alarmed, we rushed down to the yard that was the centre of the hubbub and found the said horse with its front legs and much of its body out of its stable and the remainder trapped within. The top half of the door had been left open, thus encouraging this bid for freedom, and the result was that the beast was now in loud distress. Without thinking too much about the consequences – the Health and Safety gauleiters would have a fit today – another master, two sixth-form boys and I grabbed the front legs of the horse and heaved it back inside. The headmaster's wife, who was something of an equine obsessive, was appropriately grateful at a drinks party a couple of days later.

"Thank you so much, Paul! That was terribly brave!"

"Not at all. I had lots of help and we sorted things pretty easily."

"Nonsense," boomed the reply. "That horse was balanced on its penis and you rescued it."

"Oh, I'm sure it'll do the same for me one day."

Rendcomb's cricket mattered very much to David but he was also well connected around the county and, although nearing fifty, he still played occasionally for Cirencester. Tom Graveney and also Graham Wiltshire, the Gloucestershire coach, were good friends of his and there was always a particular light in his eye when he thought he had seen someone with the sort of quality even he could not coach. One evening when we were travelling by minibus to a staff match he told me that he'd spotted a young cricketer who he absolutely knew was going to make it in the professional game. "He's got the ability, of course," said David. "That's obvious to anyone with half an eye. And he's also got it up here," he added, tapping his head.

"But the thing is, he's got it *here*," and he pointed not to his heart but to the middle of his torso. I took that to mean that there was some essential quality about the young lad – it was more than guts – that wouldn't be satisfied unless he made it as a professional cricketer. It was more than will, more than character. A few months later I realised how astute David's judgement of Jack Russell had been. And when I watched my old friend coach in the school nets those blue afternoons – it never rained, of course – I thought a kindred judgement could be applied to him. And when I sit in press boxes during Test matches or on that famous media balcony during the Cheltenham Festival I sometimes think of David and he teaches me, still.

It is over thirty years since I left Rendcomb. The school is much changed now and I have only been back twice, the last occasion being in 2014, when Worcestershire beat Gloucestershire inside three days at the College Ground and I made the most of a rare day off. I visited the Bathurst and then strolled up to North Cerney's ground, which I still think one of the most beautiful in the land. A buzzard circled in the warm air and a harvester cruised silently up and down a distant field of wheat. I looked across at Rendcomb.

Brideshead.

I am writing these lines in the midst of the strangest season cricket season any of us will ever know. Outside my flat the occasional supermarket lorry rumbles past. Otherwise the main drag from Birkdale into Southport is sepulchre-silent. This spring is a riot of poignancy; every bud and blossom seems to mock the absence of cricket. It is an April unlike any other.

And yet I do not have to close my eyes to be back in my rooms at Rendcomb. Very soon I will hear a busy step on the wooden corridor outside. In a moment there will be a brisk knock on the door. Then a weather-blessed, bright-eyed face will appear, asking me why I haven't got the kettle on and whether we should push young Bailey up to number three.

The Cricketer Online – April 2020

* * *

Since these essays were written both David Essenhigh and John Edrich have died. Jack Russell and I exchanged messages about David, who was a steadfast friend to us both. "Paul, the memories that remain are priceless. Magic days," said Jack. The words apply just as fittingly to Edrich.

6

MATCHES FROM THE DAY

Some years ago the author and Observer *journalist Neal Ascherson attended an exhibition of Hans Holbein's portraits of Henry VIII's court. "I recognised so many faces," he said recently. "I had been at school with them." Ascherson went to Eton.*

In almost every cricket pavilion in the land, faces gaze out, strangers, perhaps, but also familiar. Their expressions cover a rich emotional spectrum: confident, insecure, joyous, sullen, entitled, impassive and, just occasionally, plain barmy. These team photographs were probably taken either at the start of a season or in high summer, and the players may have regarded them as a necessary chore, one that could be completed following a moment of instruction: "Look at me, please."

But the moments have become timeless, even if a coloured blazer places an amateur in a pre-war era or a hairstyle pins a young cricketer in the 1970s. Their richness mocks the dark frames that would both preserve and confine them. Any historian finds them a challenge, these sportsmen from distant summers, senior players always sitting, in their two orderly rows: "Look at us, please."

There are, of course, many ways in which our knowledge can be extended. Autobiography, biography, letters and newspapers all help. Over the past 25 years, Stephen Chalke has interviewed hundreds of former cricketers and their recollections have deepened our understanding of county cricket, particularly in the post-war eras. If we are enthralled by individual careers, we are also often amazed that a diverse group of people could play together and work towards a common goal in a game that very often took three or four days, rather than 90 minutes, to complete.

During the first lockdown I spent much of my time writing brief essays about teams that had taken my interest. I hope they give a flavour, at least, of what it might have been like to play for these counties. The best they can manage is to send readers back to the invaluable work of other historians: David Frith, Eric Midwinter, the late Peter Wynne-Thomas, Andrew Hignell, Jeremy Lonsdale, Mick Pope and many others.

Not all the pieces describe Championship wins; one or two concern glorious failures or focus more closely on individual achievement. The first couple deal with very recent disappointments. There is another about the early years of one-day cricket. But all are bound together by the extraordinary variety of experience encompassed by county cricket. And they send me back to those team photographs and yet another attempt to understand these cricketers: their times, their lives.

Lancashire 2007 – Ramped Up

———————— THE OVAL, SEPTEMBER 22, 2007 ————————
*Surrey 427 (Ramprakash 196, Benning 51; Mahmood 4-93)
and 295-5 dec. (Ramprakash 130*) beat Lancashire 234
(Laxman 53; Nicholson 3-30, Jordan 3-50) and 464 (Laxman
100, Law 79; Hussain 4-126, Dernbach 3-85) by 24 runs*

"Come on, Pring, be honest. It's not on, is it?" said Andy Wilson, once of *The Guardian* to Derek Pringle, once of *The Daily Telegraph*.

We were sitting in the gloom that is the Oval press box. It was the evening of Friday, September 21, 2007 and Lancashire had just begun their pursuit of 489 to beat Surrey. Success would have brought a first outright title in 73 years; failure would have sealed another nearly-but-not-quite summer, Lancashire's umpteenth such campaign since Edward VIII retired hurt.

But Pringle did not abdicate his responsibilities. He agreed it wasn't on. For one thing, it would have been the second-highest successful run-chase in the history of the County Championship. For another, Lancashire were 27 without loss and therefore needed to score 462 runs in a day. True, the wicket was flat. True, Lancashire had Laxman, Law and nothing to lose. For if Sussex beat Worcestershire at Hove on Saturday morning, as they seemed certain to do, Mark Chilton's team would have to defeat Surrey to take the title. But however you diced and sliced the matter, it was not on. Wilson allowed realism to trump romance and returned home. No one thought him unwise or disloyal. The only northern journos who stayed were duty bound to do so. So the murk was fitting. Old Trafford's chances were about to be rowed across the river once again.

No one was ready for the charge of the Lancs Brigade.

How had it come to this? It is always tempting and rarely correct to view any four-day county match in its own delicate context. So enthralling is the shifting balance of a Championship game that one sometimes thinks a small war could be declared and no one watching the cricket would notice. In truth, of course, while this piece concerns one day in one match, it also embraces the other 71 played in Division One that season. (Well, 68 actually; three were abandoned.)

So the events of Saturday, September 22 were the dénouement of a five-month mystery filled with complexities, red herrings, pratfalls, heroes and hardly any villains. The penultimate chapter had seen Lancashire go top of the table when VVS Laxman's regal century guided them to a nine-wicket defeat of Warwickshire. That win was enough to enliven the PA announcer Matt Proctor's end-of-season farewell, which spectators probably considered a further bonus. Proctor's usual mid-September homily to spectators often contained so many references to darkness and long winter evenings that it might have depressed Kriss Akabusi.

Thus Lancashire's cricketers arrived at Kennington with the title beckoning them. Sky's pantechnicons had rolled up a couple of days earlier. All the visitors needed to do was beat Surrey; and in 2007 that meant they had to dismiss Mark Ramprakash. Twice. This was easier to plan than execute. Ramprakash was far and away the best batsman on the circuit. He arrived at The Oval for that final game with 1,700 Championship runs and eight centuries to his credit. "Ramps was just red-hot that summer," recalled Luke Sutton. "If you gave him a chance, he always made you pay and their whole team was built around him. He was a machine and if you could get him out, you'd gone a long way towards beating them."

And so, of course, Lancashire were given an immediate opportunity to achieve their goal. Jon Batty had fallen to Sajid Mahmood for a duck early on the first morning and Ramprakash seemed a trifle ill at ease against the new ball. He was not, as they say, 'on it'. At which point let the *Manchester Evening News* take up the story. (For this was still a time when great regional newspapers sent reporters to cover matches.)

"Ramprakash might have gone without scoring, too, attempting a jittery single after jamming a Mahmood yorker out into the off-side. The bowler picked up in his follow through and 'back handed' his throw close to the stumps, where short-leg fielder Paul Horton failed to gather – with Ramprakash retreating but still short of his ground."

Some cricketers never discover the precise cost of their errors. Poor Horton is not amongst them. It appeared to Lancashire's players that Ramprakash was galvanised by his reprieve, although there is also a thought that an unwise sledge helped things along. A little over 24 hours after that early drama Surrey's best batsman was dismissed by Glen Chapple for 196. Lancashire replied to Surrey's 427 with 234 and Ramprakash then helped himself to another 130 runs, unbeaten this time, before Mark Butcher declared late on the third evening.

It would be simplistic to say that Lancashire's failure to run out Ramprakash cost them the title. Errors in crucial games are magnified by the moment of their making. There were not many at The Oval those blissful September days who recalled Sussex's game against Lancashire at Liverpool in August. Had they done so, they might have pondered the significance of Chris Adams' brilliant one-handed diving snare at slip which removed Stuart Law off Rana Naved-ul-Hasan for 16 and helped set up the visitors' 108-run victory. No one said that was the moment when the title was decided. Just over seven weeks later Adams' bowlers duly took the last five Worcestershire wickets in less than a session and all they could do was wait, a task not helped by the fact that Sky had shifted its coverage to the World T20 and local radio was on the blink.

At The Oval Lancashire's batsmen had begun their absurd task with the words of one of the world's greatest cricketers spurring them on. "My first recollection was that the mood was pretty low on that Saturday morning," said Sutton. "It wasn't up and at 'em as I recall. Then VVS Laxman gave a speech just before the day's play and I can't remember exactly what he said but it was along the lines of, "Look, guys, we can do this. It seems impossible but the wicket's good and this side is packed full of talent". And I remember coming out of that huddle thinking we could do it. But then VVS was not just a special player, he was a special person as well."

The cricket was very special, too. Horton and Chilton put on 56 and then Chilton and Laxman added a further 58. The batting was brisk and clearly energised by the six-hour run-chase the match had become. After lunch Laxman and Law began to dominate Surrey's bowlers. Matt Nicholson was going round the park at five runs an over and only Murtaza Hussain appeared capable of restricting the flow of runs. Laxman reached his century off 97 balls and then almost immediately miscued a pull off Ian Salisbury. Ramprakash – who else? – took the catch at deepish midwicket. 229-3.

It made all the difference in the world and it made no difference whatever. Steven Croft took up where Laxman had left off and added a further 77 with Law. By now the media pack had forsaken their appointed darkroom and were sitting outside in the warm sunlight. You didn't need to be born or raised in Lancashire to hope Chilly's men would do it. Having once changed trains in Clitheroe was enough. Anyone born in Sussex kept very quiet. Croft pulled another boundary through midwicket.

"Go, Crofty!" roared Old Trafford's media officer Rebecca Trbojevich, her Sydney accent clear above the hubbub of the large crowd. "Who is that?" Michael Henderson enquired of the Reverend Malcolm Lorimer, the county's chaplain and archivist. "That's Lancashire's communications officer," replied the great cleric. A pontifical silence followed. Then Law cut Jade Dernbach savagely through point and more visiting supporters gave voice to dreams. 306-3. "You ran through the reasons why it wasn't going to happen and you got to a tipping point of thinking maybe it was," said Sutton. "As the day wore on we got to a stage when we really thought we might do it."

Law was strangled down the leg-side off Dernbach, who at once dismissed Croft in similar fashion. 307-5. But as each Lancashire batsman fell when looking for quick runs, another took their place, imbued with identical purpose. Sutton made 32 and Chapple 29 off 28 balls. Tea had long come and gone and still Sussex's players and spectators sat around at Hove, either desperately trying to hear news or desperately trying to look nonchalant. Mahmood and Dominic Cork put on 52 for the eighth wicket. By now less than a hundred runs were needed and the light was failing. When Mahmood was taken down the leg-side off Hussain, 58 were needed off 12 overs. Oliver Newby became the only Lancashire batsman not to make double figures

Only 25 were needed off 25 balls when Cork inside-edged Hussain onto his stumps...

Almost immediately at Hove there was a chorus of "Good Old Sussex by the Sea" and the small ground staged a riot of joy. It was the county's third title in five years.

In the away dressing room at The Oval there were tears and there was silence.

"For most of the day there was a significant belief we could do it and that's why we took it so hard when we didn't," said Chilton. "There were periods when they didn't look like getting a wicket and it was becoming more and more achievable. We got so close that we almost felt we'd let it slip. I was captain and it was pretty crushing for me but I was sitting opposite Corky and he was absolutely devastated. For half an hour afterwards no one spoke."

Eventually, the players trooped out onto the field. Surrey's skipper, Mark Butcher, approached Chilton, whose face was streaked with tears. "Chilly, mate," Butcher murmured and gave him a hug. He didn't need to say anything else. None of us did. It was a while before the full glory of those four days at The Oval sank in but the memory has never faded. We had seen a title lost in what we thought the most memorable fashion possible. We had seen Mark Ramprakash make two hundreds and VVS Laxman just the one. There is a fair argument that in 2007 no two batsmen in the world endowed their craft with more style or honour. And as darkness closed around The Oval that September evening, at least one of us would not have been too surprised to be told he would still be writing about that game nearly 13 years later. They say paradise is up in the stars.

Somerset 2016 – Great Days Indeed

TAUNTON, SEPTEMBER 22, 2016

Somerset 365 (Hildreth 135, Rogers 132; Ball 6-57) and
313-5 dec. (Rogers 100, Davies 59, Trego 55; Patel 3-95)*
beat Nottinghamshire 138 (Bess 5-43, Leach 3-42) and 215
(Root 66; Leach 4-69, van der Merwe 3-59) by 325 runs
Lord's, September 23, 2016

Middlesex 270 (Gubbins 125; Brooks 6-65, Bresnan 3-48) and 359-6 dec. (Malan 116, Gubbins 93, Eskinazi 78*) beat Yorkshire 390 (Bresnan 142*, Rafiq 65, Hodd 64) and 178 (Bresnan 55; Roland-Jones 6-54) by 61 runs

Among the many photographs that were taken the day after Somerset had annihilated Nottinghamshire in September 2016 there is a picture of Chris Rogers turning to look at a television. The screen itself is out of shot but we can infer roughly what it shows from the player's grim and painfully alert expression. Officially, Rogers is still Somerset's skipper but this is also his first day as a former professional cricketer. The previous afternoon he had become only the third player after William Lambert in 1817 and Len Baichan in 1982 to score two hundreds in his final first-class match. But personal achievements are now far from Rogers' mind; instead, he is wondering if there is any way in which the game between Middlesex and Yorkshire might end in a draw or maybe even a tie. Either outcome would make Somerset champions for the first time in their history. Rogers is sitting in one of the hospitality suites in what is now the Marcus Trescothick Pavilion; he is surrounded by the teammates with whom he has spent the previous six months. And they are watching their dreams being smashed.

The cricketers doing the smashing are playing at Lord's, an environment ill-suited to vandalism of any sort. But having overseen a three-and-a-half-day arm-wrestle in the game that will decide the title, Middlesex and Yorkshire's captains, James Franklin and Andrew Gale, have now set up a fourth-innings run-chase. Thus Adam Lyth and Alex Lees are deliberately bowling tripe so that their side will soon be chasing 240 in 40 overs with an agreement they will never halt their pursuit. It will prove too difficult a target on a fourth-day pitch of variable bounce but one can understand Gale's position. Yorkshire are trying to win a third successive title – it would have been the county's sixth hat-trick – and across the years there have been scores of skippers who have gambled similarly, especially in dull three-day matches on covered wickets.

And Gale's batsmen make respectable progress before Toby Roland-Jones straightens one up and Tim Bresnan is lbw for 55 when trying to clout the ball into the leg-side. The visitors now need 87 off 10 overs with five wickets in hand. Middlesex are very warm favourites but nothing prepares the spectators at Lord's or the viewers at Taunton for the final action of the season. Having dismissed Azeem Rafiq with the last delivery of his 12th over, Roland-Jones bowls Andy Hodd and Ryan Sidebottom with the first two balls of his next. The summer has ended with a hat-trick very different from the one Yorkshire supporters had envisaged. The Middlesex players and the TV commentators go berserk. Some of those watching at home may be thinking four-day county cricket is not supposed to be like this. However, it is possible that assumption has been formed by listening to those who spout about the first-class domestic game without going to the trouble of watching any of it. Such people are still about.

As it happened, 21,595 people thought that game at Lord's sufficiently important to attend in person, 7,408 of them on a final day when they saw perhaps the most gripping conclusion to a season in the Championship's 130-year history. Among those who watched the whole match was Duncan Hamilton, whose book *Kings of Summer* chronicles the game in a style which marries the virtues of the journalist to those of the poet. "It is difficult to judge something when it is actually happening," Hamilton writes in the final pages. "We wait for Time and history to bring proportion and order and rank to events. But I'm certain this match will live beyond its period, the totality of the experience too durable ever to fade." It is one of those sentences to which one responds, as Philip Larkin did to the music of Sidney Bechet, with "an enormous yes". And the warmth of one's salute is deepened by the conviction it is shared with many other people, some of whom, like myself, were at Taunton that late September evening.

When I insist that one of the most memorable days of county cricket I have seen was one on which no cricket was played, friends shake their heads in glum acknowledgement that the last marbles have left the building. I had arrived at the County Ground early that fourth morning and watched Somerset supporters greet their friends in the Stragglers' Café or the Colin Atkinson Pavilion. Whatever was going to happen, they had decided to face it together. The players had a room to themselves but some chose to take a walk on the outfield and be alone with their knowledge of cricket's iron logic. Rogers later admitted that he would have struck exactly the same sort of deal had he been in Gale or Franklin's position.

And as is often the case in such situations, one's thoughts went back to games earlier in the summer, games whose significance seemed great at the time and even greater at the end of the season. There was no doubt at all that Middlesex would be fine champions, although that was an opinion I kept to myself. They had begun their campaign with six draws, three of them at Lord's, where the county pitches were often as lively as PhDs on drainage in Grimsby. But in July Middlesex played the finest cricket of the season. At Scarborough they trampled all over Yorkshire on the final day: first Roland-Jones and Tim Murtagh thrashed 107 off 56 deliveries, at one stage hitting half-a-dozen sixes in seven balls, to give their side a first-innings lead of 171; then their attack swept aside Yorkshire's stunned batters for 167. The following morning's *Times* labelled Franklin's team the best in the country. It was a fair call.

A week later Mike Selvey's "Middle Saxons" consolidated their reputation at Taunton of all places. They were challenged to score 302 in 46 overs and got home with two balls to spare when John Simpson whacked Jim Allenby over deep square-leg for six. Each of those victories was worthy of champions and the fact that Middlesex ended the season unbeaten seemed secondary to the manner of their six wins. All the same, another close-but-no-pennant year seemed hard on Somerset and their admirable captain. Hard, too, on James Hildreth, whose ankle had been broken by a delivery from Jake Ball early on the first morning of that final game before he went on to make 135 with the help of a runner. At the end of the day Hildreth showed the media his lower leg; it was black. Defeating demoralised and relegated Nottinghamshire was then the most facile of tasks on a Bunsen but watching their spinners share 15 wickets was the joyful prelude to another disappointment for Somerset supporters. There have been so many near-misses this century that the club could have ties made, black ones with a mournful wyvern on each.

In sport it is always very tempting to pickle the distant past in the aspic of nostalgia; to think they don't make them as they used to in the candle-to-bed era. The more persuasive argument, perhaps, is that they make them just as fine or, at least, so different as to render comparisons hazardous. It is hard to think there has been a better Ashes series than 2005; or a more dramatic final day to any Test match than Headingley 2019; or a finer climax to a County Championship season than that we enjoyed in 2016. Have the debates started already? One hopes so. In the meantime let us take comfort from a slightly unlikely literary source. In the opening pages of Evelyn Waugh's *Brideshead Revisited* Sebastian Flyte says this:

"I should like to bury something precious in every place where I've been happy and then, when I was old and ugly and miserable, I could come back and dig it up and remember."

Fortunately one does not have to be a vain, alcoholic younger son of dysfunctional Roman Catholic aristocracy to empathise with Flyte's emotions. During these early months of the first non-cricket season any of us have known we should take comfort from the privileges we have enjoyed; their richness seems even greater in these strange days. Four years have not yet elapsed since Middlesex won the title but matches like those at Taunton, Scarborough and Lord's are our buried crocks of gold.

Glamorgan 1948 – Wales, Wales…

——————— BOURNEMOUTH, AUGUST 24, 1948 ———————

Glamorgan 315 (Jones 78*, DE Davies 74, Dyson 51; Bailey 6-85, Knott 3-133) beat Hampshire 84 (Muncer 5-25, Clay 3-31) and 116 (Clay 6-48) by an innings and 115 runs

"That's out, and we've won the Championship," said Dai Davies when Charlie Knott was leg before wicket to Johnnie Clay at Bournemouth in August 1948. Davies was quite correct in both respects, of course, but the rich spice of this famous story is that he was the umpire sending Knott on his way and thereby sealing Glamorgan's first title. The official later protested he had merely raised his finger but there were plenty of witnesses and Knott confirmed that Davies was the guilty – some might say 'innocent' – party.

It is a fine tale, charmingly suited to one of the grander and more unlikely triumphs in the Championship's history. Glamorgan had never finished higher than sixth in any of their 21 previous seasons, some of which had seen the county struggle to survive, let alone prosper. So no one blamed Llanelli-born Davies in the slightest. He had played for Glamorgan in the 1920s, when the county had needed to run whist drives and dances in order to soothe the imbalance in the books. He was also a regular in the 1930s when the county's finishing position in the 17-team table was in double figures far more consistently than some of their batsmen. Moreover, he was only one of thousands of Welshmen at Dean Park that Tuesday afternoon. Many supporters had booked holidays on the South Coast and some had been among the 10,000 or so who had watched Glamorgan beat Surrey at the Arms Park in their previous game.

There were other respects in which this was a deeply Welsh success. No county has the same national responsibilities as Glamorgan and it was therefore fitting that the players who won the title came from most areas of Wales. The skipper, Wilf Wooller, whose leadership was a mixture of brotherhood and bollockings, was born in Rhos-on-Sea; Willie Jones, whose two double-centuries in the space of 10 June days set up victories against Kent and Essex, hailed from Carmarthen; Clay was from Usk, while the side's most stylish batter, Gilbert Parkhouse, had his home in Swansea. The off-spinner Len Muncer, who took 139 Championship wickets in 1948, and the strike bowler 'Pete' Hever, who picked up 77, may have been vital recruits from Middlesex, but it was only to be expected that victory over Hampshire would be followed by emotional anthems from the valleys. This was a hymns and arias day, no matter that Max Boyce was still a toddler in Glynneath. Never had genteel Dean Park radiated with quite so much hwyl.

"Our leading cricketers nowadays rarely seem addicted to song," noted John Arlott drily in 1975. "But anyone who heard the Glamorgan team burst into *Land of My Fathers* after they won the Championship at Bournemouth in 1948 would have thought they were a male-voice choir." It was just a shame that Allan Watkins missed the game against Hampshire after injuring his shoulder in the final Ashes Test at The Oval. Indeed, Watkins only heard news of Glamorgan's vital game against Surrey from the stop press scores in the hourly editions of London's evening papers. "Nobody spoke to me," said Watkins after his first experience of an England dressing room. "There was no joy in the side at all." This was particularly noticeable, of course, given that Glamorgan's dressing room at this time was filled with noise and argument, most of it involving Wooller. In fairness to his England colleagues, Watkins might have realised that Arthur Morris and Ray Lindwall generally did little for their opponents' *joie de vivre*.

None of which overly concerned Glamorgan's players as they travelled to Dean Park, knowing that if they beat Hampshire and neither Surrey nor Yorkshire achieved victories, they would be champions. Glamorgan had won that previous game against Surrey at the Arms Park by an innings after Wooller had shrewdly opted to bat first on a wet pitch and let his opponents make what they could of Clay on a drying one. The answer was not very much. Surrey were not quite the power in the land they were to become a few years later and Clay – shades of Arthur Mailey – returned match figures of 10-66.

It was very much still the era of three-day cricket on uncovered pitches. If you had a useful attack, the loss of six hours' play did not end any chance of a result. So even when only 10 minutes' cricket was possible on Saturday at Bournemouth, Glamorgan supporters had reason to hope something could be conjured. It was also a more God-fearing era, albeit most Glamorgan fielders found facing Wooller when they had dropped a catch to be a Day of Judgement in itself. But Sunday remained a day of rest, not that many people noticed the difference in Bournemouth. So the Welsh supporters thronged the chapels and prayed for resilient batsmen and deadly spinners in that order.

Someone may have been listening. Fifties from Emrys Davies, Arnold Dyson and Willie Jones allowed Glamorgan to post 315 all out on Monday and Wooller exhorted his men to their greatest efforts in the hour or so that remained. "We want five of them out tonight," he told them. "We've got to get after them, I want to hear the ball hit Haydn [Davies]'s gloves every time you return it whether they run or not." A brilliant short-leg catch by Parkhouse disposed of Neville Rogers in Wooller's second over and Hampshire ended the day six down. It was entirely typical of Glamorgan's cricket during a summer in which the skipper had demanded his players become the best fielding side in the land.

"He'd always seen fielding as a prerequisite of success," wrote David Foot of Wooller. "His intrepid leg-side fields brought a new fashion to county cricket. The forward, square and backward short-legs seemed to hold on to everything, without flinching. Wooller led by example in the forward position, wearing the bruises like a Pontypool prop's battle-scars. In some respects, he never spiritually divided the two games. They were both physical, quite apart from the additional subtleties of cricket that he readily acknowledged; both were about courage and stuffing the opposition."

Chickens apart, 'stuffing' was not really Bournemouth's style, but Glamorgan did it to Hampshire all the same. "Hang on to Yorkshire, we can win here," read the telegram Wooller sent to George Woodhouse, his Somerset counterpart, at Taunton. "We will beat Yorkshire. Good luck!" was the reply. As it turned out, the match at the County Ground was drawn but that made no difference to Glamorgan. Asked to follow on 231 runs behind, the home side managed only 116 in the second innings, Clay taking 6-48. At Lord's Middlesex dispatched Surrey by an innings and Glamorgan were champions.

Amid the fizz and frolics the long moment of triumph was not lost on Johnnie Clay; nor did it ever lose its significance. Glamorgan's success was wreathed in rich emotional contexts and many of them involved him. In 1948 Clay was the 50-year-old honorary secretary of the club. In the post-war team photograph he looks more like a prudent treasurer, which was precisely the role he had undertaken in 1933 when his beloved county was on its uppers. Before that he had played for Glamorgan in 1921, their first year in the Championship. In that season he had been a fast-medium swing bowler in a struggling side; later he decided his height and build were better suited to the slow stuff.

"In what dark winter shed or sunny autumn field he practised and perfected this mutation, I do not know," wrote RC Robertson-Glasgow. "Perhaps it was a throwback to schooldays and ballistic experiments against forbidden walls. Perhaps some slow bowler had taken a wicket and Clay, weary of his own fast-medium strivings and envious of the other's facile success, put those long fingers round the ball, trundled down a vast off-break, and saw the light."

Clay had been cajoled by Wooller into playing five games in 1948; he took 27 wickets. Another spinner, the left-armer Stan Trick, could only be spared from his father's garage for seven matches, but he dismissed 36 batsmen, 22 of them in the two games at Swansea. It was all so very Glamorgan, as was the welcome the team received at Cardiff General Station when they returned late that Tuesday evening and found thousands waiting to greet them. Wooller had already gone to London to play for the Gentlemen of England against Australia but Clay, urbane and thoughtful, offered other speeches to follow those he had made at Dean Park.

"This victory for Glamorgan will do a lot of good not only for cricket generally but for similar counties like Warwickshire and Hampshire," he said. "No longer is the Championship the monopoly of the few." It was a wise saying albeit not a completely accurate prediction. Glamorgan had become only the third county outside the so-called Big Six (Surrey, Middlesex, Kent, Nottinghamshire, Yorkshire and Lancashire) to win the title. They followed Warwickshire in 1911 and Derbyshire in 1936, whose successes were, if anything, even more unlikely than Glamorgan's. It would be another 13 years before a 10th county, Hampshire, joined the list but Wooller's men had shown the way. Probably none of which troubled them late that August evening as they hightailed it to the Cardiff Athletic Club, where the celebrations continued. *Ar hyd y nos* indeed.

Hampshire 1961 – What Larks, Shack

———————————— PORTSMOUTH, JUNE 13, 1961 ————————————
Hampshire 96-0 dec. and 199-8 (Horton 51, Ingleby-Mackenzie 51; Andrew 3-20) beat Gloucestershire 176 (Shackleton 5-45, White 4-69) and 118-8 dec. (Shackleton 4-27) by two wickets

If you have 21 seconds to spare, you might do well to visit YouTube and search for 'Derek Shackleton Hampshire'. Among the available delights is a slow-motion film of the Hampshire medium-pacer bowling one ball against an unnamed and unseen Gloucestershire batsmen at Bournemouth in 1962.

At the time, cricket was still making the increasingly sham distinction between amateurs and professionals. It was also the penultimate year in which the County Championship was decided on average points per game – nine counties opting to play 28 three-day matches while the other eight contested 32 – and the last summer in which the English season would consist solely of first-class matches. "The new Knock-Out competition", as *Wisden* quaintly called the future Gillette Cup, would be introduced in 1963.

Each of the eight seasons from 1958 to 1965 was something of a voyage into the unknown for Hampshire's cricketers. How could it have been otherwise when they were led by a skipper whose life seems to have been so dedicated to hedonism that it could have been plucked straight from the pages of Scott Fitzgerald? Yet Colin Ingleby-Mackenzie, an Old Etonian socialite, was able to win over the professionals on the Hampshire staff and even persuade one or two to enjoy his own sybaritic lifestyle. Moreover, so successful was his captaincy and so skilled the players he led that Hampshire won their first County Championship in 1961. How they managed it remains one of domestic cricket's great tales.

The conventional view of Hampshire's maiden title was that Ingleby-Mackenzie used his gambler's flair to inveigle opposing skippers into making generous declarations and setting targets which his team chased to death or glory. And a few Yorkshire players, smarting because their side had been denied yet another hat-trick of titles, have stuck to this belief. But as Hampshire's former archivist, David Allen, has shown, only three of the county's 19 victories in 1961 came after their opponents' declarations and they matched Yorkshire's achievement in taking all 20 wickets in 15 of their games. Ingleby-Mackenzie's side triumphed partly because it included batsmen of the quality of Roy Marshall and Henry Horton, both of whom scored over 2,000 runs, and seam bowlers of the class of 'Butch' White and Shackleton, who each took over a hundred wickets.

At the same time, 10 of Hampshire's wins in 1961 came after Ingleby-Mackenzie had declared. That reflected well on the skipper's judgement and his bowlers' skills but it was also the result of the decision to prohibit the follow-on being enforced in any match where there was play on the first day. The rationale behind this change, which lasted only two seasons, was that it would encourage "brighter cricket" by placing an onus on skippers to set challenging targets. Ingleby-Mackenzie needed no such stimulus; his much-quoted mantra was "entertain or perish" and no game in the 1961 season epitomised either his principles or his extraordinary lifestyle better than the match against Gloucestershire at Portsmouth.

The game began on a Saturday and the opening sessions were relatively uneventful. True, Shackleton took five wickets as Gloucestershire were dismissed for 176 but he was to equal or better such a haul on 10 other occasions in the Championship season and his colleagues almost expected it of a cricketer whose qualities were perfectly captured by John Arlott: "In the dressing rooms, simply 'Shack' is enough. To the first-class cricketer, the name means shrewdly varied and utterly accurate medium-pace bowling beating down as unremittingly as February rain."

Sundays were very much a day off for county cricketers in the years before the introduction of the John Player League. Benefit matches required the attendance of some but Shackleton, who bowled 1471.3 overs in that year's Championship, probably appreciated the rest. Typically, however, Ingleby-Mackenzie preferred his own brand of relaxation and his early autobiography *Many A Slip*, published only a year later, gives an unforgettable account of his activities that weekend in June 1961:

"I soon forgot my cricketing responsibilities that evening when I drove off to Lewes for one of my rare appearances at a Deb Dance. I stayed at the hospitable home of Mr and Mrs Cosmo Crawley, and arrived late for dinner. I found myself sitting next to Susan Verney, daughter of Lord and Lady Willoughby de Broke whose interest in racing exceeded that of cricket, I was glad to discover. I did not get much sleep that night as I was scheduled to appear next day, Sunday, at the magnificent home to Lord Caenarvon at Highclere, near Newbury, to play for the Eton Ramblers against Lord Porchester's XI...

"Owing to my excessively late night, I had no time to sleep and therefore, for a change, I was one of the few people who arrived on time. The star performance among the later comers was that of Keith Miller, who arrived an hour late, shook hands with Porchy, and rushed off to be sick. He recovered so well after a lunch of champagne cocktails that he was able to score a century against us, but this was not enough to save his side. This game preceded another great party at Highclere and by the time I returned to Portsmouth next morning I was in frail condition."

Ingleby-Mackenzie admits he was "not in the least upset" when Monday's play was lost to rain, but the following morning he turned his mind to winning a match in which only 10 wickets had fallen. The best way of doing so would be to declare Hampshire's first innings in arrears and hope the Gloucestershire skipper, Arthur Milton, would respond in a similarly attacking spirit. The professionals in his team, on the other hand, saw their task as one of overhauling Gloucestershire's 176 and settling for two points for first-innings lead and two more for a faster scoring-rate when that lead was achieved. The opposition to Ingleby-Mackenzie's strategy in the home dressing-room was therefore vehement, but Milton agreed with his counterpart's gentle suggestion that one team had to win the game at Portsmouth to keep the pressure on Yorkshire, who had won seven of their first eight games.

After 70 minutes' play on the third morning, and with Hampshire 96 for no wicket, the openers, Marshall and Jimmy Gray, saw their skipper declaring. "For several moments nobody seemed to take any notice, and I had the feeling that our batsmen were deliberately ignoring my signals," wrote Ingleby-Mackenzie, an interpretation which Marshall corroborated eight years later in *Test Outcast*. "Neither of us could believe it when we saw Colin waving from the pavilion. I was furious at his apparent madness but there was nothing I could do."

Ingleby-Mackenzie was now in Milton's hands. Outright collusion was forbidden, which is not to say it didn't occur, but the captains had agreed a positive result should be achieved if possible. Gloucestershire managed 118-8 declared off 47 overs, Shackleton taking 4-27, and challenged Hampshire to score 199 in 137 minutes on a slow wicket. Typically, of course, Ingleby-Mackenzie led the charge. He and Horton scored 51 apiece but the home side had declined to 162-8 when Shackleton joined White. There were 20 minutes left in the game and no set number of overs. White, a strong man with an uncomplicated approach to such matters, whacked an unbeaten 33 and victory was secured with two minutes to spare. Bryan Timms, who was deputising for Hampshire's excellent wicketkeeper, Leo Harrison, recalls a livid Marshall and Gray showering and going for a pint before the game was won. It is interesting to ponder the repercussions had Ingleby-Mackenzie's strategy not paid off.

There was, of course, far more to Hampshire's title win in 1961 than three good batsmen, two fine seamers and a skipper with the daring to make his own luck. Peter Sainsbury was one of three spinners who each took over 40 wickets that summer and he also chipped in with 1,459 runs. Danny Livingstone also scored over a thousand runs, as did Ingleby-Mackenzie, whose total included a match-winning 132 not out against Essex at Cowes. That innings was played after a weekend in which Hampshire's captain had attempted to break the world drinking record and had also fallen in the Solent.

And so one is drawn back to two cricketers whose lifestyles could not have been more different yet who retained the greatest respect for each other. Ingleby-Mackenzie burned the candle at both ends and in the middle when he could. Now and then he was joined by Marshall and Harrison. Shackleton, on the other hand, remains the epitome of the conscientious, post-war professional, his image perfectly captured by Patrick Eagar on the cover of David Matthews' biography.

In that photograph Shackleton is coming into his delivery stride. The left arm is about to be raised in the conventional fashion but it is the right that commands the eye. The forearm is thick, the wrist cocked and the fingers grip the ball down the seam. He holds the batter in his hawk-like gaze, which is a little remarkable when one realises that he has good sight only in the right eye. His boots are heavy-soled and protect his ankles. The shirt and flannels are white as communion cloth. There is not a speck of sponsorship in sight. Every hair is in place; you might believe he has a comb back at his mark.

Shackleton's disciplines would help him take 2,857 first-class wickets, six of which were claimed on September 1, 1961 when the Championship was sealed with victory over Derbyshire at Dean Park. He stands eighth in the all-time list having reached the bowler's century in each of the 20 seasons from 1949 to 1968. No other bowler has matched that precise level of consistency.

Colin Ingleby-Mackenzie is still recalled so fondly at Hampshire that the East Stand at the Ageas Bowl is named after him. Derek Shackleton is remembered by all who saw him play cricket and in that brief film of him bowling at Bournemouth in 1962. His run-up was 12 normal paces long but, as this evidence reveals, that converted into nine long, easy strides. "He didn't leave any foot marks," said his teammate, Neville Rogers. "It was as though he bowled in slippers."

The slow-motion film of Shack lasts 21 seconds. You could watch it for hours.

Essex 1979 – It Must Be Cricket

CHELMSFORD, JUNE 22, 1979

Essex 435-9 dec. (McEwan 185, Pont 77; Kirsten 3-58) beat Derbyshire 258 (Tunnicliffe 57, Walters 54, Swarbrook 52; Lever 5-72, Phillip 4-59) and 137 (Lever 4-45, Phillip 4-28) by an innings and 40 runs

SOUTHEND-ON-SEA, JULY 13, 1979

Essex 240 (Denness 65; Hadlee 4-49, Bore 3-55) and 229 (Turner 68; Bore 5-79) beat Nottinghamshire 300 (Rice 86, Tunnicliffe 56; East 4-93, Phillip 3-54) and 123 (Acfield 5-28, East 5-76) by 46 runs*

Rather like the county they represent so proudly, Essex's cricketers go about their business with little grandeur and no fuss. If they are piqued that their club is regarded as small they rarely show it, preferring instead to win matches and see what comes of that. Perhaps only then, someone like Keith Fletcher will say how curious it is that a side of such lowly status has managed to collect seven more Championship titles in the 40 seasons since their first in 1979.

Fletcher led Essex to their first three titles before handing over to Graham Gooch, who picked up three more. The last two have been won under the leadership of Ryan ten Doeschate, most recently at a damp Taunton in September 2019 when Alastair Cook's clenched fist salute to the away dressing-room signalled the job was done. Fletcher, Gooch and Cook all captained England and played a total of 338 Test matches for their country, scoring a total of 60 hundreds. But their hearts belonged to Essex, too, and one always felt they returned to the compact ground in New Writtle Street with gratitude and relief.

Every one of those titles was celebrated with boisterous abandon, all the more so, perhaps, because there had been plenty of grim years before the pennant could be hoisted atop the Chelmsford pavilion. Admitted to the Championship in 1895, Essex had only twice finished in the top three before August 21, 1979 when the news reached Wantage Road on the dot of six o'clock that Worcestershire had drawn at Derby, thus confirming Fletcher's team as the champions. Half an hour earlier Brian Hardie's unbeaten century had taken his side to victory against Northamptonshire. It was their 11th win of the summer and there were to be two more before the season's end. Essex had first led the table on June 1 and finished the campaign 77 points ahead of Worcestershire.

"The basic philosophy of the club has not changed and the committee are determined that it will not do so," said the chairman, Doug Insole, at the end of that season, in which Essex had also won the Benson & Hedges Cup. "Cricket is for enjoyment and for entertainment. It must be profitable; it must be business-like; but most of all, it must be cricket."

That relatively simple philosophy still holds true in Chelmsford. You would struggle to find any Championship-winning team whose members do not mention team spirit, but the collective ethos seems particularly powerful at Essex. It has allowed England players to be developed and then welcomed back; it has allowed high-quality overseas cricketers to be recruited and retained; but each member of those two groups must understand that Essex does not warm to any self-anointed Billy Bigbollocks pulling his imagined rank.

Neither John Lever nor Ken McEwan were guilty of such arrogance in 1979 and both men enjoyed fine seasons. When Derbyshire were overwhelmed by an innings at Chelmsford in late June, McEwan reached his century in 85 minutes and contributed 103 of the 131 runs in his third-wicket partnership with Mike Denness. The South African's 185 helped Essex post a first-innings lead of 177, leaving Lever to add four more wickets to the five he had picked up when Derbyshire had batted on the first day. Such feats were not particularly exceptional for either cricketer that season. Over the previous fortnight Lever had taken 13 wickets in successive games against Leicestershire and Warwickshire. He dismissed 53 batsmen in June and finished the season with 106 first-class wickets, 99 of them in the Championship. It was no wonder that Derek Pringle paid particular tribute to 'JK' when he looked back on his time at Essex during the 80s in his 2018 book *Pushing the Boundaries.*

"Players considered to be a 'captain's dream' are mostly mythical beasts existing in the minds of fantasists, yet JK managed to embody it for Essex," wrote Pringle. "Need a wicket, whistle up JK. Need to keep it tight for 40 minutes, bring on JK. Need some yorkers at the death, give the ball to JK. He was a bowling everyman with the endurance to match."

Those early weeks were also memorable for McEwan, who made 787 runs in the first nine Championship matches before losing his form a little later in the season. By then, though, the South African, who had no prospect of playing Test cricket, was well-ensconced at Chelmsford. He would score over a thousand runs in each of his 12 seasons at the club and would contribute to two more Championship wins. Before him there had been Keith Boyce; after McEwan's return to South Africa there would be Allan Border, Mark Waugh and, eventually, Simon Harmer. All of them bought into the Essex approach but rarely did they earn tributes quite as affectionate as that written by David Lemmon about one of McEwan's innings in 1983:

"Once, while making a century against Kent in Tunbridge Wells, Ken McEwan straight drove, square cut and pulled Derek Underwood to the boundary in the space of one over. Each shot was executed with regal charm, and never a hint of arrogance. He batted, as did the ancients, upright, correct and magisterial. He was incapable of profaning the art of batting, incapable of an ineloquent gesture."

McEwan's own feelings towards Essex during those dozen summers were expressed in humbler but no less revealing words: "At pre-season practice we had to put up the nets ourselves and, if somebody was moving some chairs, we had to go and help them. It was a lovely atmosphere. Every day I had a good laugh. I felt very at home."

But both Lever and McEwan knew that Essex's success never revolved entirely around their performances. That was proved at Southend three weeks after the win against Derbyshire. Nottinghamshire were the visitors and for most of the three days they outplayed their hosts, gaining a 60-run first-innings lead and then dismissing Essex for 229 in their second dig. Lever had been selected in the Test squad and McEwan made just 27 runs in the match; Essex were able to set their visitors as many as 170 to win only because the invaluable Stuart Turner made an unbeaten 68 and put on 42 for the last wicket with David Acfield.

None of which seemed to matter very greatly when Nottinghamshire were 87-1 but then the spinners Ray East and Acfield took the last nine wickets for 36 runs on a deteriorating pitch. It was another triumph for Essex and for the tactical ability of a skipper whose ability and services to the game have been insufficiently recognised – except, that is, in Chelmsford.

"Fletch was tactically astute," said Gooch. "He knew the game inside out. And he had an incessant drive to win, which is important in county cricket because you're on a treadmill. Some county sides were happy for it to rain. But we weren't. 'You can't win points in the dressing room,' Fletch said. He never let things drift."

Nor were Fletcher's abilities lost on the young Derek Pringle, who rated his county captain a shrewder skipper than Mike Brearley: "Fletcher might never have been able to remember anyone's name, including most in his own team. But he knew how they played, especially Essex's opponents, and set traps accordingly. Every season Fletcher would look at the fixture list and surmise that Essex would probably need 12 or 13 victories to clinch the County Championship title. He'd then begin to identify, bad weather notwithstanding, where and against whom they might eventuate. He would also predict, broadly, how we might clinch those matches: 'JK will win us four with the ball; Goochie four with the bat; the other bowlers and batsmen a couple each,' he used to say. It was a reductive approach, and ridiculously facile for such a complex game, but it was uncanny how often his gnomic prophecies proved correct."

This determination to play attractive, winning cricket became known as The Essex Way. It brought the county their eight titles and a host of one-day trophies. Yet the Way seems little more than an aim, one that might be shared by most first-class counties. Its achievement was altogether more complex. It was founded, as is the case with any successful sports team, on the ability of the players. Its development, however, was dependent on the willingness of those players to consider their own achievement only in the context of the common pursuit; and equally, it rested on the tactical ability of a captain who was ready to take all manner of risks in pursuit of a possible victory. To lose one or two players, as Essex often did in the era of Gooch, Lever, Pringle and Neil Foster, simply made demands on others to mend any breach.

"There was no coach, no gym, no indoor nets, no standalone outdoor nets, no psychologists," wrote Pringle, "just a scorer, a physio and a captain who dared his team to win, no matter the circumstance."

To reduce The Essex Way simply to its ultimate goal is to make nearly as daft an error as to think Essex itself is no more than boy racers, cheap entertainment and TOWIE. As Gillian Darley shows in her book *Excellent Essex* the county is the "most overlooked and undersold" in England; and when Robert Macfarlane made his superb film *The Wild Places of Essex* he visited not night clubs and nail bars but Tilbury Power Station, where he saw peregrine falcons and Billericay, where there were badgers, bluebells and barn owls. Most evocatively and mysteriously of all, there is the passage in John le Carré's novel *Tinker, Tailor, Soldier, Spy* in which Peter Guillam is driving the former spymaster George Smiley to see an agent who has had to be hidden deep in England. Essex, it seems, is the natural choice.

"On the signposts were names like Little Horkesley, Wormingford and Bures Green, then the signposts stopped and Guillam had a feeling of being nowhere at all... As they got out the cold hit them and Guillam smelt a cricket field and woodsmoke and Christmas all at once; he thought he had never been anywhere so quiet or so cold or so remote."

And just as there is far more to Essex than Basildon, so there was far more to The Essex Way than a preparedness to take risks. Fletcher possessed perhaps the most instinctive and acute understanding of what could be achieved in a three-day county match during the modern era; his reward was a trio of titles which his players marked with appropriate revels. And they still enjoy their victories at Chelmsford, as journalists found when they were leaving the ground one evening in June 2017. A couple of hours earlier Harmer's 14th wicket had sealed victory in the day-night game against Middlesex with eight balls to spare. But the songs of triumph were still ringing out from the home dressing-room at near midnight.

Worcestershire 1965 – Tom, Doug and Dolly

CHELTENHAM, AUGUST 13, 1965

Worcestershire 253 (D'Oliveira 81; Allen 5-79) and 131-3 (Graveney 59*, D'Oliveira 55*) beat Gloucestershire 210 (Nicholls 99; Coldwell 4-59) and 173 (D'Oliveira 4-53, Gifford 3-50) by seven wickets

BOURNEMOUTH, AUGUST 27, 1965

Worcestershire 363-9 decl. (Headley 123, Graveney 104; Shackleton 4-66) and 0-0 decl. beat Hampshire 217-6 decl. (Caple 66, Reed 55; Coldwell 4-66) and 31 (Flavell 5-9, Coldwell 5-22) by 115 runs

For well over a decade Tom Graveney's name ended a rich debate and prompted instead some fond remembrance. A few Englishmen have been heavier scorers, others tougher to get out, but when followers of domestic cricket were asked who they would most like to watch bat for an hour, most of them settled for Tom. And first-name terms were not resented by Graveney, neither when they were used by fans of Gloucestershire, for whom he played 296 first-class games, nor by supporters of Worcestershire, where he spent that long, abundant, gorgeous autumn of his career. He understood the vulnerable affection of the man who turns up at a ground hoping to watch a favourite make a hundred and sees his dream splintered in a moment. So he relished applause all the more keenly when he played his cover drive or that top-handed ease through midwicket. Such awareness also informed the pleasure he felt when he helped Worcestershire win their first title in 1964 and then become the first county outside the Big Six to retain the Championship at Hove a year later.

Graveney's colleagues at New Road never doubted his value but statistics reinforced their opinion. His 3,985 runs in the two title-winning seasons included nine centuries and a host of vital fifties on sporting pitches against fine attacks. Then as now, professionals gauged not simply the runs a man piled up but the circumstances of their making. "People say the bowlers won us the Championship in 1964 and 1965," said the Worcestershire seamer, Len Coldwell, in a conversation recorded in Andrew Murtagh's fine biography of Graveney. "No, we didn't. That bloke over there won it for us." And he gestured across a room at Tom. The recipient of Coldwell's praise would surely have been flattered and a little embarrassed by the comment. But he would also be aware that it was not terribly fair. Worcestershire's titles, especially the second of them, were richer than even Graveney's contributions might suggest, and Coldwell knew that the bowlers did their share of work. "World is crazier and more of it than we think," wrote Louis MacNeice. Step forward, Jack Flavell; step forward, Doug Slade.

Yet even quite late in the 1965 season the idea that Don Kenyon might skipper his side to a second successive Championship seemed fanciful. It was a wet summer and six different counties had led the table by July 23 when a sodden draw at Northampton left Worcestershire with three wins from their first 17 games. The most encouraging cricket of the year had been played by a 32-year-old South African who had claimed to be three years younger when he joined the county. This was Basil D'Oliveira's first full summer on the county circuit and he was determined to make the most of a chance he had thought would never come. And D'Oliveira reached his goal partly because he strengthened his natural rapport with Graveney. In itself this was not so surprising; the pair had batted together in what is now Zimbabwe and again when on tour with a Commonwealth XI in Pakistan. But maintaining such concord against county bowlers in a damp English spring was different. That was why their partnerships of 183 and 83 in the opening match of the season against Essex were a portent of more substantial achievement. And most counties would suffer to some degree. "When we played Worcestershire we always felt that if we didn't shift Tom and Basil then we were in trouble," said the Warwickshire skipper, Mike Smith. "They had another couple of good batsmen, of course, but you always thought that if you removed those two you had a chance."

But over two months were to pass after that Essex game before Kenyon's cricketers recovered the form which had seen them win the title by 41 points the previous summer. With the simple points system then in operation – 10 for the win, two for first-innings lead – Worcestershire's margin had reflected their dominance in 1964. However, no county had opened a comparable gap by the time stand-in skipper Graveney and his players returned from

Northampton to begin the game against Kent at Dudley the following morning. In the next 39 days they were to win 10 of their 11 three-day matches.

Graveney was in the middle of his second three-year exile from the England side; D'Oliveira's international class had not yet been fully appreciated. By the next summer both would be playing Test cricket, but Worcestershire supporters were cheerily untroubled by such considerations as they saw the pair put on 131 for the fourth wicket against Kent. Then their spinners exploited the eccentricities of an outground pitch on which D'Oliveira had made a century. Indeed, five of those last 10 wins were to be achieved away from Worcestershire's headquarters, often on wickets which exposed a batsman's technical limitations. That was why, in future seasons, Worcestershire's cricketers still talked about Graveney and D'Oliveira's batting at Cheltenham.

The game on the College Ground in August was dominated by spinners. Worcestershire earned a 43-run first-innings lead and needed only 131 to complete what would have been their sixth successive victory. But by then the top had gone on the wicket, leaving conditions in which David Allen and John Mortimore needed to do little more than pitch the ball on a length and watch the fun. Worcestershire were 19-3 when D'Oliveira joined Graveney. "I can't play in this, I'm charging," he was told. Yet while Graveney went down the pitch to the spinners, D'Oliveira relied on his back-foot technique. "The fascination was in the contrast," wrote Peter Oborne in his biography of D'Oliveira. "Graveney the artist, a classical front-foot player, grand, gentlemanly and imperious; D'Oliveira the craftsman, happier drawing back into his stumps, no back-lift, the master of the short-armed jab." The pair put on an unbroken 112 for the fourth wicket. It was their second century partnership of the match and D'Oliveira's two fifties could be added to his five wickets and three catches in Gloucestershire's two innings. It was easy to see why Worcestershire's players began to believe the title could be theirs after all.

But the schedule remained unrelenting, some might say savage. The following morning Worcestershire's players were at Kidderminster where Jack Flavell's 13 wickets in the game against Somerset allowed his side to recover from conceding a 39-run first-innings lead. In a low-scoring match Kenyon's 77 took Worcestershire to the verge of a nine-wicket victory which was achieved with a precious day to spare. Perhaps no one appreciated the brief rest more than 36-year-old Flavell, who would finish the season with 132 Championship scalps having taken 10 wickets in a match on four occasions. Rather more remarkably, he missed none of Worcestershire's 28 matches. "Another time," wrote Harold Pinter.

Two days later Flavell was back at New Road where he took 4-47 in 24 overs against Northamptonshire, who harboured their own hopes of winning the title. But Worcestershire's seven-wicket victory owed more to the work of the spinners, Doug Slade and Norman Gifford, who shared eight wickets as the visitors were put out for 130 in their second innings. Graveney and D'Oliveira shared a stand of 61 to see their team home.

"Another day, another match" as Brian Brain's fine chronicle of the 1980 season put it. Brain took 33 wickets during 1965, which was a season typical of its era. Different demands were placed on a player's fitness than would be expected today; the ability to keep soldiering on was highly prized. And it was certainly true that playing two three-day games a week from May to August allowed momentum to be maintained, even when exhaustion beckoned. The day after beating Northants, Kenyon's players pitched up at New Road where Coldwell's eight wickets in the first innings and Gifford's six in the second were enough to overwhelm Surrey by an innings.

It was August 24. Northamptonshire had finished their season with a rain-affected draw against Gloucestershire. (Septembers in that era were devoted to festival cricket and, if pressed, the Gillette Cup final.) Worcestershire embarked on their southern tour to Bournemouth and Hove needing two wins to prevent Northants winning their first title. Unsurprisingly, given that Colin Ingleby-Mackenzie was involved, the game at Dean Park was one of the most bizarre of the season.

Yet there was nothing unusual about an opening day on which Graveney and Ron Headley scored centuries in Worcestershire's 363-9 declared. Rain always encouraged Ingleby-Mackenzie's gambling instincts, though, and the loss of much of the second day spurred Hampshire's skipper to declare 146 runs behind on the final morning. Kenyon was even keener to force a win and closed his own side's innings after one ball. There was little reason to suppose that the home batsmen would find scoring 147 in 160 minutes especially onerous until a warm late-summer sun got to work on a wet wicket. Hampshire were bowled out for 31; their innings lasted 16.3 overs.

Having returned figures of 5-9 at Dean Park, Flavell dismissed another seven batters the following morning at Hove where Sussex were skittled for only 72 in less than a session. But despite conceding a 94-run lead, the home side recovered in the second innings to leave Worcestershire needing 132 in two-and-a-bit sessions to win the title. That task was made more tricky when the 23-year-old John Snow removed the first four with 36 runs on the board. But Dick Richardson's patient 31 not out and Roy Booth's 38 secured a title which was celebrated with the usual Worcestershire gusto. "My goodness, we were a thirsty lot," Graveney admitted.

Perhaps there are no golden ages; perhaps there is merely our youth, a time when every good thing is burnished by first acquaintance. Yet Tom Graveney's batting had a similar effect on spectators of any age. Some might have thought it merely a natural accomplishment and forget that his skill was maintained by a daily net before play began; others might fail to note that only seven players in the game's history have scored more first-class runs and only one of those played all his cricket after 1945.

But no one missed the style, certainly not Mike Selvey, who first bowled to the 41-year-old Graveney in 1968 when he was a 20-year-old playing his fifth first-class match. Over four decades later Selvey shared the moment in a memorable *Guardian* piece. "I knew nothing," he admits. Then this…

"I bowled to Graveney and was primary witness to a single stroke that defined everything that has followed for me since. The delivery, such as it was, contained no particular merit. It was on a length, lively enough in pace from a whippy youngster and not badly directed at around middle-and-off. At least it deserved respect. What followed is as clear as day.

"Tom eased himself forward and his bat came down straight. Then, without hitting around his front pad, which had remained inside the line of the ball, he turned his top hand (not the bottom-hand shovel that so many use now) and caressed the ball away to the leg-side. There was no crack of leather on willow, no explosion from the blade.

The ball was eased with precision to the left of the fellow at midwicket and to the right of mid-on...

"In the four decades since... I have witnessed every great batsman, from Sobers and Graeme Pollock... through to Brian Lara, Sachin Tendulkar, Ricky Ponting and Jacques Kalllis. And all the aesthetes too: Gower, Mark Waugh, Mohammad Azharuddin, VVS Laxman, a host of them. But that late August boundary of Tom's, 42 years ago and in the twilight of his career, remains the single most sublime, beautiful cricket stroke I have ever seen."

There are still plenty of Worcestershire supporters who remember that 1965 team. They recall the thousand runs scored by the opener Headley; the all-round talents of D'Oliveira, who still stares out from the 1966 *Wisden* sporting a thin moustache of which Robert Donat would have been proud; then there was the tirelessness of Flavell; the keeping of Booth. But above all, they remember Graveney, batting as if put on earth for the purpose. And anyway, they will tell you, it was always 'Tom'.

Surrey 1954 – Infantry

———————————— KETTERING, AUGUST 4, 1954 ————————————
Surrey 121 (Broderick 7-38) and 139-9 (Laker 33*; Tribe 4-30) beat Northamptonshire 125 (Laker 6-38, Lock 3-31) and 133 (Laker 5-36, Lock 3-62) by one wicket

———————————— THE OVAL, AUGUST 26, 1954 ————————————
Surrey 92-3 dec. beat Worcestershire 25 (Lock 5-2) and 40 (Laker 4-27, A Bedser 3-7) by an innings and 27 runs

Retaining the County Championship is proof of sustained excellence and achieving a hat-trick of titles is an Everest few sides approach. Beyond that, though, history suggests things get even trickier, particularly since in any year there have usually been at least three or four fine teams and winning the toss in certain games is frequently vital. So what might we make of Surrey's seven successive

Championships in the 1950s, a decade in which the season was complicated by an asymmetric fixture list and enriched by uncovered pitches? Test matches deprived the side of seven players during 1955 yet the pennant flew over The Oval in late August, just as it did in the three following years. Ability does not quite explain the matter; Surrey's cricketers were driven to win, and win again.

The county's veterans will assure you the desire for victory was inculcated by Stuart Surridge, an amateur captain who successfully transcended the gulf between himself and the professionals on the staff by travelling with the players to away games, staying at the same hotels and treating them like the skilled craftsmen they were. It mattered, too, that quite apart from his tactical nous Surridge was worth his place in the team, often for his medium-pace bowling but always for his close catching where he would crouch as close to the batter as the laws permitted, uttering all manner of dark threats. The obvious parallel is with a general leading his men into battle and it is interesting that three skippers cut from similarly coarse cloth – Surridge, Wilf Wooller and Brian Close – often chose to field in positions which endangered their safety. In wartime such bravery wins medals, often posthumously. The more cerebral skippers stay at slip.

It is useful, if a shade harsh, to compare Surridge to two of his predecessors. In 1946 Nigel Bennett had accepted the Surrey captaincy but the folk tale persists at The Oval that the appointment was a delicious case of mistaken identity, one typical of the chaotic post-war era: the man the committee really wanted was another Major Bennett, Leo, who had played three games for the second eleven before the war. Nigel was a decent club player who managed 605 runs in 1946, but as *Wisden* said: "want of knowledge of county cricket on the field presented an unconquerable hindrance to the satisfactory accomplishment of arduous duties." Very well put, minister, yet the divide to be crossed was not entirely cleaved by Bennett's own tactical ignorance and general naivety. That was revealed by Jerry Lodge in his post-war history of the county: "On match days Bennett wanted to meet the players on the steps as they left their respective dressing rooms but was told that under no circumstances was this acceptable. He was informed that he must walk out on to the field of play and that the professionals must join him there."

Surridge was immediately preceded by Michael Barton, a quiet, dignified skipper, who led Surrey to a share of the Championship with Lancashire in 1950. All the same he scarcely coaxed the best out of a side which included Alec Bedser, Tony Lock and Jim Laker.

"At one time Surrey seemed to have 11 captains but this all ended abruptly when Stuart Surridge took over," wrote Dickie Dodds of Essex. "Stuart was a large man in every way. He had a large frame, a large heart, he bowled large swingers and he cracked the whip. Without question he was the boss. He led from the front and gave his orders, reprimands, encouragement and praise in language as spoken in the Borough Market. This is not to say that the Surrey players stopped chuntering as they batted, bowled and especially fielded; it was now that they had a skipper who understood their chuntering and could orchestrate it and blend it into a harmonious, constructive whole."

Few of their opponents liked Surridge's Surrey very much but not everyone can be Roger Federer. The captain bound his team to him and was loyal to them. Outsiders could think what they liked. Like Wooller, Surridge was a bollockings and brotherhood skipper, and when, at the end of 1956, he returned to his business of making bats instead of using them, the core of the side he had made won two more titles under Peter May. It was easy for the sceptics to say that anyone would have done well with an attack of Bedser, Laker, Lock and Peter Loader at their disposal; reports suggest Yorkshire and Lancashire's sides were comparably talented. However, Lancashire's skipper, Cyril Washbrook, could not have been more distant from many of his younger players had he been an old-style amateur. Surridge was never remote from the men he led, even if, on the bad days, they might have wished it so.

The results were an impressive reflection of Surrey's approach. In the seven Championship seasons they played 195 games, winning 121, losing 28 and drawing 46. The latter were more galling to Surridge – he could see little point in them – but in wet seasons like 1954 even Surrey's captain had to accept that he could not command the weather. No doubt it irked him. Yet that season's matches offered two excellent examples of his team's capabilities.

In the first game, against Northamptonshire at Kettering, Surridge did not even play. In his stead, May skippered the side and had few tactical decisions to make on the first morning apart from allowing

Laker and Lock to bowl out the home side for 125 on a spinners' pitch. By the close, though, slow left-armer Vince Broderick had taken 7-38 and his team had extended their four-run first-innings lead to 77, for the loss of four wickets. (No one thought to complain about the surface: two-day finishes were hardly unusual on the Town Ground.) On the second morning Laker completed match figures of 11-94 and Surrey needed 138 to win.

It became a day for infantrymen rather than cavalry. The broad-shouldered opener, Tom Clark, who was to finish that filthy wet season with 1,347 runs, made 32 and the 23-year-old, as yet uncapped Ken Barrington added 22. The visitors required another 38 when Jim Laker came to the wicket and still wanted 19 when he was joined by the No.10 Tony Lock. The pair added 12 before Lock became the fourth victim of George Tribe's leg-spin. Surrey's last man was Loader, for whom quick bowling was something of a laxative. Given that Frank Tyson was in the Northamptonshire team – he had so far bowled nine overs in the match – this hardly engendered much confidence in the visiting changing-room. What happened next is splendidly retold by Stephen Chalke:

"As Loader emerged from the pavilion his path was blocked by an animated Bernie Constable, who had earlier taken a few body blows from Tyson and was now waving his bat about and gesticulating repeatedly. 'What was all that about?' the others asked when Constable returned to the dressing room. 'I told him if he takes one step to leg, he'll have this bloody bat round his head when he gets back. And it will hurt a lot more than a cricket ball.'"

Mindful of Constable's gentle sanction, Loader hit two runs before Laker biffed an off-spinner from Syd Starkie to the boundary to finish the match. The whole affair had been something of a minor classic but it also makes another point about Surridge's team. If Surrey's Test players were essential to their glory years, so were cricketers like Clark and Constable and so were the second-team players who deputised during the Tests. Constable was the only other batter to reach a thousand runs in 1954 yet he predicted posterity's indifference with some accuracy. "In years to come, when they talk about this Surrey team, it will be all about the bowlers and about Peter May," he said. "There won't be one mention of the rest of us poor buggers who've had to bat on these bloody pitches."

In fact, Constable was also worth his place both as a close fielder and as one of the sharpest analysts of a batter's technique in the English game. "Bernie used to watch like a hawk when new players came in," said Micky Stewart. "Even the way they were holding their bat when they came out of the pavilion. They'd take guard and he'd come in from cover, till he was only three or four yards away, looking at the way they were holding the bat. Staring."

Rather like Worcestershire 11 years later, Surrey were well back in the chasing pack at the end of July 1954. They then won nine of their final 10 games, all of which were played between July 28 and the end of August. Five of those victories were achieved inside two days before it bucketed it down on the last, frequently preventing either Yorkshire or Derbyshire, their closest pursuers, completing their matches. Some people called it luck but they would say the same about Colin Ingleby-MacKenzie's team seven years later. Most professionals knew differently.

Perhaps, therefore, it was appropriate that the title should be secured with another two-day win that showed Surrey's attack at its most ruthless and Surridge at his most daring. Worcestershire were moored securely in mid-table when they arrived at The Oval in late August and their spinners hardly compared to Lock and Laker. The game began at two o'clock on the first day and the visitors were bowled out for 25 in 28.3 overs, Lock taking 5-2 on a pitch perfectly suited to his slow-medium left-arm. It remains Worcestershire's second-lowest total in first-class cricket. Surrey had then progressed fairly serenely to 92-3 when Barrington and May noticed Surridge waving to them from the balcony outside the upstairs dressing-room still used by the amateurs. He had declared.

"Downstairs among the rest of the side the general verdict was that the captain must have lost his senses," wrote May. "His explanation as he led us out was that it was going to rain, which did not entirely clear up the misgivings."

The location of Surridge's marbles was probably keenly debated on a few occasions during those five memorable years. All the same, an hour into Thursday morning Worcestershire had been dismissed for 40, Bedser taking 3-7. One batsman had retired with a broken finger, another had hit his wicket and a third had been sconed by a Jim Laker off-break. The whole match had lasted a little more than five hours and its 157 runs were the lowest aggregate in a completed game since 1878. One doubts Surridge made any mention of these statistics when he addressed the 3,000 spectators from the balcony. "Then the Oval was left deserted, ironically in glorious late-summer sunshine," wrote Michael Melford in *The Daily Telegraph*.

To understand Surrey's achievement 60 and more years ago we need to look behind the gold leaf at The Oval and the records in the books. It is more revealing to think of Constable and Clark or of Surridge's close fielders crouched like paparazzi around a film star. But that simile is the nearest those players will ever get to stardom; it is probably much more useful to think of them battling it out on those "bloody pitches", the sort that would get counties docked points today. And in any case, mere fame is often transitory and cheap; 20 years after his retirement Richie Benaud was asked by a young autograph-hunter whether he had ever actually played cricket.

Sussex 1963 – No Going Back

──────────── MAY 1-2, 1963, OLD TRAFFORD ────────────
Lancashire 304-9 (65 overs) (Marner 121, Grieves 57,
Booth 50; Pratt 3-75) beat Leicestershire 203 (53.3 overs)
(Hallam 106; Statham 5-28, Marner 3-49) by 101 runs

──────────── JUNE 12, 1963, HOVE ────────────
Sussex 292 (64 overs) (JM Parks 90, RJ Langridge 56;
Nicholson 3-84) beat Yorkshire 270 (63.3 overs) (Boycott
70; Thomson 3-52, Bates 3-76) by 22 runs

──────────── SEPTEMBER 7, 1963, LORD'S ────────────
Sussex 168 (60.3 overs) (JH Parks 57; Gifford 4-33) beat
Worcestershire 154 (63.2 overs) (Snow 3-13) by 14 runs

Sexual intercourse did not begin in 1963, as Philip Larkin well knew. That was partly his point in the poem "Annus Mirabilis". However, the Gillette Cup did get under way that summer and it pounded to a sweaty climax on the first Saturday in September, when Sussex beat Worcestershire by 14 runs at Lord's. The final ended in twilight and there was heavy drizzle falling when Bob Carter was run out for 2 with only 10 balls left in the match. Carter's team had needed just 169 in 65 overs but Tony Buss's 3-39 in his 15-over allotment had removed both openers and shown how testing batting would continue to be on the damp pitch. Then the three late wickets taken by the callow 21-year-old fast bowler John Snow had appeared decisive before Roy Booth's hitting forced Ted Dexter, the Sussex captain, to put all his men on the boundary. As revolutions go, it might not seem much to write home about, but that is often the way of it in England. We don't storm Bastilles; we start a new cricket competition with odd rules and celebrate with a cup of Earl Grey.

Some readers might query how far-reaching the changes were. What was this malarkey about 65 overs, all the men on the boundary and no one allowed to bowl more than 15 overs? And surely not even Psalm 55's raging wind and tempest could prevent a side overhauling 168 at only 2.6 runs an over. The answer, of course, is that you had to watch cricket nearly 60 years ago to see how difficult it was for players who had only known three-day Championship cricket to adapt to the new competition. One or two counties barely tried; they thought the thing beneath their professional dignity. Sussex succeeded and won their first-ever trophy because the whole affair appealed to Dexter, whose raffish unorthodoxy rather reflected the atmosphere in Brighton on a lively Saturday evening. The Sussex skipper thought about the tactics that might be required in a match where 170-9 would always beat 165-3 and instructed his attack accordingly, although even those directives sound quaint today: "As for the bowlers I asked nothing more of them than to bowl every ball to hit the stumps. Wide on the off-side was a no-no. Short of a length with the ball going over the top was a no-no. Up and straight allowed me to set fielders according to the strengths and weaknesses of all the different batsmen."

Snow, who was playing his first limited-overs match, followed those instructions fairly precisely, castling both Doug Slade and Norman Gifford as the evening faded into murk. But the vital wicket of Tom Graveney had been taken much earlier when Ron Headley had been tied down by Alan Oakman's off-spin and a frustrated Graveney had holed out to Dexter at long-on off Oakman, who finished the match with figures of 1-17 from 13 overs. Yes, it was a foreign country.

Yet if much of this looks very strange and staid when viewed from our momentary modernity, knockout, one-day cricket was plainly an appealing novelty to many of the game's supporters in 1963. A brief glance at the structure of the previous season suggests why this was so. In 1962 Yorkshire won the County Championship and were one of eight counties to play 32 three-day matches; the other nine played 28 and the title was decided on average points per game. There were no other competitions of any note at all in the English summer, nor had there ever been. However, Yorkshire also played first-class matches against MCC (twice), the ancient universities and the Pakistan tourists, whose own 35-match programme had begun at Arundel on April 28 and ended in Sunderland on September 10, three weeks after the end of the final Test at The Oval.

Much of this cricket was of very high quality and many games were well-attended, but they did not pay the bills. Since this was England, a series of committees had been set up over the previous decade to investigate the situation and by the early 1960s it was discovered that the counties' expenditure was exceeding normal cricket income by an average of £120,000 a year. The new competition was, in part, an attempt to deal with this shortfall by staging games that could be finished in a day and in which the number of runs scored was the sole determinant of victory. What's more, the competition was to be sponsored by Gillette, whose name the 1964 *Wisden* could not loosen itself to print. The shaving company underwrote the competition with £6,500, with £50 (about £900 now) going to the Player of the Match in each game and £1,889 (£33,500) to the winners. But even in the year following the abolition of the distinction between amateurs and professionals, much of the old authority remained. Earlier in the week of the final the Sussex players had been told by the club secretary, Lt. Col. George Grimston, that he would be trousering the prize money as the county needed the cash. In fairness, it probably did. Dexter's men received a bonus in their salary instead.

The revolution appeared a relatively modest affair. The Gillette Cup would comprise only 16 matches, with a preliminary game reducing the 17 first-class counties by one and a straight knockout format being followed thereafter. Lancashire's Peter Marner became the competition's

166

first centurion and followed his 121 against Leicestershire with 3-49 to win the Player-of-the-Match award and a gold medal, which was presented to him by Frank Woolley on the Old Trafford outfield. Marner may have appreciated the 50 quid even more; this was still an era in which some professional cricketers travelled to their work by public transport.

Most of those 16 matches in 1963 resulted in relatively comfortable victories. Eleven were won by the side batting first and only three of those by a margin of fewer than 20 runs. It was hardly surprising that teams had yet to master the intricacies of an over-limit run-chase. On the other hand, setting a target proved tricky as well. The biggest total chased down was the 159 Yorkshire overhauled in 55 overs to beat Nottinghamshire in the first round at Acklam Park, Middlesbrough. Fred Trueman made 21 batting at No.4 in that game but Brian Close forsook such off-the-wall antics when he took his side to Hove for the quarter-final, a game which encapsulated all that was vibrant and successful about the new format.

There were 15,000 people crammed into the County Ground when Close chose to field first, his decision perhaps influenced by the sea mists which drifted in throughout the day. Jim Parks, though, saw matters with perfect clarity and made 90 in his side's 292 all out in 64 overs. Trueman finished with 0-40 from 14 and Tony Nicholson, one of the most highly regarded seamers on the circuit, went for 84 runs in 15 overs, in one of which Parks twice smacked him over the covers for six. The new format was proving a midwife to innovation.

But Yorkshire were not out of it. Struggling at one stage on 100-5, they were rescued by Geoffrey Boycott, who batted superbly for 71 before being run out when trying to keep the strike. Some might think both the innings and its ending in Boycott's first List-A game offered a pithy portent of his whole career, and Ian Thomson's hard, flat throw from third-man was a tiny sign of the improvement in fielding that one-day cricket would bring. Sussex got home by 22 runs and there is a photograph of Parks being presented with his medal by Alec Bedser. Another wave of mist is covering the ground.

So to Lord's and the first of the September occasions that were to become a poignant highlight of every summer. For those watching on television, the Gillette final always marked the end of summer's lease. In later years some teams would prepare for the occasion by getting an early night but such strictures were not in place in 1963.

"While talking to the Lancashire players earlier in the season about how they would approach the game, they said that first of all they would go to Raymond's Revue Bar in Soho," recalled Oakman. "Don Bates, Ken Suttle and I agreed... and we were watching the show when a half-naked dancer walked up the aisle with a large snake hanging round her neck. She stopped by Don Bates and asked if he would like to stroke it. He nearly passed out."

Next morning there were 25,000 spectators in Lord's, one of them the nine-year-old future Sussex captain, Johnny Barclay. The banners and favours appalled some MCC members but when the *Daily Mirror*'s chief sports writer, Peter Wilson, reported on the match he marvelled that "Lord's, the temple of tradition" could have become "a reasonable replica of Wembley... a sell-out with rosettes, singing, cheers, jeers and counter-cheers. This triumphant sporting experiment... may not have been cricket to the purists but by golly it was just the stuff the doctor ordered."

There was no going back. Perhaps the patient became a trifle addicted to their medicine but by 1972 there was another one-day competition, the Benson & Hedges Cup, and the 40-over John Player Sunday League. Captains learned the value of spinners, fielding regulations prevented blanket defence of boundaries, the revolution gathered pace. And it may be that the wheel is still in spin but those who seek to saturate cricket with such matches might remember Ted Dexter's observation in 2013 that Sussex's Gillette Cup victories in 1963 and 1964 "were as nothing compared to the three Championship wins in five years". Perhaps Ted was being a shade hard on himself but it's important to note the trophy the players prize most highly. "Sweet moderation / Heart of this nation" observes Billy Bragg in one of his finest songs. Damn right.

Surrey 1925 – Got It At Last, Jack

TAUNTON, AUGUST 18, 1925

Surrey 359 (Hobbs 101, Fender 59; Young 3-9) and 183-0 (Hobbs 101*, Sandham 74*) beat Somerset 167 (Young 58; Lockton 4-36, Sadler 3-28) and 374 (MacBryan 109, Young 71, Hunt 59; Fender 5-120) by 10 wickets

For over two decades the best, and best-loved, cricketer in England was also the humblest. Records fell to him and he made more centuries than any other player, yet he maintained an unaffected serenity that wise men envied even more than his strokeplay. This is revealing because he had all the shots and played them with time to spare. He managed this even on rain-affected pitches and in matches where, as a quietly proud professional, he knew he had to earn his pay.

On flat wickets at The Oval or against weaker opposition he might give his innings away to a deserving bowler in order to allow his Surrey colleagues a chance to bat. He had received hardly any coaching; the skills at the heart of his batting were entirely natural. His first-class debut in 1905 pitted him against WG Grace and in his final Test in 1930 he watched Don Bradman make 232. He would end his career with 197 first-class hundreds but not even the great innings he played in Ashes Tests were more feted than his 126th century. That was made at Taunton in August 1925 when the County Ground was packed with spectators and the press box was as crammed as an ageing film-star's make-up box. "Fame and tranquillity can never be bedfellows," wrote Michel de Montaigne. But then Montaigne never met Jack Hobbs.

There was no touring team in 1925. That in itself was not particularly unusual: only three countries played Test matches and, as Dominic Sandbrook points out, county cricket was still the national sport, shading even football until after the Second World War. Five bowlers were to take over 200 wickets that season and the country was not short of high-class batsmen, yet Hobbs' exploits dominated the sporting pages. Beginning the summer with 113 first-class hundreds against his name, he made a dozen more in his first 27 innings. That mattered because it left him one short of the record set by Grace and once thought unchallengeable. (As things turned out, 10 of the 25 players to score a hundred hundreds overtook Grace.)

"England is waiting for news in an expectant hush," said a leader writer on *The Times*. "We shall hold our breath as hopefully as any man in Surrey and crow as lustily when the great figures break at last on the telegraph board." At which point Hobbs' form dipped a little and the weather sulked. He was dismissed by Maurice Tate for 1 at Hove, by Charlie Parker for 38 at Gloucester and by a promising

21-year-old called Harold Larwood for 1 at The Oval. For nearly a month the press pack remained in close attendance and spectators queued up, wondering if this was going to be the day. When Hobbs failed to make a century he was probably more disappointed for his supporters than himself. He may have felt responsible for their sadness. "The mental strain was beginning to tell," he admitted later. "It seemed the whole circus was following me round. The newspapers were working everybody into a fever state."

In the 10 innings after his century against Kent at Blackheath, Hobbs made 252 runs. "Centuries never bothered me, nor records really, nor averages," he said after he retired. "Of course I was earning my living but it was batting I enjoyed." And there was nothing sham about this gentle simplicity. The only false thing about Hobbs was the two dozen or so strokes he played each season that led to dismissals. For the rest of each summer he was the most technically accomplished cricketer in the land. Archie MacLaren described him as the most perfect model of what a batsman should be and wrote a book based on pre-war photographs to prove his point.

Somerset's cricketers, by contrast, were rarely cited as models of excellence in 1925. They won only three matches and finished 15th in the table. Their bowling was frequently dependent on J C 'Farmer' White, one of the nine amateurs in the team that played Surrey, who themselves fielded five unpaid players. Although White was mainly content to tend his cows in the English winters, he was a cricketer of international class and took 25 wickets as England retained the Ashes in 1928/29. None of which detracted from the general opinion that a visit to Taunton gave Hobbs an ideal opportunity to make history.

The game began on a Saturday and Somerset batted first. They managed 167 in 66.3 overs and, in an age when all counties bowled around 20 overs an hour, Hobbs had over two hours to make progress towards removing the burden from his shoulders. "We had brushed ourselves aside for the occasion," wrote RC Robertson-Glasgow, who opened the home side's bowling. But it seems that Hobbs could have been out three times that evening. He was caught at cover-point off a no-ball, might have been pouched at mid-on had Jack MacBryan moved a little more quickly, and then saw a confident lbw appeal from Robertson-Glasgow turned down. He also managed to run out Donald Knight for 34. Yet when all these tiny dramas had been completed he was unbeaten on 91. Nine runs to get and all Fleet Street in a ferment.

On Sunday Hobbs kept to his usual habit and twice went to church, but between these simple devotions he was filmed at Surrey's hotel close by the station. On the platform favoured by trains from London another carriage disgorged yet more journalists, all hip-flasks and headlines. The following morning the County Ground was quite as packed as it had been 48 hours earlier. "Somerset committee-men beamed affably alike on friends, enemies and total strangers," observed Robertson-Glasgow. Hobbs began with three singles, then a four off a Robertson-Glasgow no-ball and a single in the same over. Then he pushed a single off Jim Bridges, thereby disposing of the great matter that had bedevilled him for a month.

"Tremendous cheering, of course, greeted the accomplishment of the feat," reported *Wisden,* who gave a whole page to its match report. "Indeed, so pronounced was the enthusiasm that the progress of the game was halted some minutes while at the end of the over all the players in the field shook hands with Hobbs, and the Surrey captain brought out a drink for the hero of the occasion, who raised the glass high and bowed to the crowd before partaking of the refreshment."

The liquid in the glass Percy Fender brought out was ginger ale and toasting the crowd may have been the most ostentatious act of Hobbs's life. Leo McKinstry, his latest and best biographer, records that he also took from his pocket a telegram he had written earlier and asked the Taunton groundsman to send it to his wife, Ada, who was on holiday in Margate with their four children. It read: "Got it at last, Jack."

The rest of that game at Taunton was much more than an appendix to a great moment. The papers had their story and some sated journalists returned to the smoke. Surrey, meanwhile, having established a lead of 192, bowled out Somerset for 374, this despite a century by MacBryan. Needing 183 to win, the visitors got home by 10 wickets and Hobbs, having equalled Grace's record on Monday, surpassed it a day later. "His cares dropped from him, as the poet has it, like the needles shaken from out the gusty pine," said Robertson-Glasgow, rather sportingly given that his six overs had cost 42 runs. "The same balls which, in the first innings, he had pushed severely to cover-point he now cracked to the boundary with serene abandon."

Hobbs made 16 centuries in 1925 and finished the season with 3,024 runs. He played on until 1934, by which time he was 51. He made nearly as many hundreds after his 40th birthday as before reaching that vestibule of middle age. He was knighted in 1953, the first professional to receive the honour, yet he continued to call his former amateur colleagues Mr Jardine, Mr Fender etc. even when he was Sir Jack. He has been fortunate in his biographers and fortunate too, that one of his friends was John Arlott, who loved him very much.

"He just was the person whom I suppose I admired more than anybody else and I really believe that if he had never played cricket I would have admired him as much," Arlott told Mike Brearley in their memorable Channel 4 conversations. "He was determined to be content."

After retirement Hobbs ran his sports shop in Fleet Street and sometimes worked for the newspapers, his copy ghosted by a professional journalist. The story goes that he might be critical of one or two batsmen's dismissals in the morning session but by the time he came to file copy natural kindness had reasserted itself. "Say he's looking for his best form," he might suggest. Arlott's last poem took him six months to write. It was entitled: *To John Berry Hobbs on his Seventieth Birthday*. The fourth stanza reads as follows:

The Master: records prove the title good:
Yet figures fail you, for they cannot say
How many men whose names you never knew
Are proud to tell their sons they saw you play.

Arlott also produced a short biography of Hobbs. It details his major achievements but always places them in a context that really has little to do with cricket: "This was the man who, without believing it to be a matter of major importance, made more runs than anyone else."

In 2000 a panel of experts voted Hobbs one of *Wisden*'s Five Cricketers of the Century. In his tribute Matthew Engel noted his subject had done more than anyone to lift "the status and dignity of the English professional cricketer. He shied away from the limelight without ever resenting it. Even in old age he could be sought by all-comers at his sports shop in Fleet Street."

No doubt some customers asked Hobbs about that famous day in Taunton. He probably apologised for all the fuss he had caused.

7

ARUNDEL – SUSSEX V DURHAM 2018

These three reports recall the game at Arundel in June 2018 when Sussex defeated Durham by an innings and 64 runs. Tom Haines and Phil Salt will always remember that match but they will also know that it also gave great pleasure to very many other people. It followed the relatively recent pattern of some County Championship games which attract good attendances yet are also followed by many thousands of other supporters through conventional or social media. They also care who only sit and tweet. The reports were later incorporated into a booklet, published by the Sussex Cricket Museum, in which I expressed the hope that such marvellous days might inspire other young Sussex players and embolden them as they contemplate a career in the game. Those cricketers may not make their maiden hundreds at Arundel on an afternoon filched from the pages of Arthur Ransome but they can also enjoy memorable days when their winter work is justified. The pursuit of ambition is one of youth's greatest privileges.

And yes, I very much enjoy the afternoons when cricket bites you on the bum. By this I mean that the game offers something so remarkable that all the tentative plans you have formulated over lunch have to be ditched very quickly. Such days scare me as well but the chance to tell the story of Salt and Haines' batting at Arundel in June 2018 is one I wouldn't have missed for anything.

The re-publication of these accounts also gives me the chance to pay tribute to organisations like the Sussex Cricket Museum and Educational Trust. Instead of freezing the county's history behind glass cases, the SMT helps to show that cricketers such as Maurice Tate or young George Cox enjoyed their cricket quite as keenly as Delray Rawlins or Ben Brown. A few decades ago it was Hugh Bartlett and James Langridge; in 2018 it was Phil Salt and Tom Haines. The lifestyles and haircuts are different but the narrative is shared and the trust is passed on.

Another reason why I was so pleased to be asked to help with the booklet is that it strengthens a link with Alan Ross, the writer from whom I have learned most. Although born in India, Alan spent much of his childhood in Sussex and later lived in Clayton for 25 years. When reflecting on his time in the Royal Navy in the Second World War, he wrote this:

"During my sea-time I used to dream of Sussex; not so much a specific Sussex as a generalized romantic image conjured out of memory and hope. Sussex cricket played a large part in it, to the extent that I had only to see the word Sussex written down, in whatever context, for a shiver to run down my spine."

Tom Haines gets a lift from Mum on way to maiden hundred

——————————— DAY ONE ———————————

Sussex: 439-5 (Salt 130, Haines 124, Finch 56, Brown 50) v Durham*

John Arlott said luck was often nothing more than opportunity. In the cool of this unforgettable evening Tom Haines might admit the old boy had a point. For it was only late on Tuesday, when Chris Jordan was called into the England Lions squad, that 19-year-old Haines was told he would be playing his third County Championship match for Sussex and his first for nearly two years. He had scored 12 runs in his three previous first-class innings and may have been preferred to Laurie Evans because he bowls a bit of seam up. He needed his mum to give him a lift to Arundel from the second-team match at New Malden.

So there was no sight more glorious on an afternoon littered with blessings than Haines' eruption of joy when he reached his maiden century with a leg glance off Nathan Rimmington. It was the 19th four of an innings brimming with all the bravery of youth and none of its diffidence. To their credit Durham's players applauded the landmark but their reaction was pardonably overshadowed by the cheering of the Sussex supporters beneath the horse chestnut and the delight of Haines' teammates, almost all of whom were enjoying the shade of a blue gazebo very near the fans.

Yet Haines' achievement was literally the half of it. Three overs previously 21-year-old Phil Salt had also notched his first hundred when he pushed a single off Will Smith. Compared to Haines, Salt is a grizzled old pro; this is his 13th first-class game. But he is also a trifle more naturally aggressive, a trait made plain by his succession of on-drives and by his early pull off Matt Salisbury which sailed into the marquee nearest the chestnut. Yes, this was an afternoon of tents and trees and an occasion recognisable to Sussex supporters raised on the Langridges and the Lenhams. Two mobile phones were handed in but it was never made clear whether their owners had accidentally lost them or deliberately renounced modernity. In the morning Durham even bowled 31 overs, just one short of the notional target for the session. Unfortunately for Paul Collingwood and his bowlers it was their only achievement of the session after Salisbury's dismissal of Luke Wells. For the rest of the morning and much of the afternoon the cricket was dominated by Salt's square drives and Haines' clips off his toes.

"Grey day for the show," wrote Philip Larkin in his warm evocation of Bellingham's annual pastoral and perhaps it was Arundel's moderate cloud on the first morning that persuaded Collingwood to bowl first. Either way, his seamers could not justify his decision in the opening session and by mid-afternoon a powerful sun was coaxing spectators to the bars and refreshment vans. On a day when Durham's bowlers needed chances to go to hand, they saw them fall beyond or over fielders. When he was only 36 Haines edged Rimmington a foot or so past a diving Smith at slip; in the same bowler's next over he dishclothed a pull just over Josh Coughlin's head at mid-on; when he had made 27 Salt nearly played on but booted the ball just past the stumps; and shortly before reaching his century he lofted Smith down the ground and saw the ball land just beyond a flailing Salisbury.

Haines and Salt had put on 244 and set a new second-wicket record for matches between these counties when they departed either side of tea. Having made 124 off 167 balls, Haines nicked Cameron Steel to Collingwood at slip; in the first over after the resumption, Salt top-edged a slash off Salisbury to Gareth Harte at third man and departed for 130. Sussex supporters spent the rest of the evening enjoying Luke Wright's 32, Harry Finch's half-century and Ben Brown's unbeaten fifty. But that trio know their innings will be asterisked footnotes to the day. Durham's followers,

176

again supporting their team in good numbers, could be consoled by Salisbury's three wickets. But spectators of any stripe will remember the time they saw two freshmen cricketers take their chance on the big stage in a small corner of England. "Luck?" Sussex folk may query when reminded of that Arlott quote, "Luck was being here to see it."

Will Smith's calmness gives Durham hope of staving off Sussex

———————————— DAY TWO ————————————

Durham 202-4 (Smith 90*) trail Sussex 552 (Salt 130, Haines 124, Burgess 96, Finch 56, Brown 52) by 350 runs

When Will Smith returned to Durham last September he was moving against the flow of traffic. In the prolonged aftermath of the sanctions imposed in 2016 a number of the county's players had decided their futures lay elsewhere. Yet Smith spoke of his delight at having the chance to come home and his presence at the Riverside will be all the more welcome if he continues to fight as hard in adversity as he did on the second day of this match. His unbeaten 90 was characteristically flinty and it has encouraged Durham's hopes that they might avoid defeat even as they respond to Sussex's 552.

The intensity of the cricket at the Castle Ground stood in pleasing contrast to the serenity of the setting and both were appreciated by a large crowd, albeit most of them are hoping for a Sussex victory. At the tea interval, when Smith was unbeaten on 46, a line of spectators considered the view through the gap in this ground's many rings of trees. The Arun valley's very gentle hills were not quite blue but they will surely be remembered. Monarch's Way meandered in the distance and one almost expected the London train to billow smoke from a funnel. This is a Laurie Lee summer.

By close of play Smith could look back on a little over four hours of nudges, pushes and deflections, the unfussy stock-in-trade of the professional batsman. They had taken Durham to 202-4, still

350 shy of Sussex's total but a far better position than 96-3, the score when Graham Clark was bowled attempting to pull a Luke Wells leg break. Smith had also hit 10 fours, some of them swept, like the boundary which took him to fifty just after tea. Whatever their allegiances the large crowd had enjoyed it all, even if they reserved special cheers for the home side's four successes. As the total mounted, the soft breeze nudged the trees with no greater effect than that of rearranging the sun-shadow on the branches. Two members of Wisden's editorial staff attended the game and did some diligent fieldwork while Monty, the Almanack's dog, drowsed on a rug beside them. Perhaps he will be named one of the Five Cricketers of some future year. Yeshwant Barde, the exchange umpire, signalled Smith's boundaries so elegantly that an orchestra might have accepted his direction.

Having removed Tom Latham for two in the over before lunch, Sussex may have hoped that the pressure of facing a large total would prompt a greater clatter of wickets. If so, they underestimated both Smith and Durham. Cameron Steel slashed Danny Briggs to backward point but that success and the wicket of Clark were the home side's only successes of the afternoon session. In the evening, Collingwood helped Smith add a further 82 before he was lbw for 44 when attempting to sweep Wells. Sussex's hopes may now rest on the new ball when it becomes available six overs into the morning and on the bounce which both Briggs and Wells extracted from an otherwise blameless Arundel pitch.

There had been portents of Durham's later resilience during the first session, although limiting a side to 552 all out is rarely viewed so rosily. Instead of a score in excess of 600, Sussex had to settle for their best total at Arundel after Ben Brown had skied a pull off Chris Rushworth in the third over of the day and David Wiese had fallen leg before to his first ball. But Michael Burgess reinforced his already excellent reputation and Sussex's leading scorer in this season's Championship was only four short of his second century of the campaign when he slashed Josh Coughlin to Smith at backward point.

Arundel's charms lost on Durham after morning collapse heralds defeat

———————————————— DAY THREE ————————————————

Sussex 552 (Salt 130, Haines 124, Burgess 96, Finch 56, Brown 52; Salisbury 3-112, Rushworth 3-116) beat Durham 211 (Smith 90, Wiese 4-33, Briggs 3-57) and 277 (Poynter 84; Briggs 3-71) by an innings and 64 runs

Durham spectators arriving around an hour late at the Castle Ground on the third morning of this match would probably have been reassured to see Will Smith batting. They would also have been keen to see their side's first-innings score. Sadly their initial assumption was mistaken and their keenness was soon replaced by grisly despair.

Rather than beginning again in the manner of centurions, Smith had been dismissed for his overnight 90 when sweeping at Danny Briggs' fifth ball of the morning. And having walked off this glorious meadow at just after eleven o'clock Smith was now back again some 67 minutes later, less time than it takes the Duke of Norfolk's under-butler to clean a piece of silver. For his departure had been followed by five more as Durham lost their last six wickets for nine runs in 11 overs of mayhem. Batters arrived and departed with a rapidity that would have done credit to a hard-pressed GP's surgery. David Wiese took three wickets in seven balls and finished with 4-33; Briggs had Gareth Harte caught behind for 13 on a morning when double figures might have prompted a bat raised in irony

An already bad session soon degenerated into the worst day of a season in which Paul Collingwood's side have offered occasional indications that they are grappling their way out of their travails. By six o'clock Durham's supporters were reflecting on the loss of 16 wickets for 286 runs and their side's innings and 64-run defeat. Not even the view over the Arun valley could console the Gateshead loyalists. Only Stuart Poynter's 84 in the evening session had offered them anything to cheer.

That early clatter of wickets was an enormous bonus for Sussex. Having not needed to summon his new-ball bowlers during the bedlam, Ben Brown had no qualms about enforcing the follow-on. A disconcertingly frisky Jofra Archer then brought one sharply back off the pitch to bowl a strokeless Cameron Steel for eight and Durham lunched in the bleak knowledge they had lost seven wickets for 65 runs.

The afternoon session brought no relief as another five batsmen were dismissed while 95 runs were scored. Yet such collapses seem out of place at Arundel. Frenetic drama does not suit this absurdly idyllic setting. "Good morning, campers" said Mike Charman, the Sussex scorer and PA announcer, when welcoming the early arrivals. Such benevolence is entirely typical, for this is a ground of many perfections. It greets spectators each morning and strains their credence that such a venue exists under heaven. Charman is the sort of good-hearted bloke who does not broadcast an outgoing batter's nought. It was a kindness he had to exercise on five occasions during Friday's cricket. In the afternoon session, as our cricket drifted into the heart of the day, Charman announced the winners of the raffle, advertised other games and wished Nicola a happy birthday.

But there was little to buoy Durham's travelling band until Poynter put on 79 for the eighth wicket with Nathan Rimmington. Long before that, Tom Latham had been bowled between bad and pad by Ollie Robinson and Smith had been brilliantly caught at what was effectively third slip by Harry Finch off Wiese. Two balls later Collingwood was leg before for nought when playing across the line and Briggs then picked up Harte and Graham Clark. As so often, batting errors had spurred the bowlers to excellence and that in turn had prompted further frailty. Poynter's defiance ended when he was lbw swinging across the line to Briggs and Archer's caught and bowled in the next over ended the match.

Sussex supporters applauded it all. Their side is playing fine cricket and their only regret was that there will now be no cricket at this ground on Saturday.

> I reckon—when I count at all—
> First—Poets—Then the Sun—
> Then Summer—Then the Heaven of God—
> And then—the List is done—

To that list in Emily Dickinson's poem, supporters at Arundel, Tunbridge Wells and Scarborough would add the joys of watching cricket, even if some of those joys appear, in the eyes of outsiders, extraneous to the game. Such folk circle the county festivals on the calendar in winter's depths and they have gone out these midsummer mornings confident that life will treat them well. They have not been disappointed. They reckon – when they count at all – cricketing days at the outgrounds: the high heat of June afternoons; Academy lads like Phil Salt and Tom Haines; smoke drifting from valley cottages; ash, sycamore and Douglas-fir trees; skylarks; and the soft light of perfect evenings.

SUSSEX V DURHAM
Arundel, June 20 - 22, 2018
Specsavers County Championship Division Two
Sussex 552 — Durham (f/o) 211 & 277
Sussex won by an innings and 64 runs

SUSSEX 1ST INNINGS

BATTING

		R	B	M	4s	6s	SR
Luke Wells	c Latham b Salisbury	8	19	16	1	0	42.1
Phil Salt	c Harte b Salisbury	130	175	260	18	1	74.28
Tom Haines	c Collingwood b Steel	124	167	210	19	0	74.25
Harry Finch	c †Poynter b Salisbury	56	100	120	10	0	56
Luke Wright	c Coughlin b Steel	32	38	58	5	0	84.21
Ben Brown (c)†	c †Poynter b Rushworth	52	55	80	9	0	94.54
Michael Burgess	c Smith b Coughlin	96	95	139	11	0	101.05
David Wiese	lbw b Rushworth	0	1	2	0	0	0
Jofra Archer	c Clark b Rushworth	17	35	44	2	0	48.57
Ollie Robinson	b Clark	24	35	45	3	0	68.57
Danny Briggs	not out	0	2	4	0	0	0
Extras	(b 1, lb 5, nb 6, w 1)	13					
TOTAL	**119.5 Ov (RR: 4.60)**	**552**					

BOWLING

	O	M	R	W	E	WD	NB
Chris Rushworth	26	0	116	3	4.46	0	0
Matt Salisbury	26	5	112	3	4.3	0	0
Nathan Rimmington	23.4	3	128	0	5.4	0	1
Josh Coughlin	19	0	90	1	4.73	1	0
Will Smith	11	2	37	0	3.36	0	0
Gareth Harte	6	0	28	0	4.66	0	0
Cameron Steel	4.2	0	25	2	5.76	0	2
Graham Clark	3.5	0	10	1	2.6	0	0

FALL OF WICKETS:
1-9 (Luke Wells, 3.4 ov), 2-253 (Tom Haines, 57.2 ov), 3-283 (Phil Salt, 64.4 ov), 4-350 (Luke Wright, 79.1 ov), 5-364 (Harry Finch, 85.3 ov), 6-446 (Ben Brown, 98.2 ov), 7-446 (David Wiese, 98.3 ov), 8-500 (Jofra Archer, 108.4 ov), 9-552 (Michael Burgess, 118.4 ov), 10-552 (Ollie Robinson, 119.5 ov)

DURHAM 1ST INNINGS

BATTING

		R	B	M	4s	6s	SR
Tom Latham	c Finch b Archer	2	7	9	0	0	28.57
Cameron Steel	c Archer b Briggs	20	50	60	4	0	40
Will Smith	lbw b Briggs	90	221	247	10	0	40.72
Graham Clark	b Wells	27	56	62	5	0	48.21
Paul Collingwood (c)	lbw b Wells	44	81	95	8	0	54.32
Gareth Harte	c †Brown b Briggs	13	62	70	1	0	20.96
Stuart Poynter †	b Wiese	0	5	5	0	0	0
Josh Coughlin	b Wiese	0	1	2	0	0	0
Nathan Rimmington	c †Brown b Wiese	0	5	7	0	0	0
Matt Salisbury	b Wiese	8	22	27	0	0	36.36
Chris Rushworth	not out	0	5	10	0	0	0
Extras	(lb 5, nb 2)	7					
TOTAL	**85.4 Ov (RR: 2.46)**	**211**					

BOWLING

	O	M	R	W	E	WD	NB
Jofra Archer	18	5	50	1	2.77	0	0
Ollie Robinson	13	3	40	0	3.07	0	1
David Wiese	15.4	4	33	4	2.1	0	0
Danny Briggs	27	11	57	3	2.11	0	0
Luke Wells	12	1	26	2	2.16	0	0

FALL OF WICKETS:
1-2 (Tom Latham, 2.1 ov), 2-43 (Cameron Steel, 16.1 ov), 3-96 (Graham Clark, 35.4 ov), 4-178 (Paul Collingwood, 63.3 ov), 5-202 (Will Smith, 74.5 ov), 6-203 (Stuart Poynter, 75.5 ov), 7-203 (Josh Coughlin, 75.6 ov), 8-203 (Nathan Rimmington, 77.5 ov), 9-209 (Gareth Harte, 82.6 ov), 10-211 (Matt Salisbury, 85.4 ov)

DURHAM 2ND INNINGS (FOLLOWING ON)

BATTING		R	B	M	4s	6s	SR
Tom Latham	b Robinson	20	62	74	3	0	32.25
Cameron Steel	b Archer	8	9	13	2	0	88.88
Will Smith	c Finch b Wiese	36	102	104	6	0	35.29
Graham Clark	lbw b Briggs	49	82	91	6	0	59.75
Paul Collingwood (c)	lbw b Wiese	0	2	3	0	0	0
Gareth Harte	c †Brown b Briggs	0	5	9	0	0	0
Stuart Poynter †	lbw b Briggs	84	109	151	11	0	77.06
Josh Coughlin	c Finch b Wells	14	52	59	2	0	26.92
Nathan Rimmington	not out	49	65	72	6	1	75.38
Matt Salisbury	b Robinson	4	8	10	1	0	50
Chris Rushworth	c & b Archer	4	4	5	1	0	100
Extras	(lb 5, nb 4)	9					
TOTAL	83 Ov (RR: 3.33)	277					

BOWLING	O	M	R	W	E	WD	NB
Jofra Archer	14	2	65	2	4.64	0	0
Ollie Robinson	15	3	34	2	2.26	0	2
Danny Briggs	24	4	71	3	2.95	0	0
David Wiese	10	1	42	2	4.2	0	0
Tom Haines	11	6	22	0	2	0	0
Luke Wells	9	2	38	1	4.22	0	0

FALL OF WICKETS:
1-9 (Cameron Steel, 4.1 ov), 2-61 (Tom Latham, 21.4 ov), 3-77 (Will Smith, 34.2 ov), 4-79 (Paul Collingwood, 34.6 ov), 5-88 (Gareth Harte, 37.3 ov), 6-137 (Graham Clark, 47.3 ov), 7-189 (Josh Coughlin, 63.2 ov), 8-268 (Stuart Poynter, 79.4 ov), 9-272 (Matt Salisbury, 81.6 ov), 10-277 (Chris Rushworth, 82.6 ov)

8

GREAT DAYS AND FINALS' DAYS

Sometimes, a player or a team will take a day of an otherwise unremarkable match and make it their own; sometimes, the context of a game is worth recording. This chapter remembers a few of these occasions. The opportunity to recall a century by James Hildreth, Ian Bell's final first-class hundred, and the last time Glen Chapple wrecked a county's top-order was not to be passed up. Neither was the chance to look back on a raucously gorgeous day at Northampton or Paul Horton coming home. And there could have been half a dozen reports from Cheltenham, but this book is long enough already. I hope these pieces will encourage readers to look up the games themselves, either in Wisden or online, and even compare the pieces with their own recollections. Each spectator treasures particular images from a day at the cricket. "The more a man differs from me, the more real he seems, for he depends that much less on my subjectivity," wrote Fernando Pessoa.

Reports from five seasons are gathered here. I was delighted to include some pieces from Finals Days at Edgbaston and a longer article about a wonderful weekend at Eastbourne when a 50-over match became the context for reflections rather than the focus of them. You've probably guessed by now that I find four- and five-day cricket the game's richest and most demanding formats but I do enjoy covering limited-over matches and the atmosphere on floodlit T20 evenings at Old Trafford, Taunton or Trent Bridge is unlike anything else in English cricket. I regret that there are no reports, either in this chapter or the book, from women's cricket. This is partly because our immensely talented women's teams play very few red-ball games and partly because I have only been commissioned to cover perhaps three of their white-ball matches during my 18 years on the circuit. I hope this will change.

2015

Glamorgan v Lancashire – Colwyn Bay

———————— JULY 20 – DAY TWO ————————

Glamorgan 165-6 (Chapple 3-28) trail Lancashire 698-5dec (Petersen 286, Prince 261, Croft 57*, Brown 54; Lloyd 3-164) by 533 runs

The gulls in Colwyn Bay are probably mutants. Embittered at not landing parts in *Jurassic Park* as baby pterodactyls, they vent their savage grievance on any holiday-makers foolish enough to leave their sarnies unguarded. Their natural cinematic home would have been Alfred Hitchock's 1963 film *The Birds*, but should any director be so foolish as to attempt to remake that classic, Rhos on Sea would make an excellent setting. Yet on the second day of this match at Colwyn Bay even the massive gulls had to take second place in the avarice stakes to Lancashire's Ashwell Prince and Alviro Petersen. Then later, they may even have perched, corpulent and admiring, as Glen Chapple proved that this wicket was not quite so flat as to repel bowlers of timeless class.

Having already put on 324 for their side's third wicket when play began, Prince and Petersen extended their stand to a colossal 501 before Prince miscued a drive off David Lloyd and Andrew Salter took a good low catch running in from the long-off boundary. By that stage, the partnership was already the highest in Lancashire's history, beating the mere 371 added by Frank Watson and Ernest Tyldesley against Surrey at Old Trafford in 1928. It was also the most conceded by Glamorgan for any wicket. Prince himself had hit 35 fours and seven sixes in a career-best 261 after a morning in which he had launched a cheerful assault on the car park behind the pavilion.

As Prince ambled back to the dressing room, tossing his bat in the air as he went and accompanied by Petersen's congratulations and hugs, he probably little knew that the partnership was only 22 runs shy of the third-wicket County Championship record, which is held by Michael Carberry and Neil McKenzie, or that it was the 13th most fruitful for any wicket in first-class history. Within half an hour Petersen was gone too, also caught in the deep off the frequently punished Lloyd and also for a career-best, in his case, 286. He and

Prince had become the only Lancashire batsmen to have hit double-hundreds in the same innings. The total was then 625-4, which is really the sort of score one only reads about.

All the same, there it was, and after Steven Croft, the Lancashire skipper, had thrashed another 57 runs in 51 balls, the declaration was applied with the score having moved on to 698-5, which is the fifth highest total in Lancashire's history. Between innings there were reports that Opta's statistician was frothing at the mouth in ecstasy. Such days do not come around very often for the number crunchers.

Many debates last night and this morning concerned the flatness of this pitch. Some Glamorgan players announced that they had never played cricket on anything quite like it. At the end of Lancashire's innings the scoreboard seemed to justify their view and it was even mooted that this surface could give cricketers a standard by which the unresponsiveness of later wickets could be assessed: a Colwyn Bay quotient to rank with the Richter and Beaufort scales.

Chapple put such talk into useful perspective. When it was announced on the first morning that the 41-year-old would be in Lancashire's side, there was a sigh of loving-fondness from many in the crowd. So the happiness from the very many visiting supporters when Chapple moved one away just enough from Jacques Rudolph's loose defensive shot to clip the off stump needs little imagining. It was the beginning of a few overs to remember for Lancashire loyalists as they grab every chance they can to see Chapple in what must surely be the late autumn of his career.

Next over Colin Ingram was caught behind by Alex Davies for nought. After tea, Chris Cooke elected to leave a ball which was going to hit the off stump, and that is rarely a wise move. Chapple's figures at the end of his first spell read 11-4-27-3. For so many cricket fans, whatever their loyalties, his bowling counted for more than Petersen and Prince's stand. He had nagged away and coaxed assistance from a pitch which, hitherto, had seemed as hard as an airport runway. Lancashire's bowlers were not finished, though, as they pressed for the victory that would make them even more prohibitive favourites for promotion. Will Bragg was leg before playing across a straight one from James Faulkner and the spinners Arron Lilley and Simon Kerrigan picked up the wickets of David Lloyd and Craig Meschede, both caught in the ring for 21 apiece during a long evening session.

Mark Wallace, the epitome of Welsh resistance, is still there on 39 and Graham Wagg, in this great season for him, made so bold as to hit Lilley's penultimate ball of the day for a six over long-on. Nonetheless, Glamorgan can rarely have been so far behind in a match and an early finish is clearly on the cards. This would be a shame for those who treasure the warm friendship, grassy banks and gentle charms of this ground. The day finally ended with Petersen and Prince posing for snappers in front of a scoreboard rigged to record their partnership. Some of the resulting photographs will no doubt be auctioned at cricket dinners this winter; others will appear in county yearbooks, those annual chronicles of special weeks and afternoons of plenty.

Finals Day – 2015

AUGUST 29

Lancashire 166-7 (Davies 47, Prince 43; Afridi 3-14) beat
Northamptonshire 153-6 (Cobb 44) by 13 runs

It had scarcely promised to be a showpiece. It was a match between the county that couldn't win finals and the county that couldn't pay its bills. And it was played on a pitch that had seemed as dead as the Sogdian language. And yet, in the precise moment of victory, as Lancastrian roars echoed in the still Birmingham air, none of those things mattered a damn. Instead, as tiny knots of overjoyed red-shirted cricketers joined in the tightest of hugs, they revelled in the exultation of the moment. This was the special euphoria for which Lancashire's players had worked since they had gathered for pre-season training last December. Then they went over and shared it with their many supporters over in the Raglan Stand. Then they danced about on the field in the licensed irresponsibility of complete happiness. There were curious echoes of Taunton in 2011 when Lancashire won the County Championship outright for the first time since 1934. It was that special for them.

There were only two survivors of that team in the XI that eventually overcame Northants' brave resistance here. Cricketers like Gavin Griffiths and Liam Livingstone are nothing like regular first-team cricketers. Now they have done something that will stay with them until playing cricket is itself a memory. It didn't matter two hoots that qualifying for the quarter-finals had depended on it hosing down at Grace Road back in July. Maybe it's better that way. Only when Lancashire's players and supporters reflect on what they have done will the contexts of triumph begin to matter. Their immediate joy at Edgbaston was all the greater because they had suffered disappointment here so frequently. They are no strangers to the whips and scorns of time.

"Clearer than Scafell Pike, my heart has stamped on / The view from Birmingham to Wolverhampton" wrote WH Auden in "Letter to Lord Byron" and a few Lancashire fans may smile in grim identification with the lines. For this was their side's fifth Finals Day at Edgbaston and their second final in England's second city. In 2007, Lancashire's side included Andrew Flintoff, Stuart Law, Brad Hodge and Muttiah Muralitharan; they lost to Gloucestershire in the morning semi. Supporters have dutifully booked their hotels and travelled down the M6 on Friday evening or Saturday morning scarcely able to voice their hopes, only to return on Sunday – or even Saturday afternoon in the really bad years – cloaked in the silent gloom of defeat. It won't be like that tomorrow.

And maybe it was appropriate that the best entertainment of the day was saved until the final game. Twenty-over cricket is ideally suited to the evening and, indeed, was been played from May to early August in local tournaments across England long, long before white balls and floodlights were features of the game. The uninhibited batting of Jos Buttler and David Willey, the canny spin bowling of Shahid Afridi and Arron Lilley are all in their way very distant descendants of the skills learned by these players' amateur counterparts. The Big Bash, the IPL, the NatWest Blast are multi-million dollar operations which have revolutionised the techniques of T20 cricket. And yet they are also highly professional echoes of very enjoyable games played in Gloucestershire, Cumberland, Merseyside and elsewhere. It was just that the latter didn't have duck quacks and trumpets.

And it might be worth remembering that if Stephen Parry and Gavin Griffiths had not been playing for Lancashire today, they would have been turning out for their clubs, Formby and Ormskirk. Brook Lane is where Griffiths often bowls his seamers. Ormskirk's pavilion will be rocking tonight, as will more than a few Birmingham hotels. "It was a big call to give Gavin his debut and there was a bit of head scratching this morning but he's had a good week in practice and we had every faith in him," said Croft. "He's good under pressure and he's a good death bowler as well." Griffiths was five when Lancashire last won a one-day trophy.

If anything, Red Rose heritage made things worse. In the 30 seasons from 1970-1999 Lancashire won 16 limited-over trophies. Lord's became a second home. The county dominated the old 40-over league. There were happy Sundays at Old Trafford long before the Happy Mondays were a gleam in Shaun Ryder's eye. Since 1999, though, there had been diddly-squat one-day trophies, apart, perhaps, from the unwanted, unofficial title of champion chokers. Well, not any more, the roars from the Raglan Stand seemed to say as Griffiths bowled that final over. Not any more.

It was good to see Northants get so near to winning the trophy, too. This, after all, is the county some would exclude from such grand entertainments. Few people of sound mind talk about basing a franchise in Wantage Road, yet no ground possesses a livelier atmosphere on a T20 Friday evening. And here Alex Wakely's boys were and it was rather pleasing to see the noses of the moneyed mighty so fiercely tweaked. They pushed Croft's bowlers and fielders almost to the limit. But this, at last, was Lancashire's year. And, you know, maybe they had waited long enough.

Somerset v Hampshire – Taunton

SEPTEMBER 10 - DAY TWO

Somerset 569-5 (Trescothick 153, Abell 131, Cooper 118, Hildreth 71; Dawson 3-130) lead Hampshire 240 by 329 runs

The loveliest event of this day's cricket was one which Somerset supporters knew would occur at some time but feared they would not witness. At noon Tom Abell drove Mason Crane through the covers for three runs. His score went from 99 to 102 and he thereby reached his maiden first-class century. The first person to congratulate Abell – indeed, an enveloping hug was deemed appropriate – was his opening partner, Marcus Trescothick, who had scored the 57th century of his first-class career only 10 minutes previously. Abell was three months old when Trescothick notched his own first hundred against Surrey at Bath in 1994. The pair eventually put on 272 against Hampshire, one short of the first-wicket record for matches between the counties, and Tom Cooper later became the third Somerset centurion. By the close the home side's lead over Hampshire had been extended to 317 on what seems a flat pitch, although Dawson's three late wickets suggested it was beginning to turn.

The sporting press may say that Hampshire's bowlers stuck to their task in difficult circumstances and their judgement will be true enough. But when three of the four batsmen you dismiss have scored hundreds, it is very clear what sort of a day it has been. James Hildreth's fine 71 was little but a footnote to the play. Hampshire's batsmen got their side into this mess and they will have to get them out of it. Otherwise, James Vince's side will become warm favourites for relegation ahead of the visit of the pitiless Yorkshiremen next week. Yet for all that Cooper's first hundred for Somerset received the crowd's applause – and the ECB may care to note that yet another four-day game has been very well attended – it was the 21-year-old Abell and his partnership with Trescothick that commanded the warmest ovations. Abell was born in Taunton and attended Taunton School. He also played, and occasionally still plays, his club cricket for Taunton, so you could call him a local lad. One imagines that his three-year course at Exeter University was an awfully big adventure. The Taunton crowd rose to him because he is one of their own and that will always matter to county cricket supporters.

For his part, Keynsham-born Trescothick is loved beyond reason or measure on this ground. He is a steadfast cricketer who, rather than retiring when his England days were done, returned to county cricket and still derives deep joy from it. He has faced down tougher enemies than fast bowlers. His happiness at reaching his century was obvious and, for all his 39 years, rather boyish. His disappointment when he lost his leg stump to Fidel Edwards when he had made 153 was plain as well. He has just signed a new one-year contract simply because he wants to play professional cricket here for as long as he can. Trescothick's batting is characterised by his clattering pulls to square leg or his fearsome cover drives; Abell's, by his classical correctness, the quiet perfection of his strokes and the time he has to play them. You would pay to watch him drive off the back foot. Jack Brooks twice had him caught in the slips at Headingley last week but there is no shame in that. Hampshire's bowlers could not deal with Abell until Gareth Berg had him leg-before on the back foot for 131, half an hour after lunch. Then the crowd stood to him again and he waved back to them, which was also good to see.

They stood and applauded in all the pavilions on this ground, for Taunton is well-endowed in such structures. There is a Colin Atkinson pavilion, an Ondaatje pavilion and an Andy Caddick pavilion. In the winter, they knocked the much-loved Old Pavilion down and have replaced it with a viewing area, some corporate hospitality suites and a media centre. They have named the new building....the Somerset Pavilion. It rather reminds one of Robert Grant's 1833 hymn "O worship the King", which contains the phrase "pavilioned in splendour", itself the title of a fine book by AA Thomson. On a less-exalted level, Somerset's enthusiasm recalls the comedian Tommy Cooper's famous magic trick whereby he discovered wine bottles inside apparently empty cylinders. It seems that all Somerset need to do these days is throw up some scaffolding and a pavilion will appear. It is very like them.

For Hampshire's supporters this was a day on which they needed to show unquestioning loyalty; for Somerset's, it was a Thursday, the memory of which they will treasure when autumn's rain clouds roll down the Quantocks and into the combes like gun-smoke. But Tom Abell is not yet the answer to any vacancy that might occur in England squads. He is a talented young man learning how to play professional cricket. He has a right to remain "young and easy under the apple boughs" a while longer. Experience and responsibility will come soon enough. Abell has not even played at Lord's, The Oval or Old Trafford yet, but he will surely do so. And as the leaves grow crisp upon the trees in the sharp, brittle light of September, it was almost a reassurance to watch a batsman who, granted only a modicum of fortune, has years of cricket before him. His many supporters will remember this blue-domed day when Taunton was pavilioned in splendour and Tom was girded with praise.

2016

Gloucestershire v Essex – Cheltenham

——————————— JULY 14 – DAY TWO ———————————

*Essex 333 (Lawrence 127, ten Doeschate 52; Shaw
4-72) lead Gloucestershire 255 (Roderick 61, Miles
55; Quinn 7-76, Porter 3-67) by 78 runs*

At half-past five, midway through an evening session blessed by gentle, unexpected warmth Essex's Dan Lawrence reached the third century of his career with a pushed single off Kieran Noema-Barnett. The Cheltenham crowd gave him a generous ovation for they can spot a fine young cricketer in these parts. Lawrence only celebrated his 19th birthday two days ago and he could still play age-group cricket. But what would be the point in that now? As if liberated, Lawrence took 27 runs off his next 14 balls, repeating the straight- and cover- drives that had already elicited ripples of approval. When he lashed Noema-Barnett straight to Craig Miles at mid-wicket, he received yet more applause as he returned to the pavilion and the ex-players attending their annual get-together at the College Lawn End joined in appreciatively. Essex were all out 11 balls before the scheduled close but their 78-run lead has left them well placed in this game.

And Lawrence, of course, is only the most recent of a long line of young players to have received laurels in this sacred space…

To the right of Cheltenham College's pavilion and at the Chapel End of the ground are rows of trees, cracked willows and American limes, mostly. In front of almost every tree is a plaque marking a Cheltonian's notable performance in an important school match. For example: KS Duleepsinhji, 1921, 7-35 v Marlborough; E M Wellings, 1927, 7-113 v Marlborough; P B C Moore 1939, 197 v Malvern. In addition to being a record of achievement, the list is something of a litany, petitioning whatever power there may be for more games like this, more days on cricket's fields of praise. In many cases the request received a brutal answer; Cheltenham also has a war memorial.

And at lunchtime on the third day of this game, as Josh Shaw, Gloucestershire's loanee from Yorkshire, took refreshment in the middle of an eight-over spell in which he took three prime wickets, another tree was planted. It is a poplar and it commemorates the centenary of the death of Percy Jeeves, who died on the Somme on July 22, 1916. As many now know, thanks to Brian Halford's outstanding biography, Jeeves was playing for Warwickshire at Cheltenham in August 1913 when his style was spotted by PG Wodehouse, who wanted a name for a "gentleman's personal gentleman" in a forthcoming short story. "I remember admiring his action very much," said Wodehouse. Yet as one watched the tree being planted and the speeches made, one thought not only of Wodehouse and Jeeves but also of the other trees on the ground and, perhaps, of Edward Thomas, who might have made an elegy out of such events. Thomas died at Pas-de-Calais in 1917.

Shaw, meanwhile, whose West Riding birthplace is just six miles away from that of Jeeves, was doing his best to prevent Essex establishing a winning position in this game. After Nick Browne had edged a good ball from David Payne to Chris Dent at slip in the fifth over of the Essex innings, Shaw, another 20-year-old with all before him, had brought one back a little to have Tom Westley lbw for 24. The young seamer appealed with all the certainty of a barrister who has sweetened the jury. At the beginning of his next over Shaw inflicted a first-ball duck on Ravi Bopara, Dent again taking the catch, and when Jaik Mickleburgh, who was ailing with a strain, slapped a half volley straight to Jack Taylor at midwicket, Essex were 80-4, still trailing Gloucestershire on first innings by 175.

The visitors' recovery to 333 at the close was led by Lawrence, who treated the former players in the corporate hospitality marquee to a fine exhibition of elegant batsmanship. He adapted well to a wicket on which bowlers are dangerous if they hit an exact length but fodder if they over-pitch even a fraction. Lawrence took four boundaries off what became the last over of Shaw's first spell and added 102 with Ryan ten Doeschate, getting to his fifty in the over before the Essex skipper brought up the same landmark with a whack over midwicket off Graeme van Buuren's slow left-arm. But ten Doeschate perished more or less as Westley had to the first ball of Shaw's next over, and it was eventually left to Lawrence and James Foster to give Essex the lead with a seventh-wicket stand of 83 in 14 overs. Gloucestershire's seamers were now tiring, the ball was old and the support bowlers had to buy their wickets. Yet Lawrence's 14th four, a majestic off drive to a ball from Payne which took him to 97, was still the shot of the day and he got to three figures 11 balls later.

Once Lawrence was out, Foster bolstered Essex's position by scoring 29 more runs very rapidly but this was something of a vaudeville act after a command performance. The crowd meandered away in a thoughtful mood and a Housmanish haze lingered on the distant slopes. And on Cleeve Hill, stretching away towards Charlton Abbots, were all the trees of Gloucestershire and Oxfordshire.

2017

Sussex v Gloucestershire – Eastbourne

MAY 14 – ROYAL LONDON CUP

Gloucestershire 241-4 (Hankins 67, J Taylor 64, M Klinger 53)
beat Sussex 240 (Wright 84; Liddle 5-52) by six wickets

The Saffrons: sometimes a simple name is sufficient to prompt a confection of histories. It is over a century since the orange-yellow crocus noted for its dyeing and medicinal qualities was grown in the fields where Eastbourne's cricketers spend their summers. Yet the gentle beauty of the noun lingers and has now been coupled to a children's nursery, an apartment block and a hotel. "I'm watching cricket at Eastbourne on Sunday," I tell friends. "Oh, you're going to the Saffrons," they reply.

In Eastbourne's long 20th-century heyday there was a cricket week: two three-day county games and, as often as not, matches against the universities or the tourists as well. This was the ground on which AC Maclaren's personally selected amateur XI defeated Warwick Armstrong's seemingly invincible Australians in 1921, thereby giving Neville Cardus the only scoop of his career. There were important matches being played at The Oval and Leyton at the same time and Cardus's editor felt he should have been covering those. That opinion was strengthened when MacLaren's side were

194

bowled out for 43 on the first day. By the second morning Cardus had sent his luggage to the railway station and was ready to leave; but he stayed instead and watched Aubrey Faulkner make 153. The Australians lost by 28 runs.

"At Eastbourne cricket is played to a background of croquet and bowls, old Colonels and straight-backed memsahibs going about their daily ritual, indifferent to the pock of bat on ball and the marauding seagulls," wrote Alan Ross, for whom India and Sussex were twin lodestars and who found his loves united in the batting of Duleepsinhji in the summer of 1932.

And one scarcely has to look to see deeper histories and other aristocracies at Eastbourne. Behind the trees at the Larkin's Field End is the Compton Croquet Club, one of many references in the environs to the estate that owns acres of prime land in the town. The land on which cricket, hockey and soccer are played is still owned by the Duke of Devonshire. Seniors at the club pass on the stories they were told of the horse-drawn carriages that set off from the duke's Compton estate and travelled down the tree-lined Old Orchard Road into town. When I first visited the ground in September 2015 almost the only noise one could hear in the late afternoon was the gentle crack of mallets on croquet balls. The players were dressed in communion white and moved slowly around the lawns in the soft sunlight of early autumn.

That light, for which Eastbourne is famed, was in evidence when I returned to the Saffrons this May. It was present in the dazzling white of the bucket seats, the flounce of the marquees and in the covers protecting the pitch to be used for the next day's game. Even the pages of my notebook dazzled. It was the light which gave Eric Ravilious both a theme and a context for many of his paintings. "Everything is dazzled or is bleached out," writes Anne Wroe of Eastbourne in her wonderful *Six Facets of Light*. "A man walking a dog across the lawns becomes a radiant ghost of himself. Teapot, cups and spoons blink blindingly on a table." Or there is David Hare in his play, *The Moderate Soprano*: "In Sussex, always a feeling of air and light, of the soft Downs beyond."

Eastbourne is an outground. First-class counties visit such venues because they wish to spread their cricket more widely or because their main ground is being used for a Test match or a pop concert. There is no obligation upon officials to use outgrounds, yet Gloucestershire supporters treasure their visits to Cheltenham College and Yorkshire members voted in favour of playing two four-day games at Scarborough. The heart of a county's cricket often beats miles away from its headquarters.

I arrived in Eastbourne on the day before the 50-over game against Gloucestershire. At the ground a gaggle of officials were gazing at the pitch with the sort of attention biblical scholars might devote to a Coptic text. Both in the pavilion and beyond the boundary, club members scurried from task to task: busy, bothered, anxious, competent. County cricket was returning to the Saffrons for the first time in 17 years. On the hundreds of deckchairs was the slogan "Eastbourne: Breathe It In", accompanied by silhouettes of yachts and gulls on yet another white background. The ground has lost many of the trees it possessed when a famous photograph was taken from the Town Hall in 1929 but beeches and elms still tossed and threshed in the breeze.

In the pavilion the club's chairman, Ian Fletcher-Price, executive and articulate, talked of his pride in bringing county cricket back to the Saffrons after the bad times around the turn of the century when the pitch was not good enough, the club's committee was weak and Sussex were right to leave. He did not want Eastbourne to stretch itself too far by taking on a four-day game. On Larkin's Field, the ground at the back of the pavilion, Eastbourne's second team were taking on Crawley Eagles and a young spinner was having trouble finding his length as the end of the innings approached. "Keep at it, Henry" encouraged a team-mate as another ball disappeared into the trees bordering Saffrons Road. "Poor Henry's full tosses were hit for huge sixers". I had been in Eastbourne about two hours and I was speaking in Betjeman pastiche.

Eastbourne is fortunate. In so far as a clear trend can be discerned, it is that counties are moving away from outgrounds. Treasurers cite the cost of taking a game away from an HQ and seem oblivious to the less tangible benefits. Yet Glamorgan still play four-day games at Colwyn Bay and Swansea, while Kent visit Beckenham and Tunbridge Wells for championship matches. For some grounds, it is already too late. The Central Recreation Ground at Hastings is now the site of the Priory Meadow Shopping Centre; the name of the new development is in exquisite contrast to the ugliness of the shops. The only physical reminder that it was once one of Sussex's most precious venues is a sculpture of a batsman playing a hook. We are left with the recollections of others or the photographs: Lord Hawke signing an autograph, Denis Compton, his bat aloft and his hair tousled after he had beaten Jack Hobbs' record of 16 centuries in a season.

Dover has also gone. The last first-class game played on the Crabble Athletic Ground took place in 1976 and club cricket ceased there in 2003. The famous pavilion and the remnants of the tiered seating now look out on rugby pitches. Those wanting to know what it was like to watch cricket at the Crabble are left with Cardus's rhapsodies on Lancashire's visits. Just as powerfully, perhaps, there is a photograph of Colin Cowdrey going out to bat for Kent in the 1960s. Behind him sit the members, perhaps thinking they have summers and summers of this lovely stuff ahead of them.

At Eastbourne, Fletcher-Price need not have worried. The weather was glorious and the corporate hospitality marquees at the Meads Road End clinked and hummed from mid-morning until deep in the evening. Early on, a great woollen shark wandered in front of the press tent. Later in the Sussex innings a wicket fell and, glancing up from a photograph of the blazered Sussex team in 1927, I saw the home side's Laurie Evans ambling across to check something with the analyst after being dismissed for 48. Sweat-stained, spiky-haired and carrying a water-bottle, he could have been mistaken for a professional cyclist. So often we are told we must pay attention the here and now; yet how frequently we are tugged back to the here and then; to Cardus, MacLaren and Duleep; to the gods we worship silently; to the Saffrons in its pomp.

Sussex did not score enough runs and dropped too many catches. A target of 241 on a small ground like Eastbourne was never likely to test Gloucestershire's batting and the visitors won with eight balls to spare. The next day's press reports made much of Sussex's failure to accelerate in their later overs. A crowd of 3,000 was mentioned although there seemed more folk watching in mid-afternoon. The complimentary lines about cricket returning to Eastbourne would have pleased the club's workers as they came to terms with sudden exhaustion.

My train for London did not leave for an hour. Or maybe I just took a later train. The players threw their huge cricket bags on their shoulders and made for home. There were last circuits of the ground. The marquees were still thronged with easy affluence. The battlefield of conviviality was strewn with empty bottles and creased napkins. Hugo Boss argued with Ralph Lauren; Abercrombie and Fitch made plans for the following week with Jack Wills. I turned back again for one last look, and then another. The croquet players were still on the lawn and the Saffrons relaxed in the crystal light of a May evening.

The Cricket Monthly – May 2017

Northamptonshire v Nottinghamshire – Northampton

──────────── SEPTEMBER 22 – DAY FOUR ────────────

Northamptonshire 194 (Wood 4-52, Hutton 3-52) and 270 (Levi 115, Newton 53; Wood 4-31, Hutton 3-74) beat Nottinghamshire 151 (Kleinveldt 9-65) and 189 (Kleinveldt 4-33, Gleeson 3-52) by 124 runs

And so it will all go down to the last week of the season. So much was made clear late on a September morning stolen from May when Richard Gleeson plucked out Brett Hutton's off stump and sent it tumbling in the direction of Pitsford Water. With both promotion and the Second Division title at stake, three counties must desport themselves like the noble forces in Shakespeare's history plays:

> Northants bestir yourselves! Leicester awaits.
> The men of Durham shall to Worcester go.
> And Sussex Downs must Notts accommodate.

And it might be necessary for Nottinghamshire's cricketers to bind up a few wounds before they journey to Hove. Northants' Ben Duckett may have broken his finger and Alex Wakely copped a painful blow to his mush in this match but Nottinghamshire have lost their last two four-day games and will begin their game against

Sussex six points behind the leaders, Worcestershire, and only 13 ahead of their conquerors in this game.

Northamptonshire, for their part, will make the very short trip to Grace Road in blithe mood. They have won eight of their 13 championship matches this season and know they must win a ninth to put pressure on the counties above them. But their utterly deserved 124-run victory in this match showed them to be in excellent form Marrying professionalism with a deep and obvious enjoyment of their work, Wakely's cricketers spent the final two hours of their home season taking seven wickets for 82 runs. Then they had a laugh about it all, belted out the team song at a louder volume than head coach David Ripley had ever heard and settled into a liquid afternoon.

Ripley admitted that his team are "desperate to do well in red-ball cricket" but he also knows they will never be a bunch of humourless sobersides. On the contrary, a smile is never far from their faces and they will always choose the fearless path to victory. Richard Levi's match-transforming century on the second day of this game perfectly illustrated that approach, as did Rory Kleinveldt's career-best 13 wickets for 98. You would travel a long way to find two less isotonically-inclined cricketers – but only a fool would doubt their effectiveness.

Kleinveldt's skill was made evident after just half an hour on a morning when Nottinghamshire's final seven wickets disappeared almost as quickly as my packet of Hobnobs in the press box. For the second time in the match Cheteshwar Pujara was discomfited by Kleinveldt's lift and caught at second slip by Levi; two overs later the Job-like Jake Libby, who had spent 194 minutes over 42 runs, was tempted into an uncharacteristic fence outside the off stump and David Murphy did the rest. Belief drifted into the Ken Turner Stand and was mixed with hope. Neither fear nor Nottinghamshire's batsmen could remove it

Samit Patel and Riki Wessels attempted to resettle the innings but it was no good. Ben Sanderson had bowled beautifully on the third morning of this game but without reward. Now he beat Wessels twice outside the off stump before the batter shuffled across his stumps and was left to reflect on his overcompensation during a slow walk back to the pavilion. Tom Moores followed Wessels three overs late when a Gleeson inswinger left umpire David Millns with no option. Nottinghamshire were now 152-7 and not even halfway to their target.

Chris Read joined Patel, two of the doughtiest fighters in their county's cause, two batsmen, one thought, who were capable of rescuing that cause should it seem lost. But not this morning. Having posted a long leg and a deep square leg, Gleeson dug one in and Patel hooked it straight to the delighted substitute fielder, Saif Zaib.

Perhaps Northampton has always inspired such generosity. After the great fire of 1675 Charles II gave a thousand "tun" of timber to help with the rebuilding of All Saints church and seven years' chimney money towards the reconstruction of the town. The modern age has seen no diminution in the largesse. "Tattoo Phil's" proclaims a shop sign in the Wellingborough Road, although it is unclear whether this is an offer or a command, nor is it quite plain what portion of Phil requires decoration.

Patel stood aghast at his error and walked slowly off the field. We were nearly done. Read edged Buck to Levi and Gleeson ended the match on the stroke of lunch. It is so like Northamptonshire's players not to let cricket delay a meal. Perhaps there was satisfaction if not joy in the villas on Billing Road and in the prim, proud terraces which surround this rich and lovely ground. Perhaps the news even filtered through to Sheep Street Quality Butchers where the window already boasts an advert for Christmas Hampers. But such premature nonsense can be ignored for a week, if not a couple of months. Instead, we can ponder Hove, Worcester, Leicester. Three theatres and four days to warm us against the advancing dark. It makes you realise what Charters and Caldicott were on about.

2018

Somerset v Hampshire – Taunton

———————————— MAY 12 – DAY TWO ————————————
Somerset 324-7 (Hildreth 125*, C Overton 80; Berg 4-88) lead Hampshire 231 (Abell 3-36, Groenewald 3-59) by 93 runs

James Hildreth plays a cover-drive at Taunton on a Saturday afternoon in May. The scoreboard flicks over and something of summer is held in the moment. Barely a good hit away the County Stores is offering cream teas at two for £6. Across town, church aisles have been swept in preparation for weddings and now speeches are being smartened up, the bad jokes made a little worse. But inside the County Ground, Hildreth glides Fidel Edwards between gully and slips and down to the boundary. He is making a century and changing this game.

On Sunday morning the papers will note Hildreth's unbeaten 125 and his 133-run partnership for the sixth wicket with Craig Overton. That stand all but broke Hampshire's attack and it took Somerset into a lead which had been extended to 93 by the close of a day from which 17 overs were trimmed by bad light. Overton's dismissal when he played on to Gareth Berg for a rather cultured 80 did not end the suffering for James Vince's players. Jack Leach was also batting capably when the players finally went off.

Those papers will also make something of the absence of Kyle Abbott, who turned an ankle in the third over of Somerset's innings and could not bowl for over three hours. And they may make rather more of Edwards' dropped catch at mid-wicket which would have ended Hildreth's innings when he had only 24 and Somerset were 71-4. Both points will be valid but the folk enjoying their caramel lattes in Coffee#1 will recall the ease of Hildreth's square drives, the gentle tempo of his innings and all the pleasure it gave them.

Taunton's cricket ground, which is now squeezed between flats and offices, is woven tight into the life of the town. Hildreth moved into the nineties with the sweetest of clips through midwicket off Abbott and reached his century with a cut to the boundary off Berg. He had faced 138 balls and hit 13 fours in getting to his 41st first-class hundred for Somerset. But they still call him Hildy in The Ring of Bells.

And centuries are often made glorious by the circumstances of their making. Somerset were 40-2 when Hildreth walked out to bat. They had lost Eddie Byrom, bowled by Edwards for 10, and George Bartlett, caught at slip off Brad Wheal for one. The prize wicket, though, was that of Matt Renshaw, who had looked in the mood to reduce another county attack to weeping impotence. His flick through mid-wicket had carried the mark of Zorro; his uppercut for six off Wheal had been daring theatre. But having been dropped by a diving McManus and also survived a drum-splitting lbw shout from Edwards, Renshaw was eventually squared up by Berg and caught by Jimmy Adams at second slip when looking to play to leg. Seven balls later, local gloom deepened when Tom Abell hooked his first ball to Edwards at long leg, thus giving Berg the second of his four wickets. Hildreth strolled around the pitch like a farmer inspecting his land and something approaching calm was restored in the hour after lunch. Steve Davies and Hildreth put on 60 before the Somerset wicketkeeper was forced to retire when hit on the ankle. Lewis Gregory lasted seven balls but Overton marched out and announced his arrival with a blunderbuss off-drive to a ball from Brad Wheal. One of Instow's finest settled in and took his cue from Hildreth.

And now we are deep in the evening session. The sun has bustled its way through tissues of cloud, prompting Jeff Evans and Jeremy Lloyds to summon the cricketers out again. The outfield carries shades of the afternoon's magic. But we face only 11 balls before play is called off on this day when Hildreth made Somerset's sixth hundred of this barely adolescent season. A year ago most of the top order had difficulty reaching double figures but victory in this game may take the county to the top of the table. Spectators drift away hardly daring to dream. It is over eight hours since the gates opened and they streamed to their favoured spots in the Marcus Trescothick Stand and the Colin Atkinson Pavilion. For the first Championship match against Worcestershire they were queueing at 8.30, and the club played the William Tell overture as the members hurried to their coveted places. All for a game "nobody watches"; all for people like Hildy and days like this.

Yorkshire v Surrey – Scarborough

JUNE 26 – DAY TWO

Surrey 219-7 (Burns 59, Pope 34*; Bresnan 3-57) trail Yorkshire 342 (Tattersall 70, Ballance 54; Dernbach 4-104) by 123 runs

Mist. Mist everywhere. Mist wreathing the sightscreens and the umpires' coats. Mist masking the terraces around the ground and the refreshment stalls inside it. Mist curbing Surrey's batters as they crept to 219-7 in reply to Yorkshire's 342. Mist halting play nine times and for 25 minutes in all during the evening session as the umpires stood with the players and waited for it to clear. Mist turning Ollie Pope into a young ghost as he battled away for 34 plucky and unbeaten runs in conditions as alien as he can have known. Mist finally stopping play 14.5 overs before the close when more or less everyone gave it best and went home.

Rarely can the weather have determined the nature of a day's cricket as much as it did at North Marine Road this extraordinary Tuesday. The foghorn had sounded at six o'clock in the morning and even two hours later the cars were inching along Queens Parade past fret-gauzed hotels and pedestrians already armed with their copies of the Yorkshire Post. The mist cleared and then swirled in again, invading every crevice and seeming to make an early start unlikely. But the lexis of religious observance is not forced at Scarborough. The faithful still make their pilgrimages on days of obligation and hotels are booked before the second Sunday in Advent. Those who have been coming here since the 1960s have seen it all and remember most of it. They were not dissuaded by the mist. Instead, they talked of these being ideal conditions for seamers like Tony Nicholson who used to rumble in and create havoc in the years when Yorkshire were winning the last three of their seven titles in a decade.

This summer is not comparable to those and Steve Patterson's seamers were made to battle for almost every breakthrough on a chill Tuesday afternoon. After a morning session in which the mist lifted and 127 runs were scored, 38 of them by the home side's tailenders, Surrey's batsmen ground out the runs in a fashion which Yorkshiremen like Doug Padgett or Phil Sharpe might have admired. While Rory Burns profited from the attacking fields to hit 11 boundaries in a 46-ball fifty, the Surrey skipper's colleagues were more restrained, especially after the mist returned soon after lunch.

Before the break, Mark Stoneman was caught at the wicket off Ben Coad for 9 and Scott Borthwick also taken by Jonny Tattersall when he skied a pull off Tim Bresnan. If those blows were not bad enough, the session brought disciplinary problems for Surrey. Following a Level One offence being committed by Jade Dernbach when Jack Brooks and Patterson were extending their ninth-wicket stand to 61, Stoneman dissented when given out. The two offences in the same game led to five runs being added to the home side's total. The Scarborough crowd, ever vociferous, rather enjoyed that. The afternoon offered ideal bowling conditions and Yorkshire's seamers made the most of them. Burns was caught behind off Coad for 59 after adding only five to his lunchtime score. Ryan Patel took nearly two hours over his 32 runs before he was fourth out for 32 caught at slip by Harry Brook off Bresnan; 40 minutes later Theunis de Bruyn, after playing well for his 38, nicked Steve Patterson to Tattersall.

The murk increased in the evening session and play was stopped. Each hold up attracted barracking; each resumption brought applause. Will Jacks was leg before to Patterson for seven and Rikki Clarke caught and bowled by Bresnan for a duck. By the close Surrey could look back on a day in which they could have crumpled but did not do so. Pope's innings was a magnificent demonstration of character and resolve in one so young. Yorkshire have the advantage but this match has a long road ahead of it. Let us hope we do not need fog lamps.

Finals Day – 2018

<hr>

SEPTEMBER 15

Worcestershire 158-5 (Cox 46*, Ali 41; Briggs 2-19)
beat Sussex 157-6 (Evans 52) by five wickets

It is easy for a coach to say he wants his team to enjoy their cricket. So easy, in fact, that almost all of them do so. It is harder, though, for him to mean it and harder still for professional cricketers to take him at his word when substantial prize money is at stake. Yet Saturday's Vitality Blast final was contested by two teams whose enjoyment of their cricket was evident in everything they did.

We have to be careful here. When the Sussex coach, Jason Gillespie, tells his players to enjoy their cricket, he is not advocating cheery indifference to whatever happens, nor, we can bet, does he greet sheer sloppiness with a moon-faced smile. It would be interesting to know his reaction to Phil Salt's dozy run-out in the final against Worcestershire. Yet when Luke Wright was looking forward to the climax of this year's Blast on Friday afternoon, his words about Salt, in particular, are worth recalling.

"With Phil Salt you just let him go," he said. "He could get out first ball or he could end up smacking a hundred tomorrow. He's a match-winner...That chilled fun side of it exactly how I want to play my cricket and I think when people are happy they seem to play better. In T20 you have to risk a lot and be brave enough to go out and have a go. If Salty wants to go and hit the first ball for six tomorrow but he gets out doing it, that's just the way it is. We'll pat him on the back and we'll go again."

The serious point here – one that professional coaches develop more subtly – is that if you enjoy playing your sport, you are actually giving yourself a better chance of succeeding. Such an approach may be contrasted with the rather grim axiom that you will enjoy a game if you win it. That is an approach often espoused in some northern counties and it places the cart before the horse. It appeared present in Lancashire's run-chase against Worcestershire in the semi-final. The batsmen in that suddenly distant morning seemed haunted by the possibility of failure; there was little evidence of the natural ability so many of them possessed. And so they lost.

That analysis gives nothing like sufficient credit to Worcestershire's bowlers, of course, or to Ben Cox's fearless assault on Toby Lester's final over. Yet Cox's approach was fearless because he did not fear anything He was playing a game. And after mastering the skills required to flummox batsmen, Pat "knuckle-ball" Brown enjoyed showing them off. Such approaches come from the top. You did not need to be in Australia last winter to understand that Moeen Ali was not enjoying his cricket; yet the skipper's joy was evident in almost every aspect of his play on Finals' Day as he made 41 in each innings and took five wickets for 46 runs in eight overs. The revival in Moeen's form has been one of the themes of the summer.

Brazen enjoyment is particularly fitting on this day at Edgbaston. The whole occasion is preposterous. It is also tiring, faintly deranged and further over the top than *The Jeremy Kyle Show*. Yet it has become part of the cricket season for thousands of people, many of whom also appreciate the four-day stuff. Of course the Kiss Cam is embarrassing; of course the Scatter Blast sounds like a method of dispersing an unruly mob. But those who are not prepared to enter into the spirit of the thing would be better not attending. In a way, that includes the cricketers, too. Their seasons are judged in the main by their performances in the County Championship but their summers would be a lesser thing without the possibility of appearing in this Birmingham burlesque with its floodlights, its congregational choruses, its fancy dress and even its mascot race.

Yet this shortest of cricket's formats has also become the most analysed. Within moments of the final being completed people were noting its statistical oddities and some of them were very odd indeed. Others were more obvious. For example, Sussex became the first team from the South Group to reach the final since Surrey in 2013 but could not become the first to break the North's dominance of the Blast since Hampshire in 2012. Worcestershire became only the second team in the last eight finals to win the trophy when batting second.

Mere writers, meanwhile, are left with their images: the Worcestershire players rushing out to greet Ben Cox at the moment of victory; Moeen Ali hanging back but still accidentally copping one on the nose from an overjoyed Daryl Mitchell, who, at the age of 33, had won his first major trophy; the sight of the Worcestershire players offering a public rendition of their victory song in front of their supporters. And, yes, Kevin Sharp, who a year ago could not have dreamed he would be doing his present job. Then he was an attendant lord, one that could swell a team photograph, start a net or two. Now he is the coach of one of the season's three major trophy winners. And he will, no doubt, have appreciated the words of, Alec Stewart, his counterpart at Surrey, who as his own players celebrated the title, praised Worcestershire's cricket and took time out on Thursday evening to say they were doing things the right way by bringing on their own young players and giving them the chance to enjoy their sport.

Let us return to another fine coach and to a captain who managed to transcend the self-policed optimism of last Friday afternoon. "It's easy to put too much pressure on the day and I've told the lads to enjoy it," said Luke Wright. "Jason Gillespie has helped us to do that and I think that's why we've had so much success. The quarter-final was the most relaxed game I've ever played in really. Dizzy was so chilled in the build-up and he's the same now."

"Yeah, but you lost," the critics will smirk. They will have missed the point. Again.

Sussex v Warwickshire – Hove

———————————— SEPTEMBER 18 – DAY ONE ————————————
Warwickshire 308-2 (Bell 108*, Trott 86*, Rhodes 50) against Sussex

Just before tea on the first afternoon of this game David Wiese bowled to Ian Bell. One of his deliveries was a trifle short and a little wide of the off stump but it could scarcely be ranked as poor. Bell rocked back slightly and stroked the ball between point and cover as though not wanting to damage it. It was the fifth of his 11 fours and most of the others were similarly easeful. By the close Bell was unbeaten on 108 and had helped Jonathan Trott put on an unbroken 206 for Warwickshire's third wicket. It may be the partnership that seals a season's work.

For yes, there was significance to Bell's artistry on the opening day of this game, not that an innings of his ever requires any. Warwickshire need only a draw in this match to secure promotion and thereby keep the silent promise they made to themselves in April. Sussex, meanwhile, must win their last two games and one cannot like their chances at all. The defeat at Chester-le-Street damaged them badly and by quarter-past-twelve this morning they were watching Bell open his account with a tucked single off Wiese. Portents are rarely so decorous.

Sussex thus seem very likely to spend a fourth season in the Second Division and this will come as a great local disappointment, not least because the game has always taken its place among Brighton and Hove's bewildering variety of attractions. For example, Brighton's buses are named after notable people connected with the town and some of the vehicles honour the county's cricketers. There is a K S Ranjitsinhji, a Maurice Tate and, on Monday afternoon, CB

Fry was seen tootling down North Street. It passed Anita Roddick on the opposite side of the road, then Ivy Compton-Burnett and Ralph Vaughan Williams. It would be hazardous, though, if the buses' progress reflected the characters of any cricketers honoured: while Ken Suttle might potter along happily, Ted Dexter would hurtle down narrow roads at breakneck speed, occasionally veering off in bizarre directions.

But perhaps Sussex needed something unconventional this afternoon. Ben Brown's bowlers never allowed the batters to score at will but neither, until the last hour of play, did they induce regular error. Instead, Trott, in one of his final innings, marked out his guard like an accountant preparing his ledger while Bell remained unconsciously balletic, endowing his forward defensive shots with as much poise as his drives. In the second over after lunch he patted a full toss from Briggs to the midwicket boundary. Aggression seemed inimical to him and quite soon, Trott, after his own methodical fashion, had warmed to the theme. There were statistical niceties, too. Bell has scored more runs against Sussex than any other opponent except Australia and his fifth century against them took his aggregate to 1,506 at an average of 65.47. Trott already has six centuries against these opponents and a seventh seems likely on the morrow. And to be brutal, always an effort where Bell is concerned, Warwickshire need do nothing in this game except bat Sussex out of it.

Bell and Trott's composure was such that much of the first session became a prelude to the main business of the day. Nonetheless, for 25 overs, Dominic Sibley and Will Rhodes encountered no more difficulties than openers might expect on the first morning of a game, only for both to depart in the space of 14 balls. Sibley, having made 44, came down the pitch to drive Briggs but only skewed a catch to Michael Burgess at short mid-wicket. Then, two balls after reaching his fifty, Rhodes was bowled off the bottom edge when attempting to keep out something of a shooter from Wiese.

Thereafter, wickets never threatened to fall in the clumps beloved of the coaches; come to think of it, they rarely threatened to fall at all on an easy-paced pitch offering some low bounce and little carry. We were left, instead, with Trott tucking the ball off his hip or shaping it to third man off Chris Jordan as the Sussex attack faltered.

Jofra Archer bowled well to Trott after lunch and Briggs' accuracy always reminded both batsmen of their duties. Sussex took the new ball and Archer received an appreciative nod from Bell when he beat him outside the off stump. In the next over Trott was all but cut in two by one from Robinson that came back off the seam. But it still seemed plain that Sussex had missed the C B Fry.

Two overs before the close Bell reached the 57th century of his first-class career with a back foot four off Jordan. Another in the same over made him only the second player in the country to score a thousand championship runs this season. On such evenings, the ball becomes the context of his art, the fielders no more than obstacles to be avoided. Yet his desire is also part of the magic. For if you want to understand who Ian Bell is, then you should watch him bat for an hour. One thought of the occasion some 27 summers ago when the late Neal Abberley, then the county's batting coach, saw the nine-year-old from Coventry for the first time and wondered what the Gods had sent him. Batting is what Bell was put on earth to do and when he plays as he did at Hove on this late summer afternoon he shares his joy with others. It distracts the mind from the many recessionals of autumn; its graceful images remain when points and results are both forgotten.

2019

Middlesex v Lancashire – Lord's

——————————— APRIL 13 – DAY THREE ———————————

Middlesex 265 and 68-2 trail Lancashire 427 (Jones 122, Hameed 117, Vilas 68, Jennings 52; Murtagh 5-69) by 94 runs

Saturday morning in London: fat papers thumping onto doormats; the 319 taking its time getting to Sloane Square; Van Goghs at the Tate; Renaissance nudes at the Royal Academy; Soho's pubs opening early and the regulars meeting for convivial loneliness; pre-season practice for clubs in the Surrey Championship; Luton at Charlton and Wrexham at Barnet; Oxted Villa at Streatham Rovers,

Northampton at Harlequins and Essex at Surrey. And Rob Jones at Lord's, hoping to secure his place in Lancashire's side. This, too, is cricket in England.

Just after half past three Jones reached the century which will help him achieve his goal. He cut Steven Finn to the wide third-man boundary and, just as when he scored his maiden hundred against the same opponents in 2016, he went on a merry jig full of joyful leaps and fist pumps One could understand his euphoria. Jones has had to wait for his opportunities at Lancashire and today's showers meant he had to begin his innings on a couple more occasions than he might have expected. None of it seemed to trouble him and neither was he too bothered when rattled on the helmet by James Harris after lunch. He eventually became one of five batsmen dismissed after tea when the admirable Tim Murtagh got a leg before decision from Billy Taylor, but by the time James Harris bowled Graham Onions to end the innings Lancashire had a meaty 162-run advantage on first innings.

That lead had not been reduced at all when Nick Gubbins blamelessly nicked James Anderson's fifth ball of the innings to Glenn Maxwell at second slip. Yet that wicket was followed by such a secure 68-run stand between Sam Robson and Stevie Eskinazi that it seemed Middlesex would be going into the final day with nine wickets in hand. Then Eskinazi played across a straight ball from Onions five minutes before the close and that reverse bruised the home side's hopes. No doubt someone will say it is going to be a big first hour in the morning. But if the first hour is big, the second will be enormous and the third may well disrupt space-time altogether.

But whatever the result, Lancashire had earned their earlier advantage in a flinty manner that bodes well for them this season. The morning session, for example, had been a grim affair: only 13 overs were possible between the showers and the lingering images are of Dane Vilas and Jones defending with the resolution of Protestant pastors before the Inquisition. Both Murtagh and Steven Finn found a righteous length and Jones managed just three runs off 36 balls before the first interruption. Two fours off Harris, the second a sweet thing through mid-off, may have relaxed him a trifle but conditions were no easier for Middlesex. Their players all wore thick sweaters and between balls they stood with their hands dug deep in their armpits. On the scoreboard Haseeb Hameed's 117 shone out against Last Man, a reminder of Friday afternoon, when the ground was thronged and our talk was filled with marvellous praise.

We managed only 33 balls in the afternoon session before the rain returned. There was time for a stroll in St John's Wood: Panzers selling kumquats, yellow dates and maracuya; the 113 rumbling past Lord's on its way to Oxford Circus; young-leafed poplars in Cochrane Street; couples dawdling over a late lunch in Fego's, their gestures suggesting possibilities.

The cricket resumed just before three o'clock and the rest of the day was played in bright sunlight As if reassured by the prospect of prolonged time at the crease, the batsmen played with more assurance. Vilas reached his fifty with a tucked single off Toby Roland-Jones and one fancies it will be the first of many he will score this summer. Then Jones twice pulled James Harris savagely to the backward square boundary, as if taking revenge for that blow on the helmet. Those fours took him into the nineties and he soon reached his second championship century. It was a noble effort.

Ten minutes before tea, though, Vilas was leg before when attempting to sweep Malan. That ended his 143-run stand with Jones and it was also the prelude to a further tumble on the resumption. In all, Lancashire lost their last six wickets for 53 runs in 16 overs. One of those dismissed was Alex Davies, who was fit enough to bat but not to field after injuring his thumb on the first morning

It is late now. The newspapers have been reduced to their constituent parts and lie around suburban lounges, their crosswords half-completed. From the pubs around Lord's one hears the clink of glasses and the hum of talk on this cool spring evening. Elsewhere London's theatres are preparing for their evening performances: *The Lion King, The Book of Mormon, Top Girls*. A thousand restaurants have opened their doors. And somewhere in this sleepless metropolis Middlesex and Lancashire's cricketers are resting before the final act of this contested drama between two teams whose ambitions this summer are unapologetically grand.

Hampshire v Nottinghamshire – Newclose 2019

Hampshire 288-6 (Weatherley 66) against Nottinghamshire

When a man's desire defeats his reason he is wont to dream. He might also begin a quest that sane men dub fantasy. Little more than a decade ago there was nothing but pasture where Newclose cricket ground now stands. Then Brian Gardener, the prosperous visionary who owned the land, decided the Isle of Wight should have a venue capable of not only staging Premier League club matches, but even of tempting Hampshire to cross the Solent. And at eleven o'clock this morning, over four years after Gardener's death, Luke Fletcher bowled to Joe Weatherley at Newclose.

Nobody knows exactly how much money Gardener spent to realise his vision; estimates have settled on something above £2m. All that spectators might have noticed as they gathered on the grassy banks surrounding the arena was that the pavilion was modelled on that at Sir Paul Getty's ground at Wormsley and that the seating in front of the pavilion reminded them of somewhere…ah yes, Lord's, that was the place. Some, seeing the alders and oaks on the River Medina side of the ground, made comparisons with Arundel but Newclose is less intimate than that particular Elysium. The outfield, though, is smooth as one could wish and the pitch is clearly fit for first-class cricket even if it did not encourage free scoring on this first day.

Hampshire's 288-6 at stumps was thus an accurate reflection of three sessions in which the ball had moved about a lot yet one in which batsmen could prosper if they played straight and late. The images one remembers are not those of Stuart Broad or Jake Ball racing in but those of Steven Mullaney bowling his brisk medium pacers and taking 2-42 in 24 overs from the Carisbrooke End while Hampshire's openers, Weatherley and Oli Soames went about their business as cautiously as bomb disposal men.

Batsmen who looked to force things generally perished: Ajinkya Rahane did so in mid-afternoon when he edged a drive off Broad and was caught at around fourth slip by Chris Nash for 10. By then, Weatherley had also departed, unluckily judged caught behind off

Ball for a pleasant 66 when the ball had done no more than brush his upper arm. But that contribution represented something of a relief for an opener who had passed 30 only twice in his previous 18 first-class innings. Rather more to the point, Weatherley's 112-run stand for the first wicket with Soames had given Hampshire a foundation upon which Aneurin Donald and Ian Holland can build further on the second morning. Mullaney's bowlers might yet regret the inaccuracy which characterised their efforts in the opening session

Whatever the analysts tell them, cricketers will always be suspicious of a fresh pitch on a new ground. Both Weatherley and Soames have played second-team cricket at Newclose but only when Broad bowled an attacking length did he leak a few boundaries as they drove him through the covers. The pair put on 88 in that morning session and Weatherley looked to be in particularly sound form. By the middle of the day, Hampshire had lost two wickets and Nottinghamshire's bowlers had found a better length and line. Then just before tea, thoughts turned to self-preservation as a modest swarm of bees approached the ground from the Medina side. Some players, among them Stuart Broad, lay on the ground and one remembered wartime photographs of fielders lying in similar positions to avoid the rather more deadly danger of German bombers. By contrast, the threat this afternoon was brief and its effect faintly comical.

Having rediscovered their accuracy in the second session Nottinghamshire's bowlers got the rewards they deserved in the hour after tea. Soames' four-hour vigil for 44 runs was ended in the over after the resumption when he pushed at Ball but only nicked a catch to Matt Carter at second slip. Half an hour later Sam Northeast also departed when he attempted to force the ball through midwicket but was leg before wicket to Mullaney, who almost immediately took a second wicket when Tom Alsop was athletically caught down the leg side by Tom Moores. Hampshire's poorest period of cricket was completed when Liam Dawson drove loosely at Fletcher and was bowled for 25.

And so we got to the end of a day created by the ambition of a man who did not live to see an occasion he would have treasured. Brian Gardener was assisted in the building and development of Newclose by a number of similarly able lieutenants, among them the former Sussex chief-executive, Hugh Griffiths. As the cricket unfolded on this first day and the niggling problems which always affect such great undertakings cropped up, Griffiths and many others scurried about in the manner of outground officials across the land. And you can be sure that as they did so they were thinking of the man whose money and drive had made it all possible in the first place. "Never doubt that a small group of thoughtful and committed citizens can change the world," Jed Bartlet tells Will Bailey in *The West Wing*. But Bailey has the rejoinder to that one ready. "It's the only thing that ever has," he says.

──────────── DAY TWO ────────────

Hampshire 310 (Weatherley 66; Fletcher 4-79) and
3-1 lead Nottinghamshire 239 (Mullaney 102; Barker
3-46, Edwards 3-49, Abbott 3-61) by 74 runs

Steven Mullaney first learned about cricket in Golborne, a town which now lies in the Metropolitan Borough of Wigan. The place is no sort of Orwellian wasteland but neither is it Ambridge. And it certainly has next door to nowt in common with the pastoral glory of Newclose. Yet as we watched Nottinghamshire's captain fight like fury to keep his team in this match it was possible to discern the toughness which still characterises the league cricket he once played. Mullaney's century today was, among its other qualities, a monument to simple defiance and it should be recalled fondly by all those who saw it. But let us be crystal on two points: firstly, the resolution Mullaney displayed is not some exclusively Northern characteristic; and secondly, Nottinghamshire's skipper long ago transferred his absolute allegiance from Old Trafford to Trent Bridge. It is in the East Midlands that he has won all the honours the domestic game has to offer and his loyalty to the place is very deep. So much is clear every time he strides to the wicket and it was plain again today when he walked out with Nottinghamshire on 61-3 in reply to Hampshire's 310.

Things became much worse before they got even slightly better. Having beaten Ben Slater outside the off stump and induced a mistimed pull from Chris Nash, Kyle Abbott nipped one back to bowl Joe Clarke for 23. Then Jake Libby was leg before to Keith Barker to leave Nottinghamshire on 72-5. And all these ructions,

214

we thought, on almost the first summer's day of the season. For there was a Blyton-blue sky and so there had to be hampers. The hospitality was corporate and it was familial. The white Burgundy was chilled this afternoon and the beer needed only gravity to get it from barrel to tankard. Most in the crowd cheered happily either side of lunch as Abbott and Barker put Nottinghamshire in the toils. But then they watched in grudging admiration and near-perfect joy as Mullaney and Tom Moores, scrappers both, set about rebuilding the innings. Men under panamas and women in print dresses agreed that fast bowling looked warm work.

Warm but also productive. Having battled away for 101 minutes to stifle his attacking instincts and accumulate 34 out of a 79-run stand with Mullaney, Moores almost waved his bat at a ball from Fidel Edwards and gossamered a catch to a diving Tom Alsop down the leg side. Luke Fletcher and Stuart Broad followed him back to the pavilion in short order and the visitors took tea on 159 for eight with Mullaney 43 not out. People wondered how much batting Hampshire might have to do tonight. As things turned out, by the time Mullaney had near single-handedly reduced the deficit to 71 runs Joe Weatherley and Oli Soames needed to survive six overs, something they failed to do, Weatherley falling leg before to Fletcher when only eight balls remained. We are set for two more fine days on the abundant Island.

This afternoon, though, spectators who craved warmth had sat in the generous sun; many bared their legs and some were badly advised to do so. Those who sought the shade lounged under the scoreboard on the Medina side of the ground and ate their ice-creams in peace as Mullaney continued his innings. One well-spoken chap licking his cornet was even watched by his envious pooch. On the opposite side of the ground Jack Russell sold sketches and prints. He, perhaps above all spectators at Newclose, would have admired Mullaney's refusal to yield in the evening session. Nottinghamshire's warrior-leader reached his fifty off 113 balls but the deficit was then still over a hundred. So he buckled down again and shepherded Matt Carter through a stand of 80 for the ninth wicket. Carter played a superb supporting role as Mullaney took just 52 balls over the second fifty runs of the hundred he reached with a pulled six off Mason Crane.

This was Steven Mullaney's fourth century against Hampshire and it was nothing like a perfect demonstration of batsmanship. He was dropped three times, most noticeably on 25 when Weatherley put down a two-handed slip chance off Abbott. But faultless 30s matter little when set beside the effort Nottinghamshire's skipper summoned at Newclose. When he reached three figures he raised his arms to the pavilion as if to reinforce the message that he requires similar effort from everybody in any team he leads. When he top-edged a return catch to Ian Holland, spectators stood to him and many were wearing Hampshire badges. He had played an innings worthy of the day and worthy of the ground on which it was played. But they will read about Mullaney's hundred in places far beyond the Isle of Wight this evening; and they will smile at their warm memories.

Lancashire v Leicestershire – Liverpool

———————————— JUNE 6 – DAY FOUR ————————————

Lancashire 449 (Livingstone 114, Bohannon 98*, Bailey 57, Croft 51; Klein 3-89) drew with Leicestershire 288 (Klein 87, Cosgrove 70, Gleeson 4-58) and 151-5

As far as playing for Lancashire is concerned, Liverpudlians have had to walk alone. Only 10 cricketers either born or raised in the city have made over 20 first-class appearances for the county since 1900. It is a figure which compares most unfavourably with the heartlands of Lancastrian cricket such as Westhoughton or Accrington. One of the 10, though, is Paul Horton, so perhaps it was fitting that his 49 runs played a leading role in deciding the outcome of this game. Less fitting, of course, was that he did so wearing Leicestershire's colours, but Horton is a proud professional to his fingertips and after being released by Lancashire in 2015, he has given his very best for a county which clearly prizes his services. And yet, as this game drifted towards a draw, it was impossible to forget that Horton learned his cricket down the road at St Margaret's High School; or that he first played recreational cricket at the tearfully beautiful Sefton Park club, which is only two miles from Aigburth; or that in Lancashire's treasured title-winning summer of 2011, Horton joined his teammates in sprinting from the grand old green-and-white pavilion to acclaim famous victories against Yorkshire and Hampshire. He may be Sydney-born, and his accent is still stubbornly antipodean, but Merseyside has long been Horton's *Heimat*.

None of which counted for much this afternoon as Horton defied Lancashire and his former colleagues offered their inimitably frank commentary on his technique. Leicestershire's captain expected nothing less, of course; he has been round most of cricket's blocks and understands the informal rules of his chosen trade. He will probably have taken the comments as a compliment that he was doing his job in preventing Lancashire taking the wickets they needed to secure their fourth win in five games. But if Horton's 189-minute vigil was the centrepiece of this gentle and glorious day, Leicestershire's draw was testament to their collective effort in resisting Lancashire's attack for 94 overs on a day when the Aigburth pitch offered oodles of turn and variable bounce.

Only 146 runs had been scored and Leicestershire had not even cleared their deficit by the time Neil Bainton flicked off the bails just after six o'clock. But that didn't matter a damn. What counted was that having been 150-7 in the middle of the third afternoon, Leicestershire had lost only eight more wickets in the next 138.4 overs. Head coach Paul Nixon is building a team in his own image and they will be nobody's patsies over the next four months. Of course the cricket was slow. The ice-cream man gave up the struggle for custom at 2.40 and his van pulled out of the ground in search of a younger clientele. It returned over an hour later in the vain hope there had been a sudden influx of sweet teeth. There had not. The scene moved so gently it could have been painted: "Man with a Double-Pram at Aigburth" by Renoir.

There were some exotic statistics. Liam Livingstone's second-innings figures were 36-17-40-1, his one victim being Horton, who chopped a quicker ball onto his stumps. Livingstone's match analysis was 63-26-85-3; his labour as his side's main spinner was prodigious and it was properly praised by Nixon after the game. Livingstone wheeled away for most of this last day from the Pavilion End; partly as a consequence Lancashire's over-rate was 18 in excess of the minimum requirement, which may well be some sort of record.

Four wickets fell in the day. The first was that of nightwatchman Callum Parkinson, who had batted 216 minutes in the match when he edged Richard Gleeson to Livingstone at slip in the early afternoon. The final two, those of Hassan Azad and Neil Dexter, were taken by Steven Croft and Graham Onions in a last hour when Lancastrian hopes were suddenly raised. But Azad had batted for 177 minutes and Dexter for 88. They had done their bit. Before that last act of a great drama Lancashire's cricketers had still appealed whenever they could, although they did so more to maintain their interest in proceedings than in much hope their requests might be granted. Richard Gleeson loudly applauded a long succession of balls from Livingstone, who mixed off-spinners with the odd leggie. Fielders, as fielders will, encouraged their bowlers to go "Bang-bang". But Lancashire rarely went "Bang" on this last day. Instead they took 13 points for the draw and now lead Division Two by 11 points. They have been easily the best team in the second tier during the early part of the season.

At the end of a tough contest Leicestershire's cricketers sought to get away from Liverpool without great delay. Among them was the 20-year-old debutant, Harry Swindells, who had batted well on Wednesday and may think this game more or less the best thing in the world. And also among them was Paul Horton. He is 37 and he may have played his last first-class match at Liverpool.

Finals Day – 2019

—————————————— SEPTEMBER 21 ——————————————
Essex 148-6 beat Worcestershire 145-9 (Harmer 3-16) by four wickets

It is a curious truth that whenever one of cricket's older formats is challenged, it comes out fighting. In 2016 the decision was taken to reduce the number of County Championship matches to 14; so the competition responded by offering us Middlesex v Yorkshire at Lord's, the best climax to an English season for many years and a game so fine it even inspired an excellent book: Duncan Hamilton's *Kings of Summer*. This year, a prevailing enthusiasm among some propeller heads was a reduction in the length of Test matches to four days; so we had the most closely contested Ashes series for a decade, one in which three of the five matches had the temerity to extend themselves into a fifth day.

Next year, of course, the Hundred is to be played in the weeks hitherto reserved for the Vitality Blast. Having marketed T20 cricket superbly and seen it attract record attendances at almost all venues, the counties must now try to sell a second short-form competition much earlier in the summer at a time when many GCSE and A Level examinations are taking place. Good luck. The response of the Blast was to offer a glorious Finals Day at Edgbaston, where two of the three matches went to the last ball and one of those games, the Worcestershire Rapids v Notts Outlaws semi-final, gave us one of the most bizarre finishes in the history of T20 cricket. Old coaches are wont to suggest this is another example of the power of "Mother Cricket", a strange force by which the game rewards those who respect it and punishes those who do not. More rational individuals view this contention as so much hokum, yet even they would agree that in the summer prior to the greatest change in the English domestic game for a generation, we have had a season so fine that no one outside the ECB sees any need for fundamental alteration.

The Vitality Blast has played its part in all this. T20 Finals Day is utterly unlike any other occasion in the sporting year. It is back-slapping, brightly-coloured, belching, beery, bugger-me-sideways England in all its unapologetic finery. Decorum? Don't even think about it. Subtlety? Not unless you are referring to Pat Brown's knuckle balls or Ravi Bopara's judgement of an innings. Some people will never warm to T20 cricket yet even they admit its financial importance and concede that it has refined and extended many skills. How many misfields do you recall from this year's Finals Day? How many dropped catches?

And it is even more important to recognise the Blast's value because it appears under challenge; because, so the argument goes, if the ECB can use the Hundred to kill The Blast it will foreshadow the introduction of a hierarchy of 10 or so first-class teams with the smaller counties permanently relegated or forced out of business altogether. Counties like Essex, who won the Blast and may well win the County Championship, the greatest prize of all; counties like Somerset, who won the Royal London One-Day Cup; counties like Northamptonshire and Gloucestershire, who are on the verge of promotion to Division One; counties like Derbyshire, who so relished their first Finals Day; counties like Leicestershire, who continue to nurture great talents like Hassan Azad and Harry Swindells.

Great God, this is poisonous stuff. And a simple press release from the ECB would be a most powerful antidote to it all.

For the moment, though, we still have Finals Day and even the sceptics should treasure it a little. Sir John Betjeman would have loved the whole ridiculous rigmarole. Even though he knew next to nothing about cricket, that fine poet always appreciated English people displaying all their daft exuberance; the lines of people in fancy dress doing some version of the conga would, I suspect, have brought forth howls of laughter from him. Though capable of serious poetry, he relished popular entertainment – *Coronation Street* in its golden years was a great favourite – and Edgbaston on the third Saturday in September is a proper knees-up.

And of course it's bloody daft. From the first chorus of the morning to the final spray of champagne it is gloriously unhinged. You cannot stage an obstacle race between 18 adult humans, most of them dressed in felt animal costumes, and hope that it will look anything but absolutely bonkers. You cannot celebrate the fall of every wicket by sending people hurtling into the air in a glass pod – it is called the Bungee Blast – and think you are presenting an image of maturity. You cannot hire Mr Motivator – ask your parents – to exhort 6,000 people in the Hollies Stand to exercise when most of the people he is encouraging have been drinking for England and many are dressed as bananas / Donald Trump / chickens / Roman Catholic priests, and still hope to look sensible. Someone might have suggested to the ECB that it is tricky to exercise when you cannot stand upright. But never mind, welcome to Birmingham's House of Fun.

It is also about the beauty of seeing a great city in its crepuscular light; the beauty of seeing Birmingham's great business houses disappear into the darkness until they are revealed only by tiny pinpricks of red. The English season should always end with the last day of the County Championship but there is a certain elegiac richness about this particular Saturday evening.

And so we are left with the cricketers. They must always have the final word. We are left with Worcestershire's Daryl Mitchell going over to his teammate, Wayne Parnell, when he has been hit for four off the penultimate ball of the Final. We are left with Simon Harmer returning to console Parnell when his blows off that bowler have secured the trophy for Essex. And we are left with Harmer telling the press that his team will celebrate their victory properly but will not "go nuclear". Many of the 24,550 folk at Edgbaston, on the other hand, have been going nuclear all day. The first beach-ball was confiscated at 11.24pm. Freddie the Falcon won the Mascots' Race.

9

BOOKISH

Ted Hughes referred to poets as a tribe and I sometimes feel the same way about cricket writers. We often disagree about the game but we share so much else, not least, quite frequently, four or five working days together in a press box. This chapter features seven authors and one photographer whose work I very much like. There are features on some writers and reviews of books by others. I suspect few will be surprised that there are three pieces about Alan Ross, to whose prose and poetry I return most frequently. My justification is that each of the three covers a different area of Alan's work, but this concentration should not overshadow reviews of some exceptional recent books. One of the delights of putting this chapter together was that it gave me a chance to return to Christian Ryan's extraordinary writing in Feeling is the Thing That Happens in 1000th of a Second.

I am quite aware there are many fine authors whose work I do not consider in this chapter. Likewise, there are many great sports writers who have written barely a word about cricket. The people listed here are not necessarily members of a first XI; I don't go in for that sort of exercise anyway. I might have favourites but such things are almost always provisional and I certainly have no time for idols. All the same, the authors in this chapter are bound together by those figures in white on green and a desire to make sense of what they are doing. They have all earned my gratitude.

Preserving A Style – Alan Ross

Hector: *"The best moments in reading are when you come across something – a thought, a feeling, a way of looking at things – which you had thought special and particular to you. Now here it is, set down by someone else, a person you have never met, someone even who is long dead. And it is as if a hand has come out and taken yours."*
— Alan Bennett, *The History Boys*

Above my hearth, three Eric Ravilious prints: "Train Landscape", "Beachy Head", "Leaving Scapa Flow". As ever with Ravilious, I am attracted by their sense of perspective and the way in which the paint almost disappears, leaving one only with the mystery and immediacy of place. All three link to travel too, and I like their outward-looking attitude, the idea that with a scrap of luck the next adventure is not far away. Yet these are not the only reasons the prints hold my gaze on winter evenings when westerly rain scuds against my windows. "Leaving Scapa Flow" was reproduced on the dust-jacket of *Blindfold Games*, Alan Ross's first volume of autobiography, and "Beachy Head" on the cover of his *Poems*, which was published posthumously in 2005. The latter print features both the Sussex Downs, where Ross lived for much of his life, and the sea, where he spent much of the Second World War. Each of the prints reconnects me, albeit momentarily, to a poet and writer who, as much as anyone should, has guided my own writing life. Yet I am wary of heroes and place no one on a pedestal. I regard surveys to discover the "best" artist, poet or whatever as slightly daft exercises which deprive appreciation of its necessary subjectivity. All the same, on the very many occasions when I am dissatisfied with something I have written, I return to Ross's poetry or prose and find there something both new and reassuring.

All summer, it seems, I have been writing about Lancashire's opening batsman, Haseeb Hameed. He fascinates me because in an age when the ability to hit the ball vast distances is prized and practised, Hameed's strength is his serene occupation of the crease. Willow-thin and 19 years old, he invests the forward-defensive shot with a fastidious beauty, but one of his very best strokes is when he plays no stroke at all, instead allowing the ball to go through to the wicket-keeper. Invariably he will immediately practise that leave-alone again, as if there is some height of perfection he has not yet reached. Like all opening batsmen, Hameed will take particular satisfaction in a bowler becoming exhausted and a new ball losing its hardness. Bowling fast is a tiring activity and every four minutes or so, one of an opener's principal opponents is nearer the end of his spell. The contrast between the expenditure of great effort by the bowler and, so it appears, almost none by the batsman is wonderfully sharp. I wonder how many ways cricket writers will need to express obduracy if, as I expect, Hameed enjoys a successful Test and county career. Yet it is not the number of runs he makes but that leave-alone non-shot that enthrals me. And then, as I was skimming through Ross's first volume of autobiography in preparation for writing this piece, I came across this: "Every good batsman had his own unmistakable way of going about things, even when letting the ball go outside the off stump, bat raised in a gesture of indifference or contempt, the line of the body as expressive in its way as that of a dancer."

Ross's gravestone in the churchyard of St John the Baptist, Clayton, the Sussex village where he lived for 25 years, could hardly be much simpler or more accurate: "Alan Ross: Writer, poet and editor 1922–2001". Let us deal with each of these roles in turn. Born in Calcutta, Ross wrote or edited more than 40 books. Less than half of them are about cricket, and even those contain such a variety of digressions that the categorisation is almost mocked. No writer has taken CLR James's famous question more to heart or attempted a fuller answer to it. "War, India, cricket: these were my first subjects as a writer and they remain the preoccupations of this book," he writes in the preface to *Blindfold Games*. "In due course, the playing of games was replaced by the writing about them, and it was to the belief that the best characteristics of each derive from the same source that I nailed my colours. The searching of 'suitable similes', in Marianne Moore's phrase... whether for Hammond's off-drive, Stanley Matthews' mesmeric dribbling, or a racehorse's action, was as good a way as I could imagine of relating techniques to aesthetics."

There were also ten books of poetry before that generous selection edited by David Hughes, although Ross revised his poems

Alan Ross (r) batting with Sir Len Hutton for the Authors XI.

County cricket at Sedbergh. Lancashire v Durham, 2019.

Glorious Arundel. Hampshire v Surrey, 2020.

A County Championship game between Lancashire and Derbyshire, Southport & Birkdale CC, 2015.

John Edrich signing autographs, 1964.

Lancashire's Luke Procter completes a hundred at Southport & Birkdale CC, 2016.

Worcestershire take on Somerset at Worcester, 2018.

quite regularly and some volumes replace others. Only nine poems are about cricket but in so much of his work there is a stunning precision as a life is captured in an image or one of those "suitable similes" he sought. For example, let us take the last stanza from "Night Porter", a late poem in the pamphlet *Tropical Ice*:

With a kind of regret for the old days,
The slavish stink of condensed milk
And seaboots, the steeplechasing cockroaches;
When, among cronies, he surveyed an empire
Slung between stars and a sliding ocean
As softly sustaining as a silken pavilion.

And now this from "A Cricketer in Retirement", a poem written for and about the former Sussex player, George Cox:

I come upon
A scorecard yellow as old flannels and suddenly
I see him, smilingly prowling the covers
In soft shoes, shirt rolled to the forearm,
Light as a yacht swaying at its moorings,
Receptive to breezes.

Perhaps Ross regarded his true vocation as poetry. After all, he described *Blindfold Games* as "an attempt… to trace the manner in which a single-minded devotion to sport developed into a passion for poetry". Moreover, one of the many joys of his four volumes of autobiography is that all the chapters are followed with selections of poems, as if Ross has found a single genre insufficient to express the variety of his experience. Just as it might be when one is watching a cricket match and the eye is caught by the curving flight of the ball, a moment of graceful fielding or a young batsman arching his back and letting the ball go.

Even if his prose and poetry were not read today, Ross's influence on cultural life would still be very great. As editor of *London Magazine* for 40 years until his death, he gave a whole host of writers their first entrance into the literary world. He also published photographs and drawings and gave extensive treatment to theatre and cinema.

"Alan was, quite simply, the best and most unsung supporter of young writers there was," writes Graham Swift in his marvellous essay, "Negronis with Alan". "Unsung because trumpet-blowing was never part of his style and he hated that appropriating aspect of publishing that likes to brag about 'discovering' talent." Those who suspect that Swift's view is untypical might do well to visit the Special Collections in the library of Leeds University, which houses both *London Magazine*'s archive and the manuscripts of *Blindfold Games* and *Coastwise Lights*. There they will find notes and letters encouraging hundreds of young writers as they wondered whether they might be better trying something else. "If *London Magazine* shuts down," wrote Anthony Powell, a writer from a very different generation to Swift, "nothing else whatever of that sort will ever take its place." Ross offered hope and offers it still: hope that an aesthetic sensibility might be just as useful to a sports writer as the ability to spit out statistics or "get quotes" from a cricketer who is at his most eloquent when he is playing sport.

There were, as Swift points out, "a range of possible Alans, only some of whom you might see". There was the Calcutta-born child who was sent to school in England, yet never lost his love for India. "Through those boarding-school years what was most loved and familiar was far away was oceans away," he writes, "though it was the brown hands that I craved, and not the alternately distant and crowding affection of parents." Ross was to write both a biography of Ranji and *The Emissary*, a study of the partnership between GD Birla and MK Gandhi in the struggle for Indian independence. They are the works of an author who, when he arrived at his first school in England, spoke Hindustani better than English and who continued to use words from that early childhood throughout his life. "There were always talismans relating to India about the house," recalled Alan's son, Jonathan. "It mattered to him very much." It seems deeply appropriate, then, that some of the early drafts of Ross's autobiography are written on headed notepaper from Indian hotels. There was a part of him which never left the country of his birth.

There was also Ross the racehorse owner, Ross the naval officer, Ross the sufferer from savage depressions, Ross the lover of women, Ross the travel writer. Each of these and many others can be detected in the range of reference and sympathy employed in what are, ostensibly, cricket books, but which are like few others in that vast genre. The most famous of these is *Australia 55*, which is quite as concerned with the country visited as the Tests played on that famous tour. Indeed, Ross makes his intentions clear in the first chapter: "I am as much interested in Australia as I am in cricket (it would indeed be a dull fellow who was not) and I intend to digress as least as often as I stick to the main theme." John Woodcock regards *Australia 55* as the best cricket book ever written, yet quite as interesting in its way, albeit less lauded, is Ross's study of the famous 1963 Test, *West Indies at Lord's*, which was drawn with England needing six runs to win, West Indies one wicket shy of victory and Colin Cowdrey, his broken arm in plaster, at the non-striker's end. Ross's account of the first day's play begins with cricket at the periphery:

"Driving to Lord's from my flat in Knightsbridge, I took it easy. The sky, devoid of blue, had that grey blotting-paper texture that usually worsens rather than improves. At the Serpentine the first specks of rain pitted the placid surface unskimmed by boat and untrod by human: two figures in bathing costumes lay on the water's edge, pale as corpses and as eccentric as nudists. They looked due for arrest after such perverse exhibitionism. Deprived of light, the green foliage of Hyde Park hung dank and gloomy. It was hunting weather, not the summery high noon of the cricket season. At least, one quietly gloated, some of those Ascot hats would get their desserts; now one merely cursed their yapping owners for blocking the way to Lord's with their beige Bentleys and hearse-like Silver Clouds."

Is this a spy thriller? Or might it be a novel about a love affair, with Lord's as one of its settings? It could be either. Even better is to come when Ross describes Fred Trueman's bowling in the first innings of the game: "He had taken five wickets for 64 runs in 32 overs, demonstrating afresh that in fast bowling, as in love-making, control brings greater rewards than youthful impetuosity." Whatever it is, it is not EW Swanton.

I first wrote about Alan Ross in the winter of 2012. Since then I have read some of the *London Magazine*'s archive and I have pored over the manuscripts of *Blindfold Games* and *Coastwise Lights*. On a perfect Monday morning in June I have walked the path from Hassocks station to Clayton and stood on the village cricket ground where Ross, himself a very fine bowler in his youth, once batted, with Daisy, his beloved bearded collie, "taking up a position at square leg, from which she declined to be moved." I have tramped the Downs and felt a quite unexpected closeness to Sussex, which is merely the county of my birth, not one of the places in which I grew up. "The landscape flows and brakes, chalk-slashed, tree-shadowed, its lanes dusty, partings in squares of corn. Sheep graze on the foothills, where barns, once thatched, now tiled, catch the westering sun."

And I have visited Alan's son, Jonathan, at his lovely gallery in Earl's Court Road – the taste is clearly inherited – and drunk coffee in a mug featuring a design by Eric Ravilious. Laid out on the table were Ross's early cuttings books in which were pasted his first football reports and I read of the "smoky sunlight" on a winter's afternoon in Birmingham. There were photographs, too, one of them featuring Ross going out to bat with Sir Leonard Hutton, whose tour he described and about whom he wrote a wonderful poem. And I have returned to Hove, where Alan watched countless Sussex matches. "A raffish club always, in keeping with Regency Brighton, often in the dumps, but sometimes a shooting star. I suffered and rejoiced with them as over nothing else from the earliest of days."

It has all been very wonderful and rather dangerous. In a famous letter to his daughter, Frances, F Scott Fitzgerald wrote: "A good style simply doesn't *form* unless you read half a dozen top-flight authors every year. Or rather it forms but instead of being a subconscious amalgam of all that you have admired, it is simply a reflection of the last writer you have read, a watered-down journalese." It is one of those comments that should be pinned up above any writer's desk.

Perhaps we should end where all this began. That would be in the living-room of our family home in the Manchester suburb of Burnage. England's fortunes varied in the 1970s: there was the athletic invention of Alan Knott's batting, the grizzled experience of Ray Illingworth's off spin and the mercurial talent of John Snow, a fast bowler who helped win an Ashes series yet who seemed at the mercy of a brooding temperament. In the winter of 1974–75 England's batsmen were pitched against the Australian pair, Dennis Lillee and Jeff Thomson. It was barely a contest at times. Every evening brought brightly-coloured half-hour highlights packages:

Thomson, his run-up more a languid lope until the delivery stride and the slung missile; Lillee, his sprint to the wicket a furious declaration of implacable intent and his craft obvious, even to the untutored eye.

On the record player is an LP, *Cricket: The Sovran King of Sports*. And here is Valentine Dyall's Oxford-marmalade voice speaking the opening lines of Ross's poem, "JM Parks at Tunbridge Wells".

> *"Parks takes ten off two successive balls from Wright,*
> *A cut to the rhododendrons and a hook for six.*
> *And memory begins suddenly to play its tricks:*
> *I see his father batting, as, if here, he might.*

Our best teachers do not always work in classrooms. Their lessons are gentle and barely understood. There is merely a moment of recognition, a rough awareness of magic.

The Nightwatchman No15 – Autumn 2015

Alan and his Friends

The words on Alan Ross' gravestone could hardly be simpler: "Writer, poet and editor." They could scarcely be more accurate either. Alan is buried in the churchyard in Clayton, the Sussex village where he lived for 25 years and where he knew great happiness. That happiness was particularly precious to a man who also experienced the fathomless miseries of depression. In *Coastwise Lights*, his second volume of autobiography, Alan writes: "Our house, which in its day had been successively Roman villa, farm and, more recently, rectory, looked westwards through an orchard, past Clayton church and farm, towards the great hump of Wolstonebury, whose slopes were rusted with beech woods. Sheer to the south the sky was bisected by the line of the Downs, crowding in and falling away as far as the eye could see."

Chelsea was another of Alan's haunts and his life in literary London also features prominently in the book; he lived in an Elm

Park Gardens flat immediately after the war and died in a cottage in Elm Park Lane in 2001. This metropolitan base was essential for work: Alan was the editor of *London Magazine* for 40 years, during which time he offered encouragement and hope to very many aspiring writers who wondered doubtfully whether a literary life was for them. Such blessings are still available to those who read his four volumes of autobiography or his other prose about travel, cricket and India. Poetry, though, lies at the heart of all his work.

Coastwise Lights begins roughly where *Blindfold Games*, Alan's first volume of autobiography, ends. Having recently left the navy, we find him in the post-war world attempting to make a living by writing. Yet even more than its predecessor, the second book tries to marry a broad linear narrative with a detailed account of episodes which encapsulated Alan's passions and style of life. This impressionism is even more pronounced in his next two volumes of autobiography, *After Pusan* and *Winter Sea*. The first begins with a 30-page memoir of Alan's visit to the South Korean coastal city along with a consideration of the late 19th-century explorer Isabella Bird; it ends with 80 pages of poetry, the first Alan had written following prolonged depression. *Winter Sea* is subtitled 'War, Journeys, Writers' and is dominated by Alan's return to the Baltic, a sea where he had nearly died some 50 years previously. As always, there is poetry; as always, there is an insightful reading of somewhat neglected literary figures: the Norwegian writer Nordahl Grieg and the Estonian poet Jaan Kaplinski. These last two books are also briefer than either *Blindfold Games* or *Coastwise Lights*; perhaps they should properly be categorised as memoirs. But one is never surprised to find Alan stretching a genre, the better to reflect his experience, the better to accommodate the subtle rhythms of his prose.

These characteristics are abundantly displayed in the opening section of *Coastwise Lights*. We find Alan and the painter John Minton in Montparnasse, where they are staying in a cheap hotel en route to Corsica, the subject of their travel book, *Time Was Away*. Already two of the autobiography's themes, travel and art, have been introduced. The title of the Corsican book is taken from Louis MacNeice's famous poem but *Coastwise Lights* is also interspersed with groups of poems used, as Alan writes in the preface, "as illustrations and to fill in a few gaps".

Readers expecting to learn much about Alan's adult family life might be disappointed by all four volumes of his autobiography. They will be told relatively little about girlfriends, wives, children. Family members are glimpsed in passing before their presence is quickly woven into broader developments. This is not to say that personal relationships are omitted from *Coastwise Lights*. On the contrary, the book's richest theme is that of friendships, whether formed with painters like Keith Vaughan or authors such as Henry Green or William Plomer. Often one is sent back to writers one had heard of but did not really know. Like so many of Alan's books, *Coastwise Lights* can be an expensive purchase, not because it costs very much but because it leads one to curiously neglected authors from the second half of the last century. For if a critic as tough and sensitive as Alan liked a writer, they must have something. Alan's appreciation of writers like William Sansom or Bernard Gutteridge is warm but his assessment is unsweetened by fondness. Take, for example, this on Sansom:

"On his bad days he could be taken for a bookmaker drowning his sorrows. There was an Edwardian courtliness to Bill's sober manner – and he was usually sober three weeks out of four – a bowing to ladies and a kissing of hands. He took to wearing a musky, extremely pervasive scent, which gave him a sweet, bear-like aroma. He tended to brush his rather fine hair straight back, not quite *en brosse*, but in the manner of an Italian tenor like Tino Rossi. I never saw it remotely ruffled, not even when he had fallen over."

Much of *Coastwise Lights* is devoted to descriptions of foreign travel. Alan himself was born in Calcutta and his love of Sussex, where he was sent to school, was fostered partly by his need for an English *Heimat* and partly by his lifelong love of cricket. Yet he lost neither the urge to wander nor the desire to return to the South Downs. Kipling's lines, "Swift shuttles of an Empire's loom that weave us main to main / The Coastwise Lights of England give you welcome back again" supply much more than a title for the book. They capture its essence. Thus we begin with Alan in Montparnasse, looking out through the ventilation panel in the *toilette* of his cheap room and watching a domestic drama taking place in the apartment a few feet away. It is the sweltering summer of 1947 and all three participants he observes are naked. What Ross finds intriguing is the incongruity of the trio's behaviour; what the reader notices is the acuity of observation, the curiosity of the born writer. Other foreign trips are slightly more conventional but no less sharply realised. For four years Ross works for the British Council and accompanies its Controller of Education on a trip to Baghdad. On the flight from Rome to the Middle East he sits next to Agatha Christie. Eventually it is arranged that he will go on a shooting trip to the marsh country near Basra where he will enjoy the hospitality of the local sheikhs in their *mudhifs* on the banks of lagoons. He visits a now-vanished world made famous by Wilfred Thesiger and Gavin Maxwell. "The few days I spent in the marshes were a kind of dream, coloured the green of reeds, the blondness of corn, the gunmetal shimmer of water, the pale bronze of sky." There are echoes of Edward Thomas here. The prose, as Ross recognises, is often raw material for poems which are, to a degree, a different distillation of experience.

The trip to Iraq was Ross's first and last foreign adventure with the Council. Three years later he obeyed his obvious vocation and became a part-time freelance journalist. He had already published poetry, made translations, and written essays on American authors, but the writing life was now the whole commitment and it remains a dominant theme of *Coastwise Lights*. While becoming well connected in the literary world – Harold Nicolson and Cyril Connolly were friends – he also expressed a then unconventional desire to write about sport. Before long he was filing football reports for *The Observer* and in 1953 he became the paper's cricket correspondent, a post he occupied for 18 years.

Cricket writing is a niche activity. For every book that transcends the genre there are 10 which remain clotted by statistics and routine match reports. What Alan succeeds in doing is taking moments on the cricket field and suggesting their relationship to other arts and different skills. One of his aims, as he wrote elsewhere, was to "preserve a style, restore an action, rehearse an elegance". The result is some of the finest cricket books we have and a body of other work in which style is bound to content. Cricket may sometimes seem a little distant but poetry is never far away. I am sure Alan would be happy with this. *Blindfold Games* is, he writes, "an attempt to reconcile differing definitions of style and to trace the manner in which a single-minded devotion to sport developed into a passion for poetry". *Coastwise Lights* continues that journey as the writer grows more confident in his gifts.

In 1961 Alan took over the *London Magazine* and changed more or less everything about it. The definite article was ditched, as was the dull cover. Under Alan's editorship coverage was extended to art, cinema, architecture and music. The magazine's archive, which is housed in Leeds University's Brotherton Library, contains hundreds of letters in which young writers ask Alan to consider their poems or short stories. The swiftness of the response was legendary and further correspondence is often filled with grateful appreciation of Alan's encouragement or acceptance. The same library also contains the manuscripts of *Blindfold Games* and *Coastwise Lights*, many of the chapters written in the author's graceful hand on stationery liberated from distant hotels. One section of *Coastwise Lights* concerns Alan's involvement with *London Magazine* from the editor's perspective and chronicles the wide-ranging expansion into publishing which brought the work of Barbara Skelton, Julian Maclaren-Ross and Tony Harrison to a wider audience. "Publishing has always been for me an amateur activity in the strictest sense of the word," he writes, "it was never my livelihood, nor have I ever earned a penny out of it. But, since it was a labour of love, there was all the more reason for it to be done to the highest professional standards."

Coastwise Lights concludes with a section about horse-racing, another of Alan's passions and one facilitated in Clayton by the proximity of the small courses he loved. And so this book ends in Sussex with a description of village life and one of the finest final paragraphs in English prose. When serving on the deadly Baltic convoys in the Second World War, Alan had been sustained by the possibility of somehow returning to the county in which he eventually lives. The more remote that possibility seemed, the more vital it became to hold on to it. Earlier in *Coastwise Lights,* Alan describes his move to Clayton: "During my sea-time I used to dream of Sussex; not so much a specific Sussex as a generalised romantic image conjured out of memory and hope. Sussex cricket played a large part in it, to the extent that I had only to see the word Sussex written down, in whatever context, for a shiver to run down my spine. Such an association might properly belong to adolescence, but it has survived. Now the dream was reality and for the next 25 years Sussex was my home, London a mere work-place."

Unlike the writers whose work he published, Alan is not in want of champions. For some cricket writers he is an example to which they might, on their best days, aspire. For writers of any sort, he manages, albeit after death, to offer something of the same encouragement he did when he ran *London Magazine*. Very recently, Gideon Haigh wrote this about Alan's cricket writing: "His work stands the test, I think, precisely because of the delight Ross took in his task, of crafting prose up to the standards of the players he was watching – a writer's writer, but of his subjects like an alert and observant partner."

And then there is another writer. He has spent days in the Brotherton Library; he has wandered around Chelsea on murky autumnal evenings; and he has tramped the Downs around Clayton on summer afternoons when "the landscape flows and brakes, chalk-slashed, tree-shadowed, its lanes dusty, partings in squares of corn". He has done these things neither because Alan needs a biographer nor because he is, at least in part, a cricket writer. He has done them because he is fascinated with the mysterious process whereby one of his closest relationships has been formed with someone he never met; and because it is almost always *Alan* and hardly ever *Ross*.

First published in Slightly Foxed No66 – Autumn 2020

Alan Ross – Finding His Voices

Between my finger and my thumb
The squat pen rests.
I'll dig with it.
Seamus Heaney, "*Digging*"

When Alan Ross died on St Valentine's Day 2001, his friends and obituarists agreed that something irreplaceable had disappeared from British literary life. Writing in the *Independent*, Philip Hensher called Ross "the last of the bohemians", thus acknowledging a style that only the foolish sought to imitate. But Hensher and many others knew the matter went far deeper than that. *London Magazine*, which Ross edited for the last 40 years of his life, offered an eclectic mix of cultural life that no other English publication could match. Even more vitally, it gave greater opportunities to young writers, or older, often unpublished ones, who thought their time had passed. Financial pressure played no discernible part in this policy; rather it was Ross's belief that those who had made it (whatever "it" might be) could look after themselves. "I think writers who are on the way up, or on the way down for that matter, are much more interesting than those who are already there," he told the *Independent*'s Sabine Durrant in 1993.

The archive of *London Magazine*, which is stored in the Brotherton Library in Leeds, is a chronicle of hope, acceptance and gratitude. There are notes from now successful writers when they were on their uppers and letters from famous names when they were getting rejection slips rather than meaty cheques. For many of them Ross was an encouraging saviour, more generous with praise than fees, maybe – *London Magazine* was never flooded with cash – but generous and welcoming all the same. And the editor's own reputation was secure: *Australia 55* regularly appears in lists of the finest cricket books and his first two volumes of autobiography, *Blindfold Games* (1986) and *Coastwise Lights* (1988), are rightly judged classics of the genre. (Only his poetry, which was always the writing that mattered most to him, is under-appreciated.)

It is easy to see why Ross's writing was immediately admired and also why it continues to attract champions. In an era when tour books often consisted of little more than profoundly dull reports on matches, he was as interested in the countries he visited as the cricket that was played. Yet his accounts of the cricket reveal both a lyricism and a perception that was far beyond most of his colleagues. Take, for example, this passage from *Australia 55* on Tom Graveney:

> *A player of yacht-like character, beautiful in calm seas yet at the mercy of every change of weather. There are no obvious faults in construction but the barometer has only to fall away a point or two from fair for way to be completely lost and the boat broached to, if not turned for harbour.*

But autobiographies, however brilliant, are exercises in selection and their authors do not always make the best choices. Equally one can see that delicacy and reticence are often at work. Reviewers of *Coastwise Lights* noted that Ross's own relationships and his first marriage are barely mentioned. Unnamed girlfriends are gone in a parenthesis and no one who treasures the sanctity of their own personal relations should object to that. Instead, Ross offers rich chronicles of his varied life, aesthetic development, abiding interests, friendships. "Writing this book has been an attempt to reconcile different definitions of style and to trace the manner in which a single-minded devotion to sport developed into a passion for poetry," he wrote in the preface to *Blindfold Games*. "It was about coming to terms with war and a hunger for writing replacing a passion for cricket," he added later in *Coastwise Lights*.

Yet that love of cricket in general, and Sussex cricket in particular, never faded. In the early 1950s he was hired by the *Observer* to write about football and was soon writing about cricket as well. None of those early reports have been reprinted in hard covers; Ross's first book on the game was *Australia 55*. I therefore thought that anyone wanting to read his earliest copy would have to use the excellent newspaper libraries, although even then it would be difficult to track down the other work Ross was producing at roughly the same time, often for long-defunct papers and periodicals. The justification for such a quest was provided by a characteristic passage in the preface to *Blindfold Games*:

> *In due course, the playing of games was replaced by the writing about them, and it was to the belief that the best characteristics of each derive from the same source that I nailed my colours. The searching of "suitable similes", in Marianne Moore's phrase... whether for Hammond's off-drive, Stanley Matthews' mesmeric dribbling, or a racehorse's action, was as good a way as I could imagine of relating techniques to aesthetics.*

For my part, I also wanted to see what Ross was producing when he was around the age of some of the writers he himself later encouraged as editor of *London Magazine*. I still feel that if you don't consider his other work, your understanding of his cricket writing will be incomplete. But I couldn't examine the development of the relationship between the various genres until I was shown the four mighty books that have lain on tables in my flat these past months, unlocking lockdown and returning me to a post-war England where a different austerity prevailed. Let me explain.

* * *

In the summer of 1947 Alan Ross was a poet uncertain of his future in a country unsure of itself. The necessity of defeating fascism had been plain and worth every sacrifice. But now that was accomplished the loans had to be repaid and Britain had to bear the other obligations of victory. A nation exhausted first by war and then by rejoicing faced the complexities of peace. The 25-year-old Ross had just left the Royal Navy after five years' service in which death had twice hit his stumps but not removed the bails. Such experiences and others at sea would colour his metaphors and plague his dreams. During the war his first poems had been published by John Lehmann in *Penguin New Writing* and it was in Lehmann's flat that he first met established writers such as Louis MacNeice and Henry Green. Very pleasant, of course, hopeful even, but the pervasive uncertainty is captured perfectly in *Coastwise Lights*:

> *Before retiring my uniform I had presented myself at an officers' rehabilitation board, the function of which was to find suitable jobs for officers or suitable officers for jobs. They noted down my places of education, my naval duties, and such qualifications as I had, which were not many. The lack of a degree was unfortunate, they said, though of course many others had suffered similar interruption to their university careers. Had I thought of going back to Oxford and completing my course? Yes, I had thought of it but I had been away five years now and I wanted to get on. I had also hoped to play county cricket for a year or two, but now that chance had gone as well. If I had managed to get out of Germany six months earlier both might have been possible.*

They were sympathetic and said they would get in
touch. They never did.

Other developments may have encouraged the young writer. A few months before that careers interview in 1947, Lehmann had published *The Derelict Day*, Ross's first volume of poems. On the strength of that and a few book reviews, mainly in *Tribune* and the *Spectator*, he received an Atlantic Award of £500 from The Rockefeller Foundation. That sum would be worth close to £20,000 today and, as its recipient pointed out, "it seemed a fortune at the time". He was also getting to know painters and other poets, so perhaps it was not too surprising that Lehmann should suggest that Ross and the artist, John Minton, could do a travel book together. All the same, the notion he would eventually edit a magazine or earn much of his living writing about sport would have seemed as remote as space flight. Indeed, in *Blindfold Games* there is an air of farewell in the mentions of post-war cricket:

> *Very courteously, on the recommendation of Bert*
> *Wensley [Sussex all-rounder 1922-36 and the cricket pro*
> *at Haileybury, Ross's old school], the Sussex secretary*
> *offered me some games at the end of the 1946 season,*
> *but I could not, when the time came, get leave. I had*
> *taken part in one or two matches on the county ground*
> *at Hove… but it was a makeshift place and not the*
> *sacred arena of memory… The Sussex cricket that had*
> *sustained my adolescence and war, and since bred such*
> *durable images – Tate swinging the ball in a typical*
> *Hove sea-fret, James Langridge leaning a half-volley into*
> *the rugs of the Colonel's ladies – would have to wait for*
> *the time being, if not for ever.*

Now slow-forward some 70 years to my arrival at Gallery 286 in Earl's Court Road, the home of Jonathan Ross, Alan's son. Laid out on the table in the front room are three very large green books into which Alan pasted many of his articles and photographs.

The earliest cutting, a review of Ernest Hemingway's *Across the River and into the Trees*, was published in the weekly magazine,

Time and Tide, in September 1950. The last, a yellowing piece tipped into the third book, is from October 1962 and notes the fact that Ted Dexter's MCC tourists would play only six first-class games in Australia before the opening Test of the five-match series. But it is not the barely recognisable pattern of Ashes tours that holds my attention this summer morning. Rather it is the gradual development of Ross's career from a freelance journalist who was also working for the British Council to an established figure in sports writing and literary life. He is at ease covering an Ashes Test as he is reviewing WH Auden's poetry. In 1953 he succeeded RC Robertson-Glasgow as cricket correspondent of the *Observer* and in April 1961 he became editor of *London Magazine*. In another of the last cuttings, Ross's appointment at *LM* was noted with dry relish by his chief employer:

> *We are glad to see that our cricket correspondent has become editor of the* London Magazine. *Since the days of the Georgian poets (and they were a bit waggish about it) it's become unmodish to think that sport and literary concerns have anything in common.*
> *But Alan Ross (very good minor poet; medium-pace bowler, stylish bat) has managed to integrate both without any sign of split-mindedness. His poem about Stanley Matthews ("Now gathers speed, nursing the ball as he cruises…") is also nice soccer reporting. Numerous publications, chiefly poetry, travel and cricket. Naval service in the war. Oxford Blues for cricket and squash. Bearded, looks like a New Testament personality. Talks enthusiastically about the arts, cricket, horse-racing, cars.*

So much, so marvellous. I left Jonathan's gallery with plenty of material for the piece that appeared in *Nightwatchman 15* and the certainty that those green books needed lengthier examination. (And please do not think of them as scrapbooks; they are heavy ledgers of the sort Bob Cratchit might have written in with his battered quill.)

But I was also wondering about the period immediately prior to September 1950, the years in which Ross sought to make a writing life for himself. Then last November – why did I wait so long? – I visited Jane Ross, Alan's widow, at her home near Petersfield. Jane had a red book of cuttings ready for me, an even mightier affair than the three green ones I had seen at Jonathan's. It was bought from W Straker Ltd., a stationer whose main shop was on Ludgate Hill, and it still has the thick grey ribbons with which it can be securely tied shut. The first cutting is a poem, "Night on the Este", snipped from the November 8, 1945 issue of the *Listener*. Taken together with the other cuttings and the many books Ross wrote in those increasingly productive post-war decades, the ledger allows us to chronicle his creative development. And we can begin to see where cricket fits in to that rough narrative.

The first cricket report in the red book – and therefore perhaps the first piece Ross wrote about the game – appeared in the *Observer* on 14 May, 1950. It is, in truth, unremarkable copy, the sort written by a young reporter feeling his way in a new world. Ross comments that despite Harold Gimblett's 61, Somerset had tossed away the opportunity to bat first on a perfect wicket at Lord's. That is prescient, for Middlesex would gain a 211-run first-innings lead and win the match by eight wickets, their victory eased by Denis Compton's 144 on the Monday of the game. But at this stage of his career, Ross only reported on the Saturdays of matches for the *Observer*. If you had told him he would, in time, play cricket with Compton, whom he described as "that most charming of creatures", he might have suggested you took a little water with your Lagavulin.

Other cricket pieces followed in the same month. They are sandwiched between book reviews and long articles on both Charing Cross Road and English poetry. But some indication that a poet is now covering the County Championship can first be seen in the last paragraph of Ross's piece on the opening day of Middlesex's game against Kent at Lord's in early June:

> *A few minutes later Ridgway went off with sunstroke and with his first ball Wright completely beat Robertson. Sharp was similarly beaten at 69 after a very streaky innings but Edrich was there to guide the ball safely away from a wicket growing dusty, into the quietude of the longer shadows.*

A week later Ross was at Horsham for the game against Essex. Perhaps it was his beloved Sussex that inspired him. Anyway, here is his intro:

> *Horsham Cricket Week. Hot sun, deck chairs all round*
> *the boundary, marquees and flags and the trains*
> *moving through the trees past the river and away*
> *under the hills beyond the church. A far cry from the*
> *industrial dramas of the Test Match at Old Trafford,*
> *perhaps, but perfect enough in its way.*

Later in June he is watching Sussex play Oxford University at Chichester:

> *Sussex cricket grounds, and Chichester with its priory*
> *on the boundary edge is not the least beautiful, seem to*
> *invite stroke play. The aesthetics of their surroundings*
> *demand it. Yet since the war Sussex batsmen, perhaps*
> *aware of their bowling deficiencies, have grown*
> *increasingly firm-footed and strokeless.*

Less than two months after that game Ross would see his first cricket poem in print. It appeared in the *New Statesman and Nation* on 4 August, 1950 although, as usual for a poet who regularly revised his work, four words were changed before the poem appeared in books. Here are the last two stanzas of that first version of "Cricket at Brighton":

> *Sussex v Lancashire, the air birded and fresh after rain,*
> *Tears on syringa and cherry. Seaward the water*
> *Is satin, pale emerald, fretted with lace at the edges,*
> *The whole sky rinsed easy like nerves after pain.*
> *May here is childhood, lost somewhere between and never*
> *Recovered, but again moved nearer, as a lever*
> *Turned on the pier flickers the Past into pictures.*
> *A time of immediacy, optimism without stricture.*

Post-cards and bathing machines and old prints.
Something comes back, the inkling and momentary hint
Of what we had wanted to be, though differently now,
For the conditions are different and what we had wanted
We wanted as we were then, without conscience, unhaunted,
And given the chance must refuse to want it again.
Only, occasionally, we escape, we return to where we were:
Watching cricket at Brighton, Cornford bowling through sea-
   scented air.

One of the last pieces in the red book is a long piece for the magazine, *Contact*, about a boat trip down the Thames to Southend-on-Sea. The poet for whom the cricket at Hove was both incidental and essential is never far away:

The river widened. A heat haze hung over the coastline, but behind it a built-up façade of white houses was separated from the sand by a filling of green trees. Leigh; Westcliff-on-Sea; avenues of gentility sloping uneasily to Southend where the mile-long pier stretched out to reach the nosing pleasure trips.

The red book ends with a tiny cutting from *Radio Times* noting that Ross will be giving a talk on the poetry of Robert Lowell on the BBC Third Programme in September 1950. The first green one begins with book reviews and a wonderful piece on Tottenham Hotspur and their former ground at White Hart Lane. Then a football report from Fulham:

> *A snow-covered ground, with an aluminium sun*
> *shining on it through bare trees across the river, gave*
> *yesterday's match at Craven Cottage something of the*
> *quality of a painting by Breughel. Manchester United,*
> *on the frail edge of those who enter the second half of*
> *the season with championship possibilities, tenaciously*
> *clung to them after being two goals down at the*
> *interval.*

By 1951 Ross was becoming established as a freelance journalist with books behind him and many more to follow. Moreover he was clear about at least one of his objectives. "I wanted now to try to write poems in which football and cricket were seen in their social context," he wrote in *Coastwise Lights*. "I had visions of a poetry that would be classless, and at the same time accessible to people who had never cared for poetry or even considered it as something worth their attention."

A decade later he became editor of *London Magazine*.

September 30, 2020: Jonathan has agreed to lend me his father's cuttings books and other papers and he is helping me load three very heavy boxes onto a trolley. I totter down Earl's Court Road to the mercifully convenient parcel shop. As I negotiate crossing the road someone asks me if I am leaving home. Quite soon the very helpful assistant in the shop is putting the boxes into yet larger containers and I am filling in the various forms needed to ensure their safe arrival in Southport. Suddenly the girl looks up from behind her desk: "What is the value of these parcels, please?"

Paul Edwards would like to thank Jonathan and Jane Ross for their exceptional kindness and for their generosity in lending him Alan's cuttings books and other papers.

The Nighwatchman No33 – Spring 2021

Such Stuff As Dreams Are Made On

David Foot and Alan Gibson

The white wooden desks in the old press box at Taunton could hardly be described as custom-built. Unless one was sitting on the front row they barely allowed room for anything more than a notebook, so when laptops were introduced space became even more cramped. Each desk – they might be called "workstations" now – had at its front a curious wooden frame, above or around which one peered at the cricket. At the back of the room an old tea urn grumbled through a day's play like a church caretaker doing unpaid overtime; and in a white plastic box there were tea bags that might have interested the experts on *Antiques Roadshow*. I often wondered where Somerset acquired these media facilities; I like to think they came in a job lot that included the cinema seats above the Stragglers' Bar at the Pavilion End. It was, you might suppose, no wonder that some of us climbed the narrow ladder the roof and joined the radio chaps who, when the wind was rude, broadcast to the nation from a box little bigger than a coal shed. "Mind your head, boy!" cautioned a sign at the top of the ladder.

But none of these things mattered in the first decade of this century when I paid my first professional visit to Taunton. For one thing, I was working at a great cricket ground and in a town where people care about the game very much indeed. For another, I was writing in the room once occupied by Alan Gibson and David Foot. And now, along with recollections of eccentricity and momentary discomfort, other memories tumble out, dearer to me than cedars of Lebanon.

Ever since adolescence, Gibson and Foot had been important in my life. I marvelled at the ease with which Gibson commentated on cricket in the great era of *Test Match Special*, his erudite references woven smoothly into a description of play. And then, like many generations of undergraduates, I waited eagerly to read his match reports in *The Times* and wondered whether the cricket would receive more space than his travels and travails on the railway. On one glorious occasion in April 1976, Somerset's match against Hampshire came a distant second to his domestic life:

> *It was a relief for me to get to the cricket, even though it was not very comfortable there, because once more a bitter wind belied the sunshine. During the night our small cat, Crumbs, had given birth to kittens. She took her time about gestation and delivery. I had rung up friends in the Natural History unit of the BBC, seeking expert advice, but none of those highly-informed and highly-paid persons knew about small cats. The mating habits of Mexican spiders, yes; the battle-pattern of heated scorpions, yes; how to distinguish the song of a good thrush from a bad nightingale, yes; but domestic cats, er...*

*Well, at last Crumbs produced her kittens. They had
taken so long to get out that we had already decided
to call the first one Trevor and the second one Bailey.
I invite suggestions for the name of the third, and any
further kittens that may have arrived in my absence.*

Yes, we have read 158 words and all we have discovered about
the match is that the sun shone through a cold wind. Perhaps I
should at once counsel any current colleagues thinking of copying
Gibson's style to consider whether they are cut out for life on the
streets. These are different times and sports desks are somewhat less
tolerant of digressions, let alone whole paragraphs about pregnant
cats. All the same, there is an awareness in the best of such pieces
that writing as though cricket was the context for the rest of life is
as valid as focusing so closely on the game that other material is no
more than a speck of colour.

Something very similar informs Foot's work, although it is most
gloriously revealed in his books, particularly his biographies of
Harold Gimblett and Wally Hammond and his two collections of
portraits, *Beyond Bat and Ball* and *Fragments of Idolatry*. However,
like Gibson, Foot was very much a professional journalist whose
match reports for the *Guardian* were cameos, rich in sympathy and
insight. And when a big story was breaking and a deadline reared up
in the death of afternoon, Foot always met the challenge. In his fine
book *This Sporting Life: Cricket*, Rob Steen reports that on the June
day in 1994 when Brian Lara made 501 not out for Warwickshire
against Durham, Foot "was the only reporter at Edgbaston not to have
his knickers twisted when the computer systems went down: he had
filed two 900-word pieces before many of the others had transmitted
a word". Such skills had been learned on local newspapers in the
West Country in the years after the Second World War. That distant
age is lovingly recalled in Foot's autobiographical novel, *Country
Reporter*, which was published in 1990: "Every big town and city
had two evening papers," he wrote in the author's note before the
novel. "The reporters beat each other to the nearest phone box, and
then shared a convivial pint. I'm sure journalism was more fun."

Perhaps so, but around 2007 I could imagine nothing better
than watching Championship cricket at Taunton where the WiFi

was unreliable, the welcome was warm and the carvery lunches challenged the timorous. Yet by the time I was making almost annual visits to the ground, there was obviously no chance of meeting either of the two writers I associate most closely with the West Country. Gibson, his last years racked by alcoholism, insecurity and ill health, had died in 1997 and Foot was living with his wife Anne in serene retirement in Westbury-on-Trym. *Sixty Summers: Somerset Cricket Since the War* had seemed a lovely farewell from a man nearing his 80th birthday. And in any case I was far too amazed by the notion that I might also make something like a regular living out of reporting county cricket to worry about something that couldn't be changed...

"Paul, I'd be delighted to have a cider with you in the Stragglers' but I'm *horrified* that you have spent your money on my books." The voice is gentle, self-effacing, its tone friendly, a trifle hesitant. There is no sense of false anguish. You believe the speaker really is concerned you might have wasted your dosh. I am standing on a platform at Crewe station waiting for my connection to Taunton. It is late September 2008 and I have just checked whether my landline has received any calls. In truth I had telephoned David Foot on a mad whim, not knowing even whether he was at home, much less whether he planned to watch Somerset's final Championship game of the season. I listen to the message, put my mobile away and nearly miss my train.

David insists on buying the drinks. Rather than wait to be asked about his own writing, he enquires after mine, but the questions are practical, born of immense kindness and informed by the hard-won understanding that if a journalist can't pay his bills, he won't be around for long. "Have you got enough work? Who are you covering this for?" Eventually he talks about the Somerset cricketers he had watched in the immediate post-war era. Included in that group is Horace Hazell, a tubby slow left-armer with whom I have a growing fascination. David had written a fond essay about Hazell in *Fragments of Idolatry* and, as ever, it was intimate, accurate and sympathetic, the sort of piece a writer could manage only if he had known his subject and been trusted by him. He dwells on the spinner's greatest asset, his accuracy:

It sounds soulless and mechanical. So it probably was
for the non-partisan. But the nuances were reserved
for his teammates, as he talked incessantly in a voice
nurtured on the pastoral, Somerset side of Bristol and
which seemed to become more Quantoxhead or Creech
St Michael as the years went by. The West Country's
stonewallers were rarely bores, as CCC "Box" Case and
Alf Dipper proved. Nor were the slow bowlers who waited
for a batsman to lose patience. Once at Taunton in 1949,
against Gloucestershire, Hazell sent down 105 balls,
more than 17 maidens, without conceding a run. The
opposition included at least one renowned stroke-maker
in Tom Graveney. "Just couldn't get him away, don't ask
me why," the England batsman would later reflect.

As things turned out, I met David on two more occasions, at Taunton
in 2011 and then at the Cheltenham Festival a few years later. Indeed,
while I have dwelt upon the connections between these writers and
Somerset cricket, I am aware that this piece could have considered
their fealty to the game in Gloucestershire. Moreover, there could be
an essay about the pair of them which does not mention cricket at
all but instead examines their respective hinterlands. Alan Gibson,
after all, broadcast on a wide variety of subjects for BBC Radio, was a
producer in his own right and even stood for the Liberal Party in the
1959 General Election. He was a Baptist lay-preacher and had been
president of the Oxford Union. Clearly he was capable of charming
both the impressively godly and the incurably sceptical. David was
hardly less versatile. He appeared in a dozen episodes of the early
police drama *Softly, Softly*, wrote gags for comedians and made a BBC
documentary about glue-sniffing.

All this, of course, makes a larger point. Alan and David were
marvellous cricket writers partly because they knew about so much
more than the game. It was no effort for them to stray beyond
the boundary; indeed, they welcomed the opportunity to gauge
cricket's interplay with other pursuits. Ponder, for instance, Alan's
account of Somerset's National Westminster Bank Trophy match
against Leicestershire in 1982:

Leicestershire put Somerset in and two wickets quickly
fell: Roebuck, run out, and Richards, bowled by Taylor.
This was an encouraging beginning for Leicestershire
and for a while they kept up their aggressive spirit, and
the crowd (a large one, given the weather) was broody,
like Somerset farmers contemplating the hay harvest
once the Ring O'Bells is shut...

Denning reached his fifty out of 95 in the 36th
over. In the same over Rose put the hundred up with
a handsome cover drive. Neither batsman looked in
much trouble, though there was one confident appeal
for a catch at the wicket, austerely declined by David
Shepherd. Shepherd is popular in Somerset, now that he
has stopped batting for Gloucestershire. "Lovely decision,
sound of snick, yurs, but no deviation, see it from 'ere,"
said a farming type in the Stragglers' Enclosure, which
stands about 45 degrees from the pitch.

But while the Yorkshire-born Alan might be sent around the country
to cover matches for *The Times*, David, for the most part, remained as
close as possible to his Heimat. The result was that many cricketers
became close friends and he knew Gloucestershire and Somerset
players better than any writer has ever known a county's staff. When
they were haunted by merciless depression, as was the case with Bill
Andrews and his beloved Gimblett, David chronicled their suffering
with sympathy and love. Nor, of course, was such kindly concern
reserved only for cricketers or people he had met. One of his most
brilliant essays in *Beyond Bat and Ball* is "Inner Peace at Mid-On",
which examines the place of cricket in the life of Siegfried Sassoon, the
poet for whom the game offered some release from the memories of
the First World War trenches. It mattered not a scruple that Sassoon was
a poor cricketer:

Cricket was his game because it gave him space and
time. If his eyes misted over as he reflected again on
how his best friend died from a rifle bullet, no one
knew. Mid-on was as good a cavern as anywhere for
introspection: offering as much solitude as he found on

his daily stroll through the woodland of his estate. There were times when he needed to unburden himself, to wreak his anger on man's inhumanity: it helped when Edmund Blunden was around to share and do his best to absorb some of the pain, before lightening the gloom with a droll memory of Fenner's.

They knocked down Taunton's old pavilion stand a few years ago. The Stragglers' Bar has been replaced by a smart café which has, at least, preserved the famous name. The battered press box has been succeeded by a plush new version which is perched atop the new Marcus Trescothick Pavilion and looks rather like a Tyrolean chalet. It is air-conditioned and it is kept terribly spick. There is not much disputing the fact that the facilities are better and the view from the Thatchers Terrace is certainly very fine.

Both the written and spoken word is still revered at the County Ground. How could it be otherwise at Taunton? Eric Hill, the former player and undisputed governor of the press box, passed away in 2010 but our affairs are now guided by the gentle benevolence of Richard Walsh, who did much to ease the pain of Alan's last years, and Richard Latham, who still visits David at his home. Two doors along, Anthony Gibson, Alan's son, broadcasts on BBC Radio. His book, *Of Didcot and the Demon*, is both a jewel-laden collection of his father's finest writing and a perfectly judged account of Alan's life.

Yet I would change everything back in the beat of a swift's wing. I would return to the days when Somerset acquired its facilities rather as it used to recruit its players: by an unsystematic yet successful addition of whatever seemed appropriate and available at the time. All this would be perfectly fine if we could also have tales of cats, railway buffets and Colin Dredge, "the Demon of Frome". And above all these things, I would return to that time upon a dream when a kind-eyed master of English prose bought me a drink and asked me how my work was going.

The Nightwatchman No30 – Summer 2020

Stephen Chalke

Summer's Crown

Over the past two decades Stephen Chalke has produced a number of books describing the lives and careers of county cricketers in the quarter-century following the Second World War. Now he has written the story of the County Championship, the only competition in which the vast majority of those first-class cricketers learned, tested and practised their skills. Immediately one protests. *The* story of the County Championship? Surely there could be hundreds of stories of this glorious, ramshackle hogfeast of a competition with its long-standing aversion to order and logic. So the first of many things for which readers of this book can be grateful is that the Championship's historian has brought clear-eyed precision to his task. Those who wish to know when the counties joined the fun, and where they finished in each year, will find it all here.

Statistics and records are supplied throughout *Summer's Crown* but they never obtrude. Choosing which to leave out and how to present those included must have been very tricky but the selections have been successful. Each season since 1890 is given due attention but the book is never merely a dull chronicle. Even the controversial period from 1864 to 1890 is considered. Some critics might wish that space had been found for each year's County Championship table but Chalke has instead opted to list each team's finishing position in the book's first section, which briefly assesses each of the counties, before moving on to the many narratives within the Championship itself. The book is already 352 pages long; there seems little doubt that it could have been double that length but nothing like twice as good.

Summer's Crown is also a very clear book. The layout is easy on the eye and the colour contrast in the many tables is invariably attractive. One never has to squint to be sure of particular statistics. The illustrations are always apposite and many of them are in colour. Making production values secondary to content in a book of this type risks the content being neglected by the reader. While Chalke acknowledges the support of the England and Wales Cricket Board in bearing the costs of production, this is a handsome book because its author plainly understood the importance of making it so. Also, and this is particularly significant perhaps, readers will find which grounds a county has used and how often its cricketers have played on them. At a time when many good judges are advocating the use of outgrounds for four-day cricket, we have here a clear indication of the importance of club venues in the histories of, among others, Essex, Kent and Yorkshire. It is something to ponder for spectators as they watch fine first-class matches take place in front of a scattering of spectators in soulless concrete bowls designed for Test matches, limited-overs games, pop concerts and not much else.

But as we might expect from its civilised author, *Summer's Crown* is very short on polemic and rich in celebration. It explains the worth of the County Championship by revisiting some of its greatest matches and exploring the feats of its finest players. It is also laced with quirky incidents and barely credible facts. For example, which county did not even enter the Championship in 1919 and which, in 1925, included in its team a 57-year-old vicar whose last first-class match had been played for a Liverpool and District XI in 1893? The answer to both questions is Worcestershire, but eccentricity has not been confined to New Road, and Chalke takes obvious delight in ferreting it all out. "The quirky things always appeal to me," he writes in a prefatory paragraph.

At the same time, there is nothing self-indulgent about this book. Those who wish to understand how the format of the Championship has evolved will have their desire satisfied in the fine appendix. There is even a list of the winners of the one-day competitions, in addition to those of the Second XI and Minor County champions. We also learn how the business of county cricket has become more professional. In so far as the Championship has a single history, Chalke strives mightily and successfully to tell it. He has taken his scholarly duties very seriously; he has also, may we speculate, worked very hard and had a lot of fun.

Summer's Crown possesses a richness and variety far greater than a single review can express. To receive it is a little like being given a huge hamper at Christmas; one is still enjoying fine delicacies well past Twelfth Night. The book is also something of a love letter to all those beautiful grounds in England where Championship matches are still played and a tribute to those that will never see another ball bowled. It is also, like Chalke's best work, a tribute to the extraordinarily diverse body of men who have played first-class cricket over the 125 years this book covers. It is a magnum opus with the lightest of touches. It is a deeply humane history. Those who love the Championship have probably bought it already, but anyone who cares about English cricket, as well as supporting the national team, should possess a copy. The book cost 20 quid but that price is cheap. The County Championship is priceless.

First published by ESPN*Cricinfo, 2015*

Chris Arnot

The Past is More Important
Britain's Lost Cricket Festivals: The Idyllic Grounds
That Will Never Again Host The World's Best Players

Is there a medical condition characterised by obsessive nostalgia? If so, Chris Arnot might be a sufferer. His latest book *Britain's Lost Cricket Festivals: The Idyllic Grounds That Will Never Again Host The World's Best Players* is a fine companion to *Britain's Lost Cricket Grounds* and follows recent works on breweries, football grounds and mines. Where will Arnot visit next? Tax offices? Slag heaps? What about *Britain's Lost Slaughterhouses: Fifty Abattoirs That Will Never Stun Another Beast?*

Cricket followers, especially those old enough to remember watching the game at more than a few of the grounds celebrated here, should be grateful for Arnot's diligence. One of the most impressive aspects of this book is that rather than relying on the internet and libraries, Arnot has visited the quondam homes of first-class cricket about which he writes and has discovered what has become of them. Thus we discover that Stroud's felicitously named Erinoid Plastics ground now lies beneath the Bath Road Trading Estate and that Dover's Crabble, so wonderfully recalled by Neville Cardus, is dominated by rugby pitches.

Inevitably, in such cases, there is an overlap between this book and *Britain's Lost Cricket Grounds* but when one notices such things, one doesn't mind them. Arnot has done his leg work: he has talked to former players, county officials and local journalists. We learn a lot about grounds, some of which we'd barely considered as first-class venues. We should probably amend that nostalgia theme a little, too. While there is no mistaking Arnot's joy at being able to visit such festivals as still exist, Cheltenham or Chesterfield, for example, he is not in the business of producing some rose-tinted volume, likely to appeal only to readers of *This England*. He may regret the fact that first-class matches are no longer played at either Avenue Road, Abergavenny or The Saffrons, Eastbourne, but only Coleridge at his most cuckoo could get too romantic about the absence of the county cricket at Rushden where, according to Matthew Engel, "the members' toilets were still pretty grim" in 1963 when the final game featured a ball from Brian Statham which reared up and hit Northants' Albert Lightfoot on the nose.

Curiously, if one has an issue with this book, it concerns the absolutism of the subtitle, and it is ironic that a mild criticism may be an indirect source of encouragement to Arnot, who would clearly love to see a fair few of these grounds back on the first-class programme. How can the author, or his publishers, Aurum, know that these grounds will "never again host the world's best players". If the squabble between the county and the school can be patched up, Surrey may return to Whitgift, and Blackpool is certainly still on Lancashire's radar, even if Liverpool and Southport are ahead of Stanley Park at the moment. According to Kent's chief executive Jamie Clifford, Folkestone and Maidstone still have ambitions to be first-class venues and who says that Durham will never leave Emirates ICG? It might need nothing more than an Ashes Test and three One Direction gigs to necessitate the use of an outground.

There is another consideration that might force the nine counties who currently never play four-day matches away from their headquarters to think again. The pressure to produce good wickets for T20 matches might compel the use of outgrounds, where the attendances are larger, local sponsors may be easier to find and the game will be more of a keenly-awaited event than a routine fixture. If so, some of the venues examined by Arnot may find that their first-class lives are not yet over. In the meantime, those of us who relish watching first-class cricket at outgrounds – yes, even at Garon Park, Southend – will have to make do with the 13 venues currently used by 10 counties. If we want to find out more about the places that are no longer on the programme, we need do little more than buy Arnot's beautifully-produced books with their excellently-chosen photographs.

First published by ESPN*Cricinfo, 2014*

Too Young to Fall Asleep For Ever

Andrew Renshaw - Wisden on the Great War:
The Lives of Cricket's Fallen 1914-1918

"...Rather hoped I'd get through the whole show, go back to work at Pratt and Sons, keep wicket for the Croydon Gentlemen, marry Doris." Thus, Captain Kevin Darling in *Blackadder Goes Forth* outlines the future he knows he will never have.

Rather like Richard Curtis and Ben Elton's comedy, *Wisden on the Great War* is a work which transcends its category. The cover has Eric Ravilious's famous woodcut at the top but it also features a prominent red font and a poppy; the sombre, poetic subtitle, "the lives of cricket's fallen" completes the careful design. You can tell this book by its cover. Not that this makes the contents any less moving. By careful scholarship Andrew Renshaw has assembled brief, often very brief, lives of the cricketers who died in the First World War. He has taken their obituaries in Wisden as the substantial base for the book but has deftly edited those entries and has frequently added further information about careers and families inside and outside the game.

In addition, the first section of this fine work is taken up mainly with an account of how the first-class counties coped during the war. One notes the initial reluctance of some to stop playing cricket in the summer of 1914 and the unease of almost all about playing again in the aftermath of a conflict which had affected every club in the country. There are also tabulated lists of the first-class cricketers who died in the war and of the 407 who received gallantry awards, these sections being compiled by Steve Western and Mike Spurrier respectively. Almost at the end of the book there is a photograph of the Oakham School team in 1914: five of the XI were to die in the imminent conflict; three others also served in World War Two; Percy Chapman went on to captain Kent and England.

This last section illustrates one of the book's many strengths: Renshaw has shown a commendable willingness to depart from his strict brief, not only by supplying obituaries of the 89 first-class cricketers whose lives and deaths were not mentioned by *Wisden*, but also by explaining biographical links and adding photographs. In the torrent of births, averages and deaths, we never lose sight of the human. Inevitably, of course, some of the longer obituaries are those of famous cricketers: Colin Blythe, Kenneth Hutchings, "Tibby" Cotter, R O Schwarz. But many of the most interesting are taken up by players of whom one may never have heard: for example, we have Hugh Montagu Butterworth, a master at Wanganui Collegiate School, who had played three first-class games in 1906. Butterworth's wry letters from Flanders are given a page and a half, allowing us a glimpse into the character of the Captain who stares rather impassively into the camera on page 112.

Readers will find their own favourites. There is the Reverend Rupert Inglis, Chaplain to the Forces, who told his Frittenden parishioners of his departure in a letter and asked them simply to pray that he might be a help to those to whom he had to minister. Or there is 2nd Lt. John Howell, "for whom no honours in the game seemed unobtainable," according to H S Altham. An Old Reptonian, Howell was apparently destined to play for Surrey, if not England, when the war intervened. He died in Flanders, aged 20. Curiously, some of the most powerful entries are also the briefest. 2nd Lt Donald Tremellan of the Duke of Cornwall's Light Infantry had been a member of the Highgate School team for three years; aged 19, he was killed on April 23, 1917. Lt George Reid was, according to Wisden, "the best field in British Columbia". Although born in Greenock, he played for Coquitlam CC and was a member of the Canadian Infantry. He was killed on April 9 1917, the day after his 32nd birthday.

Given the importance attached to cricket in the public schools, it is, perhaps, to be expected that many of the dead should have been educated in the independent sector; given the number of men sent to the war by the Dominions, it is not surprising to find the large number of cricketers who came from Canada, Australia, New Zealand or South Africa. A fresh discovery for this reviewer was the Australian-born Surrey batsman Alan Marshal, one of *Wisden's* Five Cricketers of the Year in 1909. He died in Imtarfa Military Hospital, Malta, on July 23 1915, after serving in Gallipoli. Or there is Norman Callaway, who made 207 for New South Wales in his only first-class innings and died at Bullecourt on May 3, 1917 aged 21.

Every careful reader will find his own way around this book. Those looking for specific individuals would have been helped by an alphabetical index at the end of the work but that is the only serious criticism one would wish to make. Certainly it is not a book to be read in conventional fashion; rather, readers might want to dip into the major sections before going off to do something both trivial and important like buying a loaf of bread or walking the dog. *Wisden on the Great War* helps one to value the simple joys of being alive.

There could, of course, be other books on very similar themes. The fallen on the Western Front included German footballers and Austrian skiers. In due course, perhaps, Renshaw can be persuaded to assemble and enlarge upon the lives of the cricketers who died in the Second World War. For the moment he deserves a break and can relax in the confidence that he has given us one of the books of the year.

Few cricket writers produce a work which makes the game seem both irrelevant and essential. By putting together *Wisden on the Great War* Renshaw has called his almost 2000 subjects to report for duty once again and reminded us of the lives they had no chance to lead. Included in their number is the member of the Canadian Infantry who was wounded at Neuve-Chappelle and died in London on April 19, 1915. His name - wouldn't you guess it? – was Captain Darling.

First published by ESPNCricinfo, *2014*

The Blink of an Eye

Christian Ryan – Feeling is the Thing That Happens in 1000th of a Second: A Season of Cricket Photographer, Patrick Eagar

"The hardest thing of all to see is what is really there," wrote JA Baker in *The Peregrine*.

In 1975 Patrick Eagar photographed an English cricket season that included the first World Cup and a four-Test Ashes series. Now Christian Ryan has written a book about that summer, those photographs, Eagar's art and much else besides. He has helped us see what this great craftsman preserved from an age when taking pictures cost money and photographers knew what they had only when they had developed each roll of film. Baker's words might have served as an epigraph for this book.

There are no scorecards in *Feeling,* no session-by-session accounts, no chapter headings and only the roughest sense of chronological order. There are many times when Ryan strays far beyond any of cricket's wide boundaries. There is a photograph of Muhammad Ali knocking out Sonny Liston, another of the Bee Gees, and even a section of Monet's 'Water Lilies'. The penultimate picture in the book is Joel Meyerowitz's famous shot of The North Wall after 9/11. This is appropriate, not least because *Feeling*'s title is taken from Meyerowitz's words in a 1981 documentary. It is about the only unoriginal line in the book.

To an extent, *Feeling* might be seen as a companion work to Gideon Haigh's *Stroke of Genius.* In both books there is a deep curiosity about the technical aspects of the photographer's craft and the skills of cricketers; one difference, of course, is that Ryan has interviewed Eagar on Skype whereas Haigh had to explore George Beldam's technique by using more conventional historical methods. There is also the argument that Haigh's book is a biography of one cricketer, Victor Trumper, and a history of the game's most famous photograph, whereas Ryan and Eagar's collaboration ranges across many players and a vast range of images. So let us be done with comparisons; there has never been a cricket book like this.

One of the best things about *Feeling* is Ryan's detailed commentary on specific photographs. In late May 1975 the Australians practised at Lord's. Jeff Thomson faces the camera, hands on hips, while Dennis Lillee stands a little more side-on. Ryan writes this:

> *Thomson was standing, so close they were touching, beside Lillee, one's are the supple fingers of a cellist, dainty nearly, and his partner, though powerfully built, has a footman's humble air, these two most glamorous cricketers on earth. On an exposed arm, fair hairs are sprinkled. Something of their beginnings comes through, an asbestos house, anxiety nosebleeds, magpies that swooped, too shy to dance, tensed up and leaving pages blank at school exams, sport all weekend, eaten-out soup cans for golf holes, zonal hockey, fishing, soccer in the Protestant Churches League, cricket in the Municipal and Shire competition.*

It is some writer who can change tenses in a sentence, and still carry off a 98-word prose poem about what it was to be a young Australian athlete in the late 1960s. One does not need to agree with all of Ryan's observations in order to be enriched by them. And maybe it is intentional that there are white spaces at the bottom of most pages of *Feeling*; they could accommodate a reader's own queries and observations. It might therefore be useful to have two copies, one to annotate and one for best. This is one of those relatively rare books which seem to welcome argument. "What are we looking at?" wonders Ryan. "What did I take?" asks Eagar.

Some of Eagar's photographs prompt us to reconsider cricketers we thought we already knew. A particular favourite is the shot of Steve Waugh playing a forward defensive stroke, almost certainly to a ball from John Emburey, in the 1989 Lord's Test. Jack Russell has the gloves and Dickie Bird is at square-leg. Neither wicketkeeper nor umpire repel a lens but it Waugh's angular precision which commands the attention. Everything is right; there is a beautiful Aussie obduracy about the stroke but also a quietness. England lost 25 out of the next 34 Ashes Tests in which Waugh played.

The hardest thing of all to see is what is really there. "You're telling us," comes the reply from cricket writers who spend far too much of their time trying to watch the game from a hundred yards away. If the umpires were flummoxed prior to DRS what hope did they have in 1975? Cricket, after all, often seems a game which is meant to be played rather than watched. So we spend years of our lives watching it. And then a book like *Feeling* comes along, which justifies all that time and extends the parameters of our understanding.

If Chris Gayle's *Six Machine* is your thing, this book is probably not for you. If, on the other hand, you have looked at a game of cricket or even a group of players warming up and wondered, in both senses of the word, at the narratives such moments contain, one hopes your Christmas morning may be brightened by a stocking-filler richer than ripe Reblochon. And if you have a mild interest in cricket but know someone who is all but lost to the game, you should buy this book for them. Actually, buy two, because once you open *Feeling*, one doubts you'll fancy parting with it. If so, don't be too tough on yourself. In certain respects this is one of the bravest cricket books ever written. It helps us to see and then invites us to look again.

First published by ESPNCricinfo, *2017*

10

SEDBERGH – LANCASHIRE V DURHAM, 2019

If I could watch again any one of the hundreds of County Championship matches I have covered I would return to Sedbergh in the high summer of 2019 when Lancashire hosted Durham at the most spectacular first-class venue in the land. I have never stopped enjoying the game and that is the way of things with such occasions and such places; years after they have ended they inform the way we see the world. We never quite leave.

By the time my work was confirmed accommodation was rather scarce in the town, so I rented a cottage on Loftus Hill and shared it with Radio Lancashire's Scott Read. To our delight we found it overlooked the cricket field. We made daft jokes about our morning commute and ambled across the road to explore the theatre where we were going to spend the next four days. Before long we were leaning against the fence at the Evans End and gazing in silence at a ground which should brighten gloomy November in all the calendars, a ground which on the following day was to host its first County Championship match. Behind us were Winder and Crook, the two fells from which photographers take some of the best pictures of Sedbergh; to our left was Baugh Fell, its longer and more distant hump looking vaguely forbidding. We laughed in disbelief that what we do could be regarded as work.

Later that evening we went to The Dalesman, which would become our mess on each evening of the game. Almost everyone in the pub had something to do with the match. There were players, coaches, physios, scorers, umpires, journalists, administrators and spectators. For four days Sedbergh would be cricket town. I'd not seen anything like it. I returned home quite early and watched the field where I was going to work retreat into the gathering twilight. Winder and Crook were cloud-capped and the air was very still. People compare Sedbergh to Arundel but that is like comparing the poetry of Ted Hughes to that of John Betjeman.

When much younger I had read about county matches played on what were nothing more – or less – than grounds in market towns or the countryside. The vast majority of those venues are not used for first-class cricket anymore and I had given up hope that they would be called on again. I would have to be satisfied with Arundel and Tunbridge Wells. Then Lancashire's decision to play at Sedbergh gave me an opportunity that had never been available to Neville Cardus, RC Robertson-Glasgow, Alan Gibson or David Foot. I'm not sure I've ever been happier at a first-class cricket match. Whatever the deficiencies of the following four reports, I hope they reflect that joy.

Dane Vilas, Rob Jones win day for Lancashire against Durham at picturesque Sedbergh

—————————————— DAY ONE ——————————————

Lancashire 275-5 (Vilas 67, Jones 52)*

It is tempting when watching cricket on grounds like Sedbergh to toy with the notion that life might always be like this: that one's days might be spent in the stern, benevolent shadow of the Howgill Fells while batters like Dane Vilas face bowlers such as Chris Rushworth under typically Cumbrian, cloud-tossed skies. Lancashire and Durham supporters may eventually reflect on their days watching this match and judge them among the richest of their summer.

This is only partly explained by the discipline of Cameron Bancroft's bowlers, who enjoyed success when they pitched the ball up rather than digging it in on a wicket offering bounce and carry. There were also the bells of St Andrew's, which summoned us joyously to our cricket in the morning and the sun which raced across Baugh Fell in the evening. It also has something to do with the generosity of the school and its staff, who cannot do too much to make this great event memorable.

Yet this day's cricket was only given proper shape after tea once Liam Livingstone was leg-before to Nathan Rimmington for 35 and Dane Vilas began his fifth-wicket partnership with Rob Jones. Lancashire were 141-4 when Livingstone played across the line; Jones was at that point unbeaten on 27. The 23-year-old had displayed patience beyond his years yet the arrival of his captain seemed to imbue his batting with fresh urgency. It is often so with

261

inspirational captains like Vilas, who himself showed more intent than his team's top order had managed when the ball had been newer. Rather than waiting to receive deliveries, Vilas looked to meet them, thus eliminating some movement. There were the usual powerful drives and clips through midwicket and they somewhat disconcerted a Durham attack who had hitherto set the day's agenda. A Lancashire innings which had burned slowly and been filled with honest labour – only 65 runs came in 32 overs during the afternoon – suddenly acquired fresh life as Vilas demanded that Jones be alert to the possibility of quick singles.

The partnership had yielded 87 runs when Jones was pinned on the back foot for 52 by Rushworth, who had earlier bowled Keaton Jennings for 11 with one that kept low. But Rushworth was the only Durham bowler to take more than one wicket on this first day. He had Steven Croft dropped by Alex Lees before he had scored and the reprieved batsman was unbeaten on 29 when play ended in a gentle evensong of defensive strokes and watchfulness. It has been Lancashire's day and it has also been Sedbergh's.

The only problem in the whole day was certainly not of Sedbergh's making; nor indeed was it of Lancashire's, whose enterprise in taking a game to an area in the north-west from which it recruits many players should be commended. No, the stramash occurred when a charabanc hired to give home supporters free transport to the game arrived at the ground with well over an hour to spare but missed its turning and found nowhere to park. The driver, instead of letting his passengers get off, gave them a tour of Cumbrian byways for around 50 minutes, at one stage even returning south down the M6. One wonders what Francis Thompson, that great poet of Lancastrian cricket, might have made of it.

> "It is little I repair to the matches of the Northern folk
> 'Cos my own red coach will never slow.
> It is little I repair to the matches of the Northern folk
> And we've passed this pub six times before, I know."

Fortunately, when the Old Trafford Forty-Nine were allowed to escape their incarceration, they could at least enjoy some resilient

Lancastrian batting in a couple of sessions during which both sides engaged in the reconnaissance so characteristic of cricketers on fresh fields.

Having progressed, not without hazard, to 71-1 at lunch, Lancashire lost Alex Davies for 38 in the over after the resumption when he could only glove a fine lifting ball from Brydon Carse to wicketkeeper Ned Eckersley. And Lancastrian problems deepened when Haseeb Hameed, after making 24 with his customary diligence, was drawn forward by a fine ball from Ben Raine and edged a catch to Bancroft at second slip. Livingstone settled into one of his more patient innings, yet more evidence of his determination to develop his red-ball game. Jones joined him and the pair plainly steeled themselves to rebuild the innings from 81-3 on a pitch which is a credit to the school's groundsman, Martin South. The crowd at Sedbergh, some of whom had queued for 45 minutes before the gates opened, gave themselves to their cricket.

For all the racket of modernity, there remains a sense of timelessness at a venue which saw its first cricket deep in Victorian England and whose famous Knowles pavilion has celebrated its 106th birthday. Winder and Crook, the two fells closest to the ground, remained clear. Both had been shrouded in cloud on Saturday evening. Eventually even Baugh Fell doffed its cap of mist in honour of the occasion. And we are to have three days more of this stuff.

James Anderson wins Cameron Bancroft duel on the way to 950th first-class wicket

DAY TWO

Durham 199-5 (Bancroft 77) trail Lancashire 337 (Vilas 72, Jones 52; Rimmington 4-74) by 138 runs

Cricket mattered very much at Sedbergh long before Lancashire contemplated playing here. It mattered even before the Ashes were a mischievous gleam in the eye of a Melbourne lady. And it therefore mattered well over a century before James Anderson brought one back off the seam to bowl Cameron Bancroft for 77 at ten to five on this second afternoon. Yet Anderson's success, which he celebrated with a due degree of riotous joy, took its place in the honourable history of a ground on which many fine cricketers have played and celebrated. And it also reminded some spectators that the next Ashes battle begins at Edgbaston in almost exactly a month's time. As so often in cricket, a personal duel took its place within the context of a match and also extended more widely towards a future international contest. Plainly it is very doubtful whether Bancroft will make the Australian squad for that series but England v Australia requires no particular encouragement. The Howgill Fells have not seen anything like this.

For the moment, of course, Anderson's priority is his county. He was pleased to take two of the three Durham wickets which fell on 136 and rather destroyed the visitors' relatively serene pursuit of the home side's first-innings total of 337. That pursuit was all the more surprising in that it featured an opening stand of 70 between Bancroft and Alex Lees, who both profited from the waywardness of Graham Onions' new-ball spell from the Evans End. The Durham openers' partnership was their county's highest since April 8; indeed it was the only one that has exceeded 14 in 12 attempts. The odds on either Anderson or Onions making an early breakthrough were therefore very short but Saqib Mahmood took the first wicket when Lees' horrendously cramped pull only skied the ball to Anderson at mid-off.

But rather than sparking a collapse – Durham's season has not been short of them – Lees' departure was the prelude to Bancroft and Gareth Harte redoubling their efforts and putting on a further 66 runs for the second wicket before Lancashire enjoyed by far their best period of a fluctuating day. First Onions swung one in to bowl Harte for 14; next ball Anderson cleaned up Bancroft, an echo of their duels in the Ashes series 18 months ago. In the next over he had Graham Clark leg-before-wicket, thereby taking his 950th first-class wicket. Once again, there was the typical outburst of joy from a bowler who has devoted much of his professional life to his craft and who wears his supreme ability rather lightly. Having taken his 950th wicket, he turned his attention to taking his 951st, although that must wait until at least tomorrow.

"I knew I was closing in on 950 because the lads are winding Glen Chapple up about me getting close to his number of wickets [985]," said Anderson. "I think I remember my first wicket – it was Ian Ward caught behind by Warren Hegg but it was a long time ago! I'm happy to have got to where I am at but it is not something I'm that fussed about. It's about focusing on the moment and trying to do a job for the team – if I bowl well the wickets will look after themselves."

For their part Jack Burnham and Liam Trevaskis knew if they batted well, the runs would come and this they did throughout much of the rest of the evening session. Spectators who missed their early shuttle buses to Oxenholme station in the expectation that the Lancashire seamers would run amok were disappointed and had to be content with the sun racing across Baugh Fell and all the greens in creation dancing across the slopes of Winder and Crook, the fells at the Evans End. They were not short-changed.

The final wicket of the day was taken by Liam Livingstone, who, three overs before the close, had Burnham caught at slip for 26. Durham are 138 runs in arrears but have five wickets in hand. We thus seem set for a close contest, one that will honour the enormous effort of the people in this corner of Cumbria to put on a show worthy of players like Anderson and Bancroft. A day which had begun with Lancashire's last five wickets adding only 62 runs to their overnight total ended in the gentle expectation of more fine cricket tomorrow. Few who have watched this game think themselves anything but deeply fortunate to have done so.

James Anderson injury scare rocks Lancashire-Durham clash

————————————— DAY THREE —————————————
Lancashire 337 (Vilas 72, Jones 52; Rushworth 4-74)
and 204-7 (Vilas 74*) lead Durham 281 (Bancroft 77,
Rimmington 53; Onions 5-93) by 260 runs

For many devoted followers of cricket the big parade has not taken place at Sedbergh these last three days. Affairs at Edgbaston and Chester-le-Street have commanded attention, filled airwaves and ensured there are no spare seats in press boxes. Empires are being challenged in the World Cup – and perhaps replaced. For other, equally enthusiastic supporters of the game there has been nothing more worth watching than the contest in this fell-ringed theatre. International cricket passes them by until the papers arrive. So do posturing politicians; so would minor wars.

And then, at just before a quarter to 12 on this third day, a 36-year-old fast bowler bent down and felt his calf. Suddenly two worlds were joined in mild frenzy. James Anderson, England's best bowler, was injured. Mobiles sang. Texts bleeped. Where the hell was Sedbergh anyway? When do the Ashes start? Above all, how was Jimmy? Tell us, quickly, tell us NOW!

On the field Graham Onions caused some spectators to speculate for the umpteenth time as to how many Test matches he might have played had his career not coincided with that of Anderson, of whom he is a great admirer. The former Durham seamer took four wickets in 31 balls against his old mates to finish with 5-93. It is Onions' 30th haul of five or more wickets in first-class cricket. Two of the wickets were caught behind but Ned Eckersley and Nathan Rimmington were pinned lbw on the back foot, the latter for a well-struck 53. Lancashire took a 56-run lead into lunch.

News emerged of Anderson, who had only bowled eight balls this morning before clutching his leg. Two further attempts to complete his run-up had been abandoned and Sam Byrne, the Lancashire physio, had come out to meet him on the steps of the Knowles Pavilion, a building which has no doubt seen its share of tears over the decades. Burnley's finest had suffered tightness in his right calf. He would not bowl again in the game but might bat. He will be assessed. The ECB's bulletin would have to satisfy the frantic text-senders. Good luck with that. Yet perhaps it was curiously fitting that Anderson should suffer the injury at a school whose motto is *Dura Virum Nutrix* (Stern Nurse of Men). Anderson has been known to be a trifle grim, even in moments of triumph, and he was certainly in need of nursing. Certainly the motto of his own school, St Theodore's in Burnley, *Avita Pro Fide* (For the Faith of our Ancestors) is bugger all use when you've gone in the fetlock.

Almost immediately Lancashire's blazered supporters, who have gathered in the ground's two temporary stands at the Powell End, had even more pressing pains with which to deal. Chris Rushworth found the channel on or outside off stump in his first over. Keaton Jennings edged the first ball of the innings to Eckersley; Haseeb Hameed, the fourth to Cameron Bancroft at slip. Lancashire 0-2. Alex Davies was joined by Liam Livingstone, who immediately batted with his characteristic contempt for half measures. If he defended, the drawbridge was pulled up; if he attacked, the kitchen sink, washing machine and waste-bin were thrown at the ball. Six boundaries followed, some of them reminiscent of Kevin Pietersen. Livingstone flicked Brydon Carse through midwicket and drove Nathan Rimmington through mid-off. A major innings beckoned, one which might define the match and transcend the pitch's variable bounce. But the first time Livingstone could not decide between the fish or meat course he edged Raine to Bancroft and departed for 36. By then Davies had gone too, caught on the boundary when miscuing Rimmington. And in the over after Livingstone's dismissal, Rob Jones was beaten by Liam Trevaskis's throw from the boundary and run out for 5. Lancashire were 59-5 and their lead was 115.

But if Anderson is a competitor whose galaxy of skills is underpinned by a fierce professionalism, so is his county captain. Some skippers change the bowling; Dane Vilas changes the team he leads. He will not ask any young players to go into the trenches if he has not led him there and faced the bullets, too. Cricketers like Jones and Josh Bohannon could not have a better leader in seasons when they are coming to understand how tough – and how glorious – the life of professional cricketer can be.

Steven Croft, for whom this season has been a lovely late renaissance, is hewn from similar rock. He joined Vilas in an 87-run partnership which may be seen as the most important of the match. If Durham's seamers overpitched, Vilas malleted them through midwicket; if they pitched it short Croft hooked them on his way to 35. Home supporters decided that a tub of Howgill Fellside Ice Cream might be in order; it is glorious stuff. In the small hospitality area a drink or two was taken. Sedbergh staff looked at the field they knew so well and marvelled anew.

Then Croft received a ball from Rimmington that pitched on off stump and hugged the turf. The former skipper had no hope at all. He dropped his bat and then kicked it. Durham's fielders celebrated but some may have recognised that Lancashire's lead was already 202 and the visitors will have to get those runs. Bohannon made a useful 23 and Saqib Mahmood was unbeaten on 11 at the close when Vilas had 74 runs against his name. The skipper had taken blows to the arm and hand but was still there. Unvanquished as ever.

Memories of Anderson's injury began to fade a little until the evening news gatherers rang, mad with hunger for updates. They will be less ravenous tomorrow when the big parade will be at Chester-le-Street. But at Sedbergh we will watch the last day of a great game. The people up here, and the cricketers too, deserve something to cherish.

Cameron Bancroft gets warm applause after unbeaten 92 seals draw for Durham at Lancashire

———————————————— DAY FOUR ————————————————

*Lancashire 337 (Vilas 72, Jones 52; Rushworth 4-74) and 247
(Vilas 85; Rimmington 4-42) drew with Durham 281 (Bancroft
77, Rimmington 53; Onions 5-93) and 194-6 (Bancroft 92*)*

This day began with Dane Vilas driving Chris Rushworth through the off-side, the ball skimming across the perfect Cumbrian outfield to the spectators at the Powell End; but it also began with swifts swooping and banking in the blue air; and with Rough Fell sheep, motionless on the slope of Winder below Canada Wood.

This day ended with Cameron Bancroft taking a single off Rob Jones to move his score to 92; but it also ended with the players shaking hands on the draw and with Bancroft receiving the warmest of ovations as he returned to the Knowles Pavilion; and with darkly beautiful shadows on Baugh Fell behind him; and with a series of fond partings after four days filled with summer's green perfections.

"Farewell you northern hills, you mountains all goodbye," wrote Ewan MacColl. "Moorlands and stony ridges, crags and peaks, goodbye... Days in the sun and the tempered wind and the air like wine / And you drink and you drink till you're drunk on the joy of living."

Yes, we have been spoilt; yes, we have been absurdly lucky. It is not only the farmers who have made hay when the sun shone these last four days. The cricketers have been fortunate, too, and perhaps it was fitting that both sets of players were content when they left Sedbergh this rich evening. Durham's Rushworth and Nathan Rimmington paid the ground and the occasion warm compliments. "It's like a postcard wherever you look," added Bancroft.

Rimmington had a particular reason to be content. He collected career-best match figures of 8-116 when he took two of the last three Lancashire wickets to fall this morning, but by then Durham needed 304 to win in a minimum of 79 overs. Few folk fancied their chances of doing it. Then fewer still were bullish when Alex Lees was bowled playing no shot to Saqib Mahmood and Gareth Harte lost his off and middle stumps when beaten for pace and lowish bounce by the same bowler. Bancroft then cover-drove Keaton Jennings for an exquisite boundary and we had lunch, an interval enlivened by bizarre rural conversations.

"How's that lad, Anderson?" asked a spectator.

"Not good," came the reply. "He's struggling with a tight calf."

"Oh, I know what that's like."

"Really, are you an athlete of some sort?"

"No, I'm a vet."

We drifted into our afternoon's cricket and it began badly for Durham when Jack Burnham played no shot to the sixth ball after the resumption and lost his middle stump to Graham Onions. But the next 90 minutes belonged to the visitors as Bancroft grimly risked the possibility of injury by getting forward whenever he could, thus negating movement and at least limiting the impact of low bounce. Graham Clark was similarly obdurate and even some Lancashire supporters found fruition in the prospect of a full day's cricket. Sedbergh has offered an infinitude of peace these midsummer days.

Some watched from the Evans End, where, on the public footpath beyond the ground's perimeter, folk could sit on benches and watch cricket without paying a penny. It has been christened the Yorkshire End. On the field, Lancashire needed a wicket and an attack lacking both James Anderson (calf) and Liam Livingstone (side) was flagging. Then a ball from Bohannon bounced low and took out Clark's off stick. Five overs later, Onions, bowling round the wicket to encourage uncertainty about line, had the left-handed Trevaskis caught by Jones at slip. Durham were 122-5 at tea and we looked forward to a full evening session.

Yes, we have been privileged. Yes, Sedbergh is a privileged environment, but they have shared their wonderful facilities with the cricket community this week. And they have done so with glorious generosity. Cricket has mattered here for nearly two centuries. Take the school's late 19th century *Cricket Song*.

> If you've England in your veins,
> And can take a little pains,
> In the sunny summer weather, when to stay indoors is sin,
> If you've got a bit of muscle,
> And enjoy a manly tussle,
> Then go and put your flannels on and let the fun begin!

Sedbergh School Songs, in which those lines appear, was published in 1896 and looks forward to Queen Victoria's Diamond Jubilee the following year. The subtext – maybe main text – is that of the cultivation of an imperial ethos. The illustration opposite *Cricket Song* shows Sedbergh boys playing cricket in the shadow of Winder and then men playing the game in some unnamed foreign clime with the Union flag flying prominently.

These days the school is more concerned to provide the counties with players. Harry Brook, Jordan Clark, George Hill all learned their cricket on the square where Bancroft's resilience reached new heights this final evening. After Ned Eckersley played on to Mahmood he was joined by Ben Raine and the pair saw Durham through the final 22 overs. Lancashire's bowlers became provoked into experimentation, at one stage placing four short extra-covers for Raine. But nothing budged him and nothing shifted Bancroft either. The West Australian batted for 288 minutes and faced 191 balls today. He has now scored 332 runs in his last four innings and though his form may be too late to get him in the Ashes squad, he looks like a Test opener.

The rest of us must soon shift ourselves this perfect evening. The shadows are now on Winder and their patterns change with every precious moment. There is brass band music playing in the hospitality tent: hymns and tunes of glory. The players are long gone and in half an hour or so the rest of cricket's caravan must join them. But we are changed. No one who has spent the last four days at Sedbergh could be otherwise. This little world and its perfect ground will stay with us. There are children playing cricket on the outfield; there is drinking in the tent; there is new light on Baugh Fell. And enfolding it all is the joy of living.

LANCASHIRE V DURHAM

Sedbergh, June 30 - July 03, 2019
Specsavers County Championship Division Two
Lancashire 337 & 247 – Durham 281 & 194/6 (T:304)
Match drawn

LANCASHIRE 1ST INNINGS

BATTING		R	B	M	4s	6s	SR
Keaton Jennings	b Rushworth	11	32	40	2	0	34.37
Alex Davies	c †Eckersley b Carse	38	80	116	6	0	47.5
Haseeb Hameed	c Bancroft b Raine	24	77	110	2	0	31.16
Liam Livingstone	lbw b Rimmington	35	97	132	3	0	36.08
Rob Jones	lbw b Rushworth	52	150	194	6	0	34.66
Dane Vilas (c)†	c Rimmington b Rushworth	72	119	168	10	0	60.5
Steven Croft	c Bancroft b Carse	42	54	68	6	0	77.77
Josh Bohannon	not out	33	57	74	3	0	57.89
Saqib Mahmood	lbw b Rimmington	2	15	32	0	0	13.33
Graham Onions	c †Eckersley b Rimmington	0	3	8	0	0	0
James Anderson	c Clark b Rimmington	4	20	29	0	0	20
Extras	(b 1, lb 15, nb 8)	24					
TOTAL	**116.5 Ov (RR: 2.88)**	**337**					

BOWLING	O	M	R	W	E	WD	NB
Chris Rushworth	27	5	61	3	2.25	0	1
Brydon Carse	25	7	82	2	3.28	0	0
Nathan Rimmington	25.5	6	74	4	2.86	0	2
Ben Raine	24	3	62	1	2.58	0	0
Gareth Harte	11	3	27	0	2.45	0	1
Liam Trevaskis	3	0	14	0	4.66	0	0
Jack Burnham	1	0	1	0	1	0	0

FALL OF WICKETS:
1-24 (Keaton Jennings, 8.4 ov), 2-72 (Alex Davies, 27.5 ov), 3-81 (Haseeb Hameed, 35.4 ov), 4-141 (Liam Livingstone, 60.2 ov), 5-228 (Rob Jones, 84.2 ov), 6-293 (Steven Croft, 99.6 ov), 7-293 (Dane Vilas, 100.6 ov), 8-305 (Saqib Mahmood, 108.4 ov), 9-313 (Graham Onions, 110.1 ov), 10-337 (James Anderson, 116.5 ov)

DURHAM 1ST INNINGS

BATTING		R	B	M	4s	6s	SR
Cameron Bancroft (c)	b Anderson	77	139	161	12	0	55.39
Alex Lees	c Anderson b Mahmood	16	48	77	3	0	33.33
Gareth Harte	b Onions	14	53	84	1	0	26.41
Jack Burnham	c Anderson b Livingstone	26	87	118	3	0	29.88
Graham Clark	lbw b Anderson	0	9	11	0	0	0
Liam Trevaskis	c †Vilas b Onions	38	159	211	5	0	23.89
Nathan Rimmington	lbw b Onions	53	91	124	6	0	58.24
Ned Eckersley †	lbw b Onions	3	15	14	0	0	20
Ben Raine	c Croft b Jennings	5	8	9	1	0	62.5
Brydon Carse	not out	1	14	23	0	0	7.14
Chris Rushworth	c †Vilas b Onions	6	16	19	1	0	37.5
Extras	(b 4, lb 13, nb 20, w 5)	42					
TOTAL	**104.5 Ov (RR: 2.68)**	**281**					

BOWLING	O	M	R	W	E	WD	NB
James Anderson	18.2	7	39	2	2.12	0	1
Graham Onions	31.5	6	93	5	2.92	1	2
Saqib Mahmood	24	2	59	1	2.45	0	3
Josh Bohannon	12.4	1	44	0	3.47	0	4
Liam Livingstone	11	5	21	1	1.9	0	0
Keaton Jennings	7	2	8	1	1.14	0	0

FALL OF WICKETS:
1-70 (Alex Lees, 18.2 ov), 2-136 (Gareth Harte, 38.6 ov), 3-136 (Cameron Bancroft, 39.1 ov), 4-136 (Graham Clark, 41.4 ov), 5-197 (Jack Burnham, 69.3 ov), 6-263 (Liam Trevaskis, 94.5 ov), 7-269 (Ned Eckersley, 98.1 ov), 8-274 (Nathan Rimmington, 98.6 ov), 9-274 (Ben Raine, 99.5 ov), 10-281 (Chris Rushworth, 104.5 ov)

LANCASHIRE 2ND INNINGS

BATTING		R	B	M	4s	6s	SR
Keaton Jennings	c †Eckersley b Rushworth	0	1	1	0	0	0
Alex Davies	c Harte b Rimmington	15	41	66	2	0	36.58
Haseeb Hameed	c Bancroft b Rushworth	0	3	4	0	0	0
Liam Livingstone	c Bancroft b Raine	35	50	72	6	0	70
Rob Jones	run out (Trevaskis)	5	12	20	0	0	41.66
Dane Vilas (c)†	c & b Rimmington	85	135	233	9	0	62.96
Steven Croft	b Rimmington	35	92	111	5	0	38.04
Josh Bohannon	c †Eckersley b Carse	22	39	37	4	0	56.41
Saqib Mahmood	not out	31	87	107	3	0	35.63
Graham Onions	c †Eckersley b Raine	0	4	12	0	0	0
James Anderson	b Rimmington	0	8	17	0	0	0
Extras	(b 4, lb 13, nb 2)	19					
TOTAL	**78.3 Ov (RR: 3.14)**	**247**					

BOWLING	O	M	R	W	E	WD	NB
Chris Rushworth	17	5	53	2	3.11	0	0
Brydon Carse	19	1	68	1	3.57	0	1
Ben Raine	19	4	45	2	2.36	0	0
Nathan Rimmington	16.3	5	42	4	2.54	0	0
Gareth Harte	3	0	13	0	4.33	0	0
Liam Trevaskis	2	0	2	0	1	0	0
Graham Clark	1	0	6	0	6	0	0
Jack Burnham	1	0	1	0	1	0	0

FALL OF WICKETS:

1-0 (Keaton Jennings, 0.1 ov), 2-0 (Haseeb Hameed, 0.4 ov), 3-51 (Alex Davies, 14.3 ov), 4-55 (Liam Livingstone, 17.1 ov), 5-59 (Rob Jones, 18.2 ov), 6-146 (Steven Croft, 46.1 ov), 7-174 (Josh Bohannon, 54.2 ov), 8-229 (Dane Vilas, 72.3 ov), 9-236 (Graham Onions, 75.1 ov), 10-247 (James Anderson, 78.3 ov)

DURHAM 2ND INNINGS

BATTING		R	B	M	4s	6s	SR
Cameron Bancroft (c)	not out	92	191	288	7	0	48.16
Alex Lees	b Mahmood	0	6	9	0	0	0
Gareth Harte	b Mahmood	0	5	10	0	0	0
Jack Burnham	b Onions	20	29	34	4	0	68.96
Graham Clark	b Bohannon	26	76	82	2	0	34.21
Liam Trevaskis	c Jones b Onions	3	21	24	0	0	14.28
Ned Eckersley †	b Mahmood	20	42	46	1	0	47.61
Ben Raine	not out	19	83	85	1	0	22.89
Brydon Carse							
Nathan Rimmington							
Chris Rushworth							
Extras	(lb 3, nb 6, w 5)	14					
TOTAL	**75 Ov (RR: 2.58)**	**194/6**					

BOWLING	O	M	R	W	E	WD	NB
Graham Onions	17	3	38	2	2.23	0	3
Saqib Mahmood	19	2	58	3	3.05	1	0
Keaton Jennings	11	1	34	0	3.09	0	0
Josh Bohannon	19	3	44	1	2.31	0	0
Steven Croft	7	2	15	0	2.14	0	0
Rob Jones	2	1	2	0	1	0	0

FALL OF WICKETS:

1-7 (Alex Lees, 1.5 ov), 2-11 (Gareth Harte, 3.6 ov), 3-39 (Jack Burnham, 11.6 ov), 4-108 (Graham Clark, 36.1 ov), 5-117 (Liam Trevaskis, 41.5 ov), 6-149 (Ned Eckersley, 53.3 ov)

11

HEADINGLEY TEST

In the early summer of 2019 I asked Treve Whitford and Sam Gascoyne, two members of the communications staff at Yorkshire, whether the county might be interested in daily reports on that summer's Ashes Test at Headingley for their website. It was something of a hopeful pitch and I was a little surprised when Treve and Sam came back quickly with the county's wholehearted agreement. Quite soon, though, surprise gave way to understanding and to an even deeper recognition of how important cricket is to Yorkshire. No county takes the game more seriously or has a greater awareness of what an Ashes Test means. To have the Test recorded by their own correspondent would be a tiny part of that wide-ranging dedication.

But none of us were remotely ready for the dramas that lay ahead. I'm not sure I've attended a dull Test match, but it is rare to watch one with the range of emotions or the dramatic arcs of those four August days – a game famous for its climax but which contained so much more. I hope something of that is conveyed in the pieces that follow.

It's "Uz" Ground

Preview

A cricket ground without people is nothing more than concrete and metal, wood and glass, plastic and turf. You might admire the architecture or the construction but the soul of the place will elude you if you are not stirred by what has happened there. So whatever its modernity, Emerald Headingley is, and must always be, more than a stadium. Young Yorkshiremen have arrived at the ground wanting nothing more than to play for the county; veteran cricketers have walked off this sacred space after their last games not trusting themselves to say anything at all; and every springtime supporters turn up, gruff and tender, hoping to see the White Rose prosper. "It's

[uz] ground" say the county's players and supporters and dare you to correct their grammar. "[Uz] can be loving," wrote Tony Harrison, a Leeds poet, in one of his most famous 16-line sonnets, and there has never been any shortage of emotion at Headingley. It has been so since 1890 when the ground hosted its inaugural first-class match and spectators saw The North lose to the touring Australians by 160 runs. Ah yes, the Australians. I didn't think it would be long until we got round to them.

This will be Headingley's first Ashes Test for a decade and only its second in 18 years. The series began in 1890 and for 80 years after 1921 the notion that an Australian touring team should visit England and not play a Test at Leeds appeared unthinkable. Then in 2005 – the crackpot era of bids and packages – some bright spark thought it. This summer, though, Yorkshire welcomes Tim Paine's side back to a ground which possesses perhaps the richest heritage of any Ashes venue in England. And it is not absurd optimism to expect such greetings will be reciprocated, even as the rivalry assumes a fresh intensity and another great series takes shape. Where once there was Ray Lindwall, there is now Pat Cummins; where once there was Maurice Leyland, there is now Joe Root. The place is nowt without people.

And Australian players and spectators have enjoyed visiting Leeds. The visitors have won nine of their 23 Ashes Tests at Headingley and did not lose to England on the ground until defeat in 1956 began a rather gloomy period in which they were defeated in five out of eight games. Rather remarkably, Fred Trueman was the only one of the county's cricketers to be playing in that '56 Test. Perhaps he therefore felt a particular responsibility to do well, although pulling on either a Yorkshire or an England sweater was usually enough to spur him. Either way, Trueman had a big heart and a big arse. These are valuable attributes for fast bowlers and the heart is more or less compulsory. In 1961 he took six for 30 in the first innings and five for 58 in the second. His match figures, 11 for 88 in 37.2 overs, mark the only occasion on which he took ten wickets in an Ashes Test. The game did not decide a series, which was won 2-1 by Richie Benaud's tourists. But it offered some compensation to Yorkshire supporters for their team's failure to complete a hat-trick of County Championships. (Mind you, they then won five of the next seven titles.)

Even for Australians, though, and even for Yorkshire folk, there is more to it than success. When supporters from Sydney or Melbourne sit among the more knowledgeable spectators at a Leeds Test they can be encouraged they are watching cricket's supreme format in the company of people to whom the game matters just as much as it does to them. Some Yorkshire people will appreciate this accolade; others will bridle a little at it. The latter will argue there is nowhere on Earth where cricket means quite so much as the Broad Acres. In the eras when an Australian tour began at Worcester in May, ended at Scarborough in September and included at least one match against each of the first-class counties, the game with Yorkshire was frequently viewed by the tourists as a sixth Test. It is, therefore, only proper that Headingley should have witnessed many of the greatest Ashes Tests since the bail was burned. Lords may have its pomp, Trent Bridge its intimacy, The Oval its grand farewell to summer and Old Trafford… well, at this point one or two Yorkshiremen will be flummoxed since they have no idea what Old Trafford might be good for. But putting aside that question, Leeds has the expert eye and matches between England and Australia are watched there with a greater intensity than anywhere else in the kingdom.

Peter Siddle is the one survivor from the Australian team that overwhelmed England by an innings here in 2009 who has any chance of playing in this Test; and while, a trifle remarkably, five of England's squad in that series are still playing first-class cricket, only Stuart Broad and James Anderson are still in serious contention. Australian spectators, whose presence adds so much to an Ashes Test, will notice more material changes. In 2009, the players emerged from vaguely subterranean dressing rooms in the old football stand. That has been replaced by the brand new Emerald Stand and the cricketers now change at the Kirkstall Lane End where much of Leeds Beckett University and the media are also housed.

But if you can, put aside the posh new buildings for a moment. Think of Headingley as it used to be in Bradman's era; or in Laker's great series; or in 1972, when one or two Australians wanted to dig up the pitch; or in 1975 when someone actually broke in and did so. And yes, there is Botham's year and there is Mark Butcher's hundred. We may revisit these games over the next five days. For, as another Yorkshireman reminded us, a Test match is a week of your life. Before us is one of cricket's great theatres but the lines of the play can only be written by the actors. As ever, it is the people we remember.

Before A Ball is Bowled

3.10am

I look out on Wade Lane from a room a monk might regard as spartan. A man walks briskly down the road and a taxi passes. Other than that, nothing. Lights flicker in distant Roundhay and Seacroft. Even Leeds has to sleep sometime. But it is already the first day of the Third Ashes Test at Emerald Headingley.

Unbidden, my thoughts drift back to a game at Edgbaston in 2012. England Lions v Australia A. It was a rain-plagued affair with both the second and fourth days washed out. On the first blank afternoon I requested an England player for a chat and a fresh-faced 21-year-old turned up. He could not have been more generous with his time or more helpful with his answers. Courtesy came as standard with Joe Root. On the final morning I asked for an Australian, and the A team's 27-year-old wicketkeeper arrived. He explained how his career had been affected by a finger injury and showed me a digit shaped like a country lane in the Cotswolds. We talked for maybe an hour and I wished Tim Paine all the best for his future.

It is still the middle of the night in West Yorkshire. I doubt either Paine or Root recalls many details from that game and I'm certain they won't remember those conversations. But I remember them. Sleep now, perhaps.

7.20

I catch a 56 bus outside the Hedley Verity. This may sound appropriate but the pub now seems a riot of show and kitsch – everything Verity wasn't. Headingley looks relatively quiet, which is not surprising given the gates won't open for nearly two hours.

But inside the ground the various preparations for a major event jostle for one's attention. The areas where one can normally walk are occupied by vans and the perimeter of the ground is filled with every variety of food outlet. Sniffer dogs attend to the vans and there is a queue for the lift to the press box. "I'm hoping for a four-day finish because there's a beer festival in Leeds on Monday," says someone involved in television. Good to know someone's got their eyes on the prize.

Actually, one of the points about Test matches is to keep your mind off the general scrum and attend instead to what you have to do. That applies as much to journalists as it does to opening batsmen or umpires. So the seat is secured and the laptop is switched on. Then I take a stroll around the relatively quiet ground. The Emerald Stand's various suites and boxes are ready to receive around 1,800 corporate guests. My favourite, as I guess it was bound to be, is the Taverners' suite, the walls of which are filled with representations of cricketers. On one wall there is the famous portrait if Sir Leonard Hutton in which he manages to look both confident and vulnerable. Round the corner is a photograph of Sir Donald Bradman; he is looking over the photographer's shoulder and into a run-stuffed future. In front of the Long Room massed ranks of lime-bibbed stewards are being given their final instructions. In the Emerald Suite, which accommodates 500 guests and looks out on both rugby and cricket fields, waiters and waitresses, dressed rather less garishly than the stewards, you understand, are receiving their own guidelines for the day ahead. Some people think a Test match is about two teams; it actually involves about ten and that may be a great understatement. A few weeks ago Yorkshire's commercial director, Andy Dawson, told me that corporate packages for the Headingley Test cost between £500 and £700 a pop. They are sold out for the first three days of the game.

10.30

A circuit of the ground is now a rather more complex operation. Spectators fill the passageways and make their way to the stands and terraces. In one corner a musical ensemble, Flat Cap Brass is striking up. For a moment I am unsure whether the name of the group refers to their instruments or whether it is a Yorkshire motto suggesting that a wise sartorial choice will inevitably lead to wealth. Perhaps it is both. Back in the Emerald Suites the guests are tucking in to breakfast. Lunch will be smoked salmon, Yorkshire lamb and poached pear. In truth I have edited the menu; each course is an essay detailing flavours and decorations. There is also a Silent Auction. Maybe because it would be rude to speak with your mouth full.

Yes, there is a cricket match going on. Headingley is grey and overcast and it is self-evidently a bowl first morning. Normally when I have this feeling it is the prelude to a captain opting to bat. Not, however, on this occasion. Drizzle relents long enough for Root to insert Australia but the rain quickly returns and we have a delayed start.

11.55

The Test match is to begin in 15 minutes' time. "Ten past 12 start, 1.30 lunch at the moment!" booms Danny Reuben, England's Head of Elite Communications, in the press box, and one is inclined to believe the rumour that he once sold kitchen utensils off a barrow in Barnsley market.

But the cricket really is about to start. Headingley is brighter and the England bowlers are going through a final warm-up. Twenty-four hours ago I was watching Steve Patterson bowling to Liam Patterson-White at North Marine Road, Scarborough. Now anyone who has read a word of my stuff knows that I love the soul of county cricket and particularly treasure it being played on outgrounds. But some of those who played at Scarborough and Colwyn Bay over the past four days have performed on the great stages, too, and many still aspire to do so. This is still the pinnacle of the game and the four-day format plays a vital role in preparing young players for the challenge of their sporting lives.

England set up with a choir of slips and David Warner takes guard. Stuart Broad is to open the bowling from the Kirkstall Lane End. It is a run-up I have watched for over a decade. Silence. Then a crescendo of expectation as Broad approaches the crease and his arm comes over…

Australia 179 (Labuschagne 74, Warner 61, Archer 6-45) v England

There are days in this game when you can sense a cloak of responsibility being passed from one player to his successor. Jimmy Anderson is 37; he spent today proving his fitness at the Northern club in Great Crosby and he will play for Lancashire's second team again at Chester Boughton Hall next week. Jofra Archer is 24; he spent his day at Emerald Headingley, bowling the spells which have defined the current shape of the third Ashes Test. Anderson may yet take vital wickets for England and has not ruled out going on the next Ashes tour. But when Archer received a standing ovation this evening after his 6-45 had dismissed Australia for 179 one could see a new era beginning. Archer had taken the first wicket and the last; he had dismissed three of the last four Australian batsmen; he is playing in his second Test and he is already Joe Root's go-to bowler. This may yet be remembered as his series, his year. It has already been something to see.

Yet today's cricket was not all about Archer. How could it be, given that two batsmen made 135 of Australia's 179 runs and the other nine managed 31 between them? There was much more light and shade to our cricket than might be assumed from a brief glance at the scorecard. And both qualities, almost inevitably, were linked to one David Warner.

"It's important for opening batsmen to put their play-and-misses to the back of their minds," said Mike Atherton. The point is very sound but one wonders how large Warner's mind would have to be for him to obey Atherton's instruction. Put a couple of Rory Burns' innings aside and the first two Tests of this series have not been encounters to treasure for top-order batsmen. Certainly there was a ghoulish delight to be gained from watching Warner suffer in the opening four-over session we watched at Headingley this morning before rain returned. On five occasions in 12 balls one of the world's most destructive openers was reduced to foolish impotence as he groped for 85mph leg breaks from Stuart Broad. One almost thought the dismissal of Marcus Harris, caught by Jonny Bairstow off Archer, was relatively merciful, albeit Harris was probably frustrated as much as crestfallen. His departure was the immediate prelude to a long interruption for rain.

In time, though, one's pity for Warner was mixed with admiration as he took his punishment from Broad, consoled only by D:ream's assurance that things can only get better. Eventually there was a half-volley he could clip past square leg; then an over-pitched ball from Archer which was driven through the covers; and finally another delivery from Broad he could guide through point. By then Usman Khawaja had joined Harris in the pavilion, caught down the leg side after feathering a ball from Broad so thinly that it needed DRS to confirm the fact of it. But Marnus Labuschagne eventually got off the mark with a boundary off the final ball of Broad's spell and when the players were brought off for bad light, Australia were 54-2 after 18 overs. It was not a bad return after all that torture.

By teatime, that most moveable of feasts, the cricket was vaguely reminiscent of the first day of the Ashes Test 22 years ago when there was play in each of the first two sessions yet England were only 14 for nought prior to an evening session in which they lost the wickets of Mark Butcher, Alec Stewart and Nasser Hussain. I watched that day's cricket with a mate who bailed out after his third soaking of the day. I returned and sat in the evening sunlight at the Kirkstall Lane End as Glenn McGrath and Jason Gillespie did the groundwork for yet another innings victory.

For much of this long final session it seemed the cricket would bring similar satisfaction to Australian supporters massed in the North-East Stand. The light was as good as we had all day and the English bowling was poor. Warner and Labuschagne took 77 runs off 12 overs, most of them bowled by Ben Stokes and Chris Woakes. The value of keeping the ball up to the bat in heavy conditions was neglected. Warner's suffering seemed all the more worthwhile as he reached his half-century off 79 balls with successive fours off Stokes. Root recalled Archer and the game changed again as Australia lost three wickets in as many overs.

Warner's luck ran out when he didn't get far enough forward to a good length ball and edged behind for 61, thus ending his 111-run partnership with Labuschagne. Some supporters at Headingley booed the opener as he made his way off the field and were roundly condemned by Geoffrey Boycott, whose judgement on such matters is often stern but also just. Next over Travis Head was bowled for nought by a fine delivery from Broad. Seven balls later Matthew

Wade deflected a ball from Archer down into the crease from where it rolled back into the stumps, dislodging the leg bail. Australia had lost three wickets for in 15 deliveries.

Balls and their unexpected movement became something of a theme of our cricket as Labuschagne was struck a fearsome blow in the box by Broad. But by then the Queensland batsman had reached his fifty off 73 balls and had looked as secure in his technique as anyone in the series bar Steve Smith, whose approach to his craft is almost antithetical to Labuschagne's. Archer's domination of the last hour of a long day began when he removed James Pattinson and Pat Cummins via edges to Bairstow and Root. Labuschagne's fine innings ended when he was leg before to an outrageous full toss from Stokes for 74. Then England's newest star signed off by having Nathan Lyon lbw for a single. By that time he was bowling down the slope with the Kirkstall Lane at his back. That was Fred Trueman's favourite end. Jofra Archer is already moving in exalted company.

Stokes Offers Evening Defiance
After A Grim Morning

──────────── DAY TWO ────────────

Australia 179 and 171-6 (Labuschagne 53) lead*
England 67 (Hazlewood 5-30) by 283 runs

Some people complain about the price of Test match tickets and there are rain-restricted afternoons when one sees their point. Then there are days like this at Headingley when one understands why folk might pay £150 for one of the best seats in the Emerald Stand. Immediately there may be objections to this opinion. For one thing, it is pretty rich for someone who doesn't pay a penny for his cricket to pontificate about others' expenditure. For another, people may wonder quite how much satisfaction can be derived from seeing England bowled out for 67, their lowest total against Australia since 1952 and their second lowest in an Ashes Test since 1909.

Well, quite a lot as it happens, although not so much if you turn up at a cricket match interested only in seeing one team prosper. There is, one might argue, a difference between loyally supporting a side and refusing to see an opponent's merits. Let it be put more pointedly: if you were determined to boo David Warner at every opportunity this Friday morning, you were unlikely to appreciate his four slip catches, particularly the high-class efforts which removed Joe Root and Jonny Bairstow off the excellent Josh Hazlewood. Root, at least, was blameless, something which cannot be said about the other five top-order batsmen dismissed in the first session. England's lunchtime score of 54-6 was a useful corrective for those who assumed the home side would take the opportunity offered by blue skies and warm weather to establish some sort of first-innings lead. It says something about a team's fortunes when the biggest cheer from their supporters during a session greets an umpire's misjudgement and a successful DRS review. That would have been true this morning had not Chris Woakes and Jos Buttler's first boundaries been welcomed with outbursts of desperate joy from a capacity crowd struggling to cope with what they were watching.

Never mind, the optimists thought as they tucked into their fine corporate lunches, someone always comes to England's rescue. Well, not this time. Woakes was caught down the leg side off the first ball of the afternoon session and Buttler carelessly drove Hazlewood straight to the precisely placed Usman Khawaja at short extra cover. Within 20 minutes England's first innings had ended and the statisticians were battling with each other to produce the most depressing statistic. One pointed out that Joe Denly's 12 is the lowest highest score in any completed England innings. Ouch. And Denly was the only England batsman to reach double figures. Ouch again.

Cricket, like most sports, abounds with clichés: "Cricket was the winner"; "The opposition has the right to play well"; "We bowled in good areas." We've heard them all – and written a few of them. Yet one of the better ones was revived by the former England skipper, Michael Vaughan, this afternoon when he said: "You bat for your bowlers." Which is to say that a side tries to bat long enough to give the members of its attack a rest and also, in the fourth innings, a total which it can defend. The England bowlers had just two and a half hours off today before they had to crank it up again. No wonder Jofra Archer went down with cramp late in the day. The specialist batsmen, most of whom were dismissed playing poor shots this morning, know it is nothing like good enough.

And thus we return to the Australian attack and specifically to their fast bowlers, Hazlewood, Pat Cummins and James Pattinson. If the morning was grim for England, it was made so partly by the virtues and careful plans of this trio, whose pace and accuracy scrambled the minds of England's batsmen and lured them into playing shots far from their bodies. Hazlewood was the best of the Australians and finished with 5-30 from his 12.5 overs. But the trio were applauded by the massed ranks in green and gold below the scoreboard and also by plenty of supporters at the Kirkstall Lane End, which is often where the most discriminating and knowledgeable Yorkshire supporters sit.

For a while it seemed that Australia's second innings would be something of an anti-climax after the drama of England's collapse. One pundit even suggested things could get ugly for Joe Root's side as the tourists piled on the runs against demoralised opponents. Well by the end of the day Australia had carved out a lead of 283 but the cricket remained absorbing and another justification for the ticket price. Many in the Western Terrace were content when Warner was leg before to Stuart Broad for a duck in the second over but they were presumably less cheerful about the fact that five of the top seven in the tourists' order scored more than Denly had managed in England's innings. The best innings, yet again, was played by the unflappable Marnus Labuschagne, who ended this long day unbeaten on 53. England, though, had dropped him twice, Root grassing a slip catch when Labuschagne was 14 and Bairstow putting down a difficult diving chance when he was 43. Australia were 171-6 at the close and have no reason at all not to pile on the punishment in the morning.

The highlights of the day for England supporters? Jack Leach bowling Marcus Harris for 19 with his first ball of the innings; Archer returning a massive inflatable melon to the crowd when a steward was about to put it in the storeroom reserved for confiscated plastic toys; or Ben Stokes' gloriously defiant and skilful 15.2-over spell in the evening session, during which he bowled Travis Head for

25 and had Matthew Wade caught behind for 33. Beyond serious doubt, it was the latter. That was a phenomenal effort by Stokes and it was utterly in character.

Dreadful Disappointments, Ridiculous Revivals and Colossal Chases

By the time I left the press box at half past eight last evening many journalists were still working. But so were the temporary staff hired by Yorkshire to collect the litter discarded on the Western Terrace. And so were the caterers over in the spanking new stand as they prepared the tables for the next batch of corporate guests this morning, when the hospitality suites will, like the rest of the ground, be a sell-out. Yet again one was reminded how big Ashes Tests are and how precious they remain to spectators young and old, who are keen to see cricket's greatest contest flourish. The problem, as many of the papers and websites will make clear, is that unless Test cricket is viewed as precious by those in charge of the English game, it will wither due to neglect. If you sell out red-ball cricket, do not be surprised if you cannot sell out Test match venues. And please do not kid yourself that winning the World Cup will be a substitute. Nor will any other white-ball tournament, new or old, however much advertising money is thrown at it.

Now wait a moment, please. One is not resiling from the positions outlined above but Joe Root's team have yet to bat a second time. Friday evening was so miserable for patriotic Englishmen that it was all too tempting to recall other occasions when Headingley had seen Test matches turned around in fashions so spectacular that they defied all the game's logic. You now think this sentence is going to contain the word "Botham" and – curses! – you are clearly right, but we will not begin in 1981. Instead we might recall 1948, when a team was set 404 to win at Headingley and managed it.

And what a glorious occasion it was. The opener made 182, the skipper 173 not out and everyone agreed it had been a day they would remember. The only problem, if it can be designated as such, was that it was Australia doing the batting. Dammit, maybe we should try Botham instead.

Most folk remember where they were during the Headingley Test in 1981. I was teaching at the time and playing in a staff cricket match when Sir Ian was making an 87-ball century. Sadly I was not inspired by his example: as I recall, I made one in 15 balls. The following afternoon we were all gathered in the staff room, which was fugged with cigarette smoke and more or less awash with alcohol. (It was very much the end of term.) The deputy head, a rather bossy woman, poked her head round the door and asked if someone would help her organise the trophies. Then Bob Willis took another wicket and one of my braver colleagues suggested where she might put her trophies. They are the days you never forget.

And as I write this, two hours before the start of play, there is the knight of the realm himself, chatting happily to members of both squads. Against the background of England's scorecard Graham Thorpe is discussing that first innings on Sky. Good luck with that. The papers have arrived and no stone has been left unhurled. "I'm told this is the Participation Test," tweeted a mate yesterday evening. "Do you think there's any chance England will participate in it?"

Enough already. We still have time to recall one more recovery and perhaps it should encourage England supporters more than any other. Australia won the 2001 Ashes series 4-1 but the most memorable game in that series was played at Headingley. Set 315 to win on the final day, England coasted home by six wickets, Mark Butcher making 173 not out off 227 balls. The Australian attack comprised Glenn McGrath, Jason Gillespie, Brett Lee and Shane Warne. It was the innings of Butcher's life.

And that, I suppose, is what home supporters need a couple of their batsmen to do today or tomorrow. They must believe they can mock all the predictions and chase down a tall target against four very fine bowlers. Should England even be in the hunt this evening, Headingley will be rocking on Bank Holiday Sunday. The place may have new stands aplenty since 1948, 1981, 2001, but the old ground has been the scene of some great revivals. It is 9.40am. Many of the spectators are already in their seats. As so often, on a Test match morning, one is beguiled by what we may be about to see.

Root defies Australia as Emerald Headingley Test is set for a classic finish

———————————————— DAY THREE – PART TWO ————————————————

England 67 and 156-3 (Root 75*, Denly 50) need 203 runs to beat Australia 179 and 246 (Labuschagne 80, Stokes 3-56)

That was more like it. At least, it was more like the type of resistance one wishes to see from England's cricketers and it was more like a Test match as most of those at Emerald Headingley understand the term. For the day after they had been castigated for gross incompetence, Joe Root and his batsmen did the groundwork – it is really no more – for the biggest successful run-chase in their country's Test history. When England began the task of scoring 359 to win just before lunch on this third day some supporters feared they might have a free Saturday evening. Instead, Root and Ben Stokes returned to the pavilion with their side on 156-3. Root might have settled for that when his side's innings began and he has done much of the dirty work himself by making an unbeaten 75. But a moment of realism is needed. England are not even halfway to their target and Australia, whose bowlers choked the run rate quite brilliantly in this evening session, remain favourites to complete the win that would retain the Ashes. The cricketing particicution some expected has not taken place. And certainly it is better to be hopeful, as England are now, than hopeless, as they were on Friday morning.

Yet so engrossing was the cricket in the last two sessions on Saturday that it was beguiling to think our day had begun with Australia batting and England needing to take four wickets before they even knew the size of the mountain facing them. As it turned out, Australia added 75 runs in 18.2 overs during the morning session. That was frustrating enough for England but the difficulties the tourists encountered seemed grim portents for the host's next innings. Marnus Labuschagne was eventually run out for 80 by Joe Denly's fine throw from third man but by then he had been spilled by Jonny Bairstow off Stuart Broad and twice hit on the helmet by Jofra Archer. In a way it was a morning of inadequate rewards; for all that he had been dropped three times, Labuschagne's innings was worth a century, and Stokes deserved more than the wicket of Pat Cummins this morning, a success which left him with figures of 3-56.

After their team's catastrophic first innings the crowd's mood in the early overs of England's second attempt was predictably apprehensive. Though Rory Burns and Jason Roy dealt well with the four overs before lunch, the general nervousness was justified immediately on the resumption when both were dismissed within five minutes of each other. Burns was caught at slip by David Warner off Josh Hazlewood when fencing at a ball he could have left on length; and England spectators had scarcely recovered from that reverse when Roy was completely beaten by a delivery from Cummins which was angled into him before straightening and clipping the top of off stump. "A sizzler," said the radio commentator Jim Maxwell, who has seen a few such balls. "An absolute seed," added Alastair Cook, who has been dismissed by a few.

England supporters steeled themselves for disintegration but instead they saw Root and Denly edge towards competence. Whenever the pair strayed towards flamboyance they looked vulnerable. Denly's booming drives looked like blooming errors but the Kent man hit Nathan Lyon over the top without risk and pulled James Pattinson powerfully through midwicket. Yet these shots were bridged by nine overs and plenty of secure defence. Denly also took a few blows to the body from the Australian fast bowlers. Whether they hurt tomorrow will depend on the result of the match. The fifty partnership was cheered loudly on the Western Terrace and by tea the stand between Root and Denly was worth 75 runs, eight more than England's first innings total. Such comparisons with exhibits in the ECB's Black Museum are inevitable.

It was also noted that while England's innings had so far occupied 38 overs there were 39 more scheduled to be bowled. Rather than a target being chased, runs were being accumulated. Thoughts of victory could wait until Sunday and then only if England batted well in the evening session. The crowd settled again. There was far less of the uproar normally associated with a Test match Saturday at Leeds. Even people in fancy dress eschewed ostentatious parades until late in the day when the "full" signs had popped up in their eyeballs. It was difficult to remember one had followed 13 penguins up St Michael's Lane on the way to Headingley's splendid Oxfam bookshop. Their destination was The Skyrack.

Root reached his fifty off 120 balls with a cover drive off Lyon and celebrated by leg-glancing the next ball to the rope. Then applause greeted the hundred partnership but England were still not a third of the way to their target. Nonetheless, Paine modified his tactics and now sought to throttle the run rate. This tactic was successful; only 66 runs were scored off 34 overs in the evening session and England also lost Denly, who gloved a superbly directed bouncer from Hazlewood to Paine 21 balls after reaching his fifty. Denly had not managed a run off those 21 deliveries and Stokes was similarly restrained, making just two off 50 balls as a glorious day drew to its enthralling close and Headingley drew the deepest of breaths.

Some of the crowd will have gone home wishing they had tickets for tomorrow. Yet 24 hours ago there was a reasonable case that there would be no cricket to see at Headingley this Bank Holiday Sunday. Now a new ball is due eight overs into Sunday morning's cricket, when the Australian bowlers are fresh. The sensible money is on Paine's bowlers but the game abandoned good sense long ago. "This is a Test match!" someone had yelled in the Emerald Suite when England were collapsing on Friday morning. "I know it is," replied Ben Stokes with his bowling on Friday evening. "We know it, too," said Joe Root and Joe Denly as they put on 126 for their country's third wicket on Saturday afternoon. And everyone knows it, now. Suddenly we have a game on our hands.

The greatest ever innings in the greatest ever Test?

――――――――――――――――― DAY FOUR ―――――――――――――

England, 67 and 362-9 (Stokes 135*, Root 77, Denly 50,
Hazlewood 4-85), beat Australia, 179 and 246, by one wicket

At 4.20 this broiling Leeds afternoon Pat Cummins bowled to Ben Stokes. The delivery was a little short and wide and it gave Stokes the chance to swing his arms, an opportunity he is generally quick to seize. So he did again and the ball was flayed to the cover boundary.

How mundane it sounds! How matter of fact! Who would think it completed the one-wicket England victory which kept the Ashes alive after a Test which is being called the finest in the game's history?

Well, to understand all that you probably need to have been one of the 18,000 spectators at Emerald Headingley this golden Sunday or been watching the extraordinary drama unfold on television. Had you been doing either of those things you would have seen Stokes make 135 not out, an innings which helped England to score 362 in their second innings only 48 hours after they had been bowled out for 67 in their first.

This was a day of such sporting glory that no praise seems excessive. For the truth is that Stokes' century comprised three innings, each of them essential to the overall achievement. In the first, on Saturday evening, he made two runs off 50 balls when his only objective was survival; in the second he supported Jonny Bairstow and eventually reached his slowest Test fifty off 152 balls after 215 minutes of patient forbearance.

But the glory was still to come. For when England lost their ninth wicket on 286 and Stokes was joined by Somerset's Jack Leach, England were still 73 runs short of 359, the tallest total they have ever overhauled to win a Test. Stokes' response to all this was wonderful, calculated aggression. Over the course of the next 10.1 overs he hit seven sixes and scored 74 runs in the unbroken last-wicket partnership of 76 with Leach. It was a stand to which Taunton's finest contributed just a single yet defended stoutly for 17 balls against an Australian attack which suddenly saw an all-but-certain victory slipping from their grasp.

Even that does not begin to reflect the drama that took place at Headingley this afternoon. For one thing, Stokes was dropped on 116 when Marcus Harris spilled a ferociously tough low chance at third man; for another, Leach should have been run out and the destination of the Ashes settled when England's No.11 scampered madly down the wicket in the penultimate over of the game but Nathan Lyon failed to collect the throw at the bowler's end; and for yet another, Hawkeye indicated that Stokes would have been adjudged leg before to Lyon's very next ball had Australia had any reviews left with which to interrogate Joel Wilson's not out decision.

But Tim Paine had wasted both his side DRS opportunities with two footling lbw queries, one on Saturday, one on Sunday, and Australia must now bind their wounds before the Old Trafford Test a week on Wednesday. And when that game begins spectators will still be talking about the four sixes Stokes hit off Lyon, three of them orthodox straight hits, the other an outrageous reverse sweep; they will still be marvelling at the scooped six off Cummins or the two maximums over the leg side boundary off Josh Hazlewood.

Some sportsmen – there are only a very few of them – welcome the great occasions. When others withdraw, they flourish. The tension that most contemporaries and many spectators cannot bear becomes for them a natural atmosphere. The stadium becomes their workplace. Stokes is such an athlete. He did not celebrate either his fifty or his hundred because in themselves they made no difference to the result. But when that final four sped to the fence, he spread-eagled himself upright and bellowed his triumph to the world. On the Western Terrace the thousands who had supported England and quite literally cheered every run went berserk in the manner of a football crowd at Elland Road. They had heard about Headingley Tests before; now here was their own special glory, a victory they will remember for as long as they are in full possession of their marbles.

Suddenly it was 1981; suddenly it was any of three Tests in 2005 when English spectators identified with their team with a fervour no one had anticipated. Many of those on the Western Terrace were too young for any of those glories. And during this extraordinary afternoon one thought of other cricket grounds across England where club or county games were taking place. News drifted through the mayhem at Headingley that play had been stopped at the Rose Bowl in order that people could watch the conclusion of the Test. They said the score was also announced at the Tottenham Hotspur match. For the second time this summer, cricket is front page news.

Many of the Australian team stood virtually motionless when England won the match. Lyon, by contrast, sank to his knees in misery but was quickly picked up by the admirable Paine. Others trooped off the field and summoned dignity in defeat after a day they had expected to dominate. How had it come to this? To a degree one shared their disbelief. For the first eight overs of the morning session the Australian attack had been on the money, not that financial remuneration is a remotely suitable metaphor when applied to this day's epic. The cricket we saw this Sunday was of a sort cricketers dream about before they have played a first-class match or even had a county trial. Perhaps that is why the spectators identified with the batsmen so joyously; the dreams were shared.

And so was the tension, so were the disappointments. Australia bowled magnificently until they took the new ball. The first run was not scored until the 26th ball of the morning and the 33rd brought the wicket of Joe Root, who tried to work Lyon through the leg side but only inside-edged the ball onto his pad. From there it looped gently behind Smith and David Warner dived to take his sixth catch of the game.

On Saturday evening almost everyone thought it vital for England to survive the first ten overs with the second new ball. No one thought those overs would be so fruitful for England or that the momentum of the game would shift as markedly as it did. Some of that was achieved by the batsmen, particularly Bairstow, who was busy almost from the first ball he received. The Yorkshire crowd is used to such delights, of course, but the Western Terrace rarely stands for a four as it did when Bairstow drove Hazlewood through the covers and then collected another boundary when he worked the ball through gully.

Stokes was content to support Bairstow, whose speed between the wickets ensured he collected full value for every stroke. The 50 partnership came up off 58 balls and Australia's relative decline was encapsulated by Pattinson bowling a wide which went to the boundary at the Emerald Stand End. Then Stokes hooked Cummins for six. Had anyone been told it would be the first of eight such blows they would have been treated for a touch of the sun.

The cricket after lunch was a bracing corrective to English optimism. In 80 minutes the home side lost five wickets and most were self-inflicted wounds. Bairstow slashed Hazlewood to Marnus Labuschagne at second slip and trooped off with 36 to his name; Jos Buttler was run out for a single by Stokes's "yes-no" call and Travis Head's direct hit; Chris Woakes drove Hazlewood to Wade at cover; Archer clubbed 15 runs before trying the trick once too often against Lyon; Stuart Broad lasted two balls. Then Jack Leach strolled out to join Stokes. Australian spectators prepared themselves to salute the retention of the Ashes. Little did they know; little did any of us know.

And that is where this report would have ended at nearly eight o'clock on a balmy West Yorkshire evening, except that the England players have just walked out to the middle at Emerald Headingley and are sitting on the outfield savouring one of the greatest afternoons any of them will know. Jack Leach has just relived his single run and scampered down the pitch. Ben Stokes is sipping a beer at the end of a day in which he is being toasted across the land.

Ben's Match, Headingley's Test

Reflection

There are some moments in life which are so intense, so crammed with experience, that it takes a little time before they can be fully comprehended. Only when one reflects can one make order out of the chaos, however glorious that chaos might have been. Around a week ago, sitting in a hotel room in Scarborough, I wrote this:

A cricket ground without people is nothing more than concrete and metal, wood and glass, plastic and turf. You might admire the architecture or the construction but the soul of the place will elude you if you are not stirred by what has happened there.

I do not claim the slightest prescience. Nevertheless, over the last hour of the Headingley Test yesterday afternoon – Jack Leach batted for exactly 60 minutes, by the way – I saw people stirred to heights of emotion I had never thought to witness on a cricket ground. There were experienced journalists with their hands on their heads in astonishment; there was Nathan Lyon on the ground in despair; and there was the Western Terrace, a riot of movement and joy such as it has never managed before, even during a T20 Roses match. And all this on a great old ground which was wearing new clothes and winking at history as if to remind us all that an Ashes Test at Headingley is almost always something very special.

Even those who had watched the game in 1981 admitted this was something different. There were only about 5,000 spectators in the ground when Ian Botham and Bob Willis turned that match around and their transformation took something like a day to achieve. Ben Stokes managed it in the final hour of a 330-minute innings in front of a near-as-dammit full house which cheered every single and savoured each of Jack Leach's blocks. Commentators who had watched every ball of the 2005 Ashes series agreed that this atmosphere was unlike any they had known.

And when all was done, we asked three of the principal actors what they thought of it all. It is a curious feature of sport that well within an hour or so of a match finishing, we require people whose emotions have been tortured beyond decency to offer rational judgements on their performance. No journalist asks a doctor to review a heart transplant; or a teacher to reconsider a lesson; or a journo to analyse his sentences. But then in the latter case, no one gives a monkey's.

I rarely attend press conferences. What can a sportsman say that he has not already shown? Ben Stokes' fluency is not best expressed in words but in the outrageous reverse-sweep he played off Lyon or in the scoop off Pat Cummins. These were strokes of genius which Andrew Flintoff could not have produced simply because the shots had not been properly conceived in 2005. Anyway I'm glad I abandoned my rather prissy approach and listened to Joe Root, Stokes and Tim Paine on Sunday evening. Root and Stokes were excellent from their different perspectives but their comments will have been widely and exhaustively reported. Paine, as far as I could gather, was only questioned by the Australian media. He was civilised, generous, disappointed, analytical.

"It was an amazing game of cricket. Obviously we finished up on the wrong side of it but in terms of an advertisement for Test cricket it was bloody exciting. It was great to be involved in it and I thought Ben Stokes was unbelievably good. It was one of the great innings. I thought Joe Denly and Joe Root were also excellent yesterday afternoon when I thought our bowling was as good as it gets.

"That was as hard as it gets for a touring side. Sometimes people make mistakes and we made a couple today and in the end it cost us the Test match. We missed a few opportunities and a guy played out of his skin to take the game away from us. That can happen and that's okay.

"It's not yet a consolation [that he had just played in maybe the greatest Test match ever.] It certainly won't be for the next few months but I think in five or six years when we are ex-players, we'll look back and know that we played in an amazing Test series. Whenever you turn on Channel Seven, there are highlights of the 2005 Ashes series because it was unbelievable cricket, not because of who won or who lost. So far this Ashes series has been the same."

Yes, those Australian cricketers will need time to adjust to this defeat but they have only ten days before the teams meet again at Old Trafford. Then the final Test at The Oval takes place four days later. It is a brutal and bloody daft schedule. But we are in the middle of this great drama, one that is defining our summer and will warm our winter.

And so the Ashes caravan crosses the Pennines. When I left Emerald Headingley's press box at about nine o'clock last night, there were still a dozen journalists with their heads down over their laptops. Neither that room nor Yorkshire's home will ever be quite the same for me. We are all changed. Sport does that to us. It is its special gift.

Before us is one of cricket's great theatres but the lines of the play can only be written by the actors... As ever, it is the people we remember.

ENGLAND V AUSTRALIA

3rd Test, Leeds, August 22 - 25, 2019
ICC World Test Championship
Australia 179 & 246 – England 67 & 362/9 (T:359)
England won by 1 wicket

AUSTRALIA 1ST INNINGS

BATTING		R	B	M	4s	6s	SR
David Warner	c †Bairstow b Archer	61	94	148	7	0	64.89
Marcus Harris	c †Bairstow b Archer	8	12	18	2	0	66.66
Usman Khawaja	c †Bairstow b Broad	8	17	21	1	0	47.05
Marnus Labuschagne	lbw b Stokes	74	129	215	10	0	57.36
Travis Head	b Broad	0	6	8	0	0	0
Matthew Wade	b Archer	0	3	9	0	0	0
Tim Paine (c)†	lbw b Woakes	11	26	48	1	0	42.3
James Pattinson	c Root b Archer	2	8	15	0	0	25
Pat Cummins	c †Bairstow b Archer	0	13	19	0	0	0
Nathan Lyon	lbw b Archer	1	4	14	0	0	25
Josh Hazlewood	not out	1	3	5	0	0	33.33
Extras	(b 4, lb 2, nb 2, w 5)	13					
TOTAL	52.1 Ov (RR: 3.43)	179					

BOWLING	O	M	R	W	E	WD	NB
Stuart Broad	14	4	32	2	2.28	0	0
Jofra Archer	17.1	3	45	6	2.62	0	2
Chris Woakes	12	4	51	1	4.25	1	0
Ben Stokes	9	0	45	1	5	0	0

FALL OF WICKETS:
1-12 (Marcus Harris, 3.6 ov), 2-25 (Usman Khawaja, 8.4 ov), 3-136 (David Warner, 31.4 ov), 4-138 (Travis Head, 32.5 ov), 5-139 (Matthew Wade, 33.6 ov), 6-162 (Tim Paine, 42.6 ov), 7-173 (James Pattinson, 45.6 ov), 8-174 (Pat Cummins, 49.6 ov), 9-177 (Marnus Labuschagne, 51.2 ov), 10-179 (Nathan Lyon, 52.1 ov)

ENGLAND 1ST INNINGS

BATTING		R	B	M	4s	6s	SR
Rory Burns	c †Paine b Cummins	9	28	53	1	0	32.14
Jason Roy	c Warner b Hazlewood	9	15	19	2	0	60
Joe Root (c)	c Warner b Hazlewood	0	2	8	0	0	0
Joe Denly	c †Paine b Pattinson	12	49	77	1	0	24.48
Ben Stokes	c Warner b Pattinson	8	13	24	1	0	61.53
Jonny Bairstow †	c Warner b Hazlewood	4	15	33	1	0	26.66
Jos Buttler	c Khawaja b Hazlewood	5	16	29	1	0	31.25
Chris Woakes	c †Paine b Cummins	5	9	18	1	0	55.55
Jofra Archer	c †Paine b Cummins	7	8	16	1	0	87.5
Stuart Broad	not out	4	5	16	1	0	80
Jack Leach	b Hazlewood	1	7	7	0	0	14.28
Extras	(lb 3)	3					
TOTAL	27.5 Ov (RR: 2.40)	67					

BOWLING	O	M	R	W	E	WD	NB
Pat Cummins	9	4	23	3	2.55	0	0
Josh Hazlewood	12.5	2	30	5	2.33	0	0
Nathan Lyon	1	0	2	0	2	0	0
James Pattinson	5	2	9	2	1.8	0	0

FALL OF WICKETS:
1-10 (Jason Roy, 3.5 ov), 2-10 (Joe Root, 5.1 ov), 3-20 (Rory Burns, 10.4 ov), 4-34 (Ben Stokes, 14.3 ov), 5-45 (Joe Denly, 20.1 ov), 6-45 (Jonny Bairstow, 21.1 ov), 7-54 (Chris Woakes, 24.1 ov), 8-56 (Jos Buttler, 25.1 ov), 9-66 (Jofra Archer, 26.4 ov), 10-67 (Jack Leach, 27.5 ov)

AUSTRALIA 2ND INNINGS

BATTING		R	B	M	4s	6s	SR
Marcus Harris	b Leach	19	39	47	3	0	48.71
David Warner	lbw b Broad	0	2	3	0	0	0
Usman Khawaja	c Roy b Woakes	23	38	59	4	0	60.52
Marnus Labuschagne	run out (Denly/†Bairstow)	80	187	295	8	0	42.78
Travis Head	b Stokes	25	56	78	3	0	44.64
Matthew Wade	c †Bairstow b Stokes	33	59	101	6	0	55.93
Tim Paine (c)†	c Denly b Broad	0	2	5	0	0	0
James Pattinson	c Root b Archer	20	48	67	2	0	41.66
Pat Cummins	c Burns b Stokes	6	6	16	1	0	100
Nathan Lyon	b Archer	9	17	25	1	0	52.94
Josh Hazlewood	not out	4	5	10	1	0	80
Extras	(b 5, lb 13, nb 7, w 2)	27					
TOTAL	**75.2 Ov (RR: 3.26)**	**246**					

BOWLING	O	M	R	W	E	WD	NB
Jofra Archer	14	2	40	2	2.85	1	3
Stuart Broad	16	2	52	2	3.25	1	0
Chris Woakes	10	1	34	1	3.4	0	0
Jack Leach	11	0	46	1	4.18	0	0
Ben Stokes	24.2	7	56	3	2.3	0	4

FALL OF WICKETS:
1-10 (David Warner, 1.2 ov), 2-36 (Marcus Harris, 11.1 ov), 3-52 (Usman Khawaja, 14.1 ov), 4-97 (Travis Head, 32.2 ov), 5-163 (Matthew Wade, 52.6 ov), 6-164 (Tim Paine, 53.3 ov), 7-215 (James Pattinson, 67.6 ov), 8-226 (Pat Cummins, 70.2 ov), 9-237 (Marnus Labuschagne, 73.3 ov), 10-246 (Nathan Lyon, 75.2 ov)

ENGLAND 2ND INNINGS

BATTING		R	B	M	4s	6s	SR
Rory Burns	c Warner b Hazlewood	7	21	37	0	0	33.33
Jason Roy	b Cummins	8	18	42	1	0	44.44
Joe Root (c)	c Warner b Lyon	77	205	322	7	0	37.56
Joe Denly	c †Paine b Hazlewood	50	155	237	8	0	32.25
Ben Stokes	not out	135	219	330	11	8	61.64
Jonny Bairstow †	c Labuschagne b Hazlewood	36	68	110	4	0	52.94
Jos Buttler	run out (Head)	1	9	16	0	0	11.11
Chris Woakes	c Wade b Hazlewood	1	8	15	0	0	12.5
Jofra Archer	c Head b Lyon	15	33	46	3	0	45.45
Stuart Broad	lbw b Pattinson	0	2	6	0	0	0
Jack Leach	not out	1	17	60	0	0	5.88
Extras	(b 5, lb 15, nb 1, w 10)	31					
TOTAL	**125.4 Ov (RR: 2.88)**	**362/9**					

BOWLING	O	M	R	W	E	WD	NB
Pat Cummins	24.4	5	80	1	3.24	1	1
Josh Hazlewood	31	11	85	4	2.74	1	0
Nathan Lyon	39	5	114	2	2.92	0	0
James Pattinson	25	9	47	1	1.88	4	0
Marnus Labuschagne	6	0	16	0	2.66	0	0

FALL OF WICKETS:
1-15 (Rory Burns, 5.6 ov), 2-15 (Jason Roy, 6.3 ov), 3-141 (Joe Denly, 59.3 ov), 4-159 (Joe Root, 77.3 ov), 5-245 (Jonny Bairstow, 99.1 ov), 6-253 (Jos Buttler, 102.2 ov), 7-261 (Chris Woakes, 105.6 ov), 8-286 (Jofra Archer, 114.6 ov), 9-286 (Stuart Broad, 115.2 ov)

12

HAS

This chapter contains some of the pieces I have written about Haseeb Hameed. All but one of them concern his early years in Lancashire's first team. (Chapter Two includes reports about his two centuries at Worcester in 2021.) I have firmly resisted any temptation to amend them in the light of subsequent events. Most of the people reading this will know that Hameed's hundred against Middlesex at Lord's in 2019 played him false. At the end of that season he was released by Lancashire and signed by Nottinghamshire, where his career was revived by Peter Moores, one of the very best coaches in England. As these words are being written Hameed is preparing for his first Ashes tour, although it says something about the booms and slumps of his career than many people, myself included, expected him to be playing Test cricket in Australia four years ago.

Yet nothing that has happened to Hameed's cricket in the past few summers should ever eclipse the wonder that greeted his emergence in 2016. His technique has been modified and he is now a battle-toughened cricketer but the essential purity of his batsmanship remains and he is only 24. Two of these pieces refer to my first sight of him, aged 16, playing for Lancashire's second team at Southport in July 2014 when almost nobody outside Old Trafford knew how good he was. The memory of that afternoon has never faded.

Lancashire v Hampshire – May 2016

Procter and Hameed enhance
Lancashire's feel-good

―――――――――――――――――― DAY TWO ――――――――――――――――――

Hampshire 109 and 22-1 trail Lancashire 486 (Procter 137, Petersen 81, Hameed 62; Best 5-90) by 325 runs

Old Trafford on a blissful Monday morning in May. The leaves on the trees girdling the red-brick Town Hall are green with all the delicate effrontery of an English spring. Inside the ground, a medium-pace bowler runs up to the wicket and delivers a ball which passes perhaps nine inches outside off stump. The willow-thin batter lets the ball complete its journey while holding his bat extravagantly high, as if excluding the merest possibility of outrageous accident. The bowler shrugs, turns and walks back to his mark while the batter plays his leave again, as if something about the original execution displeased him. In the early stages of Ken Dodd's marathon one-man shows he encourages his audience to chant: "Time matters not one jot." One can rather imagine Haseeb Hameed nodding in fervent agreement.

Certainly the cricket seemed held in gentle suspension as Hameed completed his 291-minute 62 this morning. The pace quickened markedly after lunch as Alviro Petersen hit 13 fours in a pedigree 81 off 85 balls to extend his team's lead beyond 200 and reinforce their dominance. But Petersen is 17 years older than Hameed and has played exactly 200 more first-class matches. He is stronger, cricket-fitter and knows his game far better. At the moment Petersen has more of everything...except time.

Comparisons between the two players were therefore of limited value and they threatened to deflect attention away from the career-best 137 made by Luke Procter on a day when Lancashire had built a colossal 347-run lead by the time they were bowled out for 456. The home side's late clatter of wickets was caused largely to a splendidly defiant spell from Tino Best, who took four wickets in 23 balls, finished with 5-90 and greeted every success with a lovely explosion of joy.

This was still far and away Lancashire's day, though, not least because they claimed the important wicket of Jimmy Adams, caught at second slip by Karl Brown off James Anderson, in the hour before the close. Steven Croft's men are playing very much like a team bubbling with self-belief and this is obvious in all their disciplines. Petersen built on Hameed's work and Procter combined well with both his partners in century-plus stands.

Hameed, though, deserves credit for opening the Lancashire innings with impressive solidity and for the smooth grace with which he drove the ball through the covers. Although only 19 years old and with more than 15 cricketing summers before him, he bats as if every innings is precious. He plays a minimum of 12 shots every over, six to the balls bowled and then at least one after each of those six, as if he is still searching for a shot so perfect that it defies experience or description. He leaves the ball as a matador might manoeuvre a bull, the bat a muleta before it becomes a sword. What Hameed needs to do is develop the ability to work the ball around in the manner of Procter, who spent much of the morning pushing ones or twos and keeping things moving. The stance of Lancashire's No.3 may remind one of an arthritic rent-collector trying to see under a door of a late payer but he knows his strengths and he is revelling in his new responsibilities. Indeed, it seemed that the many Lancashire supporters at Old Trafford would be greeting at least two centurions this run-soaked afternoon but it was not to be. Hameed pushed forward to Mason Crane's penultimate ball before lunch and edged a good leg spinner to Vince at slip.

Simon Barnes once wrote of cricket as a wonderful metaphor for death and one imagines that each of his dismissals is accompanied by a sense of mild bereavement for Hameed. At one stage it seemed nip and tuck whether he was to score his first hundred for Lancashire before the county completed building their new hotel. But such frivolous speculations suddenly became as nothing. Hameed departed, smacking his bat against his pad in an abyss of disappointment. Lunch had become funeral meats.

The cricket in the afternoon session only deepened the woe for Vince's men as 146 runs were piled on in 33 overs. And only a flint-souled Jesuit would have no sympathy for Hampshire at the moment. Deprived for varying lengths of time of Fidel Edwards, Gareth Berg and Chris Wood, they are trying to make do and mend until Sean Ervine and Reece Topley are fit to wear the colours again in around a fortnight or so. James Tomlinson must feel like one of the last Texians at the Alamo, albeit Hameed currently lays the gentlest of sieges.

Lancashire v Warwickshire – June 2016

Hameed and Parkinson keep Lancashire even

——————————— DAY THREE ———————————

Lancashire 308 and 170-5 (Hameed 81; Barker 3-50) lead Warwickshire
263 (Ambrose 70*, Barker 64; Parkinson 5-49, Smith 3-30) by 215 runs*

'Mutare vel timere sperno', as they rarely say in Horwich. But the
Bolton School motto – 'I scorn to change or to fear' – carried a
rich resonance on the third day of this game at Old Trafford. For it
was one Old Boltonian, Matt Parkinson, who displayed unwavering
accuracy as he took five wickets on debut to give his side an
advantage; and it was another, Haseeb Hameed, who exhibited no
fear as he sought to preserve that advantage with an unbeaten 81
against a strong Warwickshire fightback led by the Manchester-born
seamer Keith Barker.

By the close, Lancashire had extended their 45-run lead on first
innings to 215 but they achieved that slight advantage only at the
cost of five prime wickets. This quite marvellous game remains
finely balanced going into the final day and perhaps it is only right
that two 19-year-old cricketers have played important roles in the
four-act drama. There was a childlike simplicity about much of our
cricket today and it was best expressed at 12.35 when Parkinson
turned the ball through a gap between Olly Hannon-Dalby's bat
and pad which was not so much a gate as a portico. That wicket
completed the leg spinner's first five-wicket return at a cost of 49
runs from 23.1 beautifully disciplined and skilful overs.

The recent history of English cricket is strewn with the reputations
of promising young leggies. Some are now specialist batters; others
might be selling VHS recorders. Leg spin can be a thankless calling.
So let us murmur a quiet prayer as we say that Parkinson is one to
watch. His accuracy, his economy and, more than anything else,
his ability to turn the ball suggest he has a fine future. On Tuesday
he removed Jonathan Trott and Varun Chopra. On Wednesday he
had Barker, who made 64, caught by Neil Wagner at short fine leg
when sweeping and he then mopped up the tail. Each wicket saw
him embraced by his team mates and the members rose to him as

301

he walked off into the distant dressing rooms at Old Trafford, still clutching the ball with which he had become only the second leg-spinner to take five wickets on Championship debut since the war. In less than a day Lancashire supporters have gone from: 'Who's this lad, Parkinson' to 'Parky'. If he takes more wickets in the second innings, there may be folk songs.

But this game has been the finest entertainment because both Lancashire and Warwickshire have played excellent cricket, albeit spiced with occasional fallibility. Tim Ambrose's undefeated 70 in the visitors' first innings was a tribute to understated, professional efficiency and when Lancashire had progressed smoothly if slowly to 87 for the loss of Tom Smith, Ian Bell's bowlers proved for the third time in this match that this is a wicket on which one wicket often brings four. In the third over after tea, Luke Procter's defensive push merely edged a catch to Chopra at slip. Four overs later, Alviro Petersen came down the wicket to the same bowler but only chipped a catch to Rikki Clarke at a slightly short cover. Croft, perhaps knackered by leadership, his first-innings century and over a hundred overs' wicketkeeping, played a tired defensive shot to his first ball and nicked off to Ambrose. And when Patel had Karl Brown caught at the wicket for one just three balls later, Lancashire had lost three wickets in five balls and four batsmen had been swept aside for 17 runs in five overs.

Hameed watched all this from the other end with increasing concern yet his technique remained quite unaltered. At its most serene the Lancashire opener's batting is as reassuring as the late-night shipping forecast. There were boundaries in his innings, five of them, in fact, and not all of them behind the wicket. Pulled fours off Barker and Rankin provided evidence of attacking capability yet Hameed's first instinct is, as yet, to make his wicket hard to take. 'Something there is that doesn't love a wall' wrote Robert Frost. But then Frost never saw Rahul Dravid.

And in the last 90 minutes of play Hameed was joined by Livingstone, whose lovely ability to hit the ball very hard made him a perfect foil for his partner. This pair added 66 in an unbroken stand that left Lancashire slightly ahead in this game, if only because they have the runs on the board. Livingstone's 39 not out has already included cover-driven boundaries off Patel and a wondrous pick-up for six off Clarke which sailed deep into the crowd at long on.

Hameed, for his part has batted 268 minutes, faced 223 balls and is 19 runs short of what will be the first of many hundreds. When he returned to the dressing room, he no doubt received the congratulations and perhaps it is not surprising that the pair should join forces. This area has never been short of effective double acts: Jack Simmons and David Hughes, David Lloyd and Barry Wood, Minnie Caldwell and Martha Longhurst. And now they have Has 'n' Parky, appearing soon at a cricket ground near you.

Some would counsel caution, of course. They would say that to be a young cricketer is to receive a crash course in life's turbulence. They might echo the final words of another Boltonian, the grumpy and troubled Ezra Fitton in Roy Boulting's 1966 film *The Family Way* "That's life, son. At your age it'll make you laugh but one day it'll break your bloody heart." But no. It would be better for both Hameed and Parkinson to pay no attention whatever to the words of that rather miserable old bugger. For the moment, they live in the green world of debuts, new grounds and first experiences. Maybe we all do, if we would only open our eyes...and look.

Lancashire v Yorkshire - August 2016

Hameed gets into the Roses mood

———————————— DAY ONE ————————————

Lancashire 299-7 (Hameed 114, Procter 79;
Brooks 3-51) against Yorkshire

The head is perfectly still, the stance comfortably compact. The bat is held in the air, some 30 degrees above the horizontal; it rocks, poised for potential employment, in the batter's hands. As the bowler moves into his delivery stride the rear foot moves back a shade and then the front foot goes forward a little, but these movements betoken merely readiness, not commitment. The stroke, when it is played – if it is played – is full of conviction and one could be lured into the delusion that no other shot could have been attempted to that particular delivery. If the ball is left alone, the bat describes an arc as smooth as Giotto's famous circle.

For many people, not all of them Lancastrians, the gentle budding of Haseeb Hameed's career has provided a backcloth to the summer. The first day of the Roses match saw a further flowering of this quietly precocious talent. For while medals were won in Rio and goals were scored across England, Hameed completed his third century of the season with a perfectly safe, lofted cover-drive off Adil Rashid. For all that Yorkshire's seam and swing bowlers capitalised upon some careless batting to take six wickets, one of them Hameed's, for 61 runs in a game-changing evening session, this day was still made memorable by the stroke-play of a young man who takes quite as much care over his backward defensive shots as he does over his cover drives and may even take equal pleasure from them.

Supporters travelling from across the Pennines and even some home supporters might take a different and equally valid view, of course. The dismissal of Alviro Petersen to what became the final ball of the day completed 80 minutes' cricket in which Andrew Gale's bowlers had shown why Yorkshire remain many pundits' favourites to retain their title. They understand that even when sessions are lost, days can be salvaged or even won. The limpness of Petersen's dismissal, playing on to Jack Brooks for 32, completed Yorkshire's recovery and there was little surprise that Brooks celebrated his third wicket in 29 balls by wheeling back to the Lancashire supporters in the pavilion, cupping his hand to his ear and even pointing to the name on the back of his shirt. Only 90 minutes previously, Lancashire had been 238-1 and there was even a possibility that the home side would amass a sufficiently big total to obviate the necessity of batting again on a pitch which looks likely to take increasing turn. The four Yorkshire seamers proceeded to mock such foolishness with some high quality bowling, not all of it with the new ball.

But Brooks was not the first cricketer to coax a warm reaction from the Emirates Old Trafford crowd this balmy Saturday. When Hameed reached his hundred quite shortly after tea, he swished his bat down before him in the modern fashion. He took the applause which came from all sides of the ground and reserved particular attention for his close family, who were sitting in the Red Rose Suite. He had hit 14 boundaries in the 189 balls he had needed to reach his landmark and by no means all of them had been signature cover-drives and opening batter's deflections to third man. There had been straight drives off Rashid, who did not have his best day but may yet play a crucial role in this game, and there had been cuts off Tim Bresnan and clips through square off Brooks. Just as significantly, Hameed had shown that the tempo of his run-scoring is increasing and that he is beginning to understand how to work the ball around, even when facing an attack of Yorkshire's quality. "You start to learn to adapt to different situations and learn when to put the foot on the accelerator and push on. That comes with experience and hopefully it's going in the right direction," he said. However, just as illuminating, arguably more so, was the view of the Yorkshire skipper Andrew Gale, especially when expressed in the middle of a Roses match. "Hameed is one of the best young players I've seen in a long time," he said. "He's an old-fashioned opening batter who occupies the crease and didn't get out of his shell all day. He just played beautifully."

Great batting is defined by age, magnitude and circumstance. Before he went to the wicket to face Ryan Sidebottom and Jack Brooks on a high-clouded Saturday morning 19-year-old Hameed had already become the youngest player in Lancashire's history to score a thousand first-class runs. He had reached that mark 321 days sooner than the previous record-holder, Michael Atherton, and in 23 innings, many of them played on sappy April pitches against First Division attacks. It is less than a year since he made his debut. During Hameed's 24th first-class innings he became Lancashire's leading scorer in the County Championship this season, although he and Alviro Petersen are battling day by day for that honour. During his 86-run opening stand with Tom Smith and a most fluent 152-run partnership with Luke Procter, whose own 79 was a innings studded with excellent drives, Hameed offered evidence which confirmed the view of the Lancashire coach, Ashley Giles, that he will play Test cricket in less than four years.

A Château Lafite cricketer in a wine-box world

Do you remember the first time you hit a ball with a bat?

It doesn't matter what type of ball it was or even whether you used a rough stick instead of a bat. Do you remember the thrill of making the ball travel some distance? Perhaps it went a fair way and eventually you discovered that this was achieved by "timing the stroke". Perhaps you then nagged a parent, sibling or friend to provide balls for you to hit and before long you were asking them to "bowl" in the garden, yard or street.

Some people are lost to cricket from the very start. It is a little like love.

Watching Haseeb Hameed bat is to be reminded of one's innocence and of Blake's "echoing green". Like many prodigies, he makes what he does look dangerously simple. This is because for all the technique, the coaching, the selection of shot, there is in his play a palimpsest of his childhood and an eight-year-old boy pestering his father, Ismail, to let him play cricket with his elder brothers, Safwaan and Nuaman.

Hameed is no longer pestering; he is demanding. His batting is suffused with a style both simple and cultivated; it expresses his demand that he be allowed to bat for as long as possible. He has been so successful in his 18 first-class matches, all but four of them against Division One attacks, that he is demanding to be selected for England's winter tours. Experienced Test and county bowlers try to dismiss him and then speak in admiration of his obvious skill, his preternatural self-possession at the crease, his ability to bat with a partner yet retreat into his own world, one which is inured to the comments of opponents. "Is it my turn to bat yet?"

It is a world in which shots are played to balls and then played again to imaginary deliveries as if the quest for perfection can never be completed. There is something Buddhist about all this although Hameed's only noble truth on the field is the accumulation of runs. I cannot think of another young batsman who has radiated comparable tranquillity. His opponents say he will play for England. They are right. After Hameed made a century in the Roses match, he was warmly complimented by the Yorkshire skipper, Andrew Gale. It was as if Joe Frasier has taken time out at the end of the seventh round in Manila to say that this chap Ali could actually box a bit.

Then Hameed made another hundred in the second innings. Everyone recorded the fact that he was the first Lancashire player to make two centuries in a Roses match and that he was the fifth youngest player to make a thousand runs in an English season. What was rather overlooked was that Hameed had faced 209 balls and batted for over 302 minutes to make 114 in the first innings; he then faced 124 balls and batted for 173 minutes to make 100 not out in the second dig. People on blogs have referred all season to the "Way of Hameed" – that Buddhism thing again – but Hameed's way is changing. Sharp coaches like Nottinghamshire's Mick Newell have noticed that the tempo of his batting is quickening. This is happening not because he is hitting more boundaries – he has frequently collected as many fours as his partners – but because he is learning to work the ball around for ones and twos, often against attacks of international quality.

The statistics of Hameed's short career – 18 first-class matches – have been seized on by the game's gourmands but they are satisfying to the gourmets, too.

In six innings in 2015 he averaged 42.83; after 23 innings in 2016 the average is now 53.76.

In his 29 innings he has been dismissed for single figure scores on two occasions.

He has been bowled three times in his first-class career and never with fewer than 44 runs against his name.

Hameed is an opening batsman. He is 19 years old.

Giles speaks of Hameed with deep admiration and a touch of amusement. He understands that he and sensitive coaches like Mark Chilton have been charged with developing a very special talent. In May Giles was talking about Hameed playing for England within four years; now he knows it will happen sooner than that. He laughs as he talks about not being able to "pull the wool over people's eyes any longer". He also knows that a Test career is what the young batsman has always craved. After playing for Lancashire's junior teams, almost always the one above his age, Hameed demanded to be picked for Lancashire's senior side. Now he is demanding to be selected for England. We are back with the child whose only interest was playing cricket and in scoring as many runs as possible. "Can I bat now, please?"

Hameed has never hidden his ambition. First Lancashire, then England. His heroes are Test cricketers. First and above all, there was Sachin Tendulkar, "the great Sachin" as Hameed refers to him. Now there are also Virat Kohli and Joe Root. There must be a fair chance that Root will be Hameed's England captain at some point. The two met during this year's Old Trafford Test when Hameed was one of four twelfth men and, as he said, "Joe Root changed in my place" in the dressing room before making 254. *His* spot. Lucky Joe.

Yes, I know there are many challenges ahead of Hameed and they will offer a more severe examination than he has received before. That is one of the tough delights of Test cricket. The point is that Hameed knows it as well. He wants to take his careful skills, the beautiful way in which he leaves the ball and match them against the best bowlers on Earth. He meets a bowler's gaze but he does not reply to sledges. It is not necessary. He prefers to take a few steps towards square leg as if pondering all that he has learned in the seven or so seconds it takes to face a ball in a cricket match. Then he readies himself again. One imagines Dale Steyn is looking forward to making his acquaintance; maybe one or two Australian quicks have already watched a video or two; Bay 13 at the MCG probably can't wait to greet him. The feeling will be mutual. Just give him a little time.

Among all the many judgements that have been made about Hameed one of the most illuminating is also the simplest and, paradoxically, the vaguest. "Has gets it," said Giles. What he means is that Hameed possesses a cricketing understanding beyond thought and an appreciation of the game that cannot be coached. It is this that enables him to "calibrate risk", (to take back a phrase that has passed from originality to cliché in less than two months). Hameed has all the shots but he will not play them until the odds are in his favour or the game requires him to do so. Otherwise, he might fall victim to one of the ways in which his innings can end and that is always awful. To see him walk from the wicket after someone has dismissed him for a low score is to see a young man beset with sorrow beyond consolation. He always wants to bat. "Please can I bat now?" Such, such are the joys.

Let me end with my first sight of Hameed for it has served as something of an epigraph to all that has followed. On July 3, 2014, Lancashire's second XI were playing Warwickshire at Southport. I had that morning returned from watching the first team draw their match at Taunton. I ambled down to Trafalgar Road and saw a Lancashire side that needed 217 to win collapse from 99-1 to 143-5 as a series of batters with first-team experience played half-arsed fancy-dan shots.

Although not working at the game, I had taken a notebook. Hameed batted at No.6 and he faced a Warwickshire attack that included Recordo Gordon and Josh Poysden. I watched him play a few shots and started writing down phrases: "gently impressive… his shot selection clear and correct…" Later, they were incorporated into a piece I wrote for the Lancashire website which included the following: "It was as if almost every shot Hameed played – there were three false ones in his 79 balls – was a justified consequence of intelligence he had collected."

Hameed made 30 not out and Lancashire won the game by three wickets. He did not get off the mark until his 20th ball when he cover drove a four. He didn't add to that tally until his 40th ball when he pushed a single. That stroke marked a gradual increase in his run rate. Late in his innings, when all risks had been assessed, he drove Poysden for a low, sweet, straight six. Hameed talks intelligently but he is never more eloquent than when he is batting.

He was 17 years old and just at the end of Year 12 at Bolton School. Second team coach Mark Chilton was pushing him hard, dropping him into difficult situations where he would be tested by good bowlers.

Above all, perhaps, there was calm. But then there almost always is with Hameed. Calmness is often the first impression made by watching him fulfil his vocation. He admits with a wry, self-aware grin that he has no idea what he would do in life were he not a cricketer. But that's fine because, as his former Lancashire colleague, Ashwell Prince, tweeted during the Roses match, Hameed was "born to bat".

He is a Château Lafite cricketer in a wine-box world.

ESPN*Cricinfo – September 2016*

Lancashire Yearbook – 2017

Perhaps more than most people, journalists like to be right. After all we frequently get the best view in the ground and we are meant to know something, although this latter notion is cheerily mocked in pavilions and committee rooms across the land. All the same, I felt a slightly unexpected glow of satisfaction last November when Haseeb Hameed's Test debut at Rajkot attracted what, in a more orthodox theatrical context, would have been termed "rave reviews".

In *The Times* Michael Atherton reported that Hameed had shown "preternatural poise, judgement and skill", later adding that "a veteran correspondent thought it the most accomplished debut he had seen from an English batsman in 40 years." By the time a broken little finger ended his tour of India two Tests early the Lancashire opener had done enough to suggest he has a long international career ahead of him. Which is just as well because playing five-day cricket is precisely what Hameed wants to do with his life for something like the next 15 years; indeed, it is what he and his father, Ismail, have been preparing for since he was in his early teens.

Some facts: Hameed has scored 219 runs in six Test innings; his average, albeit his career has just begun, is 43.8, four runs and a spit shy of his first-class mark; he has made two fifties, the second of them having rapidly adjusted his technique to cope with that broken digit. Yet what has been so impressive about Hameed is that he has taken the skills he showed Lancashire supporters last season and applied them seamlessly to playing Test cricket against the best team in the world. After showering praise on his young charge in 2016, Ashley Giles was always careful to say that you could never know how the lad was going to cope with Test cricket. Well, we know now.

Much has still to be proved, of course. As I write this, Hameed is in Sri Lanka with the England Lions and there are crocuses in Birkdale gardens. Lancashire have their pre-season schedule ahead of them and then the beginning of the County Championship season. It is by no means certain that Hameed will open for England in the first Test against South Africa in July. The 20-year-old knows that he must stick to the basic methods that have got him so far while making such tweaks as seem necessary. If he does that, there will be fresh gauntlets thrown down by South Africa's fast bowlers and maybe the Australian attack next winter. It cannot all be smooth sailing, although no young batsmen I have seen more aptly invites the use of metaphors involving sleek yachts on calm seas with a following breeze.

Lancashire v Middlesex – April 2019

Haseeb Hameed, Lancashire's lost talent, finds his game again

———————— DAY TWO – APRIL 11 ————————

Lancashire 267-4 (Hameed 117, Jones 55, Jennings 52) lead Middlesex 265 (Eskinazi 75, Gubbins 55; Bailey 5-67, Anderson 3-41) by two runs

Form might be temporary but its departure can cause permanent infection. A host of cricketers have lost the ability to score runs or take wickets and taken refuge in the assurances of colleagues that this was merely a brief dip in their careers. Before long, though, they have stopped believing the comforting slogans which consequently made it less likely they would ever again hear tunes of glory. In time they are found playing golf and featuring in "Whatever Happened to…" features.

Last season Haseeb Hameed made 165 runs in 17 Championship innings. Over the winter, coaches he trusts in India told him his game was in good order. Very pleasant, of course, but no one could know whether he would ever again score serious runs against high-quality pace attacks containing, say, four international bowlers.

Well, that question has been answered, though that will not prevent it being asked again. For on a bright afternoon at Lord's, with the catkins still on the alders, Hameed rediscovered the composure and assurance that had amazed former Test cricketers in Manchester and Mohali some three seasons and a few lifetimes ago. His first century since August 2016 was more than a return to form; it was reclamation of treasured territory and the firmest of reminders of the talent which brought his colleagues onto the balcony at Rajkot.

By the time he was dismissed for 117, caught and bowled by Dawid Malan when trying to pull a shortish ball, Hameed had hit 17 fours and had reached his century with a six which he smacked into the Grandstand off Toby Roland-Jones.

Ed Smith, the national selector, watched the innings and will surely have been impressed. Yet someone in the ECB should now sound a warning klaxon that it is far too soon to talk about Hameed returning to the England side. This is one century, albeit a fine one. The selectors will need more evidence before they consider Hameed for representative cricket. The innings was, however, a pleasing riposte to Paul Allott, Lancashire's director of cricket, who said recently that Hameed was "hanging on by his fingertips" at Lancashire. It is still April and it is still the springtime of Hameed's career. He is, lest we forget, 22 years old.

But it is still true that the Boltonian opener had looked good from the first delivery he faced. Rather than retreating into the meek quiescence which is so often the prelude to any batter's dismissal, he sought to get forward and score runs. In Murtagh's fourth over there was a cover drive that recalled his enchanted summer of 2016; three balls later there was an even better stroke though mid-wicket off the front foot. Throughout these early stages of Hameed's innings he was looking to play the ball rather than merely have it bowled to him. There was a scampered single, something rarely seen three years ago. There was more intent and a will to impose himself on the play. He was proactive rather than pre-emptive, adjectives which may make him sound like a yoghurt as distinct from a nuclear attack, but are still valid when applied to his smooth movement onto the front foot. His 47 pre-prandial runs included nine fours and none of them had come off thin edges.

In the early afternoon he was roughed up a little by Steven Finn, who seemed to offer a few observations on his technique. But Hameed knew rather better than anyone else the shape his game was in. The cover drives, the creams through mid-wicket, the Fort Knox forward defensive and, just as importantly, the balls he left alone, had given him all the evidence he needed. Only when Finn dug it in, and only a couple of times even then, did he look discomfited.

Yes, of course he had assistance from his colleagues. Most notably, this came from his opening partner, Keaton Jennings, who made 52 and put on 123 for the first wicket before he was tempted to poke at one outside the off stump from James Harris and nicked a catch to John Simpson. Brooke Guest, pressed into service as a No.3, made 17 before he was bowled through a Brandenburg gate by Tim Murtagh. The same bowler then tempted Glenn Maxwell into a booming drive and castled him off the inside edge. Presumably troubled by these dismissals but clearly not disturbed by them, Hameed batted on, scoring only 34 runs between lunch and tea. Four overs after the resumption he drove Toby Roland-Jones straight to the Nursery End boundary; the next ball was short and Hameed pulled it over the rope. His progress to a century was the first time he had rushed anywhere in 253 minutes; he had faced 167 balls and made maybe half a dozen errors.

In the evening session Rob Jones also batted well, reaching his own fifty and helping Dane Vilas establish what may turn out to be a very useful first-innings lead. But Jones knows whose name will be on the lips of most cricket lovers in pubs around Lord's this evening.

For one thing was made particularly clear by this innings: Hameed is, as his former colleague, Ashwell Prince, once said, born to bat. He is, one might even add, a proper cricketer to his very fingertips.

13

SEASON'S END

There is a sweet melancholy that accompanies the end of the English cricket season. Regret is tempered by gratitude and by a recognition that the year is turning. Few journalists on the county circuit would like to watch the game for much longer than six months at a stretch and my own enjoyment of autumn and winter feels like good preparation for a new season ahead. Although I'd relish the opportunity to cover cricket abroad, I welcome the chance to think about other things and not have my life regulated by the fixture list. It's also pleasant to live in the flat on which one pays a mortgage.

Dealing with other endings is far more difficult. The five end-of-season pieces that conclude this book include references to cricketers who no longer play the professional game. Retirement is inevitable, of course, but the notion that I will never again see Ian Bell play a cover-drive for Warwickshire or Daryl Mitchell go out to open the batting on a spring morning at New Road or Glen Chapple steam in for Lancashire can be countered only by a long silence or by thankfulness that I have seen these fine professionals at the peak of their powers. And it is far worse when a young player like Derbyshire's Harvey Hosein is forced to retire by injury.

Four of these pieces are relatively conventional last-day match reports. The piece from Taunton in September 2016 perhaps requires a little explanation. On the previous day I had watched Somerset defeat Nottinghamshire and go top of the table. There was a possibility, although a slim one, that Chris Rogers' team would win the first title in their county's history. Everything depended on the outcome of Middlesex's game against Yorkshire at Lord's. David Hopps, always a sucker for the bizarre, agreed that I should stay at Taunton and watch the day unfold at the County Ground. The first of the two pieces I wrote is included here; it ends in early afternoon, well before Toby Roland-Jones' hat-trick broke the hearts of the folk in the Stragglers' Café and the Colin Atkinson pavilion. Neither at Old Trafford nor Hove have I ever felt closer to a county's supporters.

2014 – Lancashire v Middlesex

Middlesex dig deep to save status

——————————— DAY FOUR, OLD TRAFFORD ———————————

*Lancashire 302-8 dec. (Croft 60; Murtagh 3-69, Roland-Jones
3-75) drew with Middlesex 214 (Procter 4-50, Chapple 4-55)
and 341-8 (Robson 75; Junaid 3-84, Kerrigan 3-106)*

Middlesex survived and Middlesex deserved to survive. At the end of a day marked not by a frenetic run-chase but by the sort of determined batting specifically designed to prevent such dramas, the players shook hands on the draw at 4.21pm at Old Trafford. At that moment Lancashire's second relegation in three years was confirmed and Middlesex could look forward with hardly expressible relief to another season among English cricket's élite.

In truth, the draw had appeared by far the most likely outcome of this match for at least an hour before it was confirmed. This was so because every single visiting batsman did his bit in the final innings of the season to deny a hard-working Lancashire attack on a pitch which never deteriorated as some players had forecast.

Resuming on 202-4 at 10.30 on the last morning of the season, Middlesex added 139 runs in 62 overs. As significant as runs scored, however, was cussed occupation of the crease, and everybody, bar Joe Denly, batted for at least an hour in the visitors' second innings. Thus, wickets fell not in the clumps Lancashire needed but at the intervals Middlesex could just about tolerate. A few home supporters may identify morning showers which trimmed 14 overs off the day's allocation as an explanation of the outcome. But most Lancashire fans will probably have more truck with the argument that it was the resilience of cricketers like Toby Roland-Jones, who batted 80 minutes for 34, or James Harris, who survived 135 minutes in accumulating 41 not out, that achieved the draw. Middlesex's performances since their first-innings collapse on the second day at Taunton have been far removed from the 'fancy-dan' image some have attached to them.

Lancashire's most successful moments of the last day came either side of the rain delay when Junaid Khan had Eoin Morgan lbw for

315

45 with a fine delivery and then induced Neil Dexter to play the ball onto his stumps for 17. Dexter's crooked shot was one of the worst of the day and it left his side on 222-6, a lead of only 134 at one o'clock. Lancashire's star was never to shine so brightly again; Rogers' lower-order batters saw to that. At the same time, it may not be lost on director of cricket Angus Fraser that Middlesex are the first Division One team to win four of their opening six games yet end the campaign outside the top three.

Their batsmen may have learned that runs are gained by application and hard work rather than resting complacently on reputations and status. Middlesex's batting collapses in high and late summer made for grim watching.

"I'm obviously relieved, and proud of the way the players have responded," said Fraser. "It's probably been one of the best four-day games of cricket you could ever see, the way it's fluctuated, and I'm proud of the way we've risen to the challenge. We've been put under the pump and shown a lot of character. That is maybe something that has been questioned in our side. It's a very talented team, with some really good cricketers in there. But we do play some soft cricket at times."

As for Lancashire, "the mood of this whole sodden place is melancholy" wrote The Beautiful South's Paul Heaton in the lyrics of *Manchester*, his wry tribute to this frequently damp city. "And everybody looks so disappointed, so, so sorry," continued the Bromborough-born bard, and that applied too on this final day of a season which had begun with Chapple's men hoping to re-establish themselves among the powerhouses of the English county game. Instead, the campaign began with a series of poor first-innings batting performances and a single victory, that against lowly Northamptonshire. There were too many weak links in the top order and the recruitment of Usman Khawaja in mid-season scarcely remedied matters. Some of the county's members have had enough and there is already talk of a petition and votes of no confidence. An EGM may be called.

Others may take a different view. Certainly some strong views were expressed at a members' forum on the first day of this game. Everyone might do well to reflect that counties which tear themselves apart do not prosper or win things. Listening to each other and attempting to reach a consensus may be a wise course of action. We shall see.

Lancashire supporters did not desert their team in droves even as their relegation became certain. The majority stayed on the ground to applaud both teams off the field and, curiously, one was reminded of the passage in John le Carré's novel *Tinker, Tailor, Soldier, Spy* when retired intelligence chief George Smiley visits MI6's former Head of Research, Connie Sachs, in Oxford. He finds her pining for her former career. "I hate the real world," she wails, in Arthur Hopcraft's faithful TV dramatisation. "I like the Circus [MI6] and all my lovely boys."

For even after the cricketers had left the field for the final time this summer, some spectators stayed in their seats, perhaps pondering what they had seen and reflecting that, for good or ill, all this was over for another year. Similar scenes may have taken place at Canterbury, Leeds and Northampton on this last day of the 2014 season. And if followers of county cricket were, indeed, reluctant to leave grounds, we may not need to look too far for the reason. Already, perhaps, they were missing their circus and its lovely boys.

2015 – Yorkshire v Sussex

Brooks brings down the blinds on Sussex

──────────────── DAY FOUR, HEADINGLEY ────────────────

Yorkshire 251 (Ballance 55, Rashid 53; Magoffin 4-57)
and 305 (Gale 67, Bresnan 55; Magoffin 3-57, Jordan
3-73) beat Sussex 286 (Yardy 70; Brooks 3-55) and 208
(Bresnan 3-30, Brooks 3-39, Rashid 3-44) by 100 runs

The large press box at Headingley, which is situated in a complex owned by Leeds Beckett University, was being used for lectures on this final day of the game. Thus, while the mighty Yorkshire bowling attack sent Sussex's rather stunned cricketers down to the Second Division, students sat in serried rows with the blinds firmly down in the Kilner Auditorium and listened to no doubt worthy lectures on important subjects such as computer science or drainage in Grimsby.

Quite right, perhaps, but for the undergraduates, many of whom were keen cricket fans, it must have been frustration itself. Jack Brooks removed the top three in Sussex's order in one of the finer new-ball spells you will see and all they could hear were muffled cheers amid the theorems. "There's music in the names I used to know / And magic when I heard them long ago", wrote Thomas Moult in *The Names*, a golden-age poem written in the persona of a cricket-loving adult remembering his schooldays.

Certainly drama students might have learned something from watching the cricket on this last day of the season. Sussex began their innings needing to bat out 92 overs for the draw or score 309 runs to win. The achievement of either goal would have prolonged their five-year stay in the first division, but they never looked like reaching either objective. Yorkshire's bowlers saw to that. First it was Brooks, cruising in as smoothly as a sports car from the Kirkstall Lane. He bowled a swinging full toss at the dreadfully out of form Ed Joyce and the Sussex skipper inside-edged it onto his stumps; then makeshift opener Chris Jordan was leg before on the back foot for 20; and in what was only Brooks' sixth over, Matt Machan chased a wideish ball and feathered a catch to Jonny Bairstow. Sussex were 39-3 in the 12th over and there was already a horrid gash below their waterline.

The crowd at Headingley enjoyed it all hugely, of course, but the students in their lecture theatre, whatever they were thinking, saw none of it. "Drone on, O teacher, you can't trouble me," Moult's poem continues. "If you choose to keep us here while cricket's in the air, / You must expect our minds to wander down the roads to Leicester, Lord's and Leeds…"

And at Leeds this final morning, things got rapidly worse for Sussex as Bresnan joined in the fun. He bowled Chris Nash through the gate for 17 and induced Luke Wright to drive most unwisely at a wider delivery of full length. Sussex were 63-5 at lunch and the writing was as clear upon the walls as the equations were on the flip-charts. When you only win one of your final 11 games, as Sussex have done, you are going to struggle; and when your seam bowlers – James Anyon, Ajmal Shahzad, Chris Jordan – are not fit for most or all of the season, while your batsmen are not in form, you are going to find things desperately hard. Hampshire may have produced a great escape worthy of Steve McQueen on his motorbike, but Sussex's relegation is hardly an enormous surprise.

There was some resistance, though, and it came from Michael Yardy, who was batting for the final time in his career, and Ben Brown, who passed a thousand runs for the season during his innings of 42. The pair added 79 in 20 overs during a stand that offered some hope that a defence worthy of mythology might be mounted. Their sixth-wicket partnership stretched deep into the afternoon, by which time a party of schoolchildren had joined the crowd, a splash of purple amid the dark anoraks and fleeces. And many spectators at Headingley probably had mixed feelings this final afternoon. They were watching their team achieve a record 11th Championship victory and win the first division by 68 points, which is greater than the margin between runners-up Middlesex and bottom-placed Worcestershire. This is a great Yorkshire team and it must be a wonderful time to follow the White Rose.

At the same time there were many who might empathise with the phrase *Gone with the Cricketers*, the evocative title chosen by the John Arlott for one of his books. For it connotes not just a physical presence but a deeper commitment. "Where's John?" friends would ask Arlott's mother, only to receive the answer: "Oh, he's gone with the cricketers." And so he was, for much of the rest of his life. And so they were at Headingley when they stood to applaud Yardy as he left first-class cricket after gloving an attempted hook to Alex Lees at first slip. There was no more touching sight than the Yorkshire team queueing up to shake the hand of the player they had just dismissed.

Yardy's dismissal by Bresnan for 41 was followed 12 balls later by that of Brown, the Sussex wicketkeeper clipping Adil Rashid straight to short-leg, where Jack Leaning grabbed a brilliant catch. That left Sussex on 142-7 and, although the last three wickets took a shade under an hour to fall, there was now no doubt which way the river was flowing. Rashid helped himself to a couple more scalps and Adam Lyth, on his 28th birthday, had Ashar Zaidi leg before for 47. At ten past three Chris Liddle was plumb enough to Rashid and the celebrations began on the outfield even as the dull realisation sunk in among the Sussex players. Dickie Bird presented the County Championship trophy to Andrew Gale, who has now received it three times in successive games. Mark Robinson, the Sussex coach, offered dignified congratulations to both Yorkshire and Hampshire; he refused to make elaborate excuses; he is a proper cricket man.

The supporters gathered on the outfield and watched their players begin the first of what will be very many celebrations. And, as is often the case at this time of year, the spectators were slow to leave, reluctant, perhaps, to forsake one home for another. Eventually they drifted away, though, and soon they must follow the different rhythms of autumn. But it will not be long before they are thinking of next April, when there will be music in the names once again and we shall be gone with the cricketers.

2016 – Somerset v Nottinghamshire

Somerset's waiting game presages the onset of winter

Prospero is right. "Our revels now are ended." Well, not quite, of course. They concluded here at Taunton on the third evening of this match with a skied catch, a retirement and much hurrahing in harvest. But as the mowers trim the County Ground's deserted square, cricket continues at half a dozen other venues around England, and at three of them matters of great moment are to be decided. All that Somerset's players and supporters can do is sit in their many pavilions and wait upon the Lord's judgement. Perhaps that is not an inappropriate occupation in this church-towered town, where Coleridge preached at Mary St Chapel in 1798. There will be prayers today, too.

And this evening the season will be done with. Both Championship and relegation will be decided and writers will be left to produce reviews of it all. Before long the players will depart for golf, for holidays with their families and for deserved rest. For over five months they have delighted and intrigued us. And perhaps it is only as the season closes that we fully appreciate the level of skill on show. Consider Jack Leach, for example: he is able to bowl a cricket ball so that it lands, more often than not, on a particular spot some 20 yards distant; not only that, but the ball will be spinning away sharply from the batsmen and looping with overspin so that the batsman may be deluded into thinking that it will land nearer to him than it eventually does.

Or there is a batsman, James Hildreth, shall we say, who can hit a ball travelling at 80mph precisely between two fielders with, among many other arts, a turn of the wrists and a transference of weight. What complexity of brain, nerve and sinew is needed to do that? Only when you reflect on these skills is their full stature revealed; in the high days of summer they can be taken for granted or remarked upon only when absent.

Something like this was noticed by William Hazlitt in his classic 1821 essay *The Indian Jugglers*:

> "Coming forward and seating himself on the ground in his white dress and tightened turban, the chief of the Indian Jugglers begins with tossing up two brass balls, which is what any of us could do, and concludes with keeping up four at the same time, which is what none of us could do to save our lives, nor if we were to take our whole lives to do it in. Is it then a trifling power we see at work, or is it not something next to miraculous?"

And county players do these things for over five months of the summer in a wide variety of conditions against opponents whose skills are quite the equal of their own. Their efforts make up a pageant which bewitches their teams' many supporters and causes them to follow their results even when living very far away.

And to most county cricketers and supporters it is the Championship which matters most of all. As I am writing this, the Stragglers Café below me is filled with Somerset supporters, all of them hoping against reason that nobody wins the game they are watching. You cannot move for wyverns on chests or anxious looks on faces. In 2012, Roy Harris, the former Somerset committee member, passed away but not before asking his grandson to promise that he would be present if his beloved county won the Championship. Yesterday, the gentleman turned up for the latter stages of the match wearing his grandfather's Somerset blazer. He had travelled from Iceland, the country not the frozen-food joint.

And this is the competition of which we must have less? This piece is being written by someone who has enjoyed T20 games and been amazed by the inventive skills on show. Yet also by someone who understood precisely what Stephen Chalke meant when he entitled his history of the County Championship *Summer's Crown*. It is easy to be seduced by enmity or to assume that those who run the ECB are double-dyed malefactors with the game's worst interests filling their evil minds. They are not. But they have done nothing for their case by failing to ask the current supporters of county clubs what they think of their ideas. Our masters look a little rude. For it is a curious plan which is based more on speculation than evidence. I'm not sure I would trust a doctor who told me my heart was not terribly important.

Advertising boards are being removed from the County Ground. An area has already been roped off for later in the afternoon when players will either be consoled by the media or begin a celebration which will last until All Souls' Day. But wherever the title ends up, cricket grounds are settling quietly into autumn and winter. Business will continue, of course. There will be conferences and Christmas parties. Press boxes will be filled with discussions of sales figures and exam papers; the members' suites will be given over to wedding receptions and retirement parties.

Then spring will come, freezing cold as likely as not, but the players will still begin their outdoor practice in England. They will be back with their gripes and their groin strains, their odd warm-ups and their lovable clichés, their absurd level of skill. Miranda is right, too. "O brave new world that has such creatures in't."

And so now we wait in this Tyrolean chalet of a press box at Taunton. Before us is perhaps the most-mentioned range of hills in county cricket. On the outfield Somerset's cricketers are now playing football with their children. Perhaps they cannot bear to watch the television. To our left is the full glory of St James' and its churchyard, and behind us are the tree-thronged humps of the Blackdowns. Throughout the town people are talking about two sessions, chuck-ups and when Middlesex might pull out. It is no good saying it will be easy to leave all this for another season but we are tougher than we think; and complex in ways beyond our imaginings.

But then, you see, Prospero is correct in another respect, too. "We are such stuff as dreams are made on."

2017 – Worcestershire v Durham

Worcestershire crown season with Division Two title

———————————— DAY FOUR, WORCESTER ————————————

Worcestershire 335 (Ashwin 82, Barnard 75, Clarke 65; Onions 4-68) and 242-3 declared (Mitchell 123*, Rhodes 51*) beat Durham 208 (Clark 60; Leach 3-30) and 232 (Clark 62; Ashwin 5-95, Leach 3-32) by 137 runs

Hunched of shoulder and a trifle bandy of gait, Daryl Mitchell works the ball square of the wicket in the manner beloved of a thousand county openers. Every April across the decades members have turned up at cricket grounds across England hoping to see batsmen like Mitchell play the innings that will win or save the game. Formats change and modernities obtrude but cricketers like Mitchell epitomise the gentle truths of time. They also win championships.

This simple fact was confirmed at 4.20 on a gorgeous September afternoon at New Road when Graham Onions drove R Ashwin to Joe Clarke at short cover. That dismissal gave Ashwin his fifth victim of the innings and it also completed Worcestershire's ninth victory of a season which ended with champagne, a trophy and all the endearing dance-about daftness that comes with them. For the fifth time in 12 seasons Worcestershire are to test themselves against the cracks of the first division and the finest bowlers in the land will try to best one of the canniest openers on the circuit.

In May, when the world sang with the ambition of spring, Mitchell went to Derby having scored 31 runs in four first-class innings. He then made 120. And on the final day of this season, under beguiling June-blue skies, Mitchell cover-drove Liam Trevaskis for three runs to reach his seventh century in this year's Championship. His unbeaten

123 set up Worcestershire's declaration and thereby their push for victory on an afternoon which had already been garlanded by the certainty of promotion.

And thus the joy of the triumphal moment was mixed with the bittersweet sadness that lies on all cricket grounds in September. "Der Sommer war sehr groß. / Leg deinen Schatten auf die Sonnenuhren" wrote Rilke. "The huge summer has gone by. / Now overlap the sundials with your shadows."

This last day passed more or less as Worcestershire intended. Mitchell reached his hundred off 134 balls and delighted the crowd when he cut a boundary between the two backward points Paul Collingwood had carefully positioned. The declaration was applied when George Rhodes notched his second fifty of the season and it left Durham to score 369 in 76 overs, a proposition they were never permitted to entertain. As if to reassure spectators that they were ready to play at a higher level, the Worcestershire seamers put on a fine show. Joe Leach pinned Cameron Steel on the back foot with the sixth ball of the innings and then ended Jack Burnham's season when Durham's No.3 played no shot at a ball which came back off the seam. "Joe Leach, Joe Leach, Joe Leach, Joe Leeeeaaaach" sang a group of Worcestershire supporters and Dolly Parton's "Jolene" will never sound the same.

It was an afternoon of last things and farewells, and when cricket has no time for such things, we might as well fold up the tents and head for the hills. Each of his teammates hugged Onions when Durham left the field as a team for the last time; Keaton Jennings' final innings for the county to which he owes so much ended on 20, when he played carefully forward to Ashwin but edged to Mitchell at first slip; and when Steve Gale came down the steps after tea to stand in his last session as a first-class umpire, both teams formed a guard of honour. The Worcestershire crowd also applauded Collingwood at almost every opportunity and Mitchell merely when he went to field at third-man. None of these fond moments weakened Durham's resolve to save the game, and it is this readiness to resist that will help sustain them over the next few years. Collingwood and Graham Clark put on 88 for the fourth wicket and both hit Ashwin for six. But both were also leg before on the back foot to Ed Barnard, whose cricket has been one of the young joys of Worcestershire's summer.

Clark made his second fifty of the match and seems likely to be one of those players upon whom Durham must build a new side. But none of his colleagues could match his intransigence on an afternoon dominated by Leach's bowlers and by the warmth of a large crowd bubbling with good humour and success. Ryan Pringle skied Ashwin to Rhodes at square-leg just before tea and Leach yorked Michael Richardson shortly after the resumption. Ashwin took care of Liam Trevaskis and Chris Rushworth with successive balls and the late high jinks of a last-wicket stand simply allowed the ECB's presentation party to ready the banners and bells.

And so ended a game which has seen all seasons but spring. Before long the spectators who had applauded the cricketers were planning to meet over the winter and saying their farewells in the meantime. "As the thin glow of summer's death / Will turn the leaves to red / May the wind blow like a lover's breath / Still warm as gingerbread" sings the matchless Nancy Kerr. If our farewells were not as eloquent, they were no less heartfelt.

It is very early evening: from the pavilion can be heard celebrations which will reach deep into the night; the tower of the cathedral is etched against a silver-blue background; through the trees boys can be seen training for a rugby match; in the distance a last spectator is leaving. Now overlap the sundials with your shadows.

2019 – Somerset v Essex

Somerset force Essex to fight for draw to seal title on dramatic final day

──────────── DAY FOUR, TAUNTON ────────────

Somerset 203 (Van der Merwe 60; Harmer 5-105, S Cook 4-26) and innings forfeited drew with Essex 141 (A Cook 53; Leach 5-32, van der Merwe 4-41) and 45-1 (A Cook 30*)

A season we thought might conclude in soggy anti-climax, with a title formally decided by a bland announcement over Taunton's public address, instead ended with warm handshakes on a sunlit outfield between two teams who had battled it out for the County Championship over the previous five months. As if to ensure that everyone remembered the value of this great title, the dear old girl had made Essex fight for the draw which secured the pennant. It was a glorious and nerve-shredding story, one they will tell often over the next few months in places like Colchester and Ilford. It may get a mention in Bridgwater and Glastonbury as well, although the remembrance will be nothing like so as warm.

It had all seemed so simple for Essex. If the showers did not put the game out of its misery, surely their batsmen would, even on a spinners' pitch. Although Nick Browne had been dismissed in the morning session, Alastair Cook and Tom Westley had shepherded their side to 102-1 by mid-afternoon. Some people were wondering when the draw could be agreed; other were simply enjoying their last cricket of the summer. Then Cook was caught at short-leg by Tom Banton off Jack Leach. A breach, to be sure, but surely nothing much more, we thought. We were wrong.

Over the next 80 minutes or so the rest of the Essex order were swept away by Leach, who finished the innings with 5-32, and Roelof van der Merwe, who took 4-41. Batters came and went like speed-daters with no interest in their partners. Encouraged by the regular fall of wickets, Leach and van der Merwe stuck to tight lines and let the pitch do the rest. It did not fail them. Dan Lawrence was caught in the gully for a second-ball duck; Ravi Bopara was taken at silly-point for a single; Tom Westley was caught at slip for a patient 36.

If only two batsmen could have stuck around for an hour there would have been nothing at all to disturb the good folk in Billericay or the Baddows. But no one stuck around. Leach bowled to an 8-1 field and six of those eight were close on the off-side. Fielders swarmed around the bat like painted ladies around buddleia. The Essex tail was swept away in a few overs. In all, the visitors lost their last nine wickets for 39 runs in a little less than 19 overs; their last six in a post-tea helter-skelter for 15 runs in 32 balls.

It was wonderful stuff for the Taunton supporters, many of whom glimpsed a miracle. But wait a moment. How could victory be achieved? The answer was simple, obvious and daring. Tom Abell forfeited his side's second innings and left Essex to score 63 in seven minutes plus a minimum of 16 overs in the last hour. Spectators hearing of the drama came to the County Ground wondering if Somerset were to win their first title in the most dramatic fashion possible. They did something similar when Harold Gimblett was batting. They watch cricket at Taunton in the full knowledge that they are passing on a sacred heritage.

At which point in this afternoon's drama, sanity was restored. Calmness re-entered the crease in the shape of Alastair Cook who, if he was as nervous as his captain Ryan ten Doeschate claimed, did not show it. Instead, he made 30 not out in 59 minutes and was one of the very first to know Essex had won the title. It was 5.20 when Abell offered the draw and Cook accepted the offer with grace. The visitors had given a little thought to winning the game but such things barely mattered a jot when set beside the title. Even the prize money, £583,000, although very useful to any county, paled when set beside the trophy and the pennant.

This is Essex's eighth title since they first won the Championship in 1979; no county has won it so frequently in that period. It is also the sixth time Somerset have finished as runners-up this century and the third time in the last four years. Such records are so simple to tap out on a laptop with the County Ground sunk in the darkness of a September evening. And then one considers the joy and sweat, the disappointment and effort, the triumphs and defeats that lie behind them. Then, if you love this game as most of those at Taunton today do, you stop for a while and ponder it all.

Marcus Trescothick fielded as a substitute for the last few overs of this match. He has been a great cricketer and he has now retired. Like Peter Wight, like Sammy Woods, like Peter Roebuck, he will never play in a title-winning Somerset side. All that is left is the respect of his fellow professionals; that was shown when the Essex players formed a guard of honour; all that is left is the unqualified love of Somerset's supporters; all that is left is his own knowledge that he has brought honour illimited to his craft.

And after all, there are bigger things than trophies. Perhaps the Essex players know that even as they are giving it large on their coach back to Chelmsford. But that will not halt their celebrations for an instant, nor should it. They are most worthy champions. The rest of us are left with memories of a glorious county season. It has offered the pastoral glory of Newclose, the rugged grandeur of Sedbergh and the warmth of so many outgrounds and fine headquarters.

The weather was glorious this afternoon at Taunton and some folk may have thought it the mockery of the gods. After all, we had seen those scarlet covers pushed on and off the County Ground far too often over the previous three days. But the sunlight was brighter than it had been throughout the entire match and it was a prelude to a wonderful conclusion to our precious season. Now there is only darkness, many darknesses really; but lighting it all like a lamp is the memory of a summer gone… and the prospect of a new season that will greet us next spring.

Note: Two months after this game the ECB's Discipline Committee ruled the pitch on which it had been played to be "poor", citing "excessive unevenness of bounce". They ruled that Somerset would begin the 2020 season on minus 12 points. I don't think anyone said what would have happened if Somerset had beaten Essex and won their first County Championship. Logic suggests the ECB would have taken the title away. My God, I'd like to have seen them try…

14

ENVOI

Roughly a decade ago I was watching Karl Brown bat on the first day of a game at Liverpool. On an impulse, I texted the dedicatee of this book: "There is literally nothing else I'd prefer to be doing." Now Karl was a fine batsman, but I was beguiled by much more than one cricketer that morning. There was the confection of skills on offer, the interplay of such disciplines, the game taking an early shape, the sight of Aigburth in her best summer clothes, the beeches on the far side of the ground, the attention of the spectators...

And in truth it had been something like that since July 21, 1965, when I saw Brian Statham lead out Lancashire at Southport. I later wrote about that distant Wednesday in *The Nightwatchman*:

"A boy is sitting on the grass behind the boundary boards at Southport's Trafalgar Road ground. He is watching his first County Championship match. Lancashire are playing Derbyshire and the white figures on the echoing green hold him quite entranced. Some of his friends get fidgety or scoff their lunch early but he ignores them. He likes everything about the game: the spectacle, the skill, the numbers. Even the delicate architecture of three stumps with two bails in their grooves, the whole construction so easily disarranged, fascinates him. He is too young for either cider or Rosie. Cricket satisfies him."

In time, Laurie Lee's attractions arrived. They did their best and worst, but the summer days kept their unspoken promise to me.

* * *

The vast majority of people who watch cricket closely feel no particular need to write about the game. Despite covering league matches for local papers and magazines, I was among them, until 2004, when my mother passed away and I suddenly found myself with no job – I had been her full-time carer for eight years – and after her death my late father's employers courteously insisted I vacate our church house within six months. Some eight weeks later, I was covering a game for the *Guardian*. As bits of good fortune go, it was a lottery win.

The game in question was a rain-wrecked non-event against Kent in one of Lancashire's relegation seasons. Only 6.3 overs were possible on the first day and none at all on the second. That didn't matter. I was hooked before play was abandoned on the opening morning. And who would not have been...

"You're a virgin! Excellent!" boomed the *Telegraph's* David Green, and his eyes lit up at the fun he was about to enjoy. In the early years of this century, Green's performance in a county press box was the best cabaret in the land.

Unencumbered by any need to tweet or blog, not that he would have obeyed any instruction to do so, he would stroll around the room during a morning's play, watching the cricket but also reminiscing about his days as a professional for Lancashire and Gloucestershire and occasionally commenting on the efforts of his colleagues. "Ah, I see Edwards is attempting to win the Booker Prize before lunch," was one observation that amused most occupants of that box at Old Trafford over 17 years ago.

Rain allowed Green even greater freedom. He would make a series of phone-calls, sometimes to berate sub-editors and, occasionally, to suggest to bank managers that, judging by their investment decisions, he would have been better off leaving his money under the mattress. Even cold callers were never so brave as to ring again. Old players were recalled, assessed and sometimes mocked, although rarely without affection. Anecdotes were told that can never appear in any book. When Green's copy appeared in the next morning's paper it would be accurate, perceptive and exactly the right length, but it would reflect none of this burlesque.

Curiously, it didn't occur to me during this extraordinary four-day induction that I knew next to nothing about working freelance for a broadsheet. Somehow I had landed in an environment where I felt utterly at home. The *Guardian's* copy-takers and sub-editors made some sense of my atrocious copy and I saw my name beneath it the following morning. (I was waiting outside the newsagent's before it opened.) As I left the old press box in the Red Rose suite after the end of the Kent game on that Friday evening, I was tempted to tell God that if He'd shown me all this, only for me never to experience it again, He and I were finished.

The next summer I covered three games; the one after, none at all. I bought a laptop and discovered its basic functions. Then I began covering

Lancashire's games for the *Liverpool Daily Post* and worked on the entire 2009 Ashes series for the same, rather civilised, newspaper. I met writers whose books I treasured. I worked for Lancashire's website and anyone else who would pay me buttons. Three years later David Hopps sent me to Worcester and in 2014 I got a regular gig with *The Times.*

And so today people might assume I would find it all so familiar, even a little routine. They should think again. I still regard it as the greatest privilege to walk through the gates at Old Trafford. The boy who watched Lancashire defeat Derbyshire inside two days in 1965 is still there somewhere. Putting this book together has helped remind me of that. The summer days hold their promise, still.

Birkdale, December 16, 2021

March 23, 2022

Jack Haynes makes hay as English summer arrives early at The Parks

Worcestershire 371 for 4 (Haynes 127, Cornall 84, D'Oliveira 58) against Oxford UCCE

"Take thermals to The Parks," said Scyld Berry. It was, of course, shrewd advice, the sort one might expect from a former editor of *Wisden.* I anticipated a cutting wind and reckoned that my thickest flannel shirt would be only one of four layers I'd need. Round the boundary, fanatics would be declaring that they hadn't missed the first day's cricket on this ground since Vic Marks was up and they were damned if a bit of frost was going to stop them now. Fielders would be wearing bobble hats and praying the ball wouldn't come to them. Jokes would feature the prospect of double pneumonia. The whole shebang was first cousin to inevitable. For what manner of loon plans to cover a cricket match before the clocks have gone forward?

But the only foolishness is my assumption. None of the Worcestershire players and coaches watching Gareth Roderick tuck Hugo Whitlock's first ball of the match backward of square is wearing anything more protective than a sweater or a tracksuit top. And hardly any of them are hypnotised by their mobile phones. "One out of one!" Brett D'Oliveira had exclaimed, having won the toss, and the visitors' new skipper scurries across to move the sightscreen. The temperature must be in the low sixties. Already some of the daffodils in Balliol's back quad are going over and the magnolias in The Parks are in riot. The Crêpes O Mania van is doing good business, although nothing like the killing it will make in the afternoon session. No one has known a March like this in Oxford. My binoculars fall apart inside the first hour's play; perhaps they can't believe their lenses.

Roderick and Taylor Cornall, Worcestershire's almost new recruit from Lancashire, put on 114 in 27.3 overs for the first wicket before Roderick chips Toby Greatwood to Karan Parmar at midwicket. Lunch is taken nine balls later. The morning's play has been watched by around a hundred spectators. The more conservatively dressed are occupying the benches, one of which is named after Martin Donnelly, the New Zealand left-hander whose batting used to empty the lecture halls here just after the war. The more unconventional groups are on the east side of The Parks. Among them have been Japanese visitors, some looking bemused, others entranced. Perhaps they thought cricket is England's answer to the tea ceremony. They may be right.

Oxford University's players are on a pre-season tour to Barbados, so this UCCE team is composed entirely of Oxford Brookes students. Their fielding in the first two sessions is particularly keen but their errors are expensive. On 38, Cornall's edged drive flies more or less unhindered between the wicketkeeper Joe Millard and first slip Whitlock. The Worcestershire opener will go on to make 84 before Millard redeems himself off the home skipper, Chris McBride.

Rather more seriously, when he has made 23, Jack Haynes nicks the slow left-armer, Connor Haddow, to first slip, where Joe Gordon just fails to pouch the chance. A few balls later Haynes drives the spinner just over a leaping McBride at mid-off. They will be more or less his last errors before Haddow bowls him off the inside edge just before the close. By then Worcestershire's finest current young batsman will have offered us drives through the covers and mid-on, although he will stroke only six fours in his hundred, and ten in his final tally of 127.

Cornall is dismissed just after half-past two and we hear our first "Let's go bang-bang" of the season. It is like spring's first cuckoo and similarly misleading. For Haynes and D'Oliveira will put on 120 either side of tea, and in the evening session Worcestershire's expected dominance is plain on a pitch that is an absolute credit to groundsman John Buddington, a Sunderland lad who arrived at The Parks via Tunbridge Wells and Horsham. Buddington is clearly a good egg and his work proves the important point that although the universities' matches may have lost first-class status, they still offer valuable preparation and are taken seriously. The counties would not play them otherwise.

And yet none of this would be quite so memorable or strangely blessed had not our afternoon been enriched by the 200 or so good-natured students, presumably from Brookes, who gathered on that sunlit eastern boundary and cheered more or less everything their friends did. Every appeal was supported by a chorus; every decent stop was applauded. There was a chorus of "Jerusalem" and for once it did not sound like brain-dead nationalism. There were other songs, too: there is, should you be in any doubt about the matter, only one Joe Gordon. To do a circuit or three was to be revived after a bleak close-season by the bugger-it exuberance of youth. Yes, there were many beer cans and plenty of wine bottles. Indeed, chuck in a few tents and a lot of mud and you had cricket's answer to Glastonbury. Even Worcestershire's players savoured the show. One wonders if any of them have had such an enjoyable first day of the season.

By seven o'clock, though, Oxford was in near darkness. The cranes that currently compete with cupolas in this enchanted city were obscured, as were the Ukrainian flags that fly from college towers, residents' windows and Blackwell's bookshop. Even in this place, where one can so easily be seduced by memories of say, snowy Decembers, present concerns cannot be avoided. But as it happens, the clocks' going forward was of little consequence. The one on the front of the famous pavilion in The Parks had not been put back in October, presumably on the sound basis that very few people would look at it outside the cricket season. And the suggestion that Oxford has its own way of reckoning time might not have surprised the spectators on the ground this balmy March. For at least one of them, Jack Haynes will always be driving the ball through the covers and there will always be a low door in the wall.

ESPN*Cricinfo, March 2022*

Acknowledgements

The life of a professional writer is a solitary one and I like that very well. But daily reporting on cricket matches is a necessarily collaborative business: one is dependent on sports editors commissioning the work; sub-editors preparing it for the paper or website; and colleagues helping out in all manner of ways. In all these respects I have been absurdly fortunate.

From a long list that includes valued friends in the press and broadcasting boxes, I must thank some specific people and the most significant of these is David Hopps. When he was UK editor of *ESPN Cricinfo*, David hired me to write my first piece for the website and, though his job-title has changed over the past decade, he has remained my boss. David has guided my work in innumerable ways: he has encouraged the writer and he has bollocked the journalist and if his suggestions were occasionally a trifle terse, there is no doubt I deserved it. But my debt to *Cricinfo* ranges more widely. Most of the pieces in this book first appeared on the site and I should like to thank Andrew Miller, the current UK editor, for giving permission that they be published. Andrew has also been a valued colleague and friend, as have others on the staff in Hammersmith: Alan Gardner, Valkerie Baynes and Matt Roller. Alan and Andrew McGlashan, the website's current Australia editor, were also sub-editors when I first began writing for *Cricinfo* and their willingness to polish and tweak, sometimes quite late in the evening, was an inspiration. Particular gratitude is also due to the editors of *The Times,* Slightly Foxed, *The Cricketer* and The Yorkshire County Cricket Club website for allowing pieces I wrote for them to be included. And my huge thanks go to George Dobell for writing the preface.

When I began to cover cricket outside Southport in 2004, Richard Williamson, the Sports Editor of the *Liverpool Daily Post*, gave me far more encouragement and far more work than my callow ignorance deserved. Then, when I was covering the 2009 Ashes, I proposed to Ken Grime that I should write some colour pieces on the series for Lancashire's website. His agreement allowed me to range far more widely than conventional match reports would allow. Readers of this book must decide whether that was a good thing. There are also two colleagues I must thank. Although born in Sussex and an enthusiastic defender of all 18 first-class teams, I have covered Lancashire most frequently. One of the many benefits of this is that I have spent many days in the company of a fellow freelancer, Graham Hardcastle, and BBC Radio Lancashire's Scott Read. Their help and steadfast friendship has been an asset on the good days and a consolation on the rough ones.

Friends and colleagues who have dined with me after a day's play know that I am prone to revisit my pieces during the evening in the hope they can be polished a little. Maybe "rescued" would be more accurate. A former girlfriend was once so exasperated by this habit that she threw the remains of her pasta at me. Others have been more tolerant. Mike Atherton, Jamie Bowman, Scyld Berry, Stephen Chalke, Kerry Donoghue, David Frith, Nathan Leamon, Gary Naylor, Duncan Hamilton, Simon Lee, Stephen Moss, Huw Richards, Jack Shantry, Nick Sharland, Richard Spiller, Graham Standring, Huw Turbervill, Ben Uglow and Graham Wood have all offered perceptive comments and encouragement while Gill Hill has continued to be the most loyal of family friends. Peter Andrews and Robert Waller deserve particular thanks, except that such a phrase seems ridiculously formal in their case. They have been with me, and with my cricket, for over 40 years and Peter is particularly generous in allowing me to stay with him when I am covering matches in the South. However, when I reported on games at the Rose Bowl I stayed with Peter's mother, Margaret, and it is by far my sharpest sadness in writing this book that she did not live to see it published. She was one of the wisest and most life-enhancing people I've ever met. Playing competitive table-tennis into her eighties probably helped.

Summer Days Promise is published by Fairfield Books and it is the fourth title to appear under the imprint since the company was bought from Stephen Chalke by Trinorth. I've greatly enjoyed working with Matt Thacker and his team and look forward to doing so again. However, when Matt offered to commission the book, I insisted that Tanya Aldred should edit it and that was one of the shrewdest decisions of my life. Tanya is the type of editor every writer should want: she is attentive, sharp, encouraging, and tough. No one wields a knife with more grace. She is also a trusted friend and that helps, too.

The only person left to thank is David Sleight. My recollection is that David first contacted me when I was covering the 2009 Ashes Test at Edgbaston. His kind text took my mind off the fact that I was sharing my Hagley Road hotel room with a variety of insects, some of whom were rather lacking in the social graces. Since then David and I have watched county cricket and talked about it with the ease of people who rarely need to explain themselves. We can be out of contact for a month or more, only to pick up where we left off. This acknowledgement goes a little deeper, though; friends are not judged by their loyalty when the score is 300 for two. But whether I have been batting on an Oval shirt-front or a Brisbane sticky-dog, David has always been available to listen and offer wise advice. I owe him a great deal yet he would never think of it in such terms. So the best I can do is dedicate *Summer Days Promise* to David, in love and friendship.